Customer Relationship Management

VSF

This book is dedicated to my children Emma and Lewis of whom I am enormously proud.

Customer Relationship Management

Concepts and Technologies

Second edition

Francis Buttle

AMSTERDAM • BOSTON • HEIDELBERG • LONDON • NEW YORK • OXFORD
PARIS • SAN DIEGO • SAN FRANCISCO • SINGAPORE • SYDNEY • TOKYO

Butterworth-Heinemann is an imprint of Elsevier

Butterworth-Heinemann is an imprint of Elsevier
Linacre House, Jordan Hill, Oxford OX2 8DP
30 Corporate Drive, Suite 400, Burlington, MA 01803, USA

First edition 2009

British Library Cataloguing-in-Publication Data
A catalogue record for this book is available from the British Library

Library of Congress Cataloging-in-Publication Data
A catalog record for this book is available from the Library of Congress

ISBN: 978-1-85617-522-7

For information on all Butterworth-Heinemann publications visit our web site at www.elsevierdirect.com

Typeset by Charon Tec Ltd., A Macmillan Company.
(www.macmillansolutions.com).

Printed and bound in Hungary

09 10 11 12 13   10 9 8 7 6 5 4 3 2 1

Working together to grow
libraries in developing countries

www.elsevier.com | www.bookaid.org | www.sabre.org

ELSEVIER   BOOK AID International   Sabre Foundation

Contents

Foreword

Customer relationship management's impact in the commercial marketplace cannot be undervalued. Despite traditional economic theory on market entry and pricing prescribing that enterprises should engage customers through prefabricated reactions and interactions given the customer event taking place, the nature, impact and reach of the power of enriching customer experiences has emerged in 2008.

Yet, one of the most common mistakes made by global companies is to view CRM as solely a technology or business challenge. CRM is first and foremost a business strategy that can be effectively executed through the appropriate business process and technology management capabilities that best match to an organization's customer-facing goals.

Long gone are the views of CRM being applications or business process methodologies for engaging customers in contact centers in the customer service functional domains within an organization. Today, every interaction or 'moment of truth' with customers can help sustain, direct, implore or resuscitate desired outcomes by enterprises. These processes transcend functional departmental silos and extend their reach across the process network to include sales and distribution partners and channels. Technology, process and organizational architectures together in concert will determine the effectiveness of how these end-to-end business processes will align to customer intents and enrich their overall experience with an organization.

The CRM strategic paradigm has gone through a three-phase generational shift over the last decade (1998–2008) with enterprises maturing from: 1) Marketing to customers the best products at the best prices, to 2) Marketing customers with the best services, to 3) Marketing customers with the dynamic services and products that they want and desire as measured by customer intent. Today, with the advent and proliferation of social communities across the internet world customers have channels for information-sharing on an enterprise's services and products that is extremely powerful. This emergence has disrupted conventional approaches towards managing customer or product information. Paradoxically, customers no longer look towards an enterprise as the best source of data or information about their own commercial product or service offerings. This sense of brand promise and brand trust has deteriorated, and today customers place their confidence in the shared and communal experiences of others through social community networks which provide transparency on valued customer experiences in the marketplace. In fact, as this book is being printed a great number of CRM Application vendors in the marketplace are vying to provide technology solutions for enterprises to integrate and use these social networks as part of core enterprise ERP and CRM solutions.

It is with distinct pleasure that I introduce you to Francis Buttle's comprehensive work on CRM. His passion for and grasp of the concepts, disruptors and application of CRM approaches will accelerate readers' abilities to grasp these exciting topics.

When considering CRM, there is no strategic alternative for enterprises but a relentless approach towards driving customer centricity in order to achieve current, future and lifetime profitability by creating customers for life.

Isher Kaila
Research Director, Global CRM Strategy
Gartner Inc.
San Jose, CA
USA

Preface

Welcome to the second edition of **Customer Relationship Management: Concepts and Technologies**.

The book provides a comprehensive and balanced review of Customer Relationship Management. It explains what CRM is, the benefits it delivers, the contexts in which it is used, the technologies that are deployed, and how it can be implemented. It shows how CRM practices and technologies are used to enhance the achievement of marketing, sales and service objectives throughout the customer life-cycle stages of customer acquisition, retention and development, whilst simultaneously supporting broader organizational goals.

The book has been written to meet the demand for an impartial, academically-sound, examination of CRM. It is a learning resource both for students of CRM and for managers wanting a better appreciation of the role that CRM can play in their own organizations.

The first edition was entitled Customer Relationship Management: Concepts and Tools. The change to the new subtitle, Concepts and Technologies, reflects the requirements of readers. In true customer-oriented manner, we surveyed readers and adopters of the first edition. They said they wanted more on CRM technologies. This book delivers it. However, although there are a number of chapters dedicated to CRM technologies, and technology matters are considered throughout the book, the book puts technology into a managerial context. This is not a book about technologies, but it is about how marketers, salespeople, service staff and their managers can use technologies to better understand and meet the requirements of customers, whilst also meeting organizational goals and objectives. Our survey of readers and adopters also discovered that they wanted more case illustrations and screenshots from CRM software applications. The book delivers them, too.

The book draws on academic and independent research to ensure that it is both theoretically sound and managerially relevant. Research from a wide range of academic disciplines contributes to the book. These include marketing, sales, customer service, human resources, technology management, strategy, change management, project management, leadership, operations, management accounting, finance and organizational behaviour. Supplementing these academic credentials, the book also makes use of research conducted by independent analysts such as Gartner and Forrester, two organizations that conduct leading-edge, state-of-the-art research into CRM and related areas.

Audience for the book

This book has been written for a number of audiences, all of whom share an interest in improving their understanding of CRM.

- MBA and Masters students, and upper-level undergraduates studying CRM or related advanced courses, such as relationship marketing, database marketing, customer management, sales management, key account management, strategic management, customer value management and customer service management.
- Those pursuing professional qualifications or accreditation in marketing through international organizations, such as the Chartered Institute of Marketing and the Institute of Direct Marketing, or national bodies such as the Marketing Institute of Ireland or the Canadian Institute of Marketing.
- Senior and mid-level managers who are involved in CRM programmes and system implementations, whether in a marketing department, the sales-force or the service centre.
- Students pursuing professional qualifications or accreditation in sales management or key account management through international organizations such as the Institute of Sales and Marketing Management or the Association of International Marketing.
- CRM users who want a better understanding of this complex area. CRM tools are deployed across the customer-facing parts of organizations. Users includes sales representatives, account managers, marketing managers, market analysts, campaign managers, market managers, customer relationship managers and customer service managers. These users are exposed to just a fragment of the CRM universe. This book can put their role into broader context.

Key features of the book

- The book provides a helicopter view, an overview, of the domain of CRM. As an impartial review of the field, it is not tied to any particular perspective on CRM. Indeed, the book identifies a number of holistic models that provide different and competing overviews of CRM.
- Although CRM is in widespread use, there is still some misunderstanding about what CRM is. The book identifies four different types of CRM: strategic, operational, analytical and collaborative.

Several chapters are dedicated to strategic CRM and others focus on operational CRM, whereas analytical CRM and collaborative CRM issues are addressed throughout the book.

- The book defines CRM as the core business strategy that integrates internal processes and functions, and external networks, to create and deliver value to targeted customers at a profit. CRM is grounded on high quality customer-related data and enabled by information technology. This definition serves as a central point-of-reference throughout the book.
- The book emphasizes a managerial perspective on CRM. Although there is plenty of content on technology, it is not a book about technology *per se*. The technology content of the book has been written so that readers who are unfamiliar with technology, or who are technophobes, can still understand what CRM technologies can deliver. Technology is secondary to management throughout the book. You don't need a degree in information systems to benefit from the book!
- The book has a strong academic foundation provided by research from a number of disciplines.
- The book contains many examples of CRM technologies and their application to marketing, selling or service functions. Screenshots are a feature of the book.
- Every chapter contains case illustrations. These are not problem-based cases, but examples of CRM in practice so that readers can come to appreciate how CRM is deployed.
- All chapters follow a common format: learning objectives, text, case illustrations, summary and references.

Improvements over the first edition

There are a number of important improvements to this edition which have been made largely as a result of input from readers and adopters.

The book is significantly expanded. At seventeen chapters, this edition is seven chapters longer than the first edition. There are three new chapters dedicated to operational CRM applications: sales-force automation, marketing automation and service automation. The chapters define important terms, identify the main vendors and actors, and set out the benefits users can expect to experience and the functionality that is available. There is a new chapter entitled 'Understanding relationships'. If CRM is about developing and maintaining relationships with customers, it is important to have clear understanding of what a relationship looks like, and how, if at all, it can be managed. This chapter defines the term 'relationship', examines whether customers want relationships with suppliers and *vice versa*, identifies attributes of successful relationships and reviews five different schools of thought that have influenced relationship management in a business context.

There is a new chapter on planning and implementing CRM projects. This takes readers through a disciplined five-stage process designed to promote successful CRM outcomes. There is a new chapter on 'Customer experience'. Customer experience has become something of a buzzword in the last few years. This chapter explores the concept of customer experience, and addresses the question of whether CRM can or does enhance customer experience.

Many new case illustrations have been added to every chapter, and all other content has been revised and updated. An added feature of this edition is the inclusion of a large number screenshots from CRM software applications. This is designed to give readers a sense of the CRM user's experience.

A final enhancement to this edition is the provision of an array of enriching online content, which is described below.

Additional online resources

Readers and adopters of the first edition said they wanted additional online resources to be available. There are now two websites linked to the book, designed to enrich the learning experience.

The website for **adopters** provides a range of pedagogical resources for instructors. Accessed by password and only available to authorized instructors, the site contains a full set of PowerPoint files; details of case studies that can be used as a basis for classroom discussion or student assignments; links to technology companies' websites where CRM technologies are demonstrated, and white papers and case histories can be viewed; links on online CRM communities and links to analysts websites where up-to-date CRM-related research is published. The adopters' website also includes a list of discussion topics, exercises, projects and assignments that engage students and promote deeper, more meaningful, learning.

The website for **readers** provides access to a range of value-adding content including chapter-by-chapter learning objectives; links to technology companies' websites where CRM technologies are demonstrated, and white papers and case histories can be viewed; links to online CRM communities; and links to analysts websites where up-to-date CRM-related research is published.

I hope you enjoy the book and find it a satisfying read. Writing a book is a little like painting a picture, or tending a garden. You never reach a point where you can safely say that the job is finished. There is always more that you can do. With that in mind, I invite you to write to me at francis@buttleassociates.com. I look forward to hearing from you.

Francis Buttle
Sydney

Acknowledgements

I'd like to express my appreciation to the many people and organizations that have contributed to this book. Most of these contributions have been requested and conscientiously delivered, but other contributors are unaware that their occasional comment or question is reflected in these pages. I thank you all.

I would particularly like to acknowledge the contribution of Isher Kaila who wrote the book's Foreword. Isher is Research Director, Global CRM Strategy for Gartner Inc., San Jose, California, USA. Gartner is the world's leading information technology research and advisory company. I first met Isher on one of his many global tours. He was visiting Australia where I had the opportunity to hear him speak insightfully and informatively about trends in CRM and customer experience management. Gartner claims 'We deliver the technology-related insight necessary for our clients to make the right decisions, every day'. Isher certainly did on that day, and he makes some similarly shrewd observations in his Foreword.

I would also like to acknowledge the input of John Turnbull and Matthew Holden. I have a strong managerial and strategic emphasis on CRM, which privileges the perspective of the user. In my 15 years or so of teaching, researching, advising and consulting on CRM I have learned much about technology, but am I by no means a match for these two technology experts.

John Turnbull is the founder and Managing Director of Customer Connect Australia (www.customerconnect.com.au). John began his working life with operational and management roles in service, sales, marketing support and project management. He has managed business transition programmes for a wide range of organizations across marketing, sales, service and operations. His experience also includes managing the sales consulting organizations in Australia and New Zealand for two major CRM vendors, PeopleSoft and Siebel (now Oracle). At Customer Connect Australia, John has helped organizations in a wide range of industries to succeed with their customer-centricity/customer management programmes. His work includes business consulting, CRM strategy, customer management education, managing business transition and customer management (CMAT™) assessment. John contributed a chapter to the first edition of this book, and the current Chapter 13, IT for CRM, draws heavily on that foundation. John and I have worked together on a number of CRM educational projects.

Matthew Holden is a highly experienced IT executive who has held senior positions at both Oracle and SAP. Currently based in Singapore, he has been a lead CRM implementation consultant at various companies including Fosters Ltd, AAPT and Cellarmaster Wines. He now works with large Asian companies and governments across the entire information technology software spectrum from ERP to CRM. More information is available at www.matthewholden.com.au. I first met Matthew when he enrolled as a PhD candidate and I had the pleasure of assisting him on the doctoral pathway. We have since worked together on a number of CRM educational projects. John and Matthew both read and commented on the technology-heavy chapters of this book. Thank you both for your input.

A number of doctoral candidates that I have supervised or advised have contributed significantly to the book. Special mention must go to Daniel Prior who identified and reviewed a number of different schools of relationship management. His thoughtful analysis provides a strong foundation for the discussion in Chapter 2. A number of chapters were read and critiqued by doctoral candidates Sergio Biggemann, Martin Williams, Reiny Iriana and Chris Baumann. Thank you, and congratulations on your own achievements: you are all Doctors now. May you continue to be successful. Jana Bowden also reviewed early drafts of chapters. You're the next to graduate.

A number of academic colleagues past, present and perhaps future, have also contributed feedback on drafts or engaged in helpful debate and discussion, amongst them Lawrence Ang, David Ballantyne, Sue Creswick, Christine Ennew, Robert East, John Murphy, Pete Naude, Sharon Murray, Adrian Payne, Thomas Ritter, Willem Selen, Alan Thomas, Ian Wilkinson, Steve Worthington and Louise Young.

I'd like to thank a number of clients with whom I've worked, including DNAML, MGSM, Microsoft, NIB, Nu-Wa, SAS and PLAUT. Special mention goes to Adam Schmidt, Bill Gates, Asha Oudit, Bob Knox, Helene Cederqvist and David Prior.

Many publishers, companies and authors have granted permission for their copyright materials to be reproduced in this book. These include photographs, line drawings, conceptual models, research data and screenshots. Every effort has been made to identify and contact copyright owners, and I am very pleased to acknowledge their contributions in the body of the book and in chapter endnotes. In the event that there has been any failure to acknowledge a source appropriately, please let me know and I'll correct the omission or amend the error at the first opportunity.

To all those at Elsevier who have been involved in the process of bringing the book to market I extend a vote of thanks: Ailsa Marks, Tim Goodfellow, Liz Burton, Sarah You and Stephani Allison. Appreciation is also extended to Lewis Buttle of eLAB Design who designed the cover.

Thanks, too, to my colleagues at Francis Buttle & Associates (www. buttleassociates.com) including Sam English, Lawrence Ang, Lee Williams, Abdullah Aldlaigan and Rizal Ahmad. Also, I appreciate the support of colleagues at Listening Post (www.listeningpost.com.au), particularly Leigh Thomas, David Young and Andrew Jones.

Finally, if you want to get in touch about the book, you can reach me at francis@buttleassociates.com

About the author

Francis Buttle, PhD, is founder and principal consultant of Francis Buttle & Associates, a Sydney, Australia-based business that helps organizations become more skilled and successful at customer acquisition, retention and development. Francis has spent most of the last 30 years in various academic roles around the world. He has been a Professor of Customer Relationship Management, Professor of Marketing, Professor of Relationship Marketing and Professor of Management at a number of leading graduate schools of management, including Manchester Business School (UK), Cranfield School of Management (UK) and Macquarie Graduate School of Management (Australia). He was appointed as the world's first Professor of CRM in 1995, and remains an Adjunct Professor at MGSM.

Francis has authored, co-authored or edited seven books, and over 100 peer-reviewed academic journal articles or conference papers. In addition, he is a frequent contributor to practitioner magazines, presenter at business conferences and a serial blogger.

Francis has developed, run or contributed to many management development programs, and has advised or consulted to numerous for-profit and not-for-profit organizations in the UK, Australia, USA, Hong Kong, Singapore and New Zealand.

Although he quit full-time academic life in 2006, he still supervises doctoral candidates and conducts customer-related research. Francis lives on Sydney's North Shore, is a qualified but reluctantly retired rugby union referee, enjoys cycling and kayaking, and rides a Suzuki.

Francis has degrees in management science, marketing and communication. His PhD was earned at the University of Massachusetts. He is an elected Fellow of the Chartered Institute of Marketing. He can be contacted at francis@buttleassociates.com.

Chapter 1

Introduction to customer relationship management

Introduction

The expression customer relationship management (CRM) has only been in use since the early 1990s. Since then there have been many attempts to define the domain of CRM, a number of which appear in Table 1.1. As a relatively immature business or organizational practice, a consensus has not yet emerged about what counts as CRM. Even the meaning of the three-letter acronym CRM is contested. For example, although most people would understand that CRM means customer relationship management, others have used the acronym to mean customer relationship marketing.[1]

Information technology (IT) companies have tended to use the term CRM to describe the software applications that automate the marketing, selling and service functions of businesses. This equates CRM with technology. Although the market for CRM software is now populated with many players, it started in 1993 when Tom Siebel founded Siebel Systems Inc. Use of the term CRM can be traced back to that period. Forrester, the technology research organization, estimates that worldwide spending on CRM technologies will reach US$11 billion per annum by 2010.[2] Others with a managerial rather than technological emphasis, claim that CRM is a disciplined approach to developing and maintaining profitable customer relationships, and that technology may or may not have a role.

Some of the differences of opinion can be explained by considering that a number of different types of CRM have been identified: strategic, operational, analytical and collaborative, as summarized in Table 1.2 and described below.

CRM is an information industry term for methodologies, software and usually Internet capabilities that help an enterprise manage customer relationships in an organized way.[3]

CRM is the process of managing all aspects of interaction a company has with its customers, including prospecting, sales and service. CRM applications attempt to provide insight into and improve the company/customer relationship by combining all these views of customer interaction into one picture.[4]

CRM is an integrated approach to identifying, acquiring and retaining customers. By enabling organizations to manage and coordinate customer interactions across multiple channels, departments, lines of business and geographies, CRM helps organizations maximize the value of every customer interaction and drive superior corporate performance.[5]

CRM is an integrated information system that is used to plan, schedule and control the pre-sales and post-sales activities in an organization. CRM embraces all aspects of dealing with prospects and customers, including the call centre, sales-force, marketing, technical support and field service. The primary goal of CRM is to improve long-term growth and profitability through a better understanding of customer behaviour. CRM aims to provide more effective feedback and improved integration to better gauge the return on investment (ROI) in these areas.[6]

CRM is a business strategy that maximizes profitability, revenue and customer satisfaction by organizing around customer segments, fostering behaviour that satisfies customers and implementing customer-centric processes.[7]

Table 1.1
Definitions of CRM

Type of CRM	Dominant characteristic
Strategic	Strategic CRM is a core customer-centric business strategy that aims at winning and keeping profitable customers
Operational	Operational CRM focuses on the automation of customer-facing processes such as selling, marketing and customer service
Analytical	Analytical CRM focuses on the intelligent mining of customer-related data for strategic or tactical purposes
Collaborative	Collaborative CRM applies technology across organizational boundaries with a view to optimizing company, partner and customer value

Table 1.2 Types of CRM

Strategic CRM

Strategic CRM is focused upon the development of a customer-centric business culture. This culture is dedicated to winning and keeping customers by creating and delivering value better than competitors. The culture is reflected in leadership behaviours, the design of formal systems of the company, and the myths and stories that are created within the firm. In a customer-centric culture you would expect resources to be allocated where they would best enhance customer value, reward systems to promote employee behaviours that enhance customer satisfaction and retention, and customer information to be collected, shared and applied across the business. You would also expect to find the heroes of the business to be those who deliver outstanding value or service to customers. Many businesses claim to be customer-centric, customer-led, customer-focused or customer-oriented, but few are. Indeed, there can be very few companies of any size that do not claim that they are on a mission to satisfy customer requirements profitably.

Customer-centricity competes with other business logics. Philip Kotler identifies three other major business orientations: product, production, and selling.[8]

Product-oriented businesses believe that customers choose products with the best quality, performance, design or features. These are often highly innovative and entrepreneurial firms. Many new business start-ups are product-oriented. In these firms it is common for the customer's voice to be missing when important marketing, selling or service decisions are made. Little or no customer research is conducted. Management makes assumptions about what customers want. The outcome is that sometimes products are overspecified or overengineered for the requirements of the market, and therefore too costly for many customers. However, marketers have identified a subset of relatively price-insensitive customers whom they dub 'innovators', who are likely to respond positively to company claims about product excellence. Unfortunately, this is a relatively small segment, no more than 2.5 per cent of the potential market.[9]

Production-oriented businesses believe that customers choose low-price products. Consequently, these businesses strive to keep operating costs low, and develop low-cost routes to market. This may well be appropriate in developing economies or in subsistence segments of developed economies, but the majority of customers have other requirements. Drivers of BMWs would not be attracted to the brand if they knew that the company only sourced inputs such as braking systems from the lowest-cost supplier.

Sales-oriented businesses make the assumption that if they invest enough in advertising, selling, public relations (PR) and sales promotion, customers will be persuaded to buy. Very often, a sales orientation follows a production orientation. The company produces low-cost products and then has to promote them heavily to shift inventory.

A **customer** or **market-oriented** company shares a set of beliefs about putting the customer first. It collects, disseminates and uses customer and competitive information to develop better value propositions for customers. A customer-centric firm is a learning firm that constantly adapts to customer requirements and competitive conditions. There is evidence that customer-centricity correlates strongly with business performance.[10]

Many managers would argue that customer-centricity must be right for all companies. However, at different stages of market or economic development, other orientations may have stronger appeal.

Strategic CRM at Boise Office Solutions

In 1998 the CEO of Itasca, Illinois-based Boise Office Solutions, decided that the only way to escape the bruising price competition and razor-thin margins of office supply superstores such as Staples and Office Depot was to provide greater value through superior customer service, with the support of a CRM system. Three years and $20 million later, the $3.5 billion subsidiary of Boise Cascade switched on a CRM system that differentiated them from other competitors in the office supplies industry. The company can now share customer data across five business units, 47 distribution centres and three customer service centres. This has allowed Boise to cross-sell, retain and service accounts much more effectively. One of the CRM system's many features is web collaboration which allows representatives to co-browse and chat with customers online while making recommendations.

Source: Greenguard (2002)[11]

Operational CRM

Operational CRM automates and improves customer-facing and customer-supporting business processes. CRM software applications enable the marketing, selling and service functions to be automated and integrated. Some of the major applications within operational CRM appear in Table 1.3. Although we cover the technology aspects of operational CRM in Chapters 14, 15 and 16, it is worth making a few observations at this point.

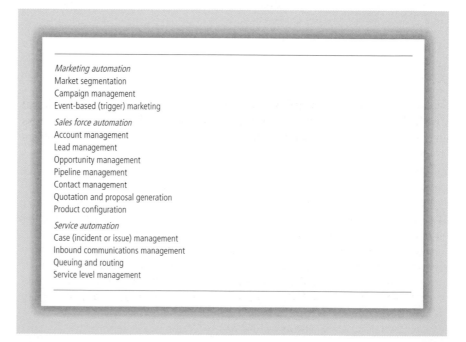

Marketing automation
Market segmentation
Campaign management
Event-based (trigger) marketing

Sales force automation
Account management
Lead management
Opportunity management
Pipeline management
Contact management
Quotation and proposal generation
Product configuration

Service automation
Case (incident or issue) management
Inbound communications management
Queuing and routing
Service level management

Table 1.3
Operational CRM

Marketing automation

Marketing automation (MA) applies technology to marketing processes. Campaign management modules allow marketers to use customer-related data in order to develop, execute and evaluate targeted communications and offers. Customer targeting for campaigning purposes is, in some cases, possible at the level of the individual customer, enabling unique communications to be designed.

In multichannel environments, campaign management is particularly challenging. Some fashion retailers, for example, have multiple transactional channels including free-standing stores, department store concessions, e-tail websites, home shopping catalogues, catalogue stores and perhaps even a television shopping channel. Some customers may be unique to a single channel, but most will be multichannel prospects, if they are not already customers of several channels. Integration of communication and offer strategies and evaluation of performance requires a substantial amount of technology-aided coordination across these channels.

Event-based, or trigger, marketing is the term used to describe messaging and offer presentation to customers at particular points in time. An event triggers the communication and offer. Event-based campaigns can be initiated by customer behaviours or contextual conditions. A call to a contact centre is an example of a customer-initiated event. When a credit-card customer calls a contact centre to enquire about the current rate of interest, this can be taken as indication that the customer is comparing alternatives and may switch to a different provider. This event may trigger an offer designed to retain the customer. Examples of contextual events are the birth of a child or a public holiday. Both of these indicate potential changes in buyer behaviour, initiating a marketing response. Event-based marketing also occurs in the business-to-business context. The event may be a change of personnel on the customer-side, the approaching expiry of a contract or a request for information (RFI).

Sales-force automation

Sales-force automation (SFA) was the original form of operational CRM. SFA systems are now widely adopted in business-to-business environments and are seen as 'a competitive imperative'[12] that offers 'competitive parity'.[13]

SFA applies technology to the management of a company's selling activities. The selling process can be decomposed into a number of stages, such as lead generation, lead qualification, needs identification, development of specifications, proposal generation, proposal presentation, handling objections and closing the sale. SFA software can be configured so that it is modelled on the selling process of any industry or organization.

Automation of selling activities is often linked to efforts to improve and standardize the selling process. This involves the implementation of a sales methodology. Sales methodologies allow sales team members and management to adopt a standardized view of the sales cycle and a common language for discussion of sales issues.

Sales-force automation software enables companies automatically to assign leads and track opportunities as they progress through the sales pipeline towards closure. Opportunity management lets users identify and progress opportunities to sell from lead status through to closure and beyond, into after-sales support. Opportunity management software usually contains lead management and sales forecasting applications. Lead management applications enable users to qualify leads and assign them to the appropriate salesperson. Sales forecasting functionality generally use transactional histories and salesperson estimates to produce estimates of future sales.

Contact management lets users manage their communications programme with customers. Computerized customer records contain customer contact histories. Contact management applications often have features such as automatic customer dialling, the salesperson's personal calendar and e-mail functionality. Quotation and proposal generation allow the salesperson to automate the production of prices and proposals for customers. The salesperson enters details such as product codes, volumes, customer name and delivery requirements, and the software automatically generates a priced quotation.

Product configuration applications enable salespeople, or the customers themselves, automatically to design and price customized products, services or solutions to problems. Configurators are useful when the product is particularly complex, such as in IT solutions. Configurators are typically based on an 'if … then' rules structure. The general case of this rule is 'If X is chosen, then Y is required or prohibited or legitimized or unaffected'. For example, if the customer chooses a particular feature (say, a particular hard drive for a computer), then this rules out certain other choices or related features that are technologically incompatible, too costly or too complex to manufacture.

Case 1.2

Operational CRM (SFA) at Roche

Roche is one of the world's leading research-based healthcare organizations, active in the discovery, development and manufacture of pharmaceuticals and diagnostic systems. The organization has traditionally been product-centric and quite poor in the area of customer management. Roche's customers are medical practitioners prescribing products to patients. Customer information was previously collected through several mutually exclusive sources, ranging from personal visits to handwritten correspondence, and not integrated into a database or central filing system, giving incomplete views of the customer. Roche identified the need to adopt a more customer-centric approach to understand their customers better, improve services offered to them and to increase sales effectiveness.

Roche implemented a sales-force automation system where all data and interactions with customers are stored in a central database which can be accessed throughout the organization. This has resulted in Roche being able to create customer profiles, segment customers and communicate with existing and potential customers. Since implementation Roche has been more successful in identifying, winning and retaining customers.

Service automation

Service automation allows companies to manage their service operations, whether delivered through call centre, contact centre, web or face-to-face.[14] CRM software enables companies to handle and coordinate their service-related inbound and outbound communications across all channels. Software vendors claim that this enables users to become more efficient and effective by reducing service costs, improving service quality, lifting productivity and increasing customer satisfaction.

Service automation differs significantly depending on the product being serviced. Consumer products are normally serviced through retail outlets, the web or a call centre as the point of first contact. These contact channels are often supported by online scripting tools to help diagnose a problem on first contact. A number of technologies are common in service automation. Call routing software can be used to direct inbound calls to the most appropriate handler. Technologies such as interactive voice response (IVR) enable customers to interact with company computers. Customers can input to an IVR system after listening to menu instructions either by telephone keypad (key 1 for option A, key 2 for option B) or by voice. If first contact problem resolution is not possible, the service process may then involve authorizing a return of goods, and a repair cycle involving a third party service provider. This process is used to service mobile phones and cameras.

Service automation for large capital equipment is quite different. This normally involves diagnostic and corrective action to be taken in the field, at the location of the equipment. Examples of this type of service include industrial air conditioning and refrigeration. In these cases, service automation may involve providing the service technician with diagnostics, repair manuals, inventory management and job information on a laptop. This information is then synchronized at regular intervals to update the central CRM system.

Many companies use a combination of direct and indirect channels especially for sales and service functions. When indirect channels are employed, operational CRM supports this function through partner relationship management (PRM). This technology allows partners to communicate with the supplier through a portal, to manage leads, sales orders, product information and incentives.

Analytical CRM

Analytical CRM is concerned with capturing, storing, extracting, integrating, processing, interpreting, distributing, using and reporting customer-related data to enhance both customer and company value.

Analytical CRM builds on the foundation of customer-related information. Customer-related data may be found in enterprise-wide repositories: sales data (purchase history), financial data (payment history, credit score), marketing data (campaign response, loyalty scheme data) and service data. To these internal data can be added data from external sources: geodemographic and lifestyle data from business intelligence organizations, for example. With the application of data mining tools, a company can then interrogate these data. Intelligent interrogation provides answers to questions such as: Who are our most valuable customers? Which customers have the highest propensity to switch to competitors? Which customers would be most likely to respond to a particular offer?

Case 1.3

Analytical CRM at AXA Seguros e Inversiones (AXA)

Spanish insurer AXA Seguros e Inversiones (AXA) has revenues of over €1.8 billion (US$2.3 billion), two million customers and is a member of global giant The AXA Group.

AXA runs marketing campaigns in Spain for its many products and services. The company wanted a better understanding of its customers, in order to be able to make more personalized offers and implement customer loyalty campaigns.

AXA used CRM vendor SAS's data mining solution to build a predictive policy cancellation model. The solution creates profiles and predictive models from customer data which enables more finely targeted campaign management, call centre management, sales-force automation and other activities involved in customer relationship management.

The model was applied to current and cancelled policies in various offices, to validate it before deploying it across Spain. Moreover, the model was used to create two control groups (subdivided into high and low probability) that were not targeted in any way, while other groups, similarly divided into high and low probability, were targeted by various marketing actions. The outcome was that the auto insurance policy cancellation rate was cut by up to nine percentage points in specific targeted segments.

With the customer insight obtained from the model, AXA is now able to design and execute personalized actions and customer loyalty campaigns tailored to the needs and expectations of high-value customers.

Source: SAS[15]

Analytical CRM has become an essential part of many CRM implementations. Operational CRM struggles to reach full effectiveness without analytical information about customers. For example, an understanding of customer value or propensities to buy underpins many operational CRM decisions, such as:

● Which customers shall we target with this offer?
● What is the relative priority of customers waiting on the line, and what level of service should be offered?
● Where should I focus my sales effort?

Analytical CRM can lead companies to decide that selling approaches should differ between customer groups. Higher potential value customers may be offered face-to-face selling; lower value customers may be contacted by telesales. Furthermore, the content and style of customer communications can be tailored, perhaps for a particular segment, using customer analytics. This enhances the probability that a given offer will be accepted by the customer.

From the customer's point of view, analytical CRM can deliver timely, customized, solutions to the customer's problems, thereby enhancing customer satisfaction. From the company's point of view, analytical CRM offers the prospect of more powerful cross-selling and up-selling programmes, and more effective customer retention and customer acquisition programmes.

Collaborative CRM

Collaborative CRM is the term used to describe the strategic and tactical alignment of normally separate enterprises in the supply chain for the more profitable identification, attraction, retention and development of customers.[16] For example, manufacturers of consumer goods and retailers can align their people, processes and technologies to serve shoppers more efficiently and effectively. They employ practices such as co-marketing, category management, collaborative forecasting, joint new product development and joint market research. Collaborative CRM uses CRM technologies to communicate and transact across organizational boundaries. Although traditional technologies such as surface mail, air mail, telephone and fax enable this to happen, the term is usually applied to more recent technologies such as electronic data interchange (EDI), portals, e-business, voice over internet protocol (VoIP), conferencing, chat rooms, web forums and e-mail. These technologies allow data and voice communication between companies and their business partners or customers. Collaborative CRM enables separate organizations to align their efforts to service customers more effectively. It allows valuable information to be shared along the supply chain.

Some CRM technology vendors have developed partner relationship management (PRM) applications that enable companies to manage complex partner or channel ecosystems and reduce the costs of partner or channel management. PRM applications are often used to manage partner promotions. A manufacturer of consumer goods might have a dozen or more different cooperative advertising programmes running simultaneously. PRM allows companies to manage the distribution of funds, plan and control promotions and measure outcomes. Sometimes the term collaborative CRM is used to describe the application of these same technologies to internal communications, for example across sales, marketing and service functions.

Case 1.4

Partner relationship management at Segway

The Segway® Personal Transporter (PT) is the world's first two-wheeled, self-balancing, electric transportation device; a product that has gained worldwide attention. Since the

Segway PT first went on sale in 2002, the company has enjoyed 50 per cent annual growth as commercial and consumer customers adopted it for its versatility, energy efficiency and ease of use.

Based in Bedford, New Hampshire, Segway has a worldwide distribution network of more than 250 outlets in 62 countries. About 90 per cent of Segway's business comes through this network of dealers and distributors.

The company wanted to deploy an integrated solution that could manage both direct and indirect sales activities in a cohesive way. The solution was the development of the Segway Partner Portal, a secure website that allows Segway employees and channel partners to manage sales processes effectively. The portal has two major functions:

1. Delivering and managing sales leads from the Segway.com website, tradeshows, advertising campaigns and various other sources.
2. Reporting retail sales for participation in Segway incentive programmes.

Segway has about 120 dealers in North America, more than 75 per cent of which have already adopted the PRM solution. Each dealership has its own account and login information, with access to the data that concerns it. Segway's regional managers can roll up the data to obtain a comprehensive view of sales and forecasts.

Source: Salesforce.com[17]

Misunderstandings about CRM

Given its recent emergence, it isn't surprising that there are a number of common misunderstandings about the nature of CRM. These are described below.

Misunderstanding 1: CRM is database marketing

Database marketing is concerned with building and exploiting high quality customer databases for marketing purposes. Companies collect data from a number of sources. These data are verified, cleaned, integrated and stored on computers, often in data warehouses or data-marts. They are then used for marketing purposes such as market segmentation, targeting, offer development and customer communication.

Whereas most large and medium-sized companies do indeed build and exploit customer databases, CRM is much wider in scope than database marketing. A lot of what we have described above as analytical CRM has the appearance of database marketing. However, database marketing is less evident in strategic, operational and collaborative CRM.

Misunderstanding 2: CRM is a marketing process

CRM software applications are used for many marketing activities: market segmentation, customer acquisition, customer retention and customer development (cross-selling and up-selling), for example. However, operational CRM extends into selling and service functions.

The deployment of CRM software to support a company's mission to become more customer-centric often means that customer-related data is shared more widely throughout the enterprise than by the marketing function alone. Operations management can use customer-related data to produce customized products and services. People management (Human Resources) can use customer preference data to help recruit and train staff for the front-line jobs that interface with customers. Research and development management can use customer-related data to focus new product development.

Customer data can not only be used to integrate various internal departments, but can also be shared across the extended enterprise with outside suppliers and partners. For example, Tesco, the international supermarket operation, has a number of collaborative new product development relationships with key suppliers. Tesco also partners with Royal Bank of Scotland to offer financial services to Tesco customers. Both these activities require the sharing of information about Tesco customers with supplier and partner. Clearly, there is more to CRM than marketing process.

Misunderstanding 3: CRM is an IT issue

Many CRM implementations are seen as IT initiatives, rather than broader strategic initiatives. True, most CRM implementations require the deployment of IT solutions. However, this should not be misunderstood. To say that CRM is about IT is like saying that gardening is about the spade or that art is about the paintbrush. IT is an enabler, a facilitator. Improvements come about in the way customers are managed through a combination of improved processes, the right competencies and attitudes (people), the right strategies and the right enabling technologies.

The importance of people and processes should not be underestimated. People develop and implement the processes that are enabled by IT. IT cannot compensate for bad processes and unskilled people. Successful CRM implementations involve people designing and implementing processes that deliver customer and company value. Often, these processes are IT-enabled. IT is therefore a part of most CRM strategies.

That said, not all CRM initiatives involve IT investments. An overarching goal of many CRM projects is the development of relationships with, and retention of, highly valued customers. This may involve behavioural changes in store employees, education of call centre staff, and a focus on empathy and reliability from salespeople. IT may play no role at all.

Misunderstanding 4: CRM is about loyalty schemes

Loyalty schemes are commonplace in many industries, such as car hire, airlines, food retail, hotels. Customers accumulate credits, such as airmiles, from purchases. These are then redeemed at some future point. Most loyalty schemes require new members to complete an application form when they join the programme. This demographic information is typically used, together with purchasing data, to help companies become more effective at customer communication and offer development. Whereas some CRM implementations are linked to loyalty schemes not all are.

Loyalty schemes may play two roles in CRM implementations. First, they generate data that can be used to guide customer acquisition, retention and development. Secondly, loyalty schemes may serve as an exit barrier. Customers who have accumulated credits in a scheme may be reluctant to exit the relationship. The credits accumulated reflect the value of the investment that the customer has made in the scheme, and therefore in the relationship.

Misunderstanding 5: CRM can be implemented by any company

Strategic CRM can, indeed, be implemented in any company. Every organization can be driven by a desire to be more customer-centric. Chief executives can establish a vision, mission and set of values that bring the customer into the heart of the business. CRM technology may play a role in that transformation. Some companies are certainly more successful than others. The banking industry has implemented CRM very widely, yet there are significant differences between the customer satisfaction ratings and customer retention rates of different banks.

Any company can also try to implement operational CRM. Any company with a sales force can automate its selling, lead management and contact management processes. The same is true for marketing and service processes. CRM technology can be used to support marketing campaigns, service requests and complaints management.

Analytical CRM is a different matter, as it is based on customer-related data. At the very least, data are needed to identify which customers are likely to generate most value in the future, and to identify within the customer base segments that have different requirements. Only then can different offers be communicated to each customer group to optimize company and customer value over the long term. If these data are missing then analytical CRM cannot be implemented.

Defining CRM

Against this background of four types of CRM and the misunderstandings about CRM, it is no easy matter to settle on a single definition of CRM.

However, we can identify a number of core CRM attributes, and integrate them into a definition that underpins the rest of this book.

CRM is the core business strategy that integrates internal processes and functions, and external networks, to create and deliver value to targeted customers at a profit. It is grounded on high quality customer-related data and enabled by information technology.

CRM is a 'core business strategy' that aims to 'create and deliver value to targeted customers at a profit'. This clearly denotes that CRM is not just about IT. CRM 'integrates internal processes and functions'. That is, it allows departments within businesses to dissolve the silo walls that separate them. Access to 'customer-related data' allows selling, marketing and service functions to be aware of each other's interactions with customers. Furthermore, back-office functions such as operations and finance can learn from and contribute to customer-related data. Access to customer-related data allows members of a business's 'external network' – suppliers, partners, distributors – to align their efforts with those of the focal company. Underpinning this core business strategy is IT: software applications and hardware.

Historically, most companies were located close to the markets they served, and knew their customers intimately. Very often there would be face-to-face, even day-to-day, interaction with customers where knowledge of customer requirements and preferences grew. However, as companies have grown larger they have become more remote from the customers they serve. The remoteness is not only geographic; it may also be cultural. Even some of the most widely admired American companies have not always understood the markets they served. Disney's development of a theme park near the French capital, Paris, was not an initial success because they failed to deliver to the value expectations of European customers. For example, Disney failed to offer visitors alcohol onsite. Europeans, however, are accustomed to enjoying a glass or two of wine with their food.

Geographic and cultural remoteness, together with business owner and management separation from customer contact, means that many, even small, companies do not have the intuitive knowledge and understanding of their customers so often found in micro-businesses, such as neighbourhood stores and hairdressing salons. This has given rise to demand for better customer-related data, a cornerstone of effective CRM.

Our definition has a strong for-profit sense. If the not-for-profit community were to replace the words business, customers and profit with appropriate equivalents, such as organization, clients and objectives, it would apply equally well in that context.

In sum, we take the view that CRM is a technology-enabled approach to management of the customer interface. Most CRM initiatives expect to have impact on the costs-to-serve and revenues streams from customers. The use of technology also changes the customer's experience of transacting and communicating with a supplier. For that reason, the customer's perspective on CRM is an important consideration in this book. CRM influences customer experience, and that is of fundamental strategic significance.

CRM constituencies

There are several important constituencies having an interest in CRM:

1. **Companies** implementing CRM: many companies have implemented CRM. Early adopters were larger companies in financial services, telecommunications and manufacturing, in the USA and Europe. Medium-sized businesses are following. There is still potential for the CRM message to reach smaller companies, public sector organizations, other worldwide markets and new business start-ups.

2. **Customers and partners of those companies**: the customers and partners of companies that implement CRM are a particularly important constituency. Because CRM influences customer experience, it can impact on customer satisfaction ratings and influence loyalty to the supplier.

3. **Vendors of CRM software**: vendors of CRM software include names such as Oracle, SAP, SAS, KANA, Microsoft and StayinFront. There has been considerable consolidation of the CRM vendor marketplace in recent years. PeopleSoft and Siebel, two of the pioneering CRM vendors, are currently owned by Oracle. Vendors sell licenses to companies, and install CRM software on the customer's servers either directly or through system integrators. The client's people are trained to use the software.

4. **CRM application service providers (ASPs)**: companies implementing CRM can also choose to access CRM functionality on a subscription basis through hosted CRM vendors such as salesforce.com, Entellium, RightNow and NetSuite. Clients upload their customer data to the host's servers and interact with the data using their web browsers. The ASP vendors deliver and manage applications and other services from remote sites to multiple users via the Internet. This is also known as SaaS (Software as a Service). Clients access CRM functionality in much the same way as they would eBay or Amazon.

5. **Vendors of CRM hardware and infrastructure**: hardware and infrastructure vendors provide the technological foundations for CRM implementations. They supply technologies such as servers, computers, handheld devices, call centre hardware, and telephony systems.

6. **Management consultants**: consultancies offer clients a diverse range of CRM-related capabilities such as strategy, business, application and technical consulting. Consultants can help companies implementing CRM in several ways: systems integration, choosing between different vendors, developing implementation plans and project management as the implementation is rolled out. Most CRM implementations are composed of a large number of smaller projects, for example, systems integration, data quality improvement, market segmentation, process engineering and culture change. The major consultancies such as Accenture, McKinsey, Bearing Point, Braxton and CGEY all offer CRM consultancy. Smaller companies sometimes offer specialized expertise. Peppers and Rogers provide strategy consulting. DunnHumby is known for its expertise in data mining for segmentation purposes.

Commercial contexts of CRM

CRM is practised in a wide variety of commercial contexts, which present a range of different customer relationship management problems. We'll consider four contexts: banks, automobile manufacturers, high-tech companies and consumer goods manufacturers.

- **Banks** deal with a large number of individual retail customers. Banks want CRM for its analytical capability to help them manage customer defection (churn) rates and to enhance cross-sell performance. Data mining techniques can be used to identify which customers are likely to defect, what can be done to win them back, which customers are hot prospects for cross-sell offers, and how best to communicate those offers. Banks want to win a greater share of customer spend (share of wallet) on financial services. In terms of operational CRM, many banks have been transferring service into contact centres and online in an effort to reduce costs, in the face of considerable resistance from some customer segments.
- **Automobile manufacturers** sell through distributor/dealer networks. They have little contact with the end-user owner or driver. They use CRM for its ability to help them develop better and more profitable relationships with their distribution networks. Being physically disconnected from drivers, they have built websites that enable them to interact with these end-users. This has improved their knowledge of customer requirements. Ultimately, they hope CRM will enable them to win a greater share of end-user spend across the car purchase, maintenance and replacement cycle.
- **High-tech companies** manufacture complex products that are generally sold by partner organizations. For example, small innovative software developers have traditionally partnered with companies such as IBM to obtain distribution and sales. However, companies like Dell have innovated channels. They go direct-to-customer (DTC). CRM helps these DTC companies to collect customer information, segment their customer base, automate their sales processes with product configurator software and deliver their customer service online. They have also developed automated relationships with suppliers, so that they carry no or low levels of inventory, which are replenished frequently in rapid response to order patterns.
- **Consumer goods manufacturers** deal with the retail trade. They use CRM to help them develop profitable relationships with retailers. CRM helps them understand costs-to-serve and customer profitability. Key account management practices are applied to strategically significant customers. IT-enabled purchasing processes deliver higher levels of accuracy in stock replenishment. Manufacturers can run CRM-enabled marketing campaigns which are highly cost-effective.

The not-for-profit context

Most of this chapter has been concerned with CRM in the for-profit context. However, CRM can also be found in the not-for-profit context. Some of the basic skills of database development and exploitation, and customer lifecycle management, are equally relevant to not-for-profit organizations.

The Salvation Army uses CRM capability to manage donor relationships, over time, using event-based fundraising. The Army also knows the value of different donor segments, and works at retaining their high value donors and at migrating first-time donors up the value ladder towards regular or long-term donor status.

Universities have deployed CRM to manage their student and alumni relationships. Today's students are thought to represent considerable potential lifetime value to Universities. For example, students who enjoy their experiences at a graduate school of business may return there for executive education. They may recommend the institution to their personal networks, or when they reach an appropriate level of seniority commission the school to consult or deliver customized training and management development. Schools as eminent as Harvard Business School have been hugely successful at fundraising from their alumni networks.

Case 1.5

Not-for-profit CRM at the city of Lynchburg

The city council of Lynchburg, VA, USA, sought to improve the levels of information and services that it provided to its 69 000 citizens. Named the 'Citizens First Program', it involved the design and implementation of an operational CRM strategy to open the lines of communication and to automate many services between the city council's 1100 employees, municipal departments and the citizens of Lynchburg. The project comprised the establishment of a website to provide citizens with 24/7 access to information concerning the city's services and facilities, in addition enabling citizens to make requests for information, inquiries and complaints. Supporting the website was CRM software and a linked call centre, providing personalized follow-up and ongoing support.

Since implementation, many benefits have been seen, namely:

- a 50% reduction in time taken to respond to citizen inquiries
- citizens can track the progress of requests for service, inquiries, etc.
- the city council can measure and report on organizational performance
- levels of communication within the city council and between municipal departments have improved.

Models of CRM

A number of comprehensive CRM models have been developed. We introduce five of them here.

The IDIC model

The IDIC model was developed by Peppers and Rogers, the consultancy firm, and has featured in a number of their books.[18] The IDIC model suggests that companies should take four actions in order to build closer one-to-one relationships with customers:

- **identify** who your customers are and build a deep understanding of them
- **differentiate** your customers to identify which customers have most value now and which offer most for the future
- **interact** with customers to ensure that you understand customer expectations and their relationships with other suppliers or brands
- **customize** the offer and communications to ensure that the expectations of customers are met.

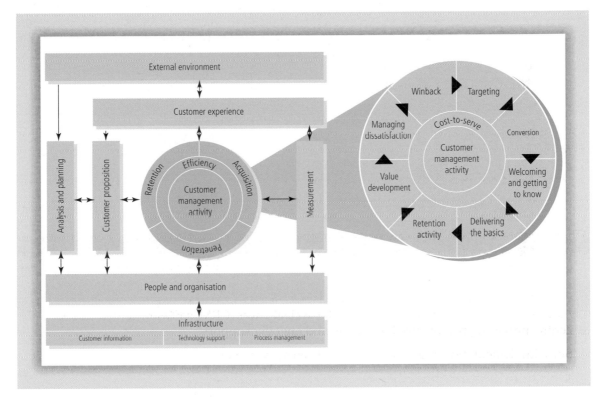

Figure 1.1 The QCi customer management model

The QCi model

The QCi model shown in Figure 1.1 is also a product of a consultancy firm.[19] The model's authors prefer to describe their model as a customer management model, omitting the word 'relationship'. At the heart of the model they depict a series of activities that companies need to perform in order to acquire and retain customers. The model features people performing processes and using technology to assist in those activities.

The CRM value chain

Francis Buttle's model was the subject of a recent book.[20] The model, as shown in Figure 1.2, consists of five primary stages and four supporting conditions leading towards the end goal of enhanced customer profitability. The primary stages of customer portfolio analysis, customer intimacy, network development, value proposition development and managing the customer lifecycle are sequenced to ensure that a company, with the support of its network of suppliers, partners and employees, creates and delivers value propositions that acquire and retain profitable customers. The supporting conditions of leadership and culture, data and IT, people and processes enable the CRM strategy to function effectively and efficiently.

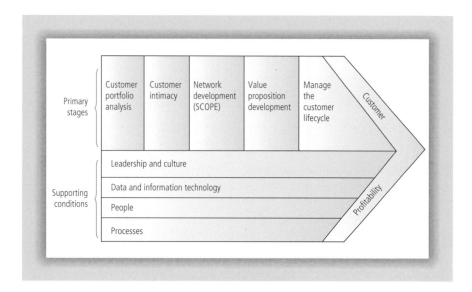

Figure 1.2
The CRM value chain

Payne's five-process model

The fourth comprehensive model was developed by Adrian Payne.[21] This model (Figure 1.3) clearly identifies five core processes in CRM: the strategy development process, the value creation process, the multichannel integration process, the performance assessment process and the information management process. The first two represent strategic CRM; the multichannel integration process represents operational CRM; the information management process is analytical CRM.

The Gartner competency model

The final comprehensive CRM model comes from Gartner Inc. Gartner Inc. is a leading IT research and advisory company that employs some 1200 research analysts and consultants in 75 countries, and has a significant place in CRM research. Figure 1.4 presents Gartner's CRM competency model.

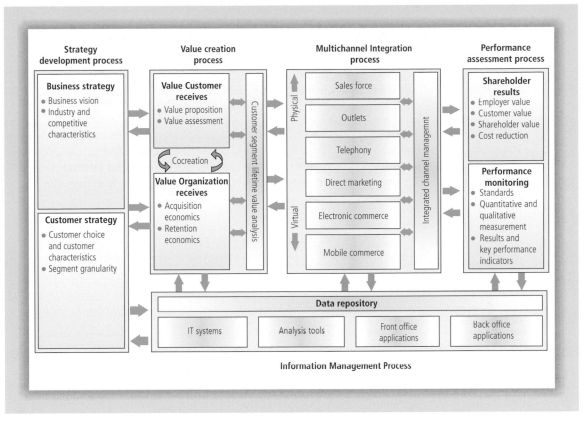

Figure 1.3 Payne's model of CRM[22]

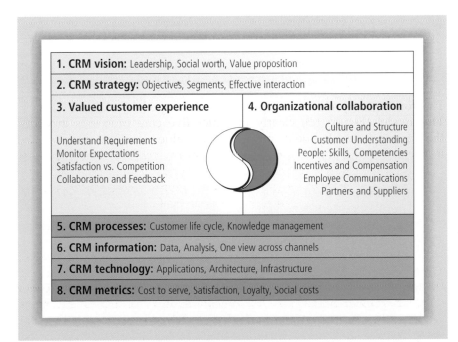

1. CRM vision: Leadership, Social worth, Value proposition

2. CRM strategy: Objectives, Segments, Effective interaction

3. Valued customer experience

Understand Requirements
Monitor Expectations
Satisfaction vs. Competition
Collaboration and Feedback

4. Organizational collaboration

Culture and Structure
Customer Understanding
People: Skills, Competencies
Incentives and Compensation
Employee Communications
Partners and Suppliers

5. CRM processes: Customer life cycle, Knowledge management

6. CRM information: Data, Analysis, One view across channels

7. CRM technology: Applications, Architecture, Infrastructure

8. CRM metrics: Cost to serve, Satisfaction, Loyalty, Social costs

Figure 1.4
Gartner's CRM
model

The model suggests that companies need competencies in eight areas for CRM to be successful. These include building a CRM vision, developing CRM strategies, designing valued customer experiences, intra and extra-organizational collaboration, managing customer lifecycle processes, information management, technology implementation and developing measures indicative of CRM success or failure.

Summary

In this chapter you have learned that the expression CRM has a variety of meanings. Four types of CRM have been identified: strategic, operational, analytical and collaborative. There are many misunderstandings about CRM. For example, some people wrongly equate CRM with loyalty programmes, whereas others think of CRM as an IT issue. Although CRM is generally thought of as a business practice, it is also applied in the not-for-profit context. A number of different constituencies have an interest in CRM, including CRM consultancies, CRM software vendors, CRM application service providers, CRM hardware and infrastructure vendors, companies that are implementing CRM and their customers. A number of different models of CRM have been developed.

Finally, we have produced a definition that underpins the rest of this book. We define CRM as the core business strategy that integrates internal processes and functions, and external networks, to create and deliver value to targeted customers at a profit. It is grounded on high quality customer-related data and enabled by information technology.

References

1. Gamble, P., Stone, M. and Woodcock, N. (1999) *Customer relationship marketing: up close and personal*. London: Kogan Page; Jain, S.C. (2005). CRM shifts the paradigm. *Journal of Strategic Marketing*, Vol. 13, December, pp. 275–291; Evans, M., O'Malley, L. and Patterson, M. (2004) *Exploing direct and customer relationship marketing*. London: Thomson.
2. http://www.forrester.com/Research/Document/Excerpt/0,7211, 43091,00.html. Accessed 13 September 2007.
3. http://whatis.techtarget.com/definition/0,289893,sid9_gci213567, 00.html. Accessed 29 November 2005.
4. http://onlinebusiness.about.com/cs/marketing/g/CRM.htm. Accessed 29 November 2005.
5. http://www.siebel.com/what-is-crm/software-solutions.shtm. Accessed 29 November 2005.
6. http://computing-dictionary.thefreedictionary.com/CRM. Accessed 29 November 2005.
7. http://www.destinationcrm.com/articles/default.asp? ArticleID=5460.

8. Kotler, P. (2000) *Marketing management: the millennium edition.* Englewood Cliffs, NJ: Prentice-Hall International.
9. Rogers, E.M. (1962) *Diffusion of innovations.* New York: Free Press.
10. Deshpandé, R. (1999) *Developing a market orientation.* London: Sage.
11. Greenguard, S. (2002) When customer focus is king. Case study: Boise Office Solutions. Brief article – company profile. http://findarticles.com/p/articles/mi_m4070/is_2002_June/ai_87430207. Accessed 20 January 2008.
12. Morgan, A. and Inks, S.A. (2001) Technology and the sales force. *Industrial Marketing Management*, Vol. 30(5), 463–472.
13. Engle, R.L. and Barnes, M.L. (2000) Sales force automation usage, effectiveness, and cost-benefit in Germany, England and the United States. *Journal of Business and Industrial Marketing*, Vol. 15(4), 216–242.
14. Contact centres differ from call centres in that they not only handle phone calls, but also communications in other media such as mail, fax, e-mail and SMS.
15. http://www.sas.com/success/axaseguros.html. Accessed 20 January 2007.
16. Kracklauer, A.H., Mills, D.Q. and Seifert, D. (eds) (2004) *Collaborative customer relationship management: taking CRM to the next level.* Berlin: Springer-Verlag.
17. http://www.salesforce.com/assets/pdf/casestudies/pdf_cs_segway.pdf. Accessed 20 January 2008.
18. Peppers, D. and Rogers, M. (1996) *The 1-to-1 future: building business relationships one customer at a time.* London: Piatkus; Peppers, D. and Rogers, M. (1998) *Enterprise 1-to-1.* London: Piatkus; Peppers, D. and Rogers, M. (1999) *The 1-to-1 fieldbook.* London: Piatkus; Peppers, D. and Rogers, M. (2000) *The 1-to-1 manager.* London: Piatkus; Peppers, D. and Rogers, M. (2001) *One-to-one B2B: CRM strategies for the real economy.* London: Piatkus; Peppers, D. and Rogers, M. (2004) *Managing customer relationships: a strategic framework.* Hoboken, NJ: John Wiley & Sons; Peppers, D. and Rogers, M. (2005) *Return on customer: creating maximum value from your scarcest resource.* New York: Doubleday.
19. http://qci.co.uk/public_tace/; Woodcock, N., Stone, M. and Foss, B. (2002) *The Customer Management Scorecard.* London: Kogan Page.
20. Buttle, F. (2004) *Customer relationship management: concepts and tools.* Oxford: Elsevier Butterworth-Heinemann.
21. Payne, A. (2005) *Handbook of CRM: achieving excellence through customer management.* Oxford: Elsevier Butterworth-Heinemann; Payne, A. and Frow, P. (2005) A strategic framework for customer relationship management. *Journal of Marketing*, Vol. 69, October, pp. 167–176.
22. Payne, A. (2005) *Handbook of CRM: achieving excellence through customer management.* Oxford: Butterworth-Heinemann.

Chapter 2
Understanding relationships

By the end of this chapter, you will understand:

1. how to recognize a relationship
2. attributes of successful relationships
3. the importance of trust and commitment within a relationship
4. why companies and customers are sometimes motivated to establish and maintain relationships with each other, and sometimes not
5. the meaning and importance of customer lifetime value
6. the five different schools of thought that contribute to our understanding of relationships and relationship management.

What is a relationship?

The 'R' of CRM stands for 'relationship'. But what do we really mean by the expression 'relationship?' Certainly, most of us would understand what it means to be in a personal relationship, but what is a relationship between a customer and supplier?

At the very least a relationship involves interaction over time. If there is only a one-off transaction, like buying a vacuum cleaner from a specialist outlet, most of us wouldn't call this a relationship. Thinking in terms of a dyadic relationship, that is a relationship between two parties, if we take this interaction over time as a critical feature, we can define the term 'relationship' as follows:

> A relationship is composed of a series of interactive episodes between dyadic parties over time.

Let's be clear about what is meant by 'interactive episode'. Episodes are time bound (they have a beginning and an end) and are nameable. Within a sales representative–customer relationship it is often possible to identify a number of discrete episodes, such as making a purchase, enquiring about a product, making a sales call, negotiating terms, dealing with a complaint, resolving an invoicing dispute and playing a round of golf.

Each episode in turn is composed of a series of interactions. Interaction consists of action and response to that action. Within each episode, each participant will act towards, and interact with, the other. The content of each episode is a range of communicative behaviours including speech, deeds (actions) and body language.

Some authorities think that it is insufficient, even naïve, to define a relationship as interaction over time. Jim Barnes, for example, suggests that there needs to be some emotional content to the interaction.[1] This implies some type of affective connection, attachment or bond.

Similarly, a relationship has been said to exist only when the parties move from a state of independence to dependence or interdependence.[2] When a customer buys an occasional latte from a coffee shop, this is a transaction not a relationship. If the customer returns repeatedly because she likes the store's atmosphere, the way the coffee is prepared or has taken a shine to the barista, this looks more like a relationship. And while, in this instance, there is dependence (of the customer on the coffee shop) there is no interdependence.

This suggests the parties within the dyad may have very different ideas about whether they are in a relationship. For example, in a professional procurement context for a multinational organization, corporate buying staff may think they are being tough and transactional. Their suppliers may feel that they have built a relationship.

We can conclude from this that a relationship is a social construct. That is to say, a relationship exists if people believe that a relationship exists and they act accordingly. It is also apparent that relationships can be unilateral or reciprocal; either one or both of the parties may believe they are in a relationship.

Change within relationships

Relationships change over time. Parties become closer or more distant; interactions become more or less frequent. Because they evolve, they can vary considerably, both in the number and variety of episodes, and the interactions that take place within those episodes. Dwyer has identified five general phases through which customer–supplier relationships can evolve.[3]

1. awareness
2. exploration
3. expansion
4. commitment
5. dissolution.

Awareness is when each party comes to the attention of the other as a possible exchange partner. Exploration is the period of investigation and testing during which the parties explore each others' capabilities and performance. Some trial purchasing takes place. If the trial is unsuccessful the relationship can be terminated with few costs. The exploration phase is thought to comprise five subprocesses: attraction, communication and bargaining, development and exercise of power, development of norms, and development of expectations. Expansion is the phase in which there is increasing interdependence. More transactions take place and trust begins to develop. The commitment phase is characterized by increased adaptation and mutually understood roles and goals. Purchasing processes that have become automated are a sure sign of commitment.

Not all relationships reach the commitment phase. Many are terminated before that stage. There may be a breach of trust that forces a partner to reconsider the relationship. Perhaps the requirements of the customer change and the supplier is no longer needed. Relationship termination can be bilateral or unilateral. Bilateral termination is when both parties agree to end the relationship. They will probably want to retrieve whatever assets they invested in the relationship. Unilateral termination is when one of the parties moves to end the relationship. Customers may exit relationships for many reasons, such as repeated service failures or changed product requirements. Suppliers may choose to exit relationships because of their failure to contribute to sales volume or profit goals. One option to resolve the problem and continue the relationship may be to reduce cost-to-serve.

This model of relationship development highlights two attributes of highly developed relationships: trust and commitment. These attributes have been the subject of a considerable amount of research.[4]

Trust

Trust is focused. That is, although there may be a generalized sense of confidence and security, these feelings are directed. One party may trust the other party's:

- **benevolence**: a belief that one party acts in the interests of the other
- **honesty**: a belief that the other party's word is reliable or credible
- **competence**: a belief that the other party has the necessary expertise to perform as required.

The development of trust is an investment in relationship building which has a long-term payoff. Trust emerges as parties share experiences, and interpret and assess each other's motives. As they learn more about each other, risk and doubt are reduced. For these reasons, trust has been described as the glue that holds a relationship together across time and experience.[5]

When mutual trust exists between partners, both are motivated to make investments in the relationship. These investments, which serve as exit barriers, may be either tangible (e.g. property) or intangible (e.g. knowledge). Such investments may or may not be retrievable when the relationship dissolves.

If trust is absent, conflict and uncertainty rise, while cooperation falls. Lack of trust clearly provides a shaky foundation for a successful customer-supplier relationship.

It has been suggested that as relationships evolve over time so does the character of trust:[6]

- **calculus-based trust**: this is present in the early stages of a relationship and is quite calculative. It is as if one party says: 'I trust you because of what I am gaining or expect to gain from the relationship'. The outcomes of creating and maintaining the new relationship are weighed against those of dissolving it.
- **knowledge-based trust**: this relies on the individual parties' interactive history and knowledge of each other, allowing each to make accurate predictions about how the other will act.

- **identification-based trust**: this happens when mutual understanding is so deep that each can act as substitute for the other in interpersonal interaction. This is found in the later stages of relationship development.

Commitment

Commitment is an essential ingredient for successful, long-term, relationships. Morgan and Hunt define relationship commitment as follows:

> Commitment is shown by 'an exchange partner believing that an ongoing relationship with another is so important as to warrant maximum effort to maintain it; that is, the committed party believes the relationship is worth working on to ensure that it endures indefinitely'. [7]

Commitment arises from trust, shared values, and the belief that partners will be difficult to replace. Commitment motivates partners to cooperate in order to preserve relationship investments. Commitment means partners eschew short-term alternatives in favour of more stable, long-term benefits associated with current partners. Where customers have choice, they make commitments only to trustworthy partners, because commitment entails vulnerability, leaving them open to opportunism. For example, a corporate customer committed to future purchasing of raw materials from a particular supplier may experience the downside of opportunistic behaviour if the supplier raises prices.

Evidence of commitment is found in the investments that one party makes in the other. One party makes investments in the promising relationship and if the other responds, the relationship evolves and the partners become increasingly committed to doing business with each other. Investments can include time, money and the sidelining of current or alternative relationships. A partner's commitment to a relationship is directly represented in the size of the investment in the relationship, since this represents termination costs. Highly committed relationships have very high termination costs, since some of these relationship investments may be irretrievable. In addition, there may be significant costs incurred in switching to an alternative supplier, such as search costs, learning costs and psychic costs.

Relationship quality

This discussion of trust and commitment suggests that some relationships can be thought to be of better quality than others. Research into relationship quality generally cites trust and commitment as core attributes of a high quality relationship.[8] However, a number of other attributes have also been identified, including relationship satisfaction, mutual goals and cooperative norms.

Relationship satisfaction is not the same as commitment. Commitment to a supplier comes as investments are made in the relationship, and investments are only made if the committed party is satisfied with their transactional history. In other words, investments are made in relationships which are satisfactory.[9] Mutual goals are present when the parties share objectives that can only be achieved through joint action and relationship continuity. Cooperative norms are seen when relational parties work together constructively and interdependently to resolve problems.

Given that CRM implementations are often designed to build closer, more value-laden relationships with customers, it makes sense for managers to be aware of the quality of the relationships they have with customers.

Why companies want relationships with customers

The fundamental reason for companies wanting to build relationships with customers is economic. Companies generate better results when they manage their customer base in order to identify, acquire, satisfy and retain profitable customers. These are key objectives of many CRM strategies.

Improving customer retention rates has the effect of increasing the size of the customer base. Figure 2.1 compares two companies. Company A has a churn rate (customer defection rate) of 5 per cent per annum; company B's churn rate is 10 per cent. Put another way, their respective customer retention rates are 95 and 90 per cent. Starting from the same position and acquiring an identical number of new customers each year, company A's customer base is 19 per cent larger than company B's after four years: 1268 customers compared with 1066 customers.

Churn rates vary considerably. The energy utilities used to enjoy very low churn levels because of their monopoly positions. However, after

Year	Company A (5% churn)			Company B (10% churn)		
	Existing customers	New customers	Total customer base	Existing customers	New customers	Total customer base
2001	1000	100	1100	1000	100	1100
2002	1045	100	1145	990	100	1090
2003	1088	100	1188	981	100	1081
2004	1129	100	1229	973	100	1073
2005	1168	100	1268	966	100	1066

Figure 2.1
The effect of customer retention on customer numbers

industry deregulation in the UK, about 25 per cent of utility customers changed suppliers within the first 24 months. The industry had been expecting 5–10 per cent churn, and were surprised at the actual levels. Most switchers were looking for better prices and to achieve a dual-fuel (gas and electricity) discount.

Case 2.1

Consequences of customer churn at Sprint Nextel

Sprint Nextel, the third largest wireless telecommunications firm in the USA, is downsizing its workforce by 4000 jobs and closing 125 stores in the first half of 2008. The moves are part of cost-saving measures prompted by anticipated decreases in the firm's subscriber base, revenues and profitability in the fourth quarter of 2007. The firm expects to save $700 to $800 million annually by cutting the jobs.

Sprint Nextel lost 190 000 subscribers and 683 000 'post-paid' customers during the fourth quarter of 2007. The subscriber losses are being attributed to a slowdown in the growth of wireless subscriptions in the USA, and continuing customer defection to larger rivals AT&T Mobile and Verizon Wireless since Sprint bought Nextel Communications for $36 billion in 2005. The firm is also struggling with service quality problems.

On this news, shares of Sprint Nextel fell to their lowest price since October 2002.

Source: http://www.allheadlinenews.com[10]

There is little merit in growing the customer base aimlessly. The goal must be to retain existing customers and recruit new customers that have future profit potential or are important for other strategic purposes.[11] Not all customers are of equal importance. Some customers may not be worth recruiting or retaining at all, for example those who have a high cost-to-serve, are debtors, late payers or promiscuous in the sense that they switch frequently between suppliers.

Other things being equal, a larger customer base does deliver better business performance. Similarly, as customer retention rates rise (or defection rates fall), so does the average tenure of a customer, as shown in Figure 2.2. Tenure is the term used to describe the length of time a customer remains a customer. The impacts of small improvements in customer retention are hugely magnified at higher levels of retention. For example, improving the customer retention rate from 75 to 80 per cent grows average customer tenure from 10 to 12.5 years. Managing tenure by reducing defection rates can be critical. For example, it can take 13 years for utility customers to break even by recovering the costs of their initial recruitment.

Managing customer retention and tenure intelligently generates two key benefits for companies; reduced marketing costs and better customer insight.

Customer retention rate (%)	Average customer tenure
50	2 years
67	3 years
75	4 years
80	5 years
90	10 years
92	12.5 years
95	20 years
96	25 years
97	33.3 years
98	50 years
99	100 years

Figure 2.2
Retention rate and
average customer
tenure

Reduced marketing costs

Improving customer retention reduces a company's marketing costs. Fewer dollars need to be spent replacing churned customers.[12] For example, it has been estimated that it costs an advertising agency at least 20 times as much to recruit a new client than it does to retain an existing client. Major agencies can spend up to $4 million on research, strategic analysis and creative work in pitching for one major client, with up to four creative teams working on different executions. An agency might incur these costs several times over as it pitches to several prospective clients to replace a lost client.[13] In addition to reducing the costs of customer acquisition, cost-to-serve existing customers also tends to fall over time. Ultimately, as in some business-to-business markets, the relationship may become fully automated. Some supply-chain relationships, for example, employ electronic data interchange (EDI) that fully automates the ordering, inventory and invoicing processes. EDI is a relationship investment that acts as an exit barrier.

Better customer insight

As customer tenure lengthens, suppliers are able to develop a better understanding of customer requirements and expectations. Customers also come to understand what a supplier can do for them. Consequently, suppliers become better placed to identify and satisfy customer requirements profitably, selling more product and service to the retained customer. Over time, as relationships deepen, trust and commitment between the parties is likely to grow. Under these circumstances, revenue and profit streams from customers become more secure. One study, for example, shows that the average online clothing customer spends 67 per cent more, and grocery customers spend 23 per cent more, in months 31–36 of a relationship than they spend in months 0–6.[14] In sum, both the cost and revenue sides of the profit equation are impacted by customer retention.

Some companies employ a model that has been variously known as a value ladder[15] or value staircase[16] to help them understand where customers are positioned in terms of their tenure with the company. Customers typically buy from a portfolio of more or less equivalent offers or suppliers. For example, large and medium-sized businesses often do business with more than one bank, and consumers may select a soft drink from a small portfolio of branded carbonated beverages. When customers climb the ladder, their value to your company grows. Your share of their portfolio expands. Put another way, your share of customer spending, or customer wallet, grows. In Table 2.1 we present a seven-stage customer journey from suspect status to advocate status.

Suspect	Does the potential customer fit your target market profile?
Prospect	The customer fits the target market profile and is being approached for the first time.
First-time customer	The customer makes a first purchase.
Repeat customer	The customer makes additional purchases. Your offer plays a minor role in the customer's portfolio.
Majority customer	The customer selects your company as supplier of choice. You occupy a significant place in the customer's portfolio.
Loyal customer	The customer is resistant to switching suppliers and has a strong positive attitude to your company or offer.
Advocate	The customer generates additional referral dollars through positive word-of-mouth.

Table 2.1 The customer journey

As in the Dwyer model cited earlier, not every customer progresses uniformly along the path from 'never-a-customer' to 'always-a-customer'. Some will have a long maturity phase (i.e. loyal customer); others will have a shorter life, perhaps never shifting from first-time customer to repeat customer; others still might never convert from prospect to first-timer. CRM software allows companies to trace where customers are on this pathway and to allocate resources intelligently to advance suitable customers along the value trajectory.

Costs and revenues vary from stage to stage of the journey. In the early stages, a company may invest significant sums in converting a prospect into a first-time customer. The investment in initiating a relationship may not be recovered for some time. For example, Reichheld and Sasser have shown that it takes a credit-card company approaching two years to recover the costs of customer acquisition.[17] Another study shows that the average online clothing customer takes four purchases (12 months) to recover the costs of their acquisition, whereas grocery customers take 18 months to break even.[18] In later years, the transactions within the relationship may become highly routinized and very low cost to complete, because each party knows and trusts the other.

Lifetime value

This leads to the core CRM idea that a customer should not be viewed as a set of independent transactions, but as a lifetime income stream. In the automobile industry, for example, it is estimated that a General Motors retail customer is worth $276 000 over a lifetime of purchasing cars (11 or more vehicles), parts and service. Fleet operators are worth considerably more.[19] When a GM customer switches to Ford, the revenue streams from that customer may be lost for ever. This makes customer retention a strategically important goal for GM.

Case 2.2

Customer lifetime value (CLV) in the banking industry

One in five banking executives does not measure CLV. Couple this with the 22 per cent who do not measure portfolio or wallet share, and it is easy to see why cross-selling is such a challenge for financial service providers. Unless a banker knows which of a customer's financial needs are being met, it is exceedingly difficult to suggest additional services. A robust business intelligence system can provide a financial services firm with a 360 degree view of the customer. Transactions can be consolidated with demographic and psychographic data, revenue and profit measures, as well as with historical customer service incidents and queries. With this total picture, the provider can see the customer from multiple perspectives and craft programmes that will satisfy a broader range of client requirements. Part of this multifaceted view of the customer is the ability to aggregate multiple customers into a household perspective. The benefits of this consolidated view are clear and strong. Multiple financial service needs can be seen in total, investment opportunities can be tied to life events for cohabiting family members and marketing costs can be driven down by providing a single, comprehensive marketing message.

Source: IBM[20]

Lifetime value (LTV), which is also known as customer lifetime value (CLV), is a measure of a customer's, or customer segment's, profit-generation for a company. LTV can be defined as follows:

> Lifetime value is the present day value of all net margins earned from a relationship with a customer, customer segment or cohort.

LTV can be estimated at the level of the individual customer, customer segment or cohort. A cohort of customers is a group that has some characteristic or set of characteristics in common. These might be customers recruited in a single year or recruited though a single campaign or channel. This type of analysis is useful, for example, to find out whether certain channels are more effective or more efficient at recruiting high value customers. A European motoring organization knows that it costs an average of $105 to recruit a new member. However, recruitment costs vary across channels. The organization's member-get-member (MGM) referral scheme costs $66, the organization's direct response TV campaign costs $300, and door drops cost $210 per newly acquired member. The

MGM scheme is most cost-effective at customer acquisition, but if these customers churn at a high rate and cost significantly more to serve, they may in fact be less valuable than customers generated at higher initial cost. In fact, customers acquired through the MGM referral scheme remain members longer, buy more and also generate word-of-mouth referrals.

To compute LTV, all historic net margins are compounded up to today's value and all future net margins are discounted back to today's value. Estimates of LTV potential look only to the future and ignore the past.

The focus on net margins rather than gross margins is because a customer that appears to be valuable on the basis of the gross margins generated might seem less profitable once cost-to-serve the customer is taken into account. Companies that do not have the processes in place to allocate costs to customers cannot use net margin data. They must work either with gross margin or sales revenue data.

For most companies, an important strategic objective is to identify and attract those customers or segments that have the highest LTV potential. They are unconcerned with the past. What matters is the future.

Research by Reichheld and Sasser indicates why it is important to look forward to compute LTV.[21] Their data suggest that profit margins tend to accelerate over time, as shown in Figure 2.3. This has four causes.

1. **Revenues grow** over time as customers buy more. In the credit-card example in Figure 2.3, users tend to grow their balances over time as they become more relaxed about using their card for an increasing range of purchases. Also, a satisfied customer may look to buy additional categories of product from a preferred supplier. An insurance company that has a loyal car insurance customer is likely to experience some success cross-selling other personal lines, for example home, property and travel insurance.

Profit (loss) per customer over time ($)						
				Year		
Service	0	1	2	3	4	5
Credit card	(51)	30	42	44	49	55
Industrial laundry		144	166	192	222	256
Industrial distribution		45	99	121	144	168
Auto servicing		25	35	70	88	88

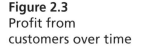

Figure 2.3
Profit from customers over time

2. **Cost-to-serve is lower** for existing customers, because both supplier and customer understand each other. For example, customers do not make demands on the company that it cannot satisfy. Similarly companies do not communicate offers that have little or no value to customers.

3. **Referrals are generated** by existing, satisfied customers through their unpaid advocacy. Lexus UK, for example, believes that every delighted customer generates £600 000 of referral business. Word-of-mouth is recognized as powerfully persuasive because it is regarded as being independent and unpaid.

4. **Higher prices are paid** by existing customers than those paid by new customers. This is partly because they are not offered the discounts that are often employed to win new customers, and partly because they are less sensitive to price offers from other potential suppliers because they are satisfied with their experience.

Computing LTV

The computation of LTV potential is, in principle, very straightforward. Several pieces of information are required. For an existing customer, you need to know:

1. what is the probability that the customer will buy products and services from the company in the future, period-by-period?
2. what will the gross margins on those purchases be, period-by-period?
3. what will the cost of serving the customer be, period-by-period?

For new customers an additional piece of information is needed:

4. what is the cost of acquiring the customer?

Finally, to bring future margins back to today's value, another question needs to be answered for both existing and new customers:

5. what discount rate should be applied to future net margins?

Some commentators suggest that LTV estimates should not be based only on future purchasing, but also on word-of-mouth (WOM) influence. The logic is that a satisfied and retained customer not only buys, but also influences others to buy. Lee and colleagues show that incorporation of WOM effects increases LTV estimates significantly.[22]

Figure 2.4 demonstrates the impact that discount rate has on customer value. Without discounting future profits, the customer appears to have an LTV of $235. However, once a 15 per cent discount rate is applied, the customer's LTV in today's dollar is only $127.43. A common practice is to use the weighted average cost of capital (WACC) as the discount factor. WACC takes into account the costs of the two sources of capital: debt and equity. Each usually has a different cost, and therefore the average cost of capital for a business will reflect the degree to which the business is funded by the two sources.

Computation of a meaningful LTV estimate requires companies to be able to forecast customer buying behaviour, product and service costs and prices, the costs of capital (for determining the discount rate) and the costs of acquiring and retaining customers. This is very demanding, especially at the level of the individual customer, but it is a challenge that analytical CRM implementations often address.

A number of companies have developed models that produce approximate LTV estimates. US Bancorp, for example, calculates a

1. Undiscounted profit earned over 5-years:			2. Discounted profit earned over 5-years (15% discount rate)		
Year	0	−$50	Year	0	−$50.00
	1	+$30		1	+$30 ÷ 1.15 = $26.09
	2	+$40		2	+$40 ÷ 1.15^2 = $30.25
	3	+$55		3	+$55 ÷ 1.15^3 = $36.16
	4	+$72		4	+$72 ÷ 1.15^4 = $41.17
	5	+$88		5	+$88 ÷ 1.15^5 = $43.76
		$235			$127.43

The net present value of 5-years profit earned from this customer is $127.43

Figure 2.4
Impact of discount rate on lifetime value

customer profitability metric called customer relationship value (CRV) in which they use historical product ownership to generate 'propensity to buy' indices. Overhead costs are not factored into the computation. Within their customer base, they have been able to identify four CRV segments, each having different value, cost, attrition and risk profiles:

- top tier, 11% of customers
- threshold, next 22%
- fence sitters, next 39%
- value destroyers, bottom 28%.

Each of these segments is treated to different value propositions and customer management programmes: product offers, lending decisions, fee waivers, channel options and retention efforts. For situations where the cost of generating accurate LTV data is thought not to be prohibitive, Berger and Nasr have developed a number of mathematical models that can be used in LTV estimation.[23]

Case 2.3

High lifetime value (LTV) customers at Barclays Bank

Barclays is a leading UK-based bank with global operations. As part of the bank's CRM strategy, it undertook customer portfolio analysis to identify which retail segments were most strategically significant. The analysis found that customers within the 25–35 year age group, who were professionally employed, who had a mortgage and/or credit-card product were most strategically significant. These were the bank's most profitable customers.

The bank also found that this segment represented the highest potential lifetime value (LTV) for the bank, 12 per cent greater than any other segment. LTV is derived from the bank's estimates of future income from fees, interest and other charges over their lifetime as a customer.

Figure 2.5 shows how to compute LTV for a cohort of customers. In year 0, the company spent $10 million in marketing campaigns to generate new customers. The result was 100 000 new customers added to the customer base at an acquisition cost of $100 per customer.

Year	$ Profit per customer	$ net present value at 15% discount	Customer retention rate (%)	No. of customers	$ Total annual profit
0	−100			100 000	−10 000 000
1	50	43.48	60	60 000	2 608 800
2	70	52.93	70	42 000	2 223 062
3	100	65.75	75	31 500	2 071 125
4	140	80.00	80	25 200	2 016 000
5	190	94.53	85	21 420	2 024 776
6	250	108.23	90	19 278	2 086 364
7	320	120.30	92	17 736	2 133 654
8	400	130.72	94	16 672	2 179 346
9	450	127.84	95	15 838	2 024 744
10	500	123.15	96	15 204	1 872 372

Figure 2.5
Computing cohort value

In year 1 the company lost 40 per cent of these new customers, but the remaining 60 per cent each generated $50 contribution to profit. If this is discounted at 15 per cent, in year 0's currency each retained customer's profit contribution is $43.48. In year 2, the retention rate rises from 60 to 70 per cent, and each of the remaining customers contributes $70 ($52.93 at discounted rate) to profit. You can see from the right hand column in Figure 2.5 that it takes nearly five years to recover the investment of acquiring this cohort. The data demonstrate two well-established phenomena. First, profit per customer rises over time, for reasons set out earlier in this chapter. Secondly, customer retention rate rises over time. It is feasible to use data such as these to manage a business for improved profitability. Several strategies are available:

1. Improve customer retention rate in the early years of the relationship. This will produce a larger number of customers to generate higher profits in the later years.
2. Increase the profit earned per customer by:
   a. reducing cost-to-serve
   b. cross-selling or up-selling additional products and services.
3. Become better at customer acquisition by:
   a. using more cost effective recruitment channels
   b. better qualification of prospects. Customers who defect early on perhaps should not have been recruited in the first place.

Don't leave this discussion of LTV by believing that if you improve customer retention business performance will automatically improve. It depends entirely on which customers are retained and how you manage those relationships.

Why companies do NOT want relationships with customers

Despite the financial benefits that can accrue from a relationship, companies sometimes resist entering into relationships with customers. In the business-to-business (B2B) context there are a number of reasons for this resistance.

Loss of control: a mature relationship involves give and take on both sides of the dyad. In bilateral relationships, suppliers may have to give up unilateral control over their own business's resources. For example, a supplier of engineering services might not want to provide free pre-sales consultancy for a new project with an established client because of the high costs involved. However, the relationship partner might have clear expectations of what activities should be performed and what resources deployed by both themselves and the other party.

Exit costs: not all relationships survive. It is not necessarily easy or cost-effective to exit a relationship. Sometimes, investments that are made in a relationship are not returned when a relationship breaks down. Relationship investments vary from the insignificant (e.g. co-branding of promotional literature) to highly significant (e.g. setting up a new production line to service a particular customer's requirements). A company might justifiably be concerned about the security of a relationship-based investment in new manufacturing operations.

Resource commitment: relationships require the commitment of resources such as people, time and money. Companies have to decide whether it is better to allocate resources to customer management or some other area of the business, such as operations or research and development. Once resources are committed, they can become sunk costs. Sunk costs are unrecoverable past expenditures. These would not normally be taken into account when deciding whether to continue in a relationship, because they cannot be recovered whether the relationship endures or not. However, it is a common instinct to consider them.

Opportunity costs: if resources are committed to one customer, they cannot be allocated to another. Relationships carry with them high opportunity costs. If you commit resources to customer A, you may have to give up the possibility of a relationship with customer B, even if that does seem to be a better proposition. An engineering consultancy that commits consultants to pre-sales activities with a current client might incur the opportunity cost of losing more lucrative work generating new business opportunities from other prospective clients.

Why customers want relationships with suppliers

B2B context

There are a number of circumstances when a B2B customer might want a long-term relationship with a supplier:

Product complexity: if the product or its applications are complex, for example, networking infrastructure.

Product strategic significance: if the product is strategically important or mission-critical, for example, supply of essential raw materials for a continuous process manufacturer.

Service requirements: if there are down-stream service requirements, for example, for machine tools.

Financial risk: if financial risk is high, for example, in buying large items of capital equipment.

Reciprocity: a financial audit practice may want a close relationship with a management consultancy, so that each party benefits from referrals by the other.

B2C context

In a business-to-consumer (B2C) context, relationships may be valued when the customer experiences benefits over and above those directly derived from acquiring, consuming or using the product or service. For example:

Recognition: customers may feel more valued when recognized and addressed by name, for example at a retail bank branch, or as a frequent flyer.

Personalization: products or services can be customized. For example, over time, a hairdresser may come to understand a customer's particular preferences or expectations.

Power: relationships with suppliers can be empowering. For example, some of the usual power asymmetry in relationships between banks and their customers may be reversed when customers feel that they have personal relationships with particular bank officers or branches.

Risk reduction: risk takes many forms – performance, physical, financial, social and psychological. High levels of perceived risk are uncomfortable for many customers. A relationship can reduce or even, perhaps, eliminate perceived risk. For example, a customer may develop a relationship with a service station to reduce the perceived performance and physical risk attached to having a car serviced. The relationship provides the assurance that the job has been skilfully performed and that the car is safe to drive.

Status: customers may feel that their status is enhanced by a relationship with a supplier, such as an elite health club or a company offering a platinum credit-card.

Affiliation: people's social needs can be met through commercially based, or non-commercially based, relationships. Many people are customers (members) of professional or community associations, for example.

Customer segments can vary in their desire to have relationships with suppliers. For example, large corporations have their own treasury departments and often get little value from a bank relationship; small private account holders have no need for the additional services that a relationship provides; small and medium-sized business and high net worth individuals may have most to gain from a closer relationship with a bank.

A number of B2C organizations deliver incremental benefits by building closer relationships with their customers. Casa Buitoni, for example, offers customers the opportunity to learn more about Italian cuisine through an online customer club. The Harley Owners Group (HOG) offers a raft of benefits to Harley Davidson owners, including club outings and preferential insurance rates. Nestlé's mother and baby club offers advice and information to new mothers.

Why customers do NOT want relationships with suppliers

While companies generally want long-term relationships with customers for the economic reasons described above, it is far less clear that customers universally want relationships with their suppliers. B2B customers cite a number of concerns.[24]

Fear of dependency: this is driven by a number of worries. Customers may be concerned that the supplier might act opportunistically, once they are in a preferred position, perhaps introducing price rises. They may also fear the reduction in their flexibility to choose alternative suppliers. There may also be concerns over a loss of personal authority and control.

Lack of perceived value in the relationship: customers may not believe that they will enjoy substantial savings in transaction costs, or that the relationship will help them create a superior competitive position, generate additional revenue or that there will be any social benefits. In other words, there is no perceived value above and beyond that obtained from the product or service.

Lack of confidence in the supplier: customers may choose not to enter a relationship because they feel the potential partner is unreliable, too small, strategically insignificant, has a poor reputation or is insufficiently innovative.

Customer lacks relational orientation: not all company cultures are equally inclined towards relationship building. Some are much more transactional. For example, some retailers make it a policy to buy a high proportion of their merchandise through special offers. The preference for transactional rather than relational business operations may be reflected in a company's buying processes and reward systems.

Rapid technological changes: in an industry with rapidly changing technology, commitment to one supplier might mean that the customer misses out on new developments available through other suppliers.

In the B2C context, consumers buy hundreds of different convenience, shopping and speciality products and services. Whereas consumers might want a relationship with their financial service advisor or their physician, they can often find no good reason for developing closer relationships with the manufacturer of their household detergent, snack foods or toothpaste. However, for consumer products and services that are personally important, customers can become more involved and become more emotionally engaged.

Customer satisfaction, loyalty and business performance

An important rationale for CRM is that it improves business performance by enhancing customer satisfaction and driving up customer loyalty, as shown in Figure 2.6. There is a compelling logic to the model, which has been dubbed the 'satisfaction–profit chain'.[25] Satisfaction increases because customer insight allows companies to understand their customers better,

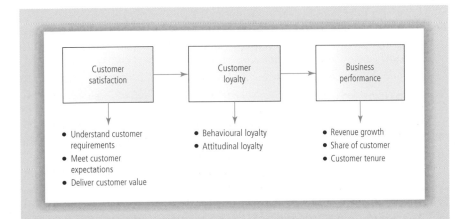

Figure 2.6
The satisfaction–profit chain

and create improved customer value propositions and better customer experiences. As customer satisfaction rises, so does customer intention to repurchase.[26] This in turn influences actual purchasing behaviour, which has an impact on business performance.

We'll examine the variables and linkages between them. First we'll define the major variables of customer satisfaction, customer loyalty and business performance.

Customer satisfaction

Customer satisfaction has been the subject of considerable research, and has been defined and measured in many ways.[27] We define customer satisfaction as follows:

> Customer satisfaction is the customer's fulfilment response to a customer experience, or some part thereof.

Customer satisfaction is a pleasurable fulfilment response. Dissatisfaction is an unpleasurable fulfilment response. The 'experience, or some part thereof' component of the definition suggests that the satisfaction evaluation can be directed at any or all elements of the customer's experience. This can include product, service, process and any other components of the customer experience.

The most common way of quantifying satisfaction is to compare the customer's perception of an experience, or some part of it, with their expectations. This is known as the expectations–disconfirmation model of customer satisfaction. This model suggests that if customers perceive their expectations to be met, they are satisfied. If their expectations are underperformed, this is negative disconfirmation and they will be dissatisfied. Positive disconfirmation occurs when perception exceeds expectation. The customer might be pleasantly surprised or even delighted. This model assumes that customers have expectations, and that they are able to judge performance. A customer satisfaction paradox has been identified by expectations–disconfirmation researchers. At times customers' expectations may be met but the customer is still not satisfied. This happens when the customer's expectations are low. 'I expected the plane to be late. It was. I'm unhappy!'

Many companies research customer requirements and expectations to find out what is important for customers, and then measure customers' perceptions of their performance compared to the performance of competitors.

Customer loyalty

Customer loyalty has also been the subject of considerable research. There are two major approaches to defining and measuring loyalty, one based on behaviour, the other on attitude.

Behavioural loyalty is measured by reference to customer purchasing behaviour. Loyalty is expressed in continued patronage and buying. There are two behavioural aspects to loyalty. First, is the customer still active? Secondly, have we maintained our share of customer spending?

In portfolio purchasing environments, where customers buy products and services from a number of more-or-less equal suppliers, the share of customer spending question is more important.

Many direct marketing companies use RFM measures of behavioural loyalty. The most loyal are those who have high scores on the three behavioural variables: recency of purchases (R), frequency of purchases (F) and monetary value of purchases (M). The variables are measured as follows:

R = time elapsed since last purchase
F = number of purchases in a given time period
M = monetary value of purchases in a given time period.

Attitudinal loyalty is measured by reference to components of attitude such as beliefs, feelings and purchasing intention. Those customers who have a stronger preference for, involvement in, or commitment to a supplier are the more loyal in attitudinal terms.

Recently, researchers have combined both views into comprehensive models of customer loyalty. The best known is Dick and Basu's model, as shown in Figure 2.7.[28] These authors identify four forms of loyalty, according to relative attitudinal strength and repeat purchase behaviour. 'Loyals' are those who have high levels of repeat buying and a strong relative attitude. 'Spurious loyals' have high levels of repeat purchase but weak relative attitude. Their repeat purchasing can be explained by inertia, high switching costs or indifference. Latent loyalty exists when a strong relative attitude is not accompanied by repeat buying. This might be evidence of weakness in the company's distribution strategy, the product or service not being available when and where customers want.

From a practical point of view, the behavioural definition of loyalty is attractive because sales and profits derive from actions not attitudes.

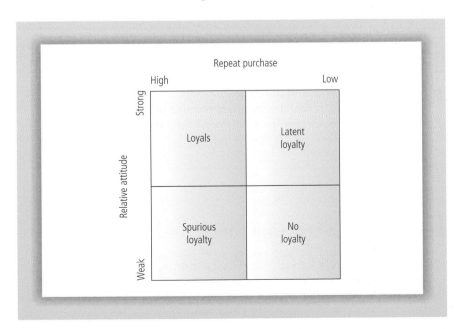

Figure 2.7
Two-dimensional model of customer loyalty

However, taking the trouble to understand the causes of weak or negative attitudes in customers can help companies identify barriers to purchase. It is equally true that knowledge of strong or positive attitudes can help companies understand the causes of competitor-resistant commitment. However, it is not clear from the Dick and Basu model whether attitude precedes behaviour or behaviour precedes attitude. Researchers generally accept that causation is circular rather unidirectional. In other words, attitudes influence behaviour, and behaviour influences attitude.

Business performance

Business performance can be measured in many ways. The recent trend has been away from simple short-term financial measures such as quarterly profit or earnings per share. Leading companies are moving towards a more rounded set of performance indicators, such as represented by the balanced scorecard.[29]

The balanced scorecard employs four sets of linked key performance indicators (KPI): financial, customer, process and learning and growth. The implied connection between these indicators is that people (learning and growth) do things (process) for customers (customer) that have effects on business performance (financial).

Customer-related KPIs that can be used to evaluate business performance following a CRM implementation include: customer satisfaction levels, customer retention rates, customer acquisition costs, number of new customers acquired, average customer tenure, customer loyalty (behavioural or attitudinal), sales per customer, revenue growth, market share and share of customer (wallet).

The balanced scorecard is highly adaptable to CRM contexts. Companies need to ask the following questions. What customer outcomes drive our financial performance? What process outcomes drive our customer performance? What learning and growth outcomes drive our process performance? The satisfaction–profit chain suggests that the customer outcomes of satisfaction and loyalty are important drivers of business performance.

Share of customer (share of wallet or SOW) is a popular measure of CRM performance. If your company makes a strategic CRM decision to serve a particular market or customer segment, it will be keen to measure and grow its share of the chosen customers' spending. As indicated in Figure 2.8, share of customer focuses on winning a greater share of targeted customers' or segments' spending, rather than market share.

Researching the satisfaction–profit chain

We'll now look at some of the research into the links between customer satisfaction, loyalty and business performance. Analysis has been done

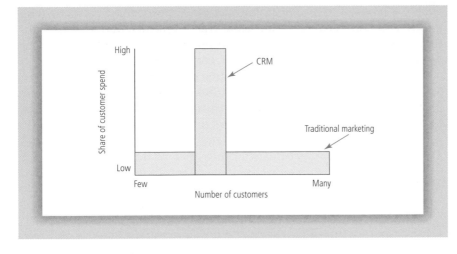

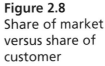

Figure 2.8
Share of market versus share of customer

on international data, national data, industry data, corporate data and individual customer data.

The American Customer Satisfaction Index (ACSI) was established in 1994. It has tracked the relationships between customer satisfaction and a number of antecedents and consequences, including customer loyalty as measured by customers' probability of buying at different price points. The ASCI model appears in Figure 2.9. Data are collected in telephone interviews with approximately 250 current customers of the larger companies in a number of industries.[30] Results from the multi-industry study show that there is a strong correlation between customer satisfaction scores and corporate earnings in the next quarter. According to the ACSI organization, 'the reason is that a satisfied customer is more profitable than a dissatisfied one. If satisfaction declines, customers become more reluctant to buy unless prices are cut. If satisfaction improves the opposite is true'.[31] An independent study, using data from the ACSI, has also found that customer satisfaction had a considerable effect on business performance, although there was variation across sectors.[32]

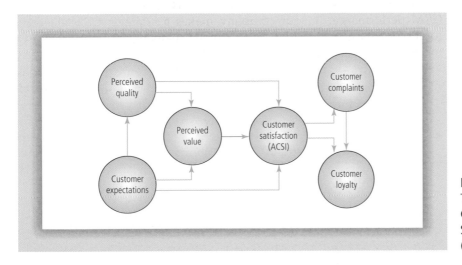

Figure 2.9
The American Customer Satisfaction Index (ACSI) model[33]

The European Customer Satisfaction Index, using a somewhat different model, analyses data from 11 European countries and also reports a strong relationship between customers' value perceptions, satisfaction levels and loyalty.[34]

At the national level, customer data from the Swedish Customer Satisfaction Barometer (SCSB) have been correlated with corporate profit performance since 1989. A lagged relationship has been identified, indicating that current customer satisfaction levels impact on tomorrow's profit performance.[35] The SCSB database matches customer-based measures with traditional financial measures of business performance, such as productivity and return on investment (ROI). The SCSB is one of several such national indices.

A number of studies in different industries and companies – telecommunications, banking, airline and automobile distribution – support the relationship between customer satisfaction, loyalty and business performance.

- **Telecommunications**: one study of the telecoms industry found that a 10 per cent lift in a customer satisfaction index predicted a 2 per cent increase in customer retention (a behavioural measure of loyalty) and a 3 per cent increase in revenues. The authors concluded that customer satisfaction was a lead indicator of customer retention, revenue and revenue growth.[36]
- **Banking**: another study found that customer satisfaction in retail banking correlated highly with branch profitability. Highly satisfied customers had balances 20 per cent higher than satisfied customers, and, as satisfaction levels went up over time, so did account balances. The reverse was also true, as satisfaction levels fell, so did account balances.[37]
- **Airlines**: a study in the airline industry examined the link between customer dissatisfaction, operating income, operating revenue and operating expense. The study identified the drivers of dissatisfaction as high load factors (i.e. seat occupancy), mishandled baggage and poor punctuality. The study concluded that as dissatisfaction rose, operating revenue (an indicator of customer behaviour) and operating profit both fell, and operating expense rose.[38]
- **Car distribution**: a study of Volvo car owners examined the links between customer satisfaction with three attributes – car purchase, workshop service and the vehicle itself – and dealer business performance. The results indicated that a one scale-point increase in overall customer satisfaction was associated with a 4 per cent increase in dealer profitability at next car purchase.[39]
- **Multi-industry**: using 400 sets of matched corporate-level data obtained from two databases – the ACSI (see above, which provided customer satisfaction scores) and Standard and Poors' Compustat (which provided business profitability data) – Yeung and colleagues found a linear relationship between customer satisfaction scores and business profitability. They rise and fall together in the same time period.[40]

Research into the satisfaction–profit chain has also been performed at the level of the individual customer. Using data collected from both customers and exporters in the Norwegian fishing industry, Helgesen finds support for both steps in the satisfaction–profit chain.[41] Satisfaction is positively associated with behavioural loyalty, which in turn is positively associated with customer profitability. However, he notes that 'the satisfaction level has to pass a certain threshold if it is to have any influence on customer loyalty', and that as satisfaction increases it has a diminishing effect on loyalty. The same effects are observed in the relationship between loyalty and customer profitability. Furthermore, only 10 per cent of the variance in each independent variable was accounted for by the dependent variable.

According to one review, there is 'growing evidence that the links in the satisfaction–profit chain are solid'.[42] However, the relationships can be both asymmetrical and non-linear. The asymmetric nature of the relationships is found by comparing the impact of an increase in one variable with an equivalent decrease. For example, a one-scale point shift up in customer satisfaction (say from three to four on a five-point scale) may not have a comparable impact on customer retention rates as a one-scale point downward shift (say from three to two on the same five-point scale). Secondly, links can be nonlinear. Nonlinearity is sometimes reflected in diminishing returns, at other times in increasing returns. For example, increasing returns may be obtained in repeat purchase levels as customers progress up the customer satisfaction scale, as shown in Figure 2.10. Diminishing returns may set in if customer expectations are already largely met. Investments in increasing customer satisfaction at already high levels of performance do not have the same impact as investments at lower levels of performance.

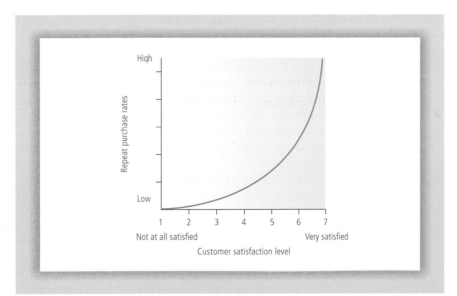

Figure 2.10
Non-linear relationship between customer satisfaction and repeat purchase

Relationship management theories

There are five main schools of thought that offer different perspectives on relationships between customers and suppliers. Although some schools are quite similar, they generally describe relationships in different terms and have different implications for relationship management. The major schools of thought are the Industrial Marketing and Purchasing (IMP) school, the Nordic school, the Anglo-Australian school, the North American school, and the Asian (*guanxi*) school. Each is briefly reviewed in the following sections. Concepts and themes from these schools have been incorporated into the preceding discussion.

The Industrial Marketing and Purchasing school

The Industrial Marketing and Purchasing school (IMP) has a dedicated focus on B2B relationships. The IMP school first emerged in the late 1970s when a number of European researchers began investigating B2B relationships with the simple goal of describing them accurately. Some of the major contributors to the IMP school are Malcolm Cunningham, David Ford, Lars-Erik Gadde, Håkan Håkansson, Ivan Snehota, Peter Naudé and Peter Turnbull.[43]

The IMP school argues that B2B transactions occur within the context of broader, long-term relationships, which are, in turn, situated within a broader network of relationships. Any single B2B relationship between supplier and customer is composed of activity links, actor bonds and resource ties. IMP researchers were among the first to challenge the view that transaction costs determined which supplier would be chosen by a customer. IMP researchers identified the important impact of relationship history on supplier selection. The characteristics of B2B relationships, from an IMP perspective, are as follows:

● Buyers and sellers are both active participants in transactions, pursuing solutions to their problems rather than simply reacting to the other party's influence.
● Relationships between buyers and sellers are frequently long-term, are close in nature, and involve a complex pattern of interaction between and within each company.
● Buyer–seller links often become institutionalized into a set of roles that each party expects the other to perform, with expectations that adaptations will be made on an ongoing basis.
● Interactions occur within the context of the relationship's history and the broader set of relationships each firm has with other firms – the firm's network of relationships. We examine the role of network members in the achievement of CRM goals in Chapter 10.
● Firms choose whom they interact with and how. The relationships that firms participate in can be many and diverse, carried out for different purposes, with different partners, and have different levels

of importance. These relationships are conducted within a context of a much broader network of relationships.

● Relationships are composed of actor bonds, activity links and resources ties, as now described.

Actor bonds

Actor bonds are defined as follows:

> Actor bonds are interpersonal contacts between actors in partner firms that result in trust, commitment and adaptation between actors.[44]

Actor bonds are a product of interpersonal communication and the subsequent development of trust. Adaptation of relationships over time is heavily influenced by social bonding.

Activity links

Activity links can be defined as follows:

> Activity links are the commercial, technical, financial, administrative and other connections that are formed between companies in interaction.

Activities might centre on buying and selling, technical cooperation or inter-firm projects of many kinds. Activities such as inter-partner knowledge exchange, the creation of inter-partner IT systems, the creation of integrated manufacturing systems such as just-in-time (JIT) and efficient consumer response (ECR), the development of jointly implemented total quality management (TQM) processes, are investments that demonstrate commitment.

IMP researchers have focused on two major streams of activity-related research: the structure and cost effectiveness of activity links, and the behavioural characteristics that enable relationships to survive. The reduction of transaction costs is an important motivation for customers forming links with suppliers. Dyer argues that search costs, contracting costs, monitoring costs and enforcement costs (the four major types of transaction cost) can all be reduced through closer B2B relationships.[45]

Resource ties

Resources are defined as follows:

> Resources are the human, financial, legal, physical, managerial, intellectual and other strengths or weaknesses of an organization.[46]

Resource ties are formed when these resources are deployed in the performance of the activities that link supplier and customer. Resources that are deployed in one B2B relationship may strengthen and deepen that relationship. However, there may be an opportunity cost. Once resources (for example, people or money) are committed to one relationship they might not be available for another relationship.

The Nordic school

The Nordic school emphasizes the role of service in supplier–customer relationships. The main proponents of the Nordic school are Christian Grönroos and Evert Gümmesson.[47]

The Nordic school emerged from research into services marketing that began in the late 1970s, particularly in Scandinavia. The key idea advocated by the Nordic school is that service is a significant component of transactions between suppliers and their customers. Their work became influential in the development of the field of relationship marketing, which presents a challenge to the transactional view of marketing that has been dominant for so long. The Nordic school's approach has application in both B2B and B2C environments. Grönroos has defined relationship marketing as follows:

> Relationship marketing is the process of identifying and establishing, maintaining, enhancing, and, when necessary, terminating relationships with customers and other stakeholders, at a profit, so that the objectives of all parties involved are met, where this is done by a mutual giving and fulfilment of promises.[48]

Gümmesson goes further, redefining marketing as follows:

> Marketing can be defined as 'interactions, relationships, and networks'. [49]

The Nordic school identifies three major characteristics of commercial relationships – interaction, dialogue and value – known collectively as the 'Triplet of Relationship Marketing'.[50]

Interaction

The Nordic school suggests that inter-firm exchanges occur in a broader context of ongoing interactions. This is a significant departure from traditional notions of marketing where interfirm exchanges are conceptualized as discrete, unrelated events, almost as if there is no history. From the Nordic school's perspective, interactions are service-dominant. As customers and suppliers interact, each performs services for the other. Customers supply information; suppliers supply solutions.

Dialogue

Suppliers and customers are in dialogue with each other. Indeed, communication between partners is essential to the functioning of the relationship. Traditional marketing thinking has imagined communication to be one way, from company to customer, but the Nordic school emphasizes the fact that communication is bilateral.

Value

The concepts of 'value', 'value creation' and 'value creation systems' have become more important to managers over the past twenty years. The Nordic school stresses the mutual nature of value. To generate value from customers, companies need to generate customer-perceived value, that is, create and deliver something that is perceived to be of value to customers. Value creation therefore requires contributions from both buyer and seller. From the Nordic school's perspective, service performance is a key contributor to customer-perceived value.

The Anglo–Australian school

The Anglo–Australian school takes the view that companies not only form relationships with customers, but also with a wide range of other stakeholders including employees, shareholders, suppliers, buyers and governments. The main proponents of this school are Martin Christopher, Adrian Payne, Helen Peck and David Ballantyne.[51]

Stakeholder relationships vary in intensity according to the level of relationship investment, commitment and longevity. Unlike the IMP school which takes a descriptive approach, the Anglo–Australian school takes a more prescriptive approach. Their work sets out to help managers to improve relationships with stakeholder groups.

The major conceptual contribution of this school is their Six-Markets Model which has been revised several times (see Figure 2.11). The model suggests that firms must satisfy six major stakeholder 'markets': internal markets (employees), supplier/alliance markets (including major suppliers, joint venture partners and the like), recruitment markets (labour markets), referral markets (word-of-mouth advocates and cross-referral networks) influence markets (these include governments, regulators, shareholders and the business press) and customer markets (both intermediaries and end-users).

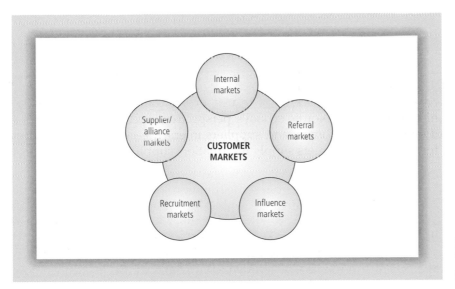

Figure 2.11
The six-markets model[52]

The school's researchers have focused on a number of topics: customer retention, customer loyalty, customer satisfaction, customer relationship economics and value creation. One of their major findings is that customer satisfaction and customer retention are drivers of shareholder value.[53]

The North American school

The North American school receives less emphasis as a separate school of relationship management than other schools. Significant contributors to this school are Jeffery Dyer, Sandy Jap, Shelby Hunt, Robert Dwyer, Jan Heide, Robert Morgan, and Jagdish Sheth. A major theme flowing through this school's work is the connection between successful inter-firm relationships and excellent business performance. The school acknowledges that relationships reduce transaction costs,[54] and that trust and commitment are two very important attributes of successful relationships. Indeed, one of the more important theoretical contributions to come from the North American school is Morgan and Hunt's 'Commitment-Trust Theory of Relationship Marketing'. This was the first time that trust was explicitly linked to commitment in the context of customer–supplier relationships. According to the theory, trust is underpinned by shared values, communication, non-opportunistic behaviour, low functional conflict and cooperation. Commitment, on the other hand, is associated not only with high relationship termination costs, but also with high relationship benefits.[55]

The North American school tends to view relationships as tools that a well-run company can manipulate for competitive advantage. They also focus on dyadic relationships rather than networks, most commonly buyer–supplier dyads or strategic alliance/joint venture partnerships.

The Asian (Guanxi) school

Guanxi is, essentially, a philosophy for conducting business and other interpersonal relationships in the Chinese, and broader Asian, context. Therefore, its effects have a significant impact on how Asian societies and economies work.

The notion of Guanxi has been known to western economists since at least 1978. This was the time when the Chinese market began to open up to the west.[56] The foundations of Guanxi are Buddhist and Confucian teachings regarding the conduct of interpersonal interactions. Guanxi refers to the informal social bonds and reciprocal obligations between various actors that result from some common social context, for example families, friendships and clan memberships. These are special types of relationships which impose reciprocal obligations to obtain resources through continual cooperation and exchange of favours.[57]

Guanxi has become a necessary aspect of Chinese and, indeed, Asian business due to the lack of codified, enforceable contracts such as those found in western markets. Guanxi determines who can conduct business with whom and under what circumstances. Business is conducted within networks, and rules based on status are invoked. Network members can only extend invitations to others to become part of their network if the invitee is a peer or a subordinate.

Summary

In this chapter you have learned that there are differing beliefs about what counts as a relationship. Although interactions over time are an essential feature of relationships, some believe that a relationship needs to have some emotional content. Although the character of a relationship can change over time, successful relationships are based on a foundation of trust and commitment. The primary motivation for companies trying to develop long-term relationships with customers is the profit motive. There is strong evidence that long-term relationships with customers yield commercial benefits as companies strive to enhance customer lifetime value. The satisfaction–profit chain suggests that customers who are satisfied are more likely to become loyal, and high levels of customer loyalty are associated with excellent business performance. However, companies are advised to focus their customer acquisition and retention efforts on those who have profit-potential or are otherwise strategically significant. Although companies generally want to develop long-term relationships with customers, there are good reasons why customers don't always share the same enthusiasm. Finally, the chapter closes with a discussion of several schools of management or marketing theory that shed light on customer relationship management. These are the IMP, Nordic, Anglo–Australian, North American and Asian (Guanxi) schools of thought.

References

1. Barnes, J.G. (2000) *Secrets of customer relationship management*. New York: McGraw-Hill.
2. Heath, R.L. and Bryant, J. (2000) *Human communication theory and research: concepts, contexts and challenges*. Mahwah, NJ: Lawrence Erlbaum Associates.
3. Dwyer, F.R., Schurr, P.H. and Oh, S. (1987) Developing buyer–seller relationships. *Journal of Marketing*, Vol. 51, pp. 11–27.
4. See, for example, Morgan, R.M. and Hunt, S.D. (1994) The commitment–trust theory of relationship marketing. *Journal of Marketing* Vol. 58(3), pp. 20–38; Rousseau, D.M., Sitkin, S.B., Burt, R.S. and Camerer, C. (1998) Not so different after all: a cross-discipline view of trust. *Academy of Management Review*, Vol. 23(3), pp. 393–404; Selnes, F. (1998) Antecedents of trust and satisfaction in buyer–seller relationships. *European Journal of Marketing*, Vol. 32(3–4), pp. 305–322; Shepherd, B.B. and Sherman, D.M. (1998) The grammars of trust: a model and general implications. *Academy of Management Review*, Vol. 23(3), pp. 422–437.
5. Singh, J. and Sirdeshmukh, D. (2000) Agency and trust mechanisms in consumer satisfaction and loyalty judgements. *Journal of Marketing Science*, Vol. 28(1), pp. 255–271.
6. Harris, S. and Dibben, M. (1999) Trust and co-operation in business relationship development: exploring the influence of national values. *Journal of Marketing Management*, Vol. 15, pp. 463–483.

7. Morgan, R.M. and Hunt, S.D. (1994) The commitment–trust theory of relationship marketing. *Journal of Marketing*, Vol. 58(3), pp. 20–38.

8. Buttle, F. and Biggemann, S. (2003) Modelling business-to-business relationship quality. Macquarie Graduate School of Management Working Paper #2003–3.

9. Wilson, D.T. and Mummalaneni, V. (1986) Bonding and commitment in supplier relationships: a preliminary conceptualization. *Industrial Marketing and Purchasing*, Vol. 1(3), pp. 44–58.

10. http://www.allheadlinenews.com/articles/7009767911. Accessed 20 January 2008.

11. The idea of strategic significance is discussed in Chapter 5.

12. Reichheld, F.F. and Detrick, C. (2003) Loyalty: a prescription for cutting costs. *Marketing Management*, September–October, pp. 24–25.

13. Ang, L. and Buttle, F.A. (2002) ROI on CRM: A Customer Journey Approach. Proceedings of the Inaugural Asia-Pacific IMP conference, Bali, December 2002.

14. Bain & Co/Mainline. (1999) *Customer spending on-line*. Bain & Co.

15. Christopher, M., Payne, A. and Ballantyne, D. (1991) *Relationship Marketing*. Oxford: Butterworth-Heinemann.

16. Gordon, I. (1998) *Relationship marketing*. Ontario: John Wiley.

17. Reichheld, F. and Sasser, W.E. Jr. (1990) Zero defections: quality comes to services. *Harvard Business Review*, September–October, pp. 105–111.

18. Bain & Co/Mainline. (1999) *Customer spending on-line*. Bain & Co.

19. Ferron, J. (2000) The customer-centric organization in the automobile industry – focus for the 21st century. In: S. Brown (ed.). *Customer Relationship Management: A Strategic Imperative in the World of e-Business*. Toronto: John Wiley, pp. 189–211.

20. IBM (2000) Business intelligence in the financial services industry: the case for differentiation. http://sysdoc.doors.ch/IBM/fss_business_intelligence_2.pdf. Accessed 20 January 2008.

21. Reichheld, F. and Sasser, W.E. Jr (1990) Zero defections: quality comes to the services. *Harvard Business Review*, September–October, pp. 105–111; see also Reichheld, F.F., Markey, R.G. and Hopton, C. (2000) The loyalty effect: the relationship between loyalty and profits. *European Business Journal*, Vol. 12(3), pp. 134–139.

22. Lee, J., Lee, J. and Fieck, L. (2006) Incorporating word of mouth effects in estimating lifetime value. *Journal of Database Marketing and Customer Strategy Management*, Vol. 14(1), pp. 29–39.

23. Berger, P.D. and Nasr, N.I. (1998) Customer lifetime value: marketing models and applications. *Journal of Interactive Marketing*, Vol. 12(1), Winter, pp. 17–30.

24. Biong, H., Wathne, K. and Parvatiyar, A. (1997) Why do some companies not want to engage in partnering relationships? In: H.-G. Gemünden, T. Ritter and A. Walter (eds). *Relationships and networks in international markets*. Oxford: Pergamon, pp. 91–108.

25. Anderson, E.W. and Mittal, V. (2000) Strengthening the satisfaction–profit chain. *Journal of Service Research*, Vol. 3(2), pp. 107–120.

26. Anderson, E.W. (1994) Cross category variation in customer satisfaction and retention. *Marketing Letters*, Vol. 5, Winter, pp. 19–30.

27. Oliver, R.L. (1997) *Satisfaction: a behavioural perspective on the consumer*. Singapore: McGraw-Hill International.
28. Dick, A.S. and Basu, K. (1994) Customer loyalty: towards an integrated framework. *Journal of the Academy of Marketing Science*, Vol. 22(2), pp. 99–113.
29. Kaplan, R.S. and Norton, D.P. (1996) *The balanced scorecard*. Boston, MA: Harvard Business School Press.
30. Fornell, C., Johnson, M.D., Anderson, E.W., Jaesung, C. and Bryant, B.E. (1996) The American customer satisfaction index: nature, purpose, and findings. *Journal of Marketing*, Vol. 60(4), October, pp. 7–18.
31. http://www.theacsi.org/predictive_capabilities.htm. Accessed 30 November 2005.
32. Yeung, M.C.H. and Ennew, C.T. (2001) Measuring the impact of customer satisfaction on profitability: a sectoral analysis. *Journal of Targeting, Measurement and Analysis for Marketing*, Vol. 19(2), pp. 106–116.
33. Copyright © 2008. ACSI, University of Michigan Business School. Used with permission.
34. Cassel, C. and Eklof, J.A. (2001) Modeling customer satisfaction and loyalty on aggregate levels: experience from the ECSI pilot study. *Total Quality Management*, Vol. 12(7–8), pp. 834–841.
35. Anderson, E.W., Fornell, C. and Lehman, D.R. (1994) Customer satisfaction, market share and profitability: findings from Sweden. *Journal of Marketing*, July, pp. 53–66.
36. Ittner, C.D. and Larcker, D.F. (1998) Are non-financial indictors of financial performance? An analysis of customer satisfaction. *Journal of Accounting Research*, Vol. 36 (supplement 1998), pp. 1–46.
37. Carr, N.G. (1999) The economics of customer satisfaction. *Harvard Business Review*, Vol. 77(2), March–April, pp. 15–18.
38. Behn, B.K. and Riley, R.A. (1999) Using non-financial information to predict financial performance: the case of the US airline industry. *Journal of Accounting, Auditing and Finance*, Vol. 14(1), pp. 29–56.
39. Gustaffson, A. and Johnson, M.D. (2002) Measuring and managing the satisfaction–loyalty–performance links at Volvo. *Journal of Targeting, Measurement and Analysis for Marketing*, Vol. 10(3), pp. 249–258.
40. Yeung, M.C.H., Ging, L.C. and Ennew, C. (2002) Customer satisfaction and profitability: a reappraisal of the relationship. *Journal of Targeting, Measurement and Analysis for Marketing*, Vol. 11(1), pp. 24–33.
41. Helgesen, O. (2006) Are loyal customers profitable? Customer satisfaction, customer (action) loyalty and customer profitability at the individual level. *Journal of Marketing Management*, Vol. 22, pp. 245–266.
42. Anderson, E.W. and Mittal, V. (2000) Strengthening the satisfaction–profit chain. *Journal of Service Research*, Vol. 3(2), pp. 107–120.
43. The IMP group has its own dedicated website, www.impgroup.org, annual conference and are prolific publishers of books and papers, a number of which follow. Cunningham, M. (1980) International marketing and purchasing: features of a European research project.

European Journal of Marketing, Vol. 14(5–6), pp. 5–21; Ford, D., Gadde, L.-E., Håkansson, H. and Snehota, I. (2003*) Managing business relationships* (2nd edn). Chichester, UK: John Wiley & Sons; Ford, D. and McDowell, R. (1999) Managing business relationships by analysing the effects and value of different actions. *Industrial Marketing Management,* Vol. 28, pp. 429–442; Ford, D. and Redwood, M. (2004) Making sense of network dynamics through network pictures: a longitudinal case study. *Industrial Marketing Management,* Vol. 34(7), pp. 648–657; Gadde, L. E., Huemer, L. and Håkansson, H. (2003) Strategizing in industrial networks. *Industrial Marketing Management,* Vol. 32, pp. 357–364; Håkansson, H. and Ford, D. (2002) How should companies interact in business networks? *Journal of Business Research,* Vol. 55, pp. 133–139; Håkansson, H. and Snehota, I. (1995) *Developing relationships in business networks.* London: Routledge; Håkansson, H. E. (1982). *International marketing and purchasing of industrial goods: an interaction approach.* Chichester: John Wiley; Turnbull, P.W. and Cunningham, M. (1980) *International marketing and purchasing: a survey among marketing and purchasing executives in five European countries.* London: Macmillan; Zolkiewski, J. and Turnbull, P. (2002) Do relationship portfolios and networks provide the key to successful relationship management? *Journal of Business and Industrial Marketing,* Vol. 17(7), pp. 575–597.

44. Håkansson, H. and Snehota, I. (1995) *Developing relationships in business networks.* London: Routledge.

45. Dyer, J.H. (1997) Effective inter-firm collaboration: how firms minimize transaction costs and maximise transaction value. *Strategic Management Journal,* Vol. 18(7), pp. 535–556; Dyer, J.H. and Chu, W. (2003) The role of trustworthiness in reducing transaction costs and improving performance: empirical evidence from the United States, Japan and Korea. *Organisation Science,* Vol. 14(1), pp. 57–68.

46. Definition based on Barney, J.B. (1991) Firm resources and sustained competitive advantage. *Journal of Management,* Vol. 17(1), pp. 99–120 and Wernerfelt, B. (1984) A resource-based view of the firm. *Strategic Management Journal,* Vol. 5(2), pp. 171–180.

47. Christian Grönroos and Evert Gummesson are prolific authors. Among their works are the following. Grönroos, C. (1996) Relationship marketing logic. *Asia-Australia Marketing Journal,* Vol. 4(1), pp. 7–18; Grönroos, C. (1997) Value-driven relational marketing: from products to resources and competencies. *Journal of Marketing Management,* Vol. 13, pp. 407–420; Grönroos, C. (2000a) Creating a relationship dialogue: communication, interaction and value. *The Marketing Review,* Vol. 1, pp. 5–14; Grönroos, C. (2000b) Relationship marketing: the Nordic School perspective. J.N. Sheth and A. Parvatiyar (eds). *Handbook of Relationship Marketing.* London: Sage Publications, pp. 95–120; Grönroos, C. (2004) The relationship marketing process: communication, interaction, dialogue, value. *Journal of Business and Industrial Marketing,* Vol. 19(2), pp. 99–113; Gummesson, E. (1990) *The part-time marketer.* Karlstad, Sweden: Center for Service Research; Gummesson, E. (1987) The new marketing: developing long-term interactive relationships. *Long Range Planning,* Vol. 20(4), pp. 10–20; Gummesson, E. (1994) Making relationship marketing operational. *International Journal of Service Industry Management,* Vol. 5(5), pp. 5–20; Gummesson, E. (1996)

Relationship marketing and imaginary organisations: A synthesis. *European Journal of Marketing*, Vol. 30, pp. 31–44; Gummesson, E. (1997a). In search of marketing equilibrium: relationship marketing versus hypercompetition. *Journal of Marketing Management*, Vol. 13, pp. 421–430; Gummesson, E. (1997b) Relationship marketing as a paradigm shift: some conclusions from the 30R approach. *Management Decision*, Vol. 35(4), pp. 267–272; Gummesson, E. (1997c) Relationship marketing: the emperor's new clothes or a paradigm shift? *Marketing and Research Today*, Vol. 25(1), pp. 53–61; Gummesson, E. (2002) Relationship marketing and a new economy: it's time for de-programming. *Journal of Services Marketing*, Vol. 16(7), pp. 585–589.

48. Grönroos, C. (1997) Value-driven relational marketing: from products to resources and competencies. *Journal of Marketing Management*, Vol. 13, pp. 407–420.

49. Gummesson, E. (1997) Relationship marketing as a paradigm shift: some conclusions from the 30R approach. *Management Decision*, Vol. 35(4), pp. 267–272.

50. Grönroos, C. (2000) Creating a relationship dialogue: communication, interaction and value. *The Marketing Review*, Vol. 1, pp. 5–14.

51. Christopher, M., Payne, A. and Ballantyne, D. (1991) *Relationship marketing: bringing quality, customer service and marketing together.* Oxford: Butterworth-Heineman; Payne, A. (2000) Relationship marketing: the UK perspective. In: J.N. Sheth and A. Parvatiyar (eds.). *Handbook of Relationship Marketing.* London: Sage Publications, pp. 39–67; Peck, H., Payne, A., Christopher, M. and Clark, M. (1999) *Relationship marketing: strategy and implementation.* Oxford: Butterworth-Heinemann.

52. Peck, H., Payne, A., Christoper, M. and Clark, M. (1999) *Relationship Marketing: strategy and implementation.* Oxford: Butterworth-Heinemann.

53. Payne, A. and Frow, P. (2005) A strategic framework for customer relationship management. *Journal of Marketing*, Vol. 69, pp. 167–176; Payne, A. and Holt, S. (2001) Diagnosing customer value: integrating the value process and relationship marketing. *British Journal of Management*, Vol. 12(2), pp. 159–182.

54. Heide, J.B. (1994) Inter-organisational governance in marketing channels. *Journal of Marketing*, Vol. 58(1), pp. 71–86; Heide, J.B. and John, G. (1990) Alliances in industrial purchasing: the determinants of joint action in buyer-supplier relationships. *Journal of Marketing Research*, Vol. 27(1), pp. 24–36.

55. Morgan, R.M. and Hunt, S.D. (1994) The commitment–trust theory of relationship marketing. *Journal of Marketing*, Vol. 58(3), pp. 20–39; Gao, T., Joseph S.M. and Bird, M.M. (2005) Reducing buyer decision-making uncertainty in organizational purchasing: can supplier trust, commitment, and dependence help? *Journal of Business Research*, Vol. 58(4), pp. 397–406.

56. Ambler, T. (1995) Reflections in China: re-orienting images of marketing. *Marketing Management*, Vol. 4(1), pp. 23–30.

57. Davies, H.A., Leung, T.K.P., Luk, S.T.K. and Wong, Y.H. (1995) The benefits of Guanxi: an exploration of the value of relationships in developing the Chinese market. *Industrial Marketing Management*, Vol. 24, pp. 207–214.

Chapter 3
Planning and implementing customer relationship management projects

By the end of this chapter, you will be aware of:

1. five major phases in a CRM implementation
2. a number of tools and processes that can be applied in each phase of an implementation
3. the importance of project management and change management throughout the implementation process.

Introduction

In the first chapter you were introduced to strategic, operational, analytical and collaborative CRM. You also learned that although CRM projects generally involve technology implementations, people and processes can also play a large part. Indeed, we said that IT cannot compensate for bad processes and inept people. Most CRM projects involve consideration of all three components.

You may have sensed from this discussion that CRM projects can vary considerably in their scope. An organization-wide CRM project that automates selling, marketing and service processes might involve process reengineering, people re-skilling and implementation of a comprehensive range of technology applications from a CRM suite vendor like SAP. The project might span several years and cost many millions of dollars. A small CRM project might involve rolling out an off-the-shelf contact management system such as GoldMine or SAGE to a sales team. This might take a couple of months to implement and cost less than a thousand dollars to complete.

CRM implementation

In this chapter we'll look at the five major phases of a CRM implementation, and the processes and tools that can be used within those phases to ensure that CRM projects deliver what is expected of them.[1] Depending on the scope of the project some of these phases, processes and tools may not be required. The key phases, as shown in Figure 3.1 are:

1. develop the CRM strategy
2. build the CRM project foundations
3. specify needs and select partner
4. implement the project
5. evaluate performance.

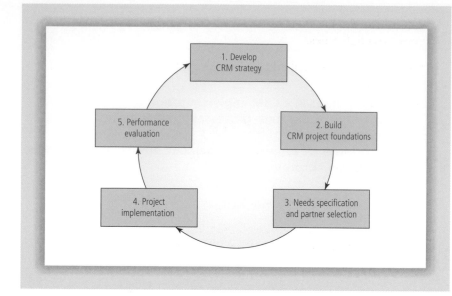

Figure 3.1
CRM project design
and planning
process

Embedded within each of these five key phases are a number of decision-points and activities, as follows:

1. Develop the CRM strategy:
   - situation analysis
   - commence CRM education
   - develop the CRM vision
   - set priorities
   - establish goals and objectives
   - identify people, process and technology requirements
   - develop the business case.
2. Build the CRM project foundations:
   - identify stakeholders
   - establish governance structures
   - identify change management needs
   - identify project management needs
   - identify critical success factors
   - develop risk management plan.
3. Specify needs and select partner:
   - process mapping and refinement
   - data review and gap analysis
   - initial technology needs specification, and research alternative solutions
   - write request for proposals (RFP)
   - call for proposals
   - revise technology needs identification
   - assessment and partner selection.
4. Implement project:
   - refine project plan
   - identify technology customization needs
   - prototype design, test, modify and roll out.

5. Evaluate performance:
    ● project outcomes
    ● business outcomes.

The rest of this chapter will add further detail to the CRM project design and planning process.

Phase 1: Develop the CRM strategy

CRM strategy can be defined as follows:

> CRM strategy is a high-level plan of action that aligns people, processes and technology to achieve customer-related goals.

Situation analysis

Development of the CRM strategy starts with a situation analysis. This analysis sets out to describe, understand and appraise the company's current customer strategy. It helps to have an organizing framework to guide your analysis. The comprehensive models of CRM that are described in Chapter 1 might be helpful. Another useful framework is the customer strategy cube. This is a three-dimensional analysis of your company's served market segments, market offerings and channels (routes to market). The situation analysis answers the questions, 'Where are we now?', and 'Why are we where we are?' in terms of the three dimensions of the cube.

Figure 3.2 illustrates the customer strategy cube of a company that sells four different offerings to five different market segments though

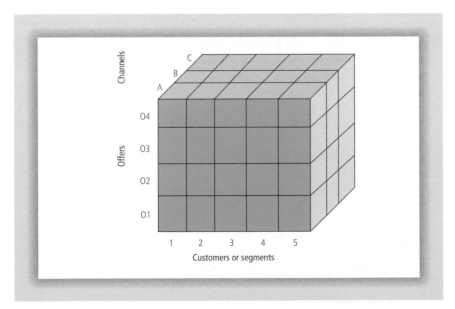

Figure 3.2
Customer strategy cube

three different channels. Each block in this cube (there are 60 (5 × 4 × 3) of them) might be a potential business unit that would be subject to a situation analysis. In fact, most businesses do not operate in all potential business units of their customer strategy cube. They operate selectively. For example, AMP sells financial products through a network of independent and tied financial planners. They do not sell direct to the consumer. Not all offerings are sold to all market segments through all channels.

The situation analysis examines the three dimensions of the customer strategy cube independently and jointly. Questions such as the following are asked.

Customers or segments

Which segments do we target? Which segments do we serve? What are our customer-related marketing and sales objectives? How much do we sell to customers? How satisfied are they? What is our market share? What is our share of customer spending? How effective are our customer acquisition strategies and tactics? How effective are our customer retention strategies and tactics? How effective are our customer development (cross-sell and up-sell) strategies and tactics? What are the customer touchpoints? What do our customers think about their experience of doing business with us? Which customer management processes have most impact on our costs or customer experience? Which technologies do we use to support our marketing, selling and service functions, and how well do they operate?

Market offerings

Which products do we offer? What is our branding strategy? How well known are our offerings? Who do we compete against? What advantages or disadvantages do we offer vis-à-vis our competitors? How do we augment and add value to our basic product offer? What benefits do customers experience from our offerings? How do our prices compare with our competitors? What are our margins?

Channels

Which channels do we use to distribute to our customers – direct and indirect? Which channels are most effective? What level of channel penetration do we have? Which channels are becoming more/less important? Where do our competitors distribute? What do channel partners think of their experience of doing business with us? What margins do channel members earn? Which channel management processes have most impact on our costs or channel member experience?

The goal of this audit is get a clear insight into the strengths and weaknesses of the company's customer strategy. Data can be collected from executives, managers, customer contact people and, importantly, customers. Business plans can be studied. One of the outcomes might be a customer interaction map, as in Figure 3.3, that identifies all customer touchpoints and the processes that are performed at those

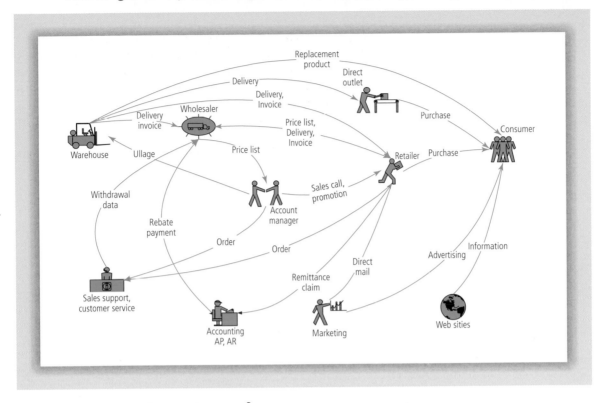

Figure 3.3 Customer interaction map[2]

touchpoints. Normally, the interactions that have important impact on customer experience or your own costs become primary candidates for reengineering and/or automation. The audit will serve as the start point for thinking about what you want to achieve from a CRM implementation.

Commence CRM education

CRM, as you have read in Chapter 1, is a term that means different things to different people. There is considerable misunderstanding about it. If you are about to embark on a CRM implementation, it is important that all stakeholders have a clear understanding of what CRM denotes. Your IT people might think that it is a technology project. Your marketing people might think it is something to do with a new approach to market segmentation. Your sales people might think it is about a new centralized database for customer records. Education has the twin benefits of allaying any fears that people might have, based on their misunderstandings, and encouraging participation from people whose jobs might be impacted. Education enables stakeholders to identify opportunities to improve their workplace.

There are very few educational programmes available. The Institute of Direct Marketing offers a suite of introductory study materials,[3] the American Marketing Association publishes a narrow range of tutorial materials, but the Chartered Institute of Marketing offers nothing.[4] Some of the richest resources are to be found in online CRM communities – self-help groups organized around a shared interest in CRM. Some of the better websites are www.customerthink.com (formerly www.crmguru.com), www.mycustomer.com (formerly www.insightexec.com, and before that www.crm-forum.com), www.sharedinsights.com, www.eccs.uk.com, searchcrm.techtarget.com, www.crm2day.com, www.crmdirectory.com and www.intelligententerprise.com. CRM vendors publish case histories which can give you a good idea of what is possible. Alternatively, you could use this book!

Develop the CRM vision

Your CRM vision is a high-level statement of how CRM will change your business as it relates to customers. The software-as-a-service (SaaS) company, salesforce.com, provides a number of examples of CRM visions.[5]

● We will work with our members in a trust-based relationship to represent their interests and to satisfy their needs for high value, security and peace of mind in motoring, travel and home.
● Nurturing relationships one cup at a time. Deliver a customer experience that consistently develops enthusiastically satisfied customers in every market in which we do business.
● Build and maintain long-term relationships with valuable customers by creating personalized experiences across all touchpoints and by anticipating customer needs and providing customized offers.
● Nothing is more important than making every user successful. (This is salesforce.com's own CRM vision.)

The CRM vision gives shape and direction to your CRM strategy. The CRM vision might be senior management's perspective, based on what they learned from the education process, or it could be the product of a wider visioning process that engages more members of your company, perhaps even customers and partners. The vision will eventually guide the development of measurable CRM outcomes.

Set priorities

CRM projects vary in their scope and can touch on one or more customer-facing parts of your business – sales, marketing or service. Clear priorities for action, normally focused on cost reduction or enhanced customer experience, might fall out of the situation analysis, but more time and debate is often necessary. Priority might be given to projects which produce quick wins, fast returns or are low-cost. Longer-term priorities might prove more difficult to implement. For example, you may want to prioritize a new segmentation of customers based on their potential profitability. An impediment to that outcome would be your company's inability to trace costs of selling, marketing and service to customers. You may need to prioritize the implementation of an activity-based costing system before performing the new segmentation.

Establish goals and objectives

Goals and objectives emerge from the visioning and prioritizing processes. Although the terms 'goals' and 'objectives' tend to be used synonymously, we use the word 'goal' to refer to a qualitative outcome and 'objective' to refer to a measurable outcome. For example, a CRM goal might be to acquire new customers. A related CRM objective could be to generate 200 additional leads by the fourth quarter of the next financial year.

Figure 3.4 reports data from Gartner Inc.[6] Their research shows that CRM goals generally cluster into three broad areas: enhancing customer satisfaction or loyalty, growing revenues or reducing costs. The bars in the chart show the percentage of respondents to their survey reporting each CRM goal. It is clear from this information that CRM strategies often pursue several goals. Among the most frequently cited goals are increased customer satisfaction and retention, reflecting the satisfaction–profit chain introduced in Chapter 2.

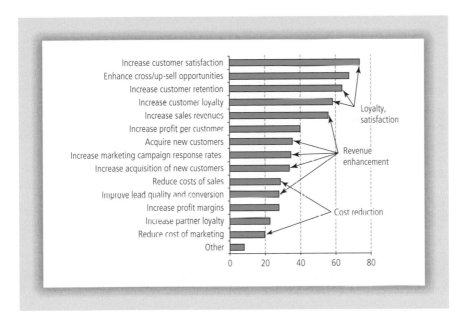

Figure 3.4
Strategic goals for CRM

Measurable objectives created at this time will later serve to evaluate the performance of the CRM implementation.

Identify people, process and technology requirements

The next step is to begin the process of identifying the people, process and technology requirements for the goals and objectives to be achieved. You'll return to these matters repeatedly as the project unfolds, but at this stage you need a general idea of the changes that are necessary so that you can begin to identify costs and construct a business case. If your goal is to enhance cross-selling opportunities you might need to invest in training sales people to ask the right questions, engineering a new opportunity management process and acquiring sales-force automation software.

Develop the business case

The business case is built around the costs and benefits of the CRM implementation and answers the question: 'Why should we invest in this CRM project?' The business case looks at both costs and revenues. CRM implementations can generate additional revenues in a number of ways:

- conversion of more leads from suspect to prospect to opportunity
- more cross-selling and up-selling
- more accurate product pricing
- higher levels of customer satisfaction and retention
- higher levels of word-of-mouth influence
- more leads and/or sales from marketing campaigns
- incremental sales from more effective selling processes.

Costs can be reduced by:

- improved lead generation and qualification
- lower costs of customer acquisition
- more efficient account management
- less waste in marketing campaigns
- reduced customer service costs
- more efficient front-office processes.

However, these benefits need to be assessed against the costs of the CRM implementation. The costs of a CRM project may extend well beyond the costs of CRM software. Additional costs may be incurred from systems integration, infrastructure costs, new desktop, laptop or handheld devices, software configuration, data modelling, beta-testing, helpdesk support, change management, project management, process reengineering, software upgrades, training and consultancy services, let alone the opportunity costs of diverting your own staff members from their routine work. For a simple CRM project IT costs may represent one quarter of the total project cost; for a complex project IT costs may be as low as one tenth of the total project cost.

Some business cases are able to ignore technology costs. Many companies using enterprise software from Oracle and SAP are already paying for CRM modules in their inclusive licence fees. A licensed SAP user, for example, might be using enterprise software only for back-office functions. However, the licence fee permits the company to use the enterprise suite's CRM modules. No additional licence costs are incurred though there may be substantial customization and implementation costs associated with switching on the unused CRM modules. Other companies that elect to deploy CRM through the SaaS approach, rather than installing software on their own hardware, treat CRM software as an operating expense. They simply treat software costs, based on a per-user monthly fee, as an operational expense that can be allocated to marketing, sales or service budgets.

Many of these costs and benefits are measurable, but there are also likely to be some important strategic benefits that are much harder to value, for example, development of a customer-centric way of doing business, better customer experience, improved responsiveness to changes in the market or competitive environments, more information sharing between business silos, improved customer service, more harmonious relationships with customers and the development of an information-based competitive advantage.

The business case should span a period equivalent to the economic life of the proposed solution. This is particularly important when comparing different implementation models such as on-premise CRM and SaaS (software–as–a–service). While the upfront costs of these two approaches are vastly different, the total cost of ownership can even out over a 3–4 year period.

The result of this analysis may be summarized in a range of statistics including total cost of ownership, payback period, internal rate of return and net present value, as shown in Figure 3.5.

CRM Business Case				Prepared by: Customer Connect Australia	
Benefit - Cost Summary	Year 1	Year 2	Year 3	Year 4	Year 5
Total Bottom Line Benefits Per Year	$150,000	$2,500,000	$2,900,000	$3,100,000	$3,100,000
Cumulative Benefits, Present Value	$150,000	$2,500,000	$4,950,000	$7,100,000	$9,100,000
Weighted Average Total Costs Per Year	$1,500,000	$1,100,000	$90,000	$250,000	$110,000
Cumulative Costs, Present Value	$1,500,000	$2,550,000	$2,600,000	$2,800,000	$2,900,000
Net Cash Flow	−$750,000	$700,000	$1,400,000	$1,450,000	$1,500,000
Cumulative Net Present Value Cash Flow	−$750,000	−$25,000	$1,100,000	$2,200,000	$3,100,000
Internal Rate of Return	129%				
Net Present Value, 5 Years	$3,100,000				
Return on Investment, Present Value, 5 Years	107%				
Payback Period, Years	2.0				

Cumulative Net Present Value Cash Flow

Figure 3.5 Business case summary data[7]

Phase 2: Build CRM project foundations

Having created the CRM strategy the next phase involves building the foundations for the CRM implementation.

Identify stakeholders

The first step is to identify stakeholders. Stakeholders include any party that will be impacted by the change – this could include senior management, users of any new system, marketing staff, salespeople, customer service agents, channel partners, customers and IT specialists. Their participation in the CRM project may be required at some future point. Research suggests that the early involvement of parties affected by change helps pre-empt later problems of resistance. Vendor experience indicates that the early involvement and participation of senior management is likely to promote a more successful implementation.

System users are important stakeholders. The importance of involving system users in the implementation of new technologies is reinforced by research conducted by Fred Davis and others. Davis found that intention to use a new technology is predicted by the perceived ease-of-use of the technology and the perceived usefulness of the technology. This is expressed in the Technology Acceptance Model which has been subjected to considerable testing and validation since Davis's initial work.[8] Early engagement of user stakeholders can help ensure that the technology is perceived as both easy-to-use and useful by users.

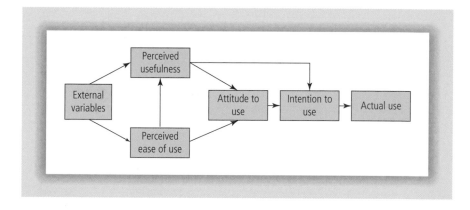

Figure 3.6
The Technology
Acceptance Model

Establish governance structures

CRM projects are designed and implemented by people. Governance structures (see Figure 3.6) need to be put in place to ensure that project roles and responsibilities are properly defined and allocated.

The programme director (PD) plays an important role in this structure. Ultimately, the PD has responsibility for ensuing that the project deliverables are achieved and that project costs are controlled. In larger projects the PD will be a full-time appointment. The PD has a boundary-spanning role – one foot is in the CRM steering committee, the other is in the programme team. Another key member of the steering committee is the executive sponsor. This is typically a board level senior executive who commits real time to the project and ensures that resources are made available. The steering committee makes policy decisions about the CRM implementation – for example, which technology to buy, which consultants to hire – and ensures that the implementation stays on track and within budget. Other senior executives may sit on the steering committee to ensure that the project remains business-focused and does not slide into becoming an IT-dominated project.

The programme team is composed of representatives from the major stakeholders (shown in Figure 3.7 as 'Lead' roles). They have the responsibility of implementing the project successfully. The Leads may have their own advisory groups that ensure that stakeholder needs and concerns are known and brought to the programme team. More importantly, the Leads are responsible for ensuring that the right people are brought in for specific project activities. For example, if the selling process is being reviewed, the sales Lead would ensure the participation of highly regarded sales representative and sales managers. CRM

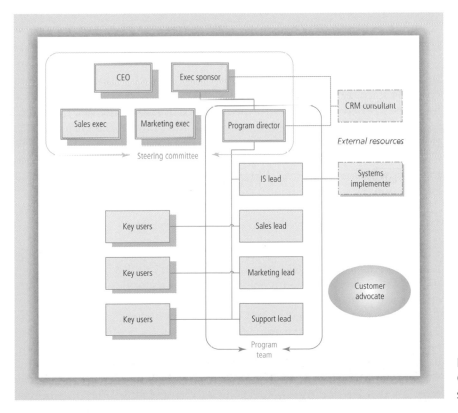

Figure 3.7
Governance
structure[9]

implementations can impose considerable demands on your company's own internal IT resources which might be called on to perform several project-related roles. The lead developer role ensures that the CRM software is customized to meet the needs of users. The database developer role ensures that customer-related data held in disparate databases is made available to end-users in the form required for operational and analytical CRM applications. The front-end developer role ensures that the user interface is easy to understand and use.

It is not uncommon for CRM projects to import resources and talents to help deliver the project. This governance structure will have a CRM consultant working with the steering committee. It is unlikely that an inhouse steering committee will have sufficient experience of CRM project implementation. An experienced consultant can help the steering committee overcome problems as the project progresses. A systems implementer is also shown in this governance structure as an important external resource. For an installed CRM system, vendors generally supply technical help to ensure that the system is properly implemented. The implementer has a boundary-spanning role, being an employee of the vendor but working onsite as the client's advocate.

A systems integrator may also be needed to align disparate systems into a coherent whole to support the project objectives. Systems integration can be defined as follows:

> Systems integration is the practice of aligning and combining system components such as people, processes, technology and data for the achievement of defined outcomes.

Very often desired CRM outcomes are impeded by the poor interoperability of IT systems. For example, the IT system that supports web operations may be incompatible with the IT system that supports the call centre. The result is that there may be two different databases containing important customer-related information. A systems integrator might be needed to programme the interface that links the two systems.

Finally, the governance chart shows that the voice of the customer has to be heard in the project team. Customers of companies that implement CRM are important stakeholders, because their experience of doing business will change. Some CRM projects fail to deliver optimal outcomes because the project team fails to ask 'What would the customer think?'

Identify change management needs

Even small CRM projects can prove challenging in terms of change management. A sales-force automation project might involve centralizing data that is presently kept on individual representatives' computers and making that information available to everyone in the team. Representatives will need to learn to share. In a distributed sales-force, these representatives may not have even met each other. If they also have to change their selling methodology, record keeping and reporting habits, there might be some worries, if not outright resistance.

According to consultants Booz Allen & Hamilton, 'Leadership teams that fail to plan for the human side of change often find themselves wondering why their best-laid plans go awry'.[10] They describe change both in terms of top-down leadership and bottom-up buy-in, as does John Kotter whose eight-step approach to managing change is widely cited and deployed.[11] The eight steps are as follows:

1. create a sense of urgency so people begin to feel 'we must do something'
2. put together a guiding team to drive the change effort
3. get the vision right, and build supporting strategies
4. communicate for buy-in
5. empower action by removing organizational barriers to change
6. produce short-term wins to diffuse cynicism, pessimism and scepticism
7. don't let up, but keep driving change and promoting the vision
8. make change stick by reshaping organizational culture.

Kotter emphasizes that successful change management programmes adopt a see–feel–change approach. To bring about change it is necessary not only to get people to see the need for change, but also to feel so emotionally engaged that they want to change. He stresses the importance of emotional engagement with the programme's vision and strategies.

Organizational culture

The idea of organizational culture has been around for many years. In everyday language, organizational culture is what is being described when someone answers the question 'what is it like working here?' More formally, organizational culture can be defined as:

> A pattern of shared values and beliefs that help individuals understand organizational functioning and thus provide them with the norms for behavior in the organization.[12]

Essentially, organizational culture is understood to comprise widely shared and strongly held values. These values are reflected in patterns of individual and interpersonal behavior, including the behavior of the business leaders, and expressed in the norms, symbols, rituals and formal systems of the organization.

A number of studies indicate that organizational culture affects business performance.[13] Recent research has also shown that organizational culture is a predictor of CRM success.[14] Adhocracy, one of four organizational cultures identified in the Competing Values model (Figure 3.8), shows the strongest association with CRM success. Adhocracies are highly flexible, entrepreneurial, externally-oriented organizations. Their core values are creativity and risk-taking.

Cameron and Quinn have developed a process for companies wishing to change their culture, as indicated by the Competing Values model.[15] They suggest that cultural change may involve adjustment to the organization's structure, symbols, systems, staff, strategy, style of leaders and skills of managers, but emphasize that individual behavioural change is the key to culture change.

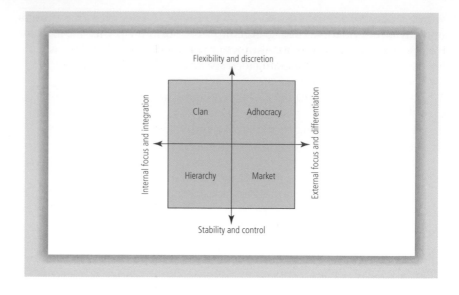

Figure 3.8
The Competing
Values model of
organizational
culture[16]

Buy-in

As noted by John Kotter, buy-in operates at an emotional or intellectual (rational) level. Intellectual buy-in is where people know what has to be changed and understand the justification for the change. New technologies are adopted more quickly when users believe that the system will be easy to use. Emotional buy-in is where there is genuine heartfelt enthusiasm, even excitement, about the change. The matrix in Figure 3.9 shows the possibility of four employee segments, reflecting the presence or absence of emotional and rational buy-in. Champions are emotionally and rationally committed. Weak links are neither emotionally nor rationally committed. Bystanders understand the changes being introduced, but feel no emotional buy-in to the change. Loose cannons are fired up with enthusiasm, but really don't understand what they have to do to contribute to the change. All these segments will be found in major change projects such as a CRM implementation.

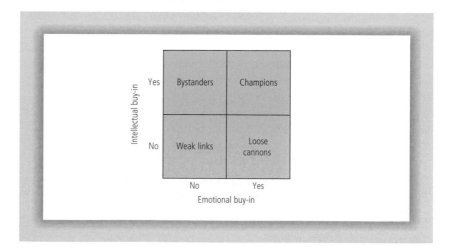

Figure 3.9
The buy-in matrix

The CRM project needs to be marketed to each of these groups in different ways. The programme team's challenges are to stir-up bystanders to become passionate about the project's goals, and to educate loose cannons on the reasoning behind CRM. Weak links can be truly problematic if they are in customer-facing roles or impact on customer experience. It has been said that it takes many years to win a customer's confidence and trust, but only one incident to break it. If efforts to win them over fail, weak links may need to be reassigned to jobs where there is no customer impact.

Identify project management needs

CRM implementations can place considerable demands on project management skills. A CRM project plan spells out the steps that will get you from where you are now (customer strategy situation analysis) to where you want to be (CRM vision, goals and objectives), on time and within budget. The CRM programme director generally performs the project management role, but sometimes it is outsourced to a consultant. A project plan sets out the tasks to be performed, the order in which they are to be executed, the time each will take, the resources required to perform the tasks (including people and money) and the deliverables from each task. Tools such as Gantt charts (see Figure 3.10), critical path analysis (CPA), programme evaluation and review techniques (PERT)

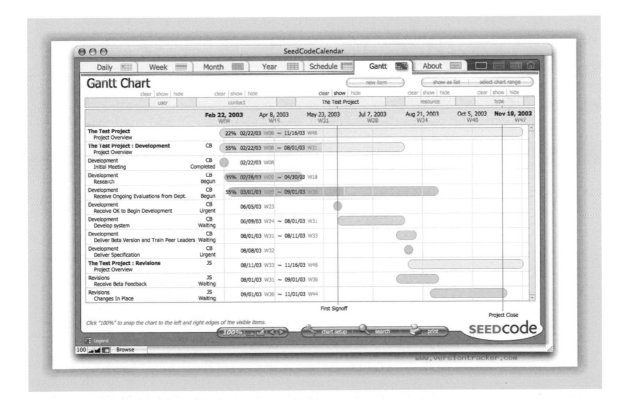

Figure 3.10 Project Gantt chart[17]

or network diagrams are useful tools for project managers. Some tasks will be performed in parallel, some in sequence. As the project rolls forward there will be periodic 'milestone' reviews to ensure that it is on time and on budget. A CRM project that has the goal of improving the productivity of marketing campaigns might be made up of a number of tasks or mini-projects, each with its own deliverable, including the following: market segmentation project, database development project, creation of a new campaign management process, management reports project, technology search and selection project, and a staff training project.

Identify critical success factors

Critical success factors (CSFs) are the 'must haves' that underpin project success. Critical success factors can be defined as follows:

> CSFs are attributes and variables that can significantly impact business outcomes.

CRM consultants and vendors offer a range of opinions on CSFs, mentioning the following: a clear customer strategy that defines your company's offers, markets and channels; an organizational culture that promotes coordination and information-sharing across business units; an agreed definition of what counts as CRM success; executive sponsorship of the CRM programme's objectives; availability and use of pertinent, accurate, timely and useable customer-related information; a clear focus on people and process issues, not only technology; starting small with quick wins that are then promoted within the company as success stories; focus on automating processes that have major implications for costs or customer experience; engagement of all stakeholders, including end-users and customers, in programme planning and roll-out.

There have been very few independent studies of CRM CSFs. Luis Mendoza and his colleagues conducted a qualitative study of CSFs that involved a panel of eight expert judges identifying 13 CSFs and 55 associated metrics covering people, process and technology aspects of CRM strategy.[18] The CSFs and their alignment with people, process and technology appear in Table 3.1, the most important being highlighted in bold.

Da Silva and Rahimi[19] conducted a single CRM case study test of three CSF models that had originally been developed in the context of enterprise resource planning (ERP) implementations. They found that CRM CSFs could be categorized as strategic and tactical. Strategic CSFs are encountered at the beginning of the project, while tactical CSFs become important later. Strategic CSFs include a clear CRM philosophy (we prefer the term 'vision'), top management commitment and project management expertise. Tactical CSFs include trouble-shooting skills, good communications and software configuration.

Croteau and Li conducted an empirical assessment of CRM CSFs in 57 large Canadian organizations.[20] Focusing only on the technology element – therefore ignoring people and process issues – they collected data about CRM's impacts on customer satisfaction, retention, loyalty

Critical success factor	People	Process	Technology
1. Senior management commitment	X		
2. Creation of a multidisciplinary team	X	X	
3. Objectives definition	X		
4. Interdepartmental integration	X	X	
5. Communication of the CRM strategy to staff	X	X	
6. Staff commitment	X		
7. Customer information management			X
8. Customer service		X	X
9. Sales automation		X	X
10. Marketing automation		X	X
11. Support for operational management	X	X	X
12. Customer contact management	X		X
13. Information systems integration			X

(Note: more important CSF's are bold typeface)

Table 3.1 Critical success factors for successful CRM strategies

and market share, and looked for associations with a number of predefined critical success factors. They conclude that the CSF most strongly associated with CRM success is an accurate and well-developed knowledge management system. This has to be supported by a suitable IT infrastructure which can capture, manage and deliver real time customer, product and service information in order to improve customer response and decision-making at all customer touchpoints. They also found that another important CSF is top management support.

Develop a risk management plan

It has been claimed that a large number of CRM projects, perhaps as many as two-thirds, fail.[21] Of course, there can be many potential causes of failure, ranging from inadequate project management to resistance of end users to the adoption of new technologies. At this stage, you'll be trying to identify the major risks to achieving the desired outcomes. Once identified, you can begin to put risk mitigation strategies and contingency plans in place. As you'd expect, some risks reflect an absence of the CSFs identified above. Gartner names a number of common causes of CRM failure: management that has little customer understanding or involvement; rewards and incentives that are tied to old, non-customer objectives; organizational culture that is not customer-focused; limited or no input from the customers; thinking that technology is the solution; lack of specifically designed, mutually reinforcing processes; poor-quality customer data and information; little coordination between departmental initiatives and projects; creation of the CRM team happening last, and the team lacks business staff; no measures or monitoring of benefits and lack of testing.[22]

Risk mitigation strategies are your responses to these risks. Let's take the risk of management having little or no customer understanding. How might you respond to this? There are a number of things you could do – management could work in the front-line serving customers (McDonalds' executives do this), listen in to call centre interactions for at least one hour a week or mystery shop your own and competitor organizations.

Phase 3: Needs specification and partner selection

Having built the CRM project foundations, the next phase involves specifying needs and selecting suitable partners.

Process mapping and refinement

The first task of Phase 3 is to identify business processes that need attention – making them more effective or efficient or flagging them as candidates for automation. Business processes can be defined as follows:

> A business process is set of activities performed by people and/or technology in order to achieve a desired outcome.

Put more simply, business processes are how things get done by your company. Processes can be classified in several ways: vertical and horizontal; front and back-office; primary and secondary.

Vertical processes are those that are located entirely within a business function. For example, the customer acquisition process might reside totally within the marketing department.

Horizontal processes are cross-functional. New product development processes are typically horizontal and span sales, marketing, finance and research and development functions.

Front-office (or front-stage) processes are those that customers encounter. The complaints handling process is an example.

Back-office (or back-stage) processes are invisible to customers, for example, the procurement process. Many processes straddle both front and back-offices: the order-fulfilment process (see Figure 3.11) is an example. The order taking part of that process sits in the front-office. The production scheduling part is back-office.

A distinction is also made between primary and secondary processes.

Primary processes have major cost implications for companies or, given their impact on customer experience, major revenue implications. The logistics process in courier organizations – from picking up a package, through moving the package, to delivering the package – constitutes about 90 per cent of the cost base of the business, and is therefore a primary process. Customers may have a different perspective on what is important. They typically do not care about back-office processes. They care about the processes that touch them. In the insurance industry these are the claims process, the policy renewal process and the new policy purchase process. In the courier business they are the pick-up, delivery and tracking processes.

Secondary processes have minor implications for costs or revenues, or little impact on customer experience.

Strategic CRM aims to build an organization that is designed to create and deliver customer value consistently better than its competitors. Designing processes that create value for customers is clearly vital to this outcome. 3M's mission is 'to solve unsolved problems innovatively'. It does this in part through new product development processes that are designed to identify good ideas and bring them to the market quickly.[23] For 3M, the innovation process is a primary process that enables the company to differentiate itself from its competitors.

Operational CRM involves the automation of the company's selling, marketing and service processes, and generally requires the support of analytical CRM. Figure 3.12 shows the campaign management process for a particular customer offer made by First Direct, a UK-based telephone bank. It shows that the propensity of a customer to open a high interest savings account is determined by a scoring process that considers both demographic and transactional data. The propensity

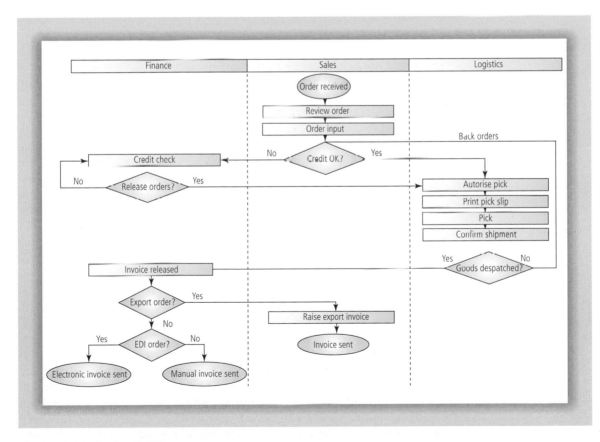

Figure 3.11 Order fulfilment process

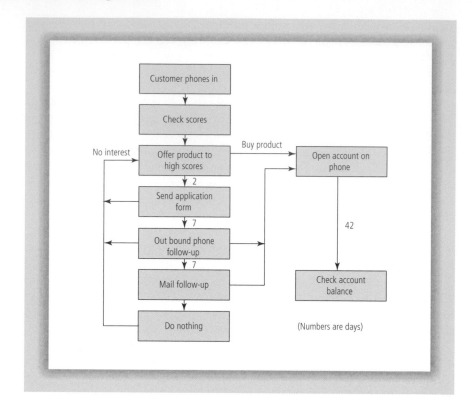

Figure 3.12
Campaign
management
process for high
interest savings
account

modelling process is an illustration of analytical CRM. If a target score is reached an offer is made, either by the customer service agent during a phone call or at a later time by mail. This automation of the selling process is an example of operational CRM.

Flowcharting, which is also known as blueprinting and process mapping, is a tool that can be used to make processes visible. The flowchart sets out the steps involved in performing the process. It may also identify the people (or roles) that contribute to the process, and the standards by which the process is measured, such as time, accuracy or cost. Processes always have customers, who may be either internal or external to a company. Customers receive process outputs. Figure 3.11 shows the order fulfilment process for an exporter. The flowchart shows that the process is cross-functional and is completed by a number of internal supplier–customer relationships in series.

Software such as Microsoft Visio, ABC Flowcharter and ConceptDraw is readily available to help generate process flowcharts. Major vendors and consultants may use their own proprietary applications. Oracle, for example uses Oracle Designer which allows them to model processes and generate the associated software code. Flowcharts can be used to identify fail points where a process frequently breaks down, redundancies and duplications. They can also be used for induction and training of new people and for illustrating internal customer–supplier relationships. Processes can be rated according to the degree to which they can be improved. It has been suggested, for example, that processes be rated according to the criteria in Table 3.2.

	Process rating
Best practice (superiority)	The process is substantially defect-free and contributes to CRM performance. Process is superior to comparable competitors and other benchmarks
Parity	A good process which largely contributes to CRM performance
Stability	An average process which meets expectations with no major problems, but which presents opportunities for improvement
Recoverability	The process has identified weaknesses which are being addressed
Criticality	An ineffective and/or inefficient process in need of immediate remedial attention

Table 3.2 Evaluating processes[24]

Data review and gap analysis

Having identified processes that require attention, the next step is to review the data requirements for the CRM implementation and to identify shortfalls.

Strategic CRM uses customer-related data to identify which customers to target for acquisition, retention and development, and what to offer them. Operational CRM uses customer-related data in the everyday running of the business, for example in handling billing queries in the contact centre or mounting campaigns in the marketing department. Analytical CRM uses customer-related data to answer questions such as 'who are our most profitable customers' and 'which customers are most likely to churn'?. Collaborative CRM uses customer-related data to enable channel partners to target their communications more precisely. The fundamental issue companies have to ask is: what customer-related data do we need for strategic, operational, analytical and collaborative CRM purposes?

Members of the programme team should be well placed to answer the question 'what information is needed?' For example, the programme team's marketing lead would be expected to appreciate the information needs of direct marketers running event-based campaigns. Typically, these marketers want to know response rates to previous mailings broken down by customer group, the content of those offers, sales achieved by the mailings and the number of items returned unopened. They would also want to know the names and addresses of selected targets, their preferred method of communication (mail? e-mail? phone?), their preferred form of salutation (first name? Mr? Ms?) and the offers that have been successful in the past. In a globalized business world, it is important to respect cultural connections.

At this stage of planning the CRM project, you are identifying the data that is needed for CRM purposes and creating an inventory of data that is available for these purposes. The gap between what is available and what is needed may be quite significant. A useful distinction can be made between 'need-to-know' and 'like-to-know' that is, between information needed for CRM purposes and information that might be useful at some future point. Given the costs of developing and maintaining customer-related databases, companies need to be rigorous in screening data requirements.

Initial technology needs specification and research alternative solutions

Earlier in this process you began to consider technology requirements. Now you can return to this question with a clearer focus on the process and data issues. There are a huge number of software applications that fall under the heading of CRM. They are shown in Figure 3.13. You need to decide what applications will deliver your CRM vision and meet the business case requirements. You can learn about these applications by visiting vendor websites, joining online communities such as www. customerthink.com, or attending physical or virtual (online) exhibitions. There is more coverage on IT issues in Chapters 13–16 of this book. Chapter 13 presents an overview of IT for CRM, and Chapters 14, 15

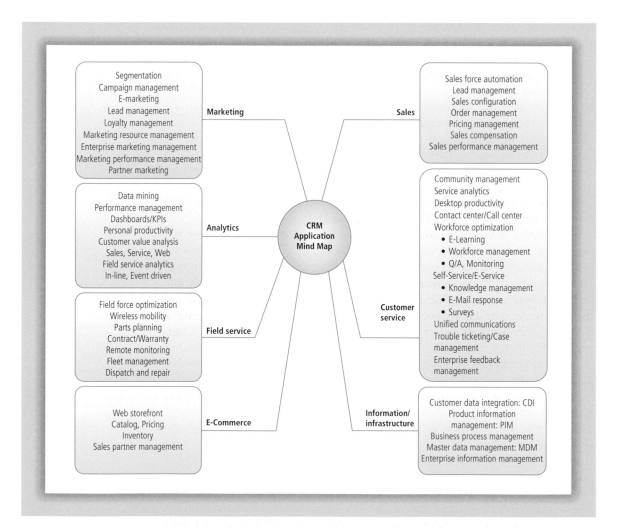

Figure 3.13 CRM applications (Source: Gartner Inc)

and 16 review sales-force automation, marketing automation and service automation respectively.

A decision has to be made about whether to build, buy or rent the CRM applications that are chosen. Your options are to build your CRM applications from scratch, to buy an on-premise site licence or pay a monthly per-user charge for an on-demand solution. If you opt to build from scratch you may find that some open source modules provide much or all of what you need. Open source software is peer-reviewed software that gives CRM application developers the opportunity to view and evaluate source code. Open source advocates suggest that being able to modify source code leads to improved software with fewer bugs, and that free distribution leads to more developers working to improve the software. The second alternative is to license CRM applications. Yearly licence fees typically vary according to the number of users. Licence fees give you the right to use the CRM software, but additional costs may be incurred for CRM application support and maintenance, training, customization, integration, IT infrastructure and end-user support. The final alternative is to pay a monthly per-user cost for an on-demand solution which generally includes implementation, maintenance, training, support and application management services delivered directly by the application vendor. Most companies opt for either hosted (on-demand) or installed (on-premise) solutions.

Hosted or on-premise CRM

One important decision is how to access CRM functionality. CRM software is distributed in two ways. It can be installed on your company's own servers or it can be accessed from another party's servers via the Internet. The former is known as on-premise, offline or installed CRM, an option that has been the preferred mode for many large-scale enterprises and early adopters. The alternative is known as hosted or online CRM, web-service, the ASP (Application Service Provider) model or the Software-as-a-Service (SaaS) model.

The hosted option is becoming more popular as CRM solutions are adopted by mid-market and smaller enterprises. Some larger organizations are also opting for online CRM solutions particularly for tactical or departmental-level issues, and many enterprises are using a hybrid mix of hosted and on-premise solutions, which is feasible when the underlying data model is the same.[25]

SaaS vendors deliver and manage applications and other services from remote sites to multiple users via the Internet. The software is installed on the ASP's servers or those of their partners. For example, Siebel's hosting partner is IBM. Access is on a pay-as-you-go or subscription basis. Some vendors offer a variety of options for their software. Oracle sells both on-premise and hosted versions of siebel CRM. Stayinfront sells on-premise owner-operated, on-premise hosted (whereby the software is on your site but managed by Stayinfront) and off-site hosted versions. Some vendors offer a 'peppercorn' arrangement whereby, after several years of rental, the software can be purchased for a token sum.

In the early days, hosted CRM applications offered much less functionality than their on-premise competitors. Currently, the gap is closing. Some SaaS vendors are providing advanced functionality for competitive intelligence, pricing, content management, data warehousing and analytics, and workflow design.[26]

There are a number of players in hosted CRM, some of whom are shown in Table 3.3.

Hosted CRM vendor	url
Salesforce.com	http://www.salesforce.com/
Siebel Systems	http://www.crmondemand.com/
Red CRM	http://redcrm.com/
Sugar CRM	http://www.sugarcrm.com
Entellium CRM Solutions	http://www.entellium.com/
SalesLogix	http://www.saleslogix.com/home/default.php3
Soffront Software Inc.	http://www.soffront.com/
RightNow Technologies	http://www.rightnow.com/
NetSuite	http://www.netsuite.com/portal/products/crm_plus/main.shtml
Oracle	http://www.oracle.com/ondemand/ebso.html
Aplicor Inc.	http://www.aplicor.com/

Table 3.3 Hosted CRM vendors

It is widely claimed that there are significant cost advantages to the hosted model. Costs are fixed and known. Companies pay a per-user monthly fee. If you have 50 users, and the monthly fee is $100 per user, you can expect annual user fees of $60 000. Upgrades are performed by the vendor away from the users' premises. On-premise implementations, in contrast, can impose significant burdens on in-house IT staff and budgets. There can be upfront investments in IT hardware and infrastructure, software purchase and customization, and training. Implementation costs can be significant. User support and software upgrade costs are additional to initial software licence costs. Essentially, the hosted model converts capital expenditure and fixed costs into variable costs. Hosted CRM costs have fallen to US$50 per user per month, and are expected to fall further as the growth in the market attracts new vendors.

One analysis has compared the total costs of ownership (TCO) of installed and hosted sales-force automation, using a hypothetical 500-user installation.[27] The TCO of the installed solution was eight times that of the hosted solution in year one (Table 3.4); in subsequent years the relative costs appear to even out, largely because the hosted solution requires clients to pay monthly or annual subscription fees based on the number of users.

Additional research by the Meta Group indicates that hosted CRM has a cost advantage in the first three years, but thereafter the annual charges incurred make on-premise solutions a more attractive proposition. They conclude:

'for a typical mid-market on-premises CRM application, total first year costs are nearly 50 per cent more than for a typical first year hosted application. However, a different picture emerges when costs

Cost item	On-premise CRM	Hosted CRM
Number of users	500	500
Application licence/subscription	$1 250 000	$750 000
Implementation and customization	$6 250 000	$187 000
Training	$150 000	$75 000
IT infrastructure/hardware	$500 000	$0
IT personnel	$500 000	$0
Support/upgrade costs	$225 000	$0
Year one expenditure	**$8 875 000**	**$1 012 500**

Sources: Triple Tree; Software & Information Industry Association (SIAA); salesforce.com; Yankee Group. Table originally appeared in eMarketer 2005.

Table 3.4 Hosted versus installed CRM – first year costs for a 500-user deployment

are projected over a few years … When long term costs are analysed, hosted products approach an equivalent total cost of ownership (TCO) to that of on-premise products in approximately three years. Beyond this time, a hosted TCO will exceed an on-premise TCO'.[28]

A contrary analysis, conducted by the Yankee Group, estimated that the TCO of an on-premise solution is almost 60 per cent higher over a five year period.[29] These conflicting results point to the need for CRM adopters to conduct their own TCO analysis.

You will also need to consider hardware issues. What types of hardware are required by sales, service and marketing users? Perhaps salespeople need a personal digital assistant (PDA) for easy portability, whereas marketing people will be satisfied with a desktop computer. Mobile road warriors in remote locations may require both a laptop in their home office and a PDA on the road. Table 3.5 offers a comparison of PDA and laptop attributes.

You now need to finalize your thinking about systems integration. For example, you might want your CRM system to 'talk to' or share data with back-end systems for finance, inventory management and order processing. You might want it to integrate with other third-party systems that provide added functionality for sales, marketing and service staff. For example, your marketing people might want integration with a mapping system, while salespeople might want integration with a global positioning system.

Write request for proposals (RFP)

Before calling for proposals you need to write a detailed RFP. This document becomes the standard against which vendors' proposals are evaluated. It summarizes your thinking about the CRM programme and invites interested parties to respond in a structured way. Typical contents of the RFP include:

1. Instructions to respondents
2. Company background

Attribute	Laptop	PDA
Content	Full	Narrow
Size	XXXX	X
Portability	Moderate	High
Start time	Moderate	Fast
Speed of input	Fast	Slow
Dialogue barrier	Yes	No
Stickiness	Moderate	High
Walk and use	No	Yes
Presentations	Excellent	Good
Replacement cost	High	Moderate
Synchronization	Good	Excellent

(Source: Customer Connect Australia)

Table 3.5
Comparing laptops and PDAs

3. The CRM vision and strategy
4. Strategic, operational, analytical and collaborative CRM requirements
5. Process issues:
   a. customer interaction mapping
   b. process re-engineering.
6. Technology issues:
   a. delivery model – SaaS, on-premise, blended
   b. functionality required – sales, marketing and service
   c. management reports required
   d. hardware requirements and performance measures
   e. architectural issues
   f. systems integration issues
   g. customization requirements
   h. upgrades and service requirements.
7. People issues:
   a. project management services
   b. change management services
   c. management and staff training.
8. Costing issues – TCO targets
9. Implementation issues – pilot, training, support, roll-out, timeline
10. Contractual issues
11. Criteria for assessing proposals
12. Timeline for responding to proposals.

Call for proposals

The next step is to invite potential partners to respond to the RFP. You'll see from the RFP contents that CRM projects sometimes require input from several process, people and technology partners. On the technology side, if your company is already paying for CRM modules as part of its enterprise IT system, you'll certainly want to add this technology vendor to the list of those invited to respond. Between three and six potential technology vendors are typically invited.

Revised technology needs identification

Proposals from technology vendors will sometimes identify opportunities for improved CRM performance that you may not have considered. Perhaps there is some functionality or an issue that you had not considered. For example, you might not have considered the need to provide implementation support to sales representatives in the field. A vendor who indicates that they'll be able to help representatives learn the new technology in remote locations might be very attractive.

Assessment and partner selection

The next stage is to assess the proposals and select one or more partners. This task is generally performed by an evaluation team formed for this purpose and reporting to the steering committee. Assessment is made easier if you have a structured RFP and scoring system. There are two types of scoring system – unweighted and weighted. An unweighted system simply treats each assessment variable as equally important. A weighted system acknowledges that some variables are more important than others. These are accorded more significance in the scoring process.

Evaluation and selection should involve more than just the written vendor proposals. Short-listed vendors should be invited to demonstrate their solutions in relevant scenaries. Vendors may be required to provide proof-of-concept for technical solutions such as e-mail integration or mobile synchronization. Finally, preferred vendors should be subject to reference checks. The results of all these inputs are then scored to support the final decision.

Phase 4: Project implementation

By now, you have developed the CRM strategy, built the CRM project foundations, specified your needs and selected one or more partners. It is now implementation time!

Refine project plan

The first step of Phase 4 requires you to cooperate with your selected partners in refining the project plan. Remember, this was originally defined without consideration of the needs and availability of your partners. You may find that your partner's consultants are already committed to other projects and that you'll have to wait. Your partners will be able to help you set new milestones and refine the budget.

Identify technology customization needs

It is very common that off-the-shelf technology fails to meet all the requirements of users. Some vendors have industry-specific versions of their CRM software. Oracle, for example, offers a range of CRM suites for banking, retail, public sector and other verticals. Even so, some customization is often required. The lead developer, database developer and front-end developer, in partnership with vendors, can perform these roles.

Customization needs are typically specified using a gap analysis approach. The required business process is supplied to the vendor, who (after some preparation) presents how this process is supported in the software. Any gaps are highlighted for subsequent analysis and action. This continues until all business processes have been examined. The resultant gap register is then assessed, priorities are established and customization of their software and/or modification of the business process begins.

Customization raises problems of ownership of Intellectual Property that both vendors and clients will want to reslove. Vendors have invested millions, perhaps billions, of dollars to create, code, test and protect their product. The view of most software companies is that they will maintain the rights to any customized code and the right to incorporate it into future releases of the software. It is not unusual for a client's legal team to contest this position.

Prototype design, test, modify and roll-out

The output of this customization process will be a prototype that can be tested by users on a duplicated set, or a dummy set, of customer-related data. End-user tests will show whether further customization is required. Final adjustments to marketing, selling and service processes are made at this stage, and further training needs are identified and met. After a final review, a roll-out programme is implemented. In larger companies this often is a phased roll-out. For example, a new sales-force automation system might be rolled out first to the 'champions', those identified earlier as buying in both emotionally and rationally. A new service automation solution might be rolled out to newly acquired customers first, before the existing customer base is imported. The idea is to iron out any problems before company-wide adoption.

Phase 5: Evaluate performance

The final phase of the CRM project involves an evaluation of its performance. How well has it performed? Two sets of variables can be measured: project outcomes and business outcomes. Project outcomes focus on whether the project has been delivered on time and to budget. Your evaluation of the business outcomes requires you to return to the project objectives, your definition of CRM success and the business case, and ask whether the desired results have been achieved.

If your single goal was to enhance customer retention rates, with a measurable lift from 70 to 80 per cent, and this is accomplished then your CRM project has been successful. Congratulations! However, most projects have multiple objectives and it is common for some objectives to be achieved while others are not. Lead conversion by the sales team might rise, but lead generation by campaign managers might fall short of objectives. A critical issue concerns the timing of any business performance evaluation. It can take users several months to become familiar with new processes and competent in using new technology. Periodic measures of business outcomes can be taken over time, to ensure that the programme outcomes are achieved. Ongoing training, timed to coincide with software upgrades, can enhance business outcomes.

Summary

In this chapter, you've learned about the five major phases of a CRM implementation, and the processes and tools that are used to ensure that CRM projects deliver what is expected of them. The key phases are:

1. Develop the CRM strategy
2. Build the CRM project foundations
3. Specify needs and select partner
4. Implement project
5. Evaluate performance.

CRM projects vary in scope, duration and cost, but it is always important to be clear about what business outcomes are desired and to measure the performance of the CRM implementation accordingly.

References

1. The content in this section is drawn from a number of sources. Important contributions are made by John Turnbull, Managing Director of Customer Connect (www.customerconnect.com.au) and Gartner Inc. (www.gartner.com).
2. Copyright©2008. Customer Connect Australia. Used with permission.
3. See http://www.theidm.com/index.cfm?fuseAction=contentDisplay.&chn=3&tpc=149. Accessed 25 June 2007.
4. See http://www.marketingpower.com/content24634.php. Accessed 25 June 2007.
5. http://blogs.salesforce.com/ask_wendy/files/how_to_create_your_crm_vision_5.16.05.PDF. Accessed 26 June 2007.
6. www.gartner.com.
7. Copyright©2008. Customer Connect Australia. Used with permission.
8. Davis, F.D. (1989). Perceived usefulness, ease of use and user acceptance of information technology. *MIS Quarterly*, Vol. 13(3), pp. 319–339.
9. Copyright©2008. Customer Connect Australia. Used with permission.

10. http://www.boozallen.de/media/file/guiding_principles.pdf. Accessed 27 June 2007.

11. Kotter, J.P. and Cohen, D.S. (2002) *The heart of change: real-life stories of how people change their organizations.* Boston, MA: Harvard Business School Press.

12. Deshpandé, R. and Webster, F.E. Jr. (1989) Organizational culture and marketing: defining the research agenda. *Journal of Marketing*, Vol. 53, pp. 3–15, January.

13. Deshpandé, R., Farley, J.U. and Webster, F.E. Jr. (1993) Corporate culture, customer orientation, and innovativeness in Japanese firms: a quadrad analysis. *Journal of Marketing*, Vol. 57, pp. 23–37, January.

14. Iriana, R. and Buttle, F. (in press). The impacts of organizational culture on customer relationship management outcomes. *International Journal of Research in Marketing.*

15. Cameron, K.S. and Quinn, R.E. (1999) *Diagnosing and changing organisational culture.* Reading, MA: Addison Wesley.

16. Cameron, K.S. and Quinn, R.E. (1999) *Diagnosing and changing organisational culture.* Reading, MA: Addison Wesley.

17. Copyright©2008. SeedCode LLC. Used with permission.

18. Mendoza, L.E., Marius, A., Perez, M. and Griman, A.C. (2007) Critical success factors for a CRM strategy. *Information and Software Technology*, Vol. 49, pp. 913–945.

19. Da Silva, R.V. and Rahimi, I.D. (2007) A critical success factor model for CRM implementation. *International Journal of Electronic Customer Relationship Management*, Vol. 1(1), pp. 3–15.

20. Croteau, A.-M. and Li, P. (2003) Critical success factors of CRM technological initiatives. *Canadian Journal of Administrative Sciences*, Vol. 20(1), pp. 21–34.

21. Buttle, F. and Ang, L. (2004) ROI on CRM: a customer journey approach. http://www.crm2day.com/library/EpFlupuEZVRmkpZCHM.php; Davids, M. (1999) How to avoid the 10 biggest mistakes in CRM. *Journal of Business Strategy*, November–December, pp. 22–26.

22. www.gartner.com

23. Treacy, M. and Wiersema, F. (1995) *The discipline of market leaders.* London: Harper Collins.

24. Adapted from Jones, P.A. and Williams, T. (1995) *Business improvement made simple.* Northampton: Aegis Publishing.

25. A data model is an abstract description of how data is organized in an information system or database.

26. For a review of hosted CRM, refer to Buttle, F. (2006) Hosted CRM: literature review and research questions. Macquarie Graduate School of Management, working paper 2006–1.

27. eMarketer. (2005) *CRM Spending and Trends.* http://www.emarketer. com/Report.aspx?crm_aug05. Accessed 21 August 2005.

28. Meta Group. (2004) Hosted CRM: the real cost. http://www. metagroup.com/us/displayArticle.do?oid=47816. Accessed 11 November 2005.

29. Kane, R. (2004) The top 10 myths of hosted CRM. http://www.aplicor. com/4%20Company/10%20Myths%20of%20Hosted%20CRM% 20Whitepaper.pdf. Accessed 20 October 2005.

Chapter 4
Developing, managing and using customer-related databases

By the end of this chapter, you will understand:

1. the central role of customer-related databases to the successful delivery of CRM outcomes
2. the importance of high quality data to CRM performance
3. the issues that need to be considered in developing a customer-related database
4. what data integration contributes to CRM performance
5. the purpose of a data warehouse and data mart
6. how data access can be obtained by CRM users
7. the data protection and privacy issues that concern public policy makers.

Introduction

In this chapter we discuss the importance of developing an intimate knowledge and understanding of customers. This is essential to achieving CRM success. Strategic CRM, which focuses on winning and keeping profitable customers, relies on customer-related data to identify which customers to target, win and keep. Operational CRM, which focuses on the automation of customer-facing processes such as selling, marketing and customer service, needs customer-related data to be able to deliver excellent service, run successful marketing campaigns and track sales opportunities. Analytical CRM mines customer-related data for strategic or tactical purposes. Collaborative CRM involves the sharing of customer-related data with organizational partners, with a view to enhancing company, partner and customer value. Customer-related databases are the foundation for the execution of CRM strategy. Proficiency at acquiring, enhancing, storing, distributing and using customer-related data is critical to CRM performance.

What is a customer-related database?

You may have already noted that this chapter is not about customer databases. Rather, it is about customer-related databases. Why? Companies typically do not have a single customer database; instead, they have a number of customer-related databases. Large organizations, such as financial services companies, can have 20 or more customer systems, each with a separate database. These databases capture customer-related data from a number of different perspectives. Customer-related databases might be maintained in a number of functional areas – sales, marketing, service, logistics and accounts – each serving different operational purposes. Respectively, these databases might record quite different customer-related data – opportunities, campaigns, enquiries, deliveries and billing. Customer-related data might also be maintained by different channel managers – company-owned retail stores, third-party retail outlets and online retail, for example. Similarly, different product managers might maintain their own customer-related data. Customer-related data can have a current, past or future perspective, focusing upon current opportunities, historic sales or potential opportunities. Customer-related data might be about individual customers, customer cohorts, customer segments, market segments or entire markets. They might also contain product information, competitor information, regulatory data or anything else pertinent to the development and maintenance of customer relationships.

Developing a customer-related database

Most databases share a common structure of files, records and fields (also called tables, rows and columns). Files (tables) hold information on a single topic such as customers, products, transactions or service requests. Each file (table) contains a number of records (rows). Each record (row) contains a number of elements of data. These elements are arranged in common sets of fields (columns) across the table. The modern customer-related database therefore resembles a spreadsheet. There are six major steps in building a customer-related database, as shown in Figure 4.1.[1]

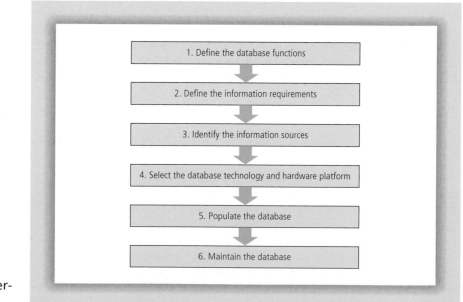

Figure 4.1
Building a customer-related database

Define the database functions

Databases support the four forms of CRM – strategic, operational, analytical and collaborative.

Strategic CRM needs data about markets, market offerings, customers, channels, competitors, performance and potential to be able to identify which customers to target for customer acquisition, retention and development, and what to offer them. Collaborative CRM implementations generally use the operational and analytical data as described below, so that partners in distribution channels can align their efforts to serve end-customers.

Customer-related data is necessary for both operational and analytical CRM purposes.

Operational CRM uses customer-related data to help in the everyday running of the business. For example:

- a telecoms customer service representative (CSR) needs to access a customer record when she receives a telephone query
- a hotel receptionist needs access to a guest's history so that she can reserve the preferred type of room – smoking or non-smoking, standard or de-luxe
- a salesperson needs to check a customer's payment history to find out whether the account has reached the maximum credit limit.

Analytical CRM uses customer-related data to support the marketing, sales and service decisions that aim to enhance the value created for and from customers. For example:

- the telecoms company might want to target a retention offer to customers who are signalling an intention to switch to a different supplier
- the hotel company might want to promote a weekend break to customers who have indicated their complete delight in previous customer satisfaction surveys
- a sales manager might want to compute his sales representatives' customer profitability, given the level of service that is being provided.

Customer-related data are typically organized into two subsets, reflecting these operational and analytical purposes. Operational data resides in an OLTP (online transaction processing) database, and analytical data resides in an OLAP (online analytical processing) database. The information in the OLAP database is normally a summarized, restructured, extract of the OLTP database, sufficient to perform the analytical tasks. The analytical database might also draw in data from a number of internal and external sources. OLTP data needs to be very accurate and up to date. When a customer calls a contact centre to enquire about an invoice, it is no use the CSR telling the customer what the average invoice is for a customer in her postcode. The customer wants personal, accurate, contemporary, information. OLAP databases can perform well with less current data.

Define the information requirements

The people best placed to answer the question 'what information is needed?' are those who interact or communicate with customers for sales, marketing and service purposes, and those who have to make strategic CRM decisions.

A direct marketer who is planning an e-mail campaign might want to know open and click-through rates, and click-to-open rates (CTOR) for previous e-campaigns, broken down by target market, offer and execution. She would also want to know e-mail addresses, e-mail preferences (html or plain text), and preferred salutation (first name? Mr? Ms?). Operational and analytical needs like these help define the contents of customer-related databases.

Senior managers reviewing your company's strategic CRM decisions will require a completely different set of information. They may want to know the following. How is the market segmented? Who are our current customers? What do they buy? Who else do they buy from? What are our customers' requirements, expectations and preferences across all components of the value proposition, including product, service, channel and communication?

With the advent of packaged CRM applications, much of the database design work has been done by the software vendors. The availability of industry-specific CRM applications, with their corresponding industry-specific data models, allows for a much closer fit with a company's data needs. Where there is a good fit out of the box, the database design process for both operational and analytical CRM applications becomes one of implementing exceptions that have been overlooked by the generic industry model. Some CRM vendors have also built in the extract, transform and load processes to move information from OLTP to OLAP databases although it is highly likely that a client will need to modify and customize the standard processes.

Customer information fields

Most CRM software has predefined fields in different modules, whether for sales, marketing or service applications. For example, in a sales application, a number of fields (columns) of information about customers are common: contact data, contact history, transactional history, current pipeline, future opportunities, products and communication preferences.

Contact data

Who is the main contact (name) and who else (other names) is involved in buying decisions? What are their roles? Who are the decision-makers, buyers, influencers, initiators and gatekeepers? What are the customer's invoice addresses, delivery addresses, phone numbers, fax numbers, e-mail addresses, street addresses and postal addresses?

Contact history

Who has communicated with the customer, when, about what, in which medium and with what outcome?

Transactional history
What has the customer bought and when? What has been offered to the customer, but not been purchased?

Current pipeline
What opportunities are currently in the sales pipeline? What is the value of each opportunity? What is the probability of closing? Is there a 10 per cent, 20 per cent … 90 per cent chance of making a sale? Some CRM applications enable sales people to allocate red, amber or green signals to opportunities according to the probability of success.

Opportunities
Whereas 'transactional history' looks backwards, 'opportunity' looks forwards. This is where opportunities that have not yet been opened or discussed are recorded.

Products
What products does the customer have? When were these products purchased, and when are they due for renewal? Have there been any service issues related to these products in the past?

Communication preferences
What is the preferred medium of communication – mail, telephone, e-mail, face-to-face, etc.? If it is e-mail, is plain text or html preferred? What is the preferred salutation? And the preferred contact time and location? Customers may prefer you to contact them by phone for some communications (e.g. an urgent product recall), by mail for others (e.g. invoicing), by e-mail (e.g. for advice about special offers) and face-to-face for other reasons (e.g. news about new products). These preferences can change over time. When a customer's preferences are used during customer communications, it is evidence that the company is responsive to customer expectations. Many companies allow customers to opt in to, or out of, different forms of communication. Customers may prefer to adjust their own preferences. Amazon.com, for example, allows customers to opt to receive e-mail about six different types of content: terms and conditions of shopping at Amazon; new products; research surveys; magazine subscription renewal notices; information about and from Amazon's partners and special offers.

Identify the information sources

Information for customer-related databases can be sourced internally or externally. Prior to building the database it is necessary to audit the company to find out what data are available. Internal data are the foundation of most CRM programmes, though the amount of information available about customers depends on the degree of contact that the company has with the customer. Some companies sell through partners, agents and distributors and have little knowledge about the demand chain beyond their immediate contact.

Internal data can be found in various functional areas.

- Marketing might have data on market size, market segmentation, customer profiles, customer acquisition channels, marketing campaign records, product registrations and requests for product information.
- Sales might have records on customer purchasing history including recency, frequency and monetary value, buyers' names and contact details, account number, SIC code, important buying criteria, terms of trade such as discounts and payment period, potential customers (prospects), responses to proposals, competitor products and pricing, and customer requirements and preferences.
- Customer service might have records of service histories, service requirements, customer satisfaction levels, customer complaints, resolved and unresolved issues, enquiries, and loyalty programme membership and status.
- Finance may have data on credit ratings, accounts receivable and payment histories.
- Your webmaster may have click-stream data.

Enhancing the data

External data can be used to enhance the internal data and can be imported from a number of sources including market research companies and marketing database companies. The business intelligence company Claritas, for example, offers clients access to their Behaviourbank and Lifestyle Selector databases. These databases are populated with data obtained from many millions of returned questionnaires. Experian, another intelligence company, provides geodemographic data to its clients. External data can be classified into three groups:[2]

1. compiled list data
2. census data
3. modelled data.

Compiled list data

Compiled list data are individual level data assembled by list bureaux or list vendors. They build their lists from a variety of personal, household and business sources. They might use local or council tax records, questionnaire response data, warranty card registrations or businesses' published annual reports. Lists can be purchased outright or rented for a period of time and a defined number of uses. Once the list or its permitted use has expired, it must be removed from the database.

If you were a retailer thinking of diversifying from leisurewear into dancewear and had little relevant customer data of your own, you might be interested in buying or renting data from an external source. Data could have been compiled by the bureau or vendor from a variety of sources, such as:

- memberships of dance schools
- student enrolments on dance courses at school and college
- recent purchasers of dance equipment

- lifestyle questionnaire respondents who cite dance as an interest
- subscribers to dance magazines
- purchasers of tickets for dance and musical theatre.

Census data

Census data are obtained from government census records. In different parts of the world, different information is available. Some censuses are unreliable; others do not make much data available for non-governmental use.

In the USA, where the census is conducted every ten years, you cannot obtain census data at the household level, but you can at a more aggregated geodemographic level, such as zip code, census tract and block group. Census tracts are subdivisions of counties. Block groups are subdivisions of census tracts, the boundaries of which are generally streets. In the USA there are about 225 000 block groups, with an average of over 1000 persons per group. Census data available at geodemographic level includes:

- median income
- average household size
- average home value
- average monthly mortgage
- percentage ethnic breakdown
- marital status
- percentage college educated.

For the UK census there are 155 000 enumeration districts, each comprising about 150 households and ten postcodes. The enumeration district is the basis for much geodemographic data.

Individual-level data are better predictors of behaviour than aggregated geodemographic data. However, in the absence of individual-level data, census data may be the only option for enhancing your internal data. For example, a car reseller could use census data about median income and average household size to predict who might be prospects for a purchase promotion.

Modelled data

Modelled data are generated by third parties from data that they assemble from a variety of sources. You buy processed, rather than raw, data from these sources. Often they have performed clustering routines on the data. For example, Claritas has developed a customer classification scheme called PRIZM. In Great Britain, PRIZM describes the lifestyles of people living in a particular postcode. Every postcode is assigned to one of 72 different clusters on the basis of their responses to a variety of lifestyle and demographic questions. Eighty per cent of the data used in the clustering process is less than three years old.

Figure 4.2 provides the PRIZM profile of residents of one postcode in the London suburb of Twickenham. They are assigned to PRIZM code A101, which applies to about one-third of one per cent of households in the country. The figure profiles their occupational status, living accommodation, car ownership, vacation choices and media consumption.

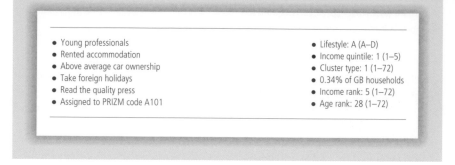

Figure 4.2
PRIZM analysis of
TW9 1UU, England

If you want to use external data to enhance your internal data, you'll need to send a copy of the data that you want to enhance to the external data source. The source will match its files to yours using an algorithm that recognizes equivalence between the files (often using names and addresses). The source then attaches the relevant data to your files and returns them to you.

Secondary and primary data

Customer-related data are either secondary or primary. Secondary data are data that have already been collected, perhaps for a purpose that is very different from your CRM requirement. Primary data are that collected for the first time, either for CRM or other purposes.

Primary data collection through traditional means, such as surveys, can be very expensive. Companies have, therefore, had to find relatively low cost ways to generate primary customer data for CRM applications. Among the data-building schemes that have been used are the following:

● **Competition entries**: customers are invited to enter competitions of skill or lotteries. They surrender personal data on the entry forms.
● **Subscriptions**: customers may be invited to subscribe to a newsletter or magazine, again surrendering personal details
● **Registrations**: customers are invited to register their purchase. This may be so that they can be advised on product updates.
● **Loyalty programmes**: many companies run loyalty programmes. These enable companies to link purchasing behaviour to individual customers and segments. When joining a programme, customers complete application forms providing the company with personal, demographic and even lifestyle data.

Select the database technology and hardware platform

Customer-related data can be stored in a database in a number of different ways.

1. hierarchical
2. network
3. relational.

Hierarchical and network databases were the most common form between the 1960s and 1980s. The hierarchical database is the oldest form and not well suited to most CRM applications. You can imagine the hierarchical model as an organization chart or family tree, in which a child can have only one parent, but a parent can have many children. The only way to get access to the lower levels is to start at the top and work downwards. When data is stored in hierarchical format, you may end up working through several layers of higher-level data before getting to the data you need. Product databases are generally hierarchical. A major product category will be subdivided repeatedly until all forms of the product have their own record.

To extend the family tree metaphor, the network database allows children to have one, none or more than one parent. Before the network database had the chance to become popular, the relational database superseded it, eventually becoming an ANSI standard in 1971.[3]

Relational databases

Relational databases are now the standard architecture for CRM applications (see Figure 4.3). Relational databases store data in two dimensional tables comprised of rows and columns. Relational databases have one or more fields that provide a unique form of identification for each record. This is called the primary key. For sales databases, each customer is generally assigned a unique number which appears in the first column. Therefore, each row has a unique number. Companies also have other databases for marketing, service, inventory, payments and so on. The customer's unique identifying number enables linkages to be made between the various databases.

Let's imagine you are a customer of an online retailer. You buy a book and supply the retailer with your name, address, preferred delivery choice and credit-card details. A record is created for you on the 'Customer' database, with a unique identifying number. An 'Orders received' database records your purchase and preferred delivery choice. An 'Inventory' database records that there has been a reduction in the stock of the item you ordered. This may trigger a re-ordering process when inventory reaches a critical level. A 'Payment' database records your payment by credit-card. There will be one-to-many linkages between your customer record and these other databases. With the advent of enterprise suites from vendors such as Oracle and SAP, all of these databases may reside in the one system and be preintegrated. The choice of hardware platform is influenced by several conditions:

1. The size of the databases. Even standard desktop PCs are capable of storing huge amounts of customer data. However, they are not designed for this data to be shared easily between several users.

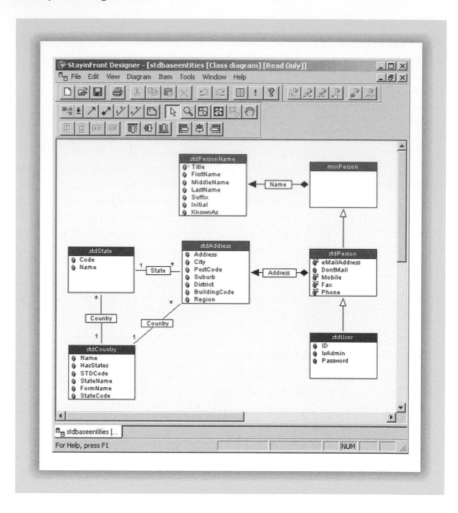

Figure 4.3
Relational database
model[4]

2. Existing technology. Most companies will already have technology that lends itself to database applications.
3. The number and location of users. Many CRM applications are quite simple, but in an increasingly global marketplace the hardware may need very careful specification and periodic review. For example, the hardware might need to enable a geographically dispersed, multilingual, user group to access data for both analytical and operational purposes.

Relational database management system (RDBMS)

A relational database management system can be defined as follows:

> An RDBMS is a software programme that allows users to create, update and administer a relational database.

There are a number of relational database management systems available from technology firms that are well suited to CRM applications. Leading RDBMS products are Oracle, DB2 from IBM, and Microsoft's SQL server. Most RDBMS products use SQL to access, update and query the database.

The selection of the CRM database can be done in parallel with the next step in this process, selection of CRM applications. Modern database applications come together with their own database schema, which predetermines the tables and columns in the database structure. Each CRM vendor then supports a specified list of database technologies, for example, Oracle or SQL server.

Indeed, it is possible to buy an entire platform, consisting of integrated hardware, operating system (OS), database and CRM applications. Leading platforms include UNIX, Microsoft and IBM. The UNIX platform offers a number of hardware/OS/database options, such as Hewlett-Packard hardware, Digital UNIX operating system and Oracle database. The IBM platform employs AS/400 hardware, OS/400 operating system and DB2/400 database. Microsoft NT servers are becoming more popular for CRM applications, due to the ease with which they can be scaled and expanded.

Populate the database

Having decided what information is needed and the database and hardware requirements, the next task is to obtain the data and enter it onto the database. CRM applications need data that are appropriately accurate. We use the 'appropriately' because the level of accuracy depends upon the function of the database. As noted earlier, operational CRM applications generally need more accurate and contemporary data than analytical applications.

You may have personally experienced the results of poor quality data. Perhaps you have received a mailed invitation to become a donor to a charity, to which you already donate direct from your salary. This could have happened when a prospecting list that has been bought by the charity was not been checked against current donor lists. Perhaps you have been addressed as Mrs although you prefer Ms. This is caused because the company has either not obtained or not acted or checked your communication preferences.

One of the biggest issues with customer data is not so much incorrect data as missing data. Many organizations find it difficult to obtain even basic customer data, such as e-mail addresses and preferences. The main steps in ensuring that the database is populated with appropriately accurate data are as follows:

1. source the data
2. verify the data
3. validate the data
4. de-duplicate the data
5. merge and purge data from two or more sources.

Sourcing: organizations must develop explicit processes to obtain information from customers, such as on initial sign-up or when concluding a service call. Organizations cannot rely on customer goodwill; data must be collected whenever interaction occurs.

Verification: this task is conducted to ensure that the data has been entered exactly as found in the original source. This can be a very labour-intensive process since it generally involves keying the data in twice with the computer programmed to flag mismatches. An alternative is to check visually that the data entered match the data at the primary source.

Validation: this is concerned with checking the accuracy of the data that are entered. There are a number of common inaccuracies, many associated with name and address fields: misspelt names, incorrect titles, inappropriate salutations. A number of processes can improve data accuracy.

- range validation: does an entry lie outside the possible range for a field?
- missing values: the computer can check for values that are missing in any column.
- check against external sources: you could check postcodes against an authoritative external listing from the mail authorities.

De-duplication: also known as de-duping. Customers become aware that their details appear more than once on a database when they receive identical communications from a company. This might occur when external data is not cross-checked against internal data, when two or more internal lists are used for the mailing or when customers have more than one address on a database. There may be sound cost reasons for this (de-duplication does cost money), but from the customer's perspective it can look wasteful and unprofessional. De-duplication software is available to help in the process.

The de-duplication process needs to be alert to the possibility of two types of error:

1. Removing a record that should be retained. For example, if a property is divided into unnumbered apartments and you have transactions

DupID	FirstName	LastName	CompanyName	StreetAddress	City	State
483	Stephen	Ayres	US Veterans Affairs Med. Ctr.	1601 SW Archer Rd.	Gainesville	FL
483	Stephen	Aires	US Affairs Medical Center	1601 SW Archer Rd.	Gainesville	Fl
573	Karl	Asha	ClearCommerce Corporation	11500 Metric Blvd.	Austen	TX
573	DanieleCarl	Asha	ClearCommerce Corporation	11500 Metric Boulevard	Austen	TX
870	Sherrell	Ballard	Southern Farm Bureau Life Ins.	Box 78	Jackson	MS
870	Cheryl	Ballard	Southern Farm Bur Lf Insur Co	P O Box 78	Jackson	MS
1359	Timothy	Bremere	General Cslty Co of Wisconsin	1 General Dr.	Sun Prairie	WI
1359	Tim	Bremer	General Casualty Companies	One general Drive	Sun Prairie	WI
2101	Mike	Condry	Celina Financial Corp.	One Insurance Sq.	Celina	OH
2101	Mike	Condry	Celina Insurance Group	One Insurance Square	Celina	OH
2800		Carmer	Indiana Lumbermans Insurance	Box 68600	Indianapolis	IN
2800	Patty	Carmer	Indiana Lumbermens Mutl Insur	P O Box 68600	Indianapolis	IN
3363	Robert	Delaney	Principal Mutual Life Insurance	711 High St	Des Moines	IA
3363	B	Delaney	THE PRINCIPAL FINANCIAL GROUP	711 High St	Des Moines	IA
3532	Danny	Teo	Bosley Medical	91 wilsheer	Beverly Hills	CA
3532	Danny	Teo	Bosley	9100 Wilshire	Beverly Hills	CA

Figure 4.4 Output from merge–purge operation[5]

with more than one resident, then it would be a mistake to assume duplication and delete records. Similarly, you may have more than one customer in a household, bearing the same family name or initials.

2. Retaining a record that should be removed. For example, you may have separate records for a customer under different titles such as Mr and Dr.

Merge and purge: also known as merge–purge (see Figure 4.4), this is a process that is performed when two or more databases are merged. This might happen when an external database is merged to an internal database, when two internal databases are merged (e.g. marketing and customer service databases), or when two external lists are bought and merged for a particular purpose such as a campaign. There can be significant costs savings for marketing campaigns when duplications are purged from the combined lists.

Maintain the database

Customer databases need to be updated to keep them useful. Consider the following statistics:

- 19% of managing directors change jobs in any year
- 8% of businesses relocate in any year
- in the UK, 5% of postcodes change in an average year
- in western economies about 1.2% of the population dies each year
- in the USA, over 40 million people change addresses each year.

It does not take long for databases to degrade. Companies can maintain data integrity in a number of ways.

1. Ensure that data from all new transactions, campaigns and communications is inserted into the database immediately. You will need to develop rules and ensure that they are applied.
2. Regularly de-duplicate databases.
3. Audit a subset of the files every year. Measure the amount of degradation. Identify the source of degradation: is it a particular data source or field?
4. Purge customers who have been inactive for a certain period of time. For frequently bought products, the dormant time period might be six months or less. For products with a longer repeat purchase cycle, the period will be longer. It is not always clear what a suitable dormancy period is. Some credit-card users, for example, may have different cards in different currencies. Inactivity for a year only indicates that the owner has not travelled to a country in the previous year. The owner may make several trips in the coming year.
5. Drip-feed the database. Every time there is a customer contact there is an opportunity to add new or verify existing data.
6. Get customers to update their own records. When Amazon customers buy online, they need to confirm or update invoice and delivery details.

7. Remove customers' records when they request this.
8. Insert decoy records. If the database is managed by an external agency, you might want to check the effectiveness of the agency's performance by inserting a few dummy records into the database. If the agency fails to spot the dummies, you may have a problem with their service standards.

Users with administrative rights can update records. Database updating and maintenance is also enabled by database query language. Common languages are SQL (Structured Query Language) and QBE (Query By Example). Maintenance queries available in SQL include UPDATE, INSERT and DELETE commands. You can use the commands to update your customer-related data. INSERT, for example, adds a new record to the database.

Desirable data attributes

Maintaining the database means that users will be more likely to have their need for accurate and relevant data met. Accuracy and relevance are two of six desirable data attributes that have been identified – data should be shareable, transportable, accurate, relevant, timely and secure.[6] You can remember these desirable data attributes through the mnemonic STARTS.

Data need to be **shareable** because several users may require access to the same data at the same time. For example, profile information about customers who have bought annual travel insurance might need to be made available to customer service agents in several geographic locations simultaneously as they deal with customer enquiries in response to an advertising campaign.

Data need to be **transportable** from storage location to user. Data need to be made available wherever and whenever users require. The user might be a hot-desking customer service representative, a delivery driver en route to a pick-up, an independent mortgage consultant or a salesperson in front of a prospect. Today's international corporations with globally distributed customers, product portfolios across several categories and multiple routes to market face particularly challenging data transportation problems. Electronic customer databases are essential for today's businesses, together with enabling technologies, such as data synchronization, wireless communications and web browsers to make the data fully transportable.

Data **accuracy** is a troublesome issue. In an ideal world it would be wonderful to have 100 per cent accurate data. But data accuracy carries a high costs. Data are captured, entered, integrated and analysed at various moments. Any or all of these processes may be the source of inaccuracy. Keystroke mistakes can cause errors at the point of data entry. Inappropriate analytical processes can lead to ill-founded conclusions. In CRM, data inaccuracy can lead to undue waste in marketing campaigns, inappropriate prospecting by salespeople and general suboptimal customer experience. It also erodes trust in the CRM system, thus reducing usage. This leads to further degrading of data quality. To counter this, usage volumes and data quality should be monitored. Data need to be entered at source rather than second hand; user buy-in needs to be managed; data quality processes such as de-duplication need to be introduced. Newsagency and book retailer WH Smith attribute high response rates of CRM-enabled direct marketing to the accuracy of their database. For example, an offer of Delia Smith's *How to Cook* book achieved an 8 per cent response rate, significantly more than was the norm before their data quality project was implemented.

Relevant data is pertinent for a given purpose. To check a customer's credit worthiness you need their transaction and payment histories, and their current employment and income status. To flag customers who are hot prospects for a cross-sell campaign, you need their propensity-to-buy scores. In designing a data management system to support a CRM strategy, relevance is a major issue. You need to know what decisions will be made and what information is needed to enable them to be made well.

Timely data is data that is available as and when needed. Data that is retrieved after a decision is made is not helpful. Equally, decision-makers do not want to be burdened with data before the need is felt. Bank tellers need to have propensity-to-buy information available to them at the time a customer is being served.

Data **security** is a hugely important issue for most companies. Data, particularly data about customers, is a major resource and a source of competitive advantage. It provides the foundation for delivery of better solutions to customers. Companies do need to protect their data against loss, sabotage and theft. Many companies regularly back-up their data. Security is enhanced through physical and electronic barriers such as firewalls. Managing data security in a partner environment is particularly challenging, as it is essential that competing partners do not see each other's sales leads and opportunity information, despite being signed into the same CRM system through the same portal.

Data integration

As noted earlier, in most companies there are several customer-related databases, maintained by different functions or channels. There might also be customer data in product or production databases, as well as call centres and websites, as suggested in Figure 4.5. External data from suppliers, business partners, franchisees and others may also need to be integrated.

Failure to integrate databases may lead to inefficiency, duplication and damaged customer relationships. Poor integration is indicated when you have bought an item online, only to be offered the same item at a later time through a different channel of the same company.

Customer data integration relies on standardization of data across databases. An indicator of the magnitude of the problem is that when Dun & Bradstreet was integrating data from several sources to create

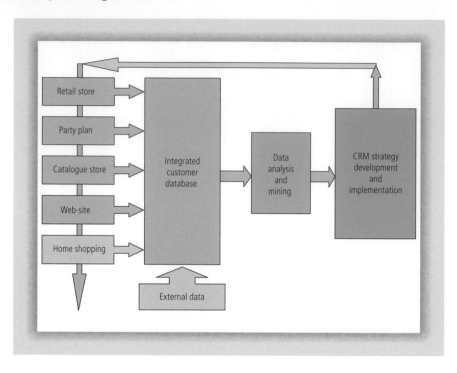

Figure 4.5
A single view of the customer

a marketing database it found 113 different entries for AT&T alone. These included ATT, A.T.T., AT and T and so on.

Companies often face the challenge of integrating data from several sources into a coherent single view of the customer. Sometimes this becomes a significant challenge in a CRM project, and a necessary hurdle to cross before implementing marketing, sales or service CRM applications.

The major on-premise CRM vendors, such as Oracle and SAP, offer solutions to this problem. SAP, for example, offers Master Data Management as part of its NetWeaver business integration platform. This enables companies to capture and consolidate data from different sources into a centralized database.

For companies with older mainframe (legacy) systems, another solution to the problem of database integration is to convert to newer systems with a centralized database that can accept real time inputs from a number of channels.[7] However, where there is considerable investment in legacy systems and a huge number of records this may not be cost effective. Legacy systems are typically batch-processing systems. In other words, they do not accept real time data. Many technology firms have developed software and systems to allow companies to integrate databases held on different legacy systems. Sometimes middleware has to be written to integrate data from diverse sources. Middleware is a class of software that connects different parts of a system that would not otherwise be able to communicate to each other. Middleware acts as a broker of information between systems, receiving information from source systems, and passing it to destination systems in a format that can be understood. It is often referred to as a kind of 'glue' that holds a network together.

Data integration at the American Heart Association

The American Heart Association (AHA) is a not-for-profit US health organization dedicated to reducing disability and death from heart attack, stroke and related cardiovascular disorders.

One of the AHA's major goals has been improving its relationships with stakeholders, including many thousands of volunteers conducting unpaid work for the organization, donors, businesses and the media. However, a challenge facing the AHA in achieving this goal was integrating the organization's data, which was previously located in over 150 separate databases, often geographically isolated and specific to certain departments within the organization. These provided a fragmented view of customers' profiles and history of activities.

AHA chose to implement a CRM software system across the organization to integrate all existing databases. Since implementation the AHA has found its staff is far more productive, it is able to respond to customers more quickly and provide more personalized service. Donations from customers have increased by over 20 per cent, using the system to contact potential donors compared to previous activities.

Data warehousing

As companies have grown larger they have become separated both geographically and culturally from the markets and customers they serve. Disney, an American corporation, has operations in Europe, Asia and Australasia, as well as in the USA. Benetton, the French fashion brand has operations across five continents. In retailing alone it operates over 7000 stores and concessions. Companies such as these generate a huge volume of data that needs to be converted into information that can be used for both operational and analytical purposes.

The data warehouse is a solution to that problem. Data warehouses are really no more than repositories of large amounts of operational, historical and other customer-related data. Data volume can reach terabyte levels, i.e. 2^{40} bytes of data. A warehouse is a repository for data imported from other databases. Attached to the front end of the warehouse is a set of analytical procedures for making sense out of the data. Retailers, home shopping companies and banks have been early adopters of data warehouses.

Watson describes a data warehouse as follows:[8]

- **subject-oriented**: the warehouse organizes data around the essential subjects of the business (customers and products) rather than around applications such as inventory management or order processing.
- **integrated**: it is consistent in the way that data from several sources is extracted and transformed. For example, coding conventions are standardized: M = male, F = female.

- **time-variant**: data are organized by various time-periods (e.g. months).
- **non-volatile**: the warehouse's database is not updated in real time. There is periodic bulk uploading of transactional and other data. This makes the data less subject to momentary change.

There are a number of steps and processes in building a warehouse. First, you must identify where the relevant data is stored. This can be a challenge. When the Commonwealth Bank opted to implement CRM in its retail banking business, it found that relevant customer data were resident on over 80 separate systems. Secondly, data must be extracted from those systems. It is possible that when these systems were developed they were not expected to align with other systems.

The data then needs to be transformed into a standardized, consistent and clean format. Data in different systems may have been stored in different forms, as Figure 4.6 indicates. Also, the cleanliness of data from different parts of the business may vary. The culture in sales may be very driven by quarterly performance targets. Getting sales representatives to maintain their customer files may be not straightforward. Much of their information may be in their heads. On the other hand, direct marketers may be very dedicated to keeping their data in good shape.

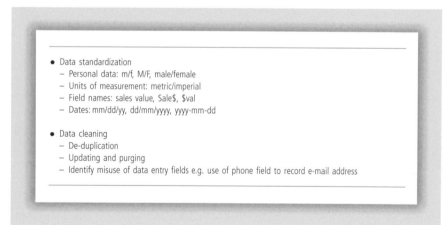

Figure 4.6
Data transformation

After transformation, the data then needs to be uploaded into the warehouse. Archival data that have little relevance to today's operations may be set aside, or only uploaded if there is sufficient space. Recent operational and transactional data from the various functions, channels and touchpoints will most probably be prioritized for uploading.

Refreshing the data in the warehouse is important. This may be done on a daily or weekly basis depending upon the speed of change in the business and its environment.

Data marts

A data mart is a scaled down version, or subset, of the data warehouse, customized for use in a particular business function or department.

Marketing and sales may have their own data marts enabling them to conduct separate analyses and make strategic and tactical decisions. Some large data warehousing projects have taken years to implement and have yielded few measurable benefits. According to a Gartner Inc., 75 per cent of data warehouse implementations will fail to meet their delivery targets. The Meta Group says 20 per cent fail outright and 50 per cent fall short of expectations.[9] Data mart project costs are lower because the volume of data stored are reduced, the number of users is capped, and the business focus is more precise. Technology requirements are less demanding.

Case 4.2

Data warehousing at Owens & Minor Inc.

Owens & Minor Inc., a Fortune 500 company headquartered in Richmond, VA, is the USA's leading distributor of national name brand medical/surgical supplies. The company's data warehouse project was first implemented in April 1997, starting with a single subject area – sales. Today, the data warehouse environment has grown to integrate over 20 different subject areas with over ten years of history. The size of the warehouse is just under 2 terabytes of total space. Internally there are over 900 users out of a total employee base of 3000, which is a very high percentage of business intelligence users. Externally Owens & Minor has four different extranet user groups that total around 600 users.

Source: The Data Warehousing Institute[10]

Data access and interrogation

CRM applications allow users to interact with customer-related databases for operational purposes. Sales representatives add data to customer records after a call is completed; CSRs in call centres log inbound calls on customer records; marketers update online brochures as product specifications change.

In addition, CRM users want to interrogate data for analytical purposes, or receive management reports. There are three main ways of doing this – standard reports, database queries, and data mining.[11]

Standard reports

Standard reports are automatically generated periodically by the CRM system. Examples include monthly reports to sales management about sales representatives' activity and performance against quota, and daily reports of call centre activity. OLAP technologies allow users to drill down into the data on a screen rather than resorting to a flat, fixed-format, report. Starting with aggregated sales data for a region, a sales manager can drill down into data about individual sales representatives and their customers, to reveal where causes of underperformance lie. Special reports can also be produced when ad hoc queries are made of a database, data warehouse or data mart. Most database management systems incorporate some reporting capability.

Database queries

A number of different types of query languages are available to CRM users when they want to raise a database query. Some are graphical – users can click and drag the data they want, and then drill down until they reach the level of granularity they require. Database managers may prefer to use SQL, which is now the standard query language for relational databases. SQL queries employing standard commands, such as SELECT, INSERT, DELETE, UPDATE, CREATE, DROP, can be used to access required data.

Data mining

In the CRM context, data mining can be defined as follows:

> Data mining is the application of descriptive and predictive analytics to support the marketing, sales and service functions.[12]

Although data mining can be performed on operational databases, it is more commonly applied to the more stable datasets held in data marts or warehouses. Higher processing speeds, reduced storage costs and better software packages have made data mining more attractive and economical.

Data mining can provide answers to questions that are important for both strategic and operational CRM purposes. For example:

1. How can our market and customer base be segmented?
2. Which customers are most valuable?
3. Which customers offer most potential for the future?
4. What types of customers are buying our products? Or not buying?
5. Are there any patterns of purchasing behaviour in our customer base?
6. Should we charge the same price to all these segments?
7. What is the profile of customers who default on payment?
8. What are the costs of customer acquisition?
9. What sorts of customer should be targeted for acquisition?
10. What offers should be made to specific customer groups to increase their value?
11. Which customers should be targeted for customer retention efforts?
12. Which retention tactics work well?

Data mining helps CRM in a number of ways. It can find **associations** between data. For example, the data may reveal that customers who buy low fat desserts are also big buyers of herbal health and beauty aids, or that consumers of wine enjoy live theatre productions. One analyst at Wal-Mart, the American retailer, noted a correlation between diaper sales and beer sales, which was particularly strong on Fridays. On investigating further he found that fathers were buying the diapers and picking up a six-pack at the same time. The company responded to this information by locating these items closer to each other. Sales of both rose strongly.[13]

Case 4.3

Data mining at Marks & Spencer

Data mining has proven to be a successful strategy for the UK retailer Marks & Spencer (M&S). The company generates large volumes of data from the ten million customers per week it serves in over 300 stores. The organization claims data mining lets it build one-to-one relationships with every customer, to the point that whenever individual customers come into a store the retailer knows exactly what products it should offer in order to build profitability.

Marks & Spencer believes two factors are important in data mining. First is the quality of the data. This is higher when the identity of customers is known, usually as a result of e-commerce tracking or loyalty programme membership. Second is to have clear business goals in mind before starting data mining. For example, M&S uses data mining to identify 'high margin', 'average margin' or 'low margin' customer groups. The company then profiles 'high margin' customers. This is used to guide customer retention activities with appropriate targeted advertising and promotions. This technique can also be used to profile 'average margin' or 'low margin' customers who have the potential to be developed into 'high margin' customers.

Sequential patterns often emerge from data mining. Data miners look for 'if ... then' rules in customer behaviour. For example, they might find a rule such as 'If a customer buys walking shoes in November, then there is a 40 per cent probability that they will buy rainwear within the next six months', or 'If a customer calls a contact centre to request information about interest rates, then there is a 50 per cent probability the customer will churn in the next three months'. Rules such as these enable CRM users to implement timely tactics. In the first instance, there is an opportunity for cross-selling. Secondly, there may be an opportunity to save the customer.

Data-mining also works by **classifying**. Customers can be classified into mutually exclusive groups. For example, you might be able to segment your existing customers into groups according to the value they produce for your company. You can then profile each group. When you identify a potential new customer you can judge which group the prospect most resembles. That will give you an idea of the prospect's potential value.

You could also classify customers into quintiles or deciles in terms of important transactional information such as the recency, frequency and monetary value of the purchases they have made. This is called RFM

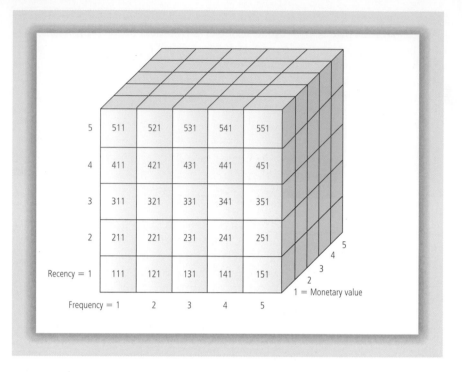

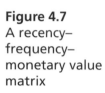

Figure 4.7
A recency–
frequency–
monetary value
matrix

analysis. Then you can experiment with different treatments, making different offers and communicating in different ways to selected cells of the RFM matrix (see Figure 4.7). You can expect to find that customers who have bought most recently, frequently or spend most with you are the most responsive in general terms.

Another approach in data mining is **clustering**. CRM practitioners attempt to cluster customers into groups. The general objective of clustering is to minimize the differences between members of a cluster while also maximizing the differences between clusters. Clustering techniques work by using a defined range of variables to perform the clustering procedure. You might, for example, use all available transaction data to generate customer segments. There are a number of techniques, such as cluster analysis, which find the hidden clusters.[14] Once statistical clusters have been formed they need to be interpreted. Lifestyle market segments are outputs of cluster analysis on large sets of data. Cluster labels such as 'Young working class families' or 'Wealthy suburbanites' are often used to capture the essence of the cluster.

Finally, data mining can contribute to CRM by **making predictions**. CRM practitioners might use historic purchasing behaviour to predict future purchasing behaviour and customer lifetime value.

These five major approaches to data mining can be used in various sequences. For example, you could use clustering to create customer segments, then within segments use transactional data to predict future purchasing and customer lifetime value.

According to Gartner Inc., market leaders SAS and SPSS offer broad data mining solutions that meet most market needs.[15] There are many other vendors. Successful vendors of CRM analytics provide the following:

- packaged applications to support common CRM decisions such as cross-sell and customer churn prediction
- a user interface suitable for business users
- the capability to access data from various sources including data warehouses, data marts, call centres, e-commerce or web-tracking systems, as well as third party data sources
- robust data mining statistical tools such as cluster analysis, decision trees and neural networks that can provide reliable insights into different types and volumes of data
- reporting tools that make the results of analysis available to decision-makers such as campaign managers and call centre agents.

Privacy issues

Privacy and data protection are major concerns to legislators around the world. Customers are increasingly concerned about the amount of information commercial organizations have about them, and the uses to which that information is put. In fact, consumers are not aware of just how much information is available to companies. When you use the Internet, small programmes called cookies are downloaded onto your hard disk from the sites you visit. A very small number of websites obtain permission from their site visitors prior to the download; most do not.

There have been two major responses to the privacy concerns of customers. The first is self-regulation by companies and associations. For example, a number of companies publish their privacy policies and make a commercial virtue out of their transparency. Professional bodies in fields such as direct marketing, advertising and market research have adopted codes of practice that members must abide by.

The second response has been legislation. In 1980, the Organization for Economic Cooperation and Development (OECD) developed a set of principles that has served the foundation for personal data protection legislation around the world.[16] These principles are voluntary guidelines that member nations can use when framing laws to protect individuals against abuses by data gatherers. The principles are as follows:

- **Purpose specification**: at the time of data collection, the consumer should be provided with a clear statement of the purposes for which the data is being collected.
- **Data collection processes**: data should be collected only by fair and lawful means.
- **Limited application**: data should be used only for valid business purposes.
- **Data quality**: personal data should be relevant for the purposes used and kept accurate, complete and up to date.
- **Use limitation**: personal data should not be disclosed, sold, made available or otherwise used for purposes than as specified at the time

of collection unless the consumer gives consent or as required by law. Consumer consent can be obtained either through an opt-in or opt-out process. Opt-in means than consumers agree that their data may be used for a particular purpose. Opt-out means that consumers prohibit use for that purpose.

- **Openness**: consumers should be able to receive information about developments, practices and policies with regard to their personal data. They should be able to find out what data has been collected and the uses to which it has been put. Consumers should have access to the data controller.
- **Access**: consumers should be able to access their data in readable form, to challenge the data and, if the challenge is successful, have the data erased, corrected or completed.
- **Data security**: personal data should be protected against risks such as loss, unauthorized access, destruction, use, modification or disclosure.
- **Accountability**: a data controller should be accountable for compliance with these measures.

Legislation has been enacted at a number of levels. In 1995, the Council of the European Union issued Directive 95/46/EC on the 'Protection of Individuals with Regard to the Processing of Personal Data and on the Free Movement of Such Data'. This applies to all forms of data and information processing including e-commerce. It required all member states to upgrade their legislation to a common standard by 1998. Companies are now only allowed to process personal data where the individual has given consent or where, for legal or contractual reasons, processing is necessary. EU countries are not allowed to export personal data to countries where such exacting standards do not apply. Legislation guarantees certain rights to citizens of the EU:

- **notification**: individuals are to be advised without delay about what information is being collected, and the origins of that data, if not from the individual
- **explanation** of the logic behind the results of automated decisions based on customer data (e.g. why a credit application was rejected)
- **correction/deleting/blocking** of data that do not comply with legislation
- **objection**: individuals can object to the way in which their data are processed (opt-out). Where the objection is justified, the data controller must no longer process the information.

Data controllers are also required to comply with certain obligations, including:

- Only collect and process data for legitimate and explicit purposes.
- Only collect personal data when individual consent has been granted, or is required to enter into or fulfil a contract, or is required by law.
- Ensure the data is accurate and up to date.
- At the point of data collection, to advise the individual of the identity of the collector, the reason for data collection, the recipients of the

data, and the individual's rights in respect of data access, correction and deletion.
- Ensure that the data is kept secure and safe from unauthorized access and disclosure.

The USA has not adopted these legislative standards, but in order to enable US companies to do business with EU organizations, the US Commerce Department has devised a set of 'Safe Harbor' principles. US organizations in the Safe Harbor are assumed to adhere to seven principles regarding notice (as in notification, above), choice, onward transfer (disclosure to third parties), security, data integrity, access and enforcement (accountability). US companies obtain Safe Harbor refuge by voluntarily certifying that they adhere to these principles. This enables data transfers to be made to the USA. Two areas of difference between the EU Directive and these Safe Harbor principles are in access and enforcement. The Safe Harbor wording for access is weaker. The Safe Harbor principle states that 'individuals must have *reasonable* access to personal information about them that an organization holds, and to be able to correct or amend the information *where it is inaccurate*'. The enforcement principle is unclear about sanctions should a company breach the standard and it allows no possibility of enforcement by government agencies.

In the USA, there is a tendency to rely on self-regulation by individual or associated companies, rather than legislation at state or federal level. For example, the World-Wide Web Consortium (W3C) has developed a Platform for Privacy Preferences (P3P) standard for improving privacy protection in e-commerce. This comprises three major elements:

1. A personal profile: each Internet user creates a file consisting of personal data and privacy rules for use of that data. Personal data might include demographic, lifestyle, preference and click-stream data. Privacy rules are the rules that the user prescribes for use of the data, e.g. opt-in or opt-out rules, and disclosure to third parties. The profile is stored in encrypted form on the user's hard drive, can be updated at any time by the users and is administered by the user's web browser.
2. A profile of website privacy practices: each website discloses what information has been accessed from the user's personal profile and how it has been used.
3. Automated protocols for accessing and using the user's data: these allow either the user or the user's agent (perhaps the web browser) automatically to ensure that the personal profile and the privacy rules are being complied with. If compliance is assured, then users can enter websites and transact without problems.

This is now being complemented with a more rigorous approach to legislation. In Australia, privacy legislation has been enacted at state and federal levels.

Summary

In this chapter you've read about the development, management and use of customer-related databases. CRM cannot deliver its promised benefits without appropriate customer-related data. Customer-related data are used for strategic, operational, analytical and collaborative CRM purposes. Customer-related databases need to be constructed with a very clear idea of the applications for which the data are needed. These applications range across the full territory of CRM strategy development and implementation. Customer-related data can be used to answer strategic questions such as 'Which customers should we serve?' and tactical questions such as 'What is the best day to communicate with a given customer?'

We described a six-step approach to developing a high quality customer-related database, consisting of defining the database functions, establishing the information requirements, identifying the information sources, selecting the database technology and hardware platform, populating and maintaining the database. We saw how compiled list data, census data and modelled data can be imported to enhance the basic data available in company-maintained databases, most of which adopt the standard relational architecture. Data integration from disparate databases is often a barrier to the delivery of desired CRM outcomes. Attached to the front end of many databases are data mining systems that allow users to make sense of the data. We ended by looking at data warehouses, data marts and privacy issues.

References

1. Based on O'Connor, J. and Galvin, E. (2001) *Marketing in the digital age*, (2nd edn). Harlow, England: Financial Times/Prentice Hall.
2. Drozdenko, R.G. and Drake, P.D. (2002) *Optimal database marketing: strategy, development and data mining*. Thousand Oaks, CA: Sage.
3. ANSI is the American National Standards Institute.
4. Courtesy of StayinFront Inc., www.stayinfront.com Used with permission.
5. Courtesy of Intelligent Search Technology Ltd, www.intelligentsearch.com
6. Based on Watson, R.T. (1999) *Data management: databases and organisations*. New York: John Wiley.
7. Drozdenko, R.G. and Drake, P.D. (2002) *Optimal database marketing: strategy, development and data mining*. Thousand Oaks, CA: Sage.
8. Watson, R.T. (1999) *Data management: databases and organizations*. New York: John Wiley.
9. D'Addario, J. (2002) *The application revolution*. http://www.tdwi.org/Publications/display.aspx?id=6460&t=y. Accessed 11 September 2007.
10. The Data Warehousing Institute. http://www.tdwi.org/display.aspx?ID=7145. Accessed 11 September 2007.

11. Zikmund, W.G., McLeod, R. Jr. and Gilbert, F.W. (2003) *Customer relationship management: integrating marketing strategy and information technology*. Hoboken, NJ: John Wiley.
12. Gartner Inc. (2006) *Magic quadrant for data mining*, 1Q06. www.gartner.com
13. Dempsey, M. (1995) Customers compartmentalised. *Financial Times*, 1 March.
14. Saunders, J. (1994) Cluster analysis. In: G.J. Hooley and M.K. Hussey (eds). *Quantitative methods in marketing*. London: Dryden Press, pp. 13–28.
15. Gartner Inc. (2006) *Magic quadrant for data mining*, 1Q06. www.gartner.com
16. Swift, R.S. (2001) *Accelerating customer relationships using CRM and relationship technologies*. Upper Saddle River, NJ: Prentice Hall.

Chapter 5
Customer portfolio management

By the end of this chapter you will understand:

1. the benefits that flow from managing customers as a portfolio
2. a number of disciplines that contribute to customer portfolio management: market segmentation, sales forecasting, activity-based costing, lifetime value estimation and data mining
3. how customer portfolio management differs between business-to-consumer and business-to-business contexts
4. how to use a number of business-to-business portfolio analysis tools
5. the range of customer management strategies that can be deployed across a customer portfolio.

What is a portfolio?

The term portfolio is often used in the context of investments to describe the collection of assets owned by an individual or institution. Each asset is managed differently according to its role in the owner's investment strategy. Portfolio has a parallel meaning in the context of customers. A customer portfolio can be defined as follows:

> A customer portfolio is the collection of mutually exclusive customer groups that comprise a business's entire customer base.

In other words, a company's customer portfolio is made up of customers clustered on the basis of one or more strategically important variables. Each customer is assigned to just one cluster in the portfolio. At one extreme, all customers can be treated as identical; at the other, each customer is treated as unique. Most companies are positioned somewhere between these extremes.

One of strategic CRMs fundamental principles is that not all customers can, or should, be managed in the same way, unless it makes strategic sense to do so. Customers not only have different needs, preferences and expectations, but also different revenue and cost profiles, and therefore should be managed in different ways. For example, in the B2B context, some customers might be offered customized product and face-to-face account management; others might be offered standardized product and web-based self-service. If the second group were to be offered the same product options and service levels as the first, they might end up being value-destroyers rather than value-creators for the company.

Customer portfolio management (CPM) aims to optimize business performance – whether that means sales growth, enhanced customer profitability, or something else – across the entire customer base. It does this by offering differentiated value propositions to different segments of customers. For example, the UK-based NatWest Bank manages its business customers on a portfolio basis. It has split customers into three segments based upon their size, lifetime value and creditworthiness. As Figure 5.1 shows, each cluster in the portfolio is treated to a different value proposition. When companies deliver tiered service levels such as these, they face a number of questions. Should the tiering be based upon current or future customer value? How should the sales and service support vary across tiers? How can customer expectations be managed to avoid the problem of low tier customers resenting not being offered high tier service? What criteria should be employed when shifting customers up and down the hierarchy? Finally, does the cost of managing this additional complexity pay off in customer outcomes such as enhanced retention levels, or financial outcomes such as additional revenues and profit?

- Corporate Banking Services has three tiers of clients ranked by size, lifetime value and credit worthiness.
  - The top tier numbers some 60 multinational clients. These have at least one **individual relationship manager** attached to them.
  - The second tier numbering approximately 150 have **individual client managers** attached to them.
  - The third tier representing the vast bulk of smaller business clients have access to a **'Small Business Advisor'** at each of the 100 business centres.

Figure 5.1
Customer portfolio management in NatWest Corporate Banking Services

Who is the customer?

The customer in a B2B context is different from a customer in the B2C context. The B2C customer is the end consumer: an individual or a household. The B2B customer is an organization: a company (producer or reseller) or an institution (not-for-profit or government body). CPM practices in the B2B context are very different from those in the B2C context.

The B2B context differs from the B2C context in a number of ways. First, there are fewer customers. In Australia, for example, although there is a population of twenty million people, there are only one million registered businesses. Secondly, business customers are much larger than household customers. Thirdly, relationships between business customers and their suppliers typically tend to be much closer than between household members and their suppliers. You can read more about this in Chapter 2. Often business relationships feature reciprocal trading. Company A buys from company B, and company B buys from company A. This is particularly common among small and medium-sized enterprises.

Fourthly, the demand for input goods and services by companies is derived from end user demand. Household demand for bread creates organizational demand for flour. Fifthly, organizational buying is conducted in a professional way. Unlike household buyers, procurement officers for companies are often professionals with formal training. Buying processes can be rigorously formal, particularly for mission-critical goods and services, where a decision-making unit composed of interested parties may be formed to define requirements, search for suppliers, evaluate proposals and make a sourcing decision. Often, the value of a single organizational purchase is huge: buying an airplane, bridge or power station is a massive purchase few households will ever match. Finally, much B2B trading is direct. In other words, there are no channel intermediaries and suppliers sell direct to customers.

These differences mean that the CPM process is very different in the two contexts. In the B2B context, because suppliers have access to much more customer-specific information, CPM uses organization-specific data, such as sales volume and cost-to-serve, to allocate customers to strategic clusters. In the B2C context, individual level data is not readily available. Therefore, the data used for clustering purposes tends not to be specific to individual customers. Instead, data about groups of customers, for example geographic market segments, is used to perform the clustering.

Basic disciplines for CPM

In this section, you'll read about a number of basic disciplines that can be useful during CPM. These include market segmentation, sales forecasting, activity-based costing, customer lifetime value estimation and data mining.

Market segmentation

CPM can make use of a discipline that is routinely employed by marketing management: market segmentation. Market segmentation can be defined as follows:

> Market segmentation is the process of dividing up a market into more-or-less homogenous subsets for which it is possible to create different value propositions.

At the end of the process the company can decide which segment(s) it wants to serve. If it chooses, each segment can be served with a different value proposition and managed in a different way. Market segmentation processes can be used during CPM for two main purposes. They can be used to segment potential markets to identify which customers to acquire, and to cluster current customers with a view to offering differentiated value propositions supported by different relationship management strategies.

In this discussion we'll focus on the application of market segmentation processes to identify which customers to acquire. What distinguishes market segmentation for this CRM purpose is its very clear focus on customer value. The outcome of the process should be the identification of the value potential of each identified segment. Companies will want to identify and target customers that can generate profit in the future: these will be those customers that the company and its network are better placed to serve and satisfy than their competitors.

Market segmentation in many companies is highly intuitive. The marketing team will develop profiles of customer groups based upon their insight and experience. This is then used to guide the development of marketing strategies across the segments. In a CRM context, market segmentation is highly data dependent. The data might be generated internally or sourced externally. Internal data from marketing, sales and finance records are often enhanced with additional data from external sources such as marketing research companies, partner organizations in the company's network and data specialists (see Figure 5.2).

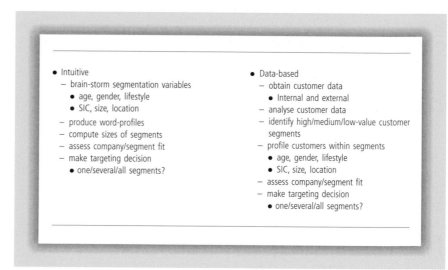

Figure 5.2
Intuitive and data-based segmentation processes

The market segmentation process can be broken down into a number of steps:

1. identify the business you are in
2. identify relevant segmentation variables
3. analyse the market using these variables
4. assess the value of the market segments
5. select target market(s) to serve.

Identify the business you are in

This is an important strategic question to which many, but not all, companies have an answer. Ted Levitt's classic article, 'Marketing Myopia' warned companies of the dangers of thinking only in terms of product-oriented answers.[1] He wrote of a nineteenth century company that defined itself as being in the buggy-whip industry. It has not survived. It is important to consider the answer from the customer point of view. For example, is Blockbuster in the video-rental business or some other business, perhaps home entertainment or retailing? Is a manufacturer of kitchen cabinets in the timber processing industry, or the home-improvement business?

A customer-oriented answer to the question will enable companies to move through the market segmentation process because it helps identify the boundaries of the market served, it defines the benefits customers seek, and it picks out the company's competitors.

Let's assume that the kitchen furniture company has defined its business from the customer's perspective. It believes it is in the home value improvement business. It knows from research that customers buy its products for one major reason: they are home owners who want to enhance the value of their properties. The company is now in a position to identify its markets and competitors at three levels:

1. **benefit competitors**: other companies delivering the same benefit to customers. These might include window replacement companies, heating and air-conditioning companies and bathroom renovation companies
2. **product competitors**: other companies marketing kitchens to customers seeking the same benefit
3. **geographic competitors**: these are benefit and product competitors operating in the same geographic territory.

Identify relevant segmentation variables and analyse the market

There are many variables that are used to segment consumer and organizational markets. Companies can enjoy competitive advantage through innovations in market segmentation. For example, before Häagen-Dazs, it was known that ice-cream was a seasonally sold product aimed primarily at children. Häagen-Dazs upset this logic by targeting an adult consumer group with a different, luxurious product, and all-year-round purchasing potential. We'll look at consumer markets first.

Consumer markets

Consumers can be clustered according to a number of shared characteristics. These can be grouped into user attributes and usage attributes, as summarized in Figure 5.3.

In recent years there has been a trend away from simply using demographic attributes to segment consumer markets. The concern has been that there is too much variance within each of the demographic clusters to regard all members of the segment as more-or-less homogenous. For example, some 30–40 year olds have families and mortgaged homes; others live in rented apartments and go clubbing at weekends. Some members of religious groups are traditionalists; others are progressives.

User attributes	*Demographic attributes*: age, gender, occupational status, household size, marital status, terminal educational age, household income, stage of family lifecycle, religion, ethnic origin, nationality
	Geographica attributes: country, region, TV region, city, city size, postcode, residential neighbourhood
	Psychographic attributes: lifestyle, personality
Usage attributes	Benefits sought, volume consumed, share of category spend

Figure 5.3
Criteria for segmenting consumer markets

The family lifecycle (FLC) idea has been particularly threatened. The FLC traces the development of a person's life along a path from young and single, to married with no children, married with young children, married couples with older children, older married couples with no children at home, empty nesters still in employment, retired empty nester couples, to sole survivor working or not working. Life for many, if not most people, does not follow this path. It fails to take account of the many and varied life choices that people make: some people never marry, others marry late, there are also childless couples, gay and lesbian partnerships, extended families, single-parent households and divorced couples.

Let's look at some of the variables that can be used to define market segments. Occupational status is widely used to classify people into social grades. Systems vary around the world. In the UK, the JICNARS social grading system is employed. This allocates households to one of six categories (A, B, C1, C2, D and E) depending on the job of the head of household. Higher managerial occupations are ranked A; casual, unskilled workers are ranked E. Media owners often use the JICNARS scale to profile their audiences.

A number of data analysis companies have developed geodemographic classification schemes. CACI, for example, has developed ACORN which allocates individuals, households and postcodes to one of the five categories shown in Figure 5.4, and beyond into 17 groups and 56 types. ACORN data suggest that clusters of like households exhibit similar buying behaviours. This clustering outcome is based on data covering over 400 variables, from online behaviour to housing type, education and family structure.

Lifestyle research became popular in the 1980s. Rather than using a single descriptive category to classify customers as had been the case with demographics, it uses multivariate analysis to cluster customers. Lifestyle analysts collect data about people's activities, interests and opinions. A lifestyle survey instrument may require answers to 400 or 500 questions, taking several hours to complete. Using analytical processes such as factor analysis and cluster analysis, the researchers are able to produce lifestyle or psychographic profiles. The assertion is made

1. Wealthy achievers	25.4%
2. Urban prosperity	11.5%
3. Comfortably off	27.4%
4. Moderate means	13.8%
5. Hard pressed	21.2%
6. Unclassified	0.7%

The number represents the % of UK households falling into each category

Figure 5.4
Geodemographics,
ACORN

that we buy products because of their fit with our chosen lifestyles. Lifestyle studies have been done in many countries, as well as across national boundaries. A number of companies conduct lifestyle research on a commercial basis and sell the results to their clients.

Usage attributes can be particularly useful for CRM purposes. Benefit segmentation has become a standard tool for marketing managers. It is axiomatic that customers buy products for the benefits they deliver, not for the products themselves. Nobody has ever bought a 5mm drill bit because they want a 5mm drill bit. They buy because of what the drill bit can deliver: a 5mm hole. CRM practitioners need to understand the benefits that are sought by the markets they serve. The market for toothpaste, for example, can be segmented along benefit lines. There are three major benefit segments: white teeth, fresh breath, and healthy teeth and gums. When it comes to creating value propositions for the chosen customers, benefit segmentation becomes very important.

The other two usage attributes, volume consumed and share of category spend, are also useful from a CRM perspective. Many companies classify their customers according to the volume of business they produce. For example, in the B2C context, McDonald's USA found that 77 per cent of their sales are to males aged 18 to 34 who eat at McDonald's three to five times per week, despite the company's mission to be the world's favourite family restaurant. Assuming that they contribute in equal proportion to the bottom line, these are customers that the company must not lose. The volume they provide allows the company to operate very cost-effectively, keeping unit costs low.

Companies that rank customers into tiers according to volume, and are then able to identify which customers fall into each tier, may be able to develop customer migration plans to move lower volume customers higher up the ladder from first-time customer to repeat customer, majority customer, loyal customer, and onwards to advocate status. This only makes sense when the lower volume customers present an opportunity. The key question is whether they buy product from other suppliers in the category. For example, customer Jones buys five pairs of shoes a year. She only buys one of those pairs from 'Shoes4less' retail outlets. She therefore presents a greater opportunity than customer

Smith who buys two pairs a year, but both of them from Shoes4less. Shoes4less has the opportunity to win four more sales from Jones, but none from Smith. This does not necessarily mean that Jones is more valuable than Smith. That depends on the answers to other questions. First, how much will it cost to switch Jones from her current shoe retailer(s), and what will it cost to retain Smith's business? Secondly, what are the margins earned from these customers? If Jones is very committed to her other supplier, it may not be worth trying to switch her. If Smith buys high margin fashion and leisure footwear and Jones buys low margin footwear, then Smith might be the better opportunity despite the lower volume of sales.

Most segmentation programmes employ more than one variable. For example, a chain of bars may define its customers on the basis of geography, age and music preference. Figure 5.5 shows how the market for chocolate can be segmented by usage occasion and satisfaction. Four major segments emerge from this bivariate segmentation of the market.

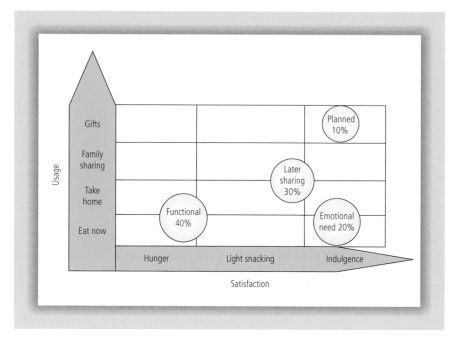

Figure 5.5
Bivariate segmentation of the chocolate market (Source: Mintel 1998)

Business markets

Business markets can also be segmented in a number of ways, as shown in Figure 5.6

The basic starting point for most B2B segmentation is the International Standard Industrial Classification (ISIC), which is a property of the United Nations Statistics Division. While this is a standard that is in widespread use, some countries have developed their own schemes. In the USA, Canada and Mexico, there is the North American Industry Classification System (NAICS). A 1400 page NAICS manual was

Business market segmentation criteria	Illustration
International Standard Industrial Classification	An internationally agreed standard for classifying goods and service producers
Dispersion	Geographically concentrated or dispersed
Size	Large, medium, small businesses: classified by number of employees, number of customers, profit or turnover
Account status	Global account, National account, Regional account, A or B or C class accounts
Account value	<$50 000, <$100 000, <$200 000, <$500 000
Buying processes	Open tender, sealed bid, internet auction, centralized, decentralized
Buying criteria	Continuity of supply (reliability), product quality, price, customization, just-in-time, service support before or after sale
Propensity to switch	Satisfied with current suppliers, dissatisfied
Share of customer spend in the category	Sole supplier, majority supplier, minority supplier, non-supplier
Geography	City, region, country, trading bloc (ASEAN, EU)
Buying style	Risk averse, innovator

Figure 5.6
How business markets are segmented

published in 2007. In New Zealand and Australia there is the Australia and New Zealand Standard Industrial Classification (ANZSIC).

The ISIC classifies all forms of economic activity. Each business entity is classified according to its principal product or business activity, and is assigned a four-digit code. These are then amalgamated into 99 major categories. Figure 5.7 illustrates several four-digit codes.

ISIC 4-digit code	Activity
1200	Mining of uranium and thorium ores
2511	Manufacture of rubber tyres and tubes; re-treading and rebuilding of rubber tyres
5520	Restaurants, bars and canteens
8030	Higher education

Figure 5.7
Examples of ISIC codes

Governments and trade associations often collect and publish information that indicates the size of each ISIC code. This can be a useful to guide when answering the question, 'Which customers should we acquire?' However, targeting in the B2B context is often conducted not at the aggregated level of the ISIC, but at an individual account level. The question is not so much, 'Do we want to serve this segment?' as much as 'Do we want to serve this customer?'

Several of these account-level segmentation variables are specifically important for CRM purposes: account value, share of category (share of wallet) spend and propensity-to-switch.

Case 5.1

Customer segmentation at Dell Computer

Dell was founded in 1984 with the revolutionary idea of selling custom-built computers directly to the customer. Dell has grown to become one of the world's larger PC manufacturers and continues to sell directly to individual consumers and organizations.

The direct business model of Dell and the focus on serving business customers has resulted in the organization investing heavily in developing an advanced CRM system to manage its clearly segmented customers. Dell has identified eight customer segments, these being: Global Accounts, Large Companies, Midsize Companies, Federal Government, State and Local Government, Education, Small Companies and Consumers. Dell has organized its business around these eight segments, where each is managed by a complete business unit with its own sales, finance, IT, technical support and manufacturing arms.

Account value

Most businesses have a scheme for classifying their customers according to their value. The majority of these schemes associate value with some measure of sales revenue or volume. This is not an adequate measure of value, because it takes no account of the costs to win and keep the customer. We address this issue later in the chapter.

Share of wallet (SOW)

Share of category spend gives an indication of the future potential that exists within the account. A supplier with only a 15 per cent share of a customer company's spending on some raw material has, on the face of it, considerable potential.

Propensity-to-switch

Propensity-to-switch may be high or low. It is possible to measure propensity-to-switch by assessing satisfaction with the current supplier, and by computing switching costs. Dissatisfaction alone does not indicate a high propensity to switch. Switching costs may be so high that, even in the face of high levels of dissatisfaction, the customer does not switch. For example, customers may be unhappy with the performance of their telecommunications supplier, but may not switch because of the disruption that such a change would bring about.

Assess the value in a market segment and select which markets to serve

A number of target market alternatives should emerge from the market segmentation process. The potential of these to generate value for the company will need to be assessed. The potential value of the segmentation opportunities depends upon answers to two questions:

1. How attractive is the opportunity?
2. How well placed is the company and its network to exploit the opportunity?

Figure 5.8 identifies a number of the attributes that can be taken into account during this appraisal. The attractiveness of a market segment is related to a number of issues, including its size and growth potential, the number of competitors and the intensity of competition between them, the barriers to entry, and the propensity of customers to switch from their existing suppliers. The question of company fit revolves around the issue of the relative competitive competency of the company and its network members to satisfy the requirements of the segment.

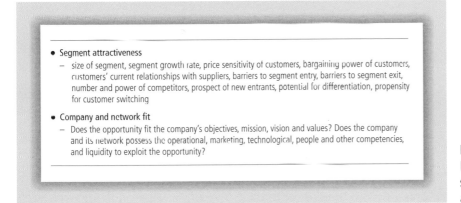

- Segment attractiveness
  - size of segment, segment growth rate, price sensitivity of customers, bargaining power of customers, customers' current relationships with suppliers, barriers to segment entry, barriers to segment exit, number and power of competitors, prospect of new entrants, potential for differentiation, propensity for customer switching

- Company and network fit
  - Does the opportunity fit the company's objectives, mission, vision and values? Does the company and its network possess the operational, marketing, technological, people and other competencies, and liquidity to exploit the opportunity?

Figure 5.8
Evaluating segmentation alternatives

In principle, if the segment is attractive and the company and network competencies indicate a good fit, the opportunity may be worth pursuing. However, because many companies find that they have several opportunities, some kind of scoring process must be developed and applied to identify the more valuable opportunities. The matrix in Figure 5.9 can be used for this purpose.[2] To begin with, companies need to identify attributes that indicate the attractiveness of a market segment (some are listed in Figure 5.8), and the competencies of the company and its network. An importance weight is agreed for each attribute. The segment opportunity is rated against each attribute and a score is computed. The opportunities can then be mapped into Figure 5.9.

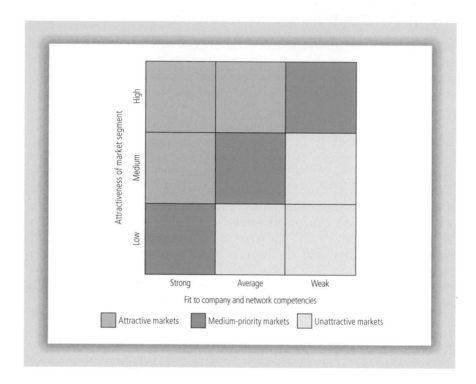

Figure 5.9
McKinsey/General Electric customer portfolio matrix

Sales forecasting

The second discipline that can be used for CPM is sales forecasting. One major issue commonly facing companies that conduct CPM is that the data available for clustering customers takes a historical or, at best, present day view. The data identifies those customers who have been, or presently are, important for sales, profit or other strategic reasons. If management believes the future will be the same as the past, this presents no problem. However, if the business environment is changeable, this does present a problem. Because CPMs goal is to identify those customers that will be strategically important in the future, sales forecasting can be a useful discipline.

Sales forecasting, some pessimists argue, is a waste of time, because the business environment is rapidly changing and unpredictable. Major world events such as terrorist attacks, war, drought and market-based changes, such as new products from competitors or high visibility promotional campaigns, can make any sales forecasts invalid.

There are a number of sales forecasting techniques that can be applied, providing useful information for CPM. These techniques, which fall into three major groups, are appropriate for different circumstances.

- **qualitative methods:**
  - customer surveys
  - sales team estimates
- **time-series methods:**
  - moving average
  - exponential smoothing
  - time-series decomposition
- **causal methods:**
  - leading indicators
  - regression models.

Qualitative methods are probably the most widely used forecasting methods. Customer surveys ask consumers or purchasing officers to give an opinion on what they are likely to buy in the forecasting period. This makes sense when customers forward-plan their purchasing. Data can be obtained by inserting a question into a customer satisfaction survey. For example, 'In the next six months are you likely to buy more, the same or less from us than in the current period?' And, 'If more, or less, what volume do you expect to buy from us?' Sometimes, third party organizations such as industry associations or trans-industry groups such as the Chamber of Commerce or the Institute of Directors collect data that indicate future buying intentions or proxies for intention, such as business confidence.

Sales team estimates can be useful when salespeople have built close relationships with their customers. A key account management team might be well placed to generate several individual forecasts from the team membership. These can be averaged or weighted in some way that reflects the estimator's closeness to the customer. Account managers for Dyno Nobel, a supplier of commercial explosives for the mining and quarrying industries, are so close to their customers that they are able to forecast sales two to three years ahead.

Operational CRM systems support the qualitative sales forecasting methods, in particular sales team estimates. The CRM system takes into account the value of the sale, the probability of closing the sale and the anticipated period to closure. Many CRM systems also allow management to adjust the estimates of their sales team members, to allow for overly optimistic or pessimistic salespeople.

Time-series approaches take historical data and extrapolate them forward in a linear or curvilinear trend. This approach makes sense when there are historical sales data, and the assumption can be safely made that the future will reflect the past. The moving average method is the simplest of these. This takes sales in a number of previous periods and averages them. The averaging process reduces or eliminates random variation. The moving average is computed on successive periods of data, moving on one period at a time, as in Figure 5.10. Moving averages based on different periods can be calculated on historic data to generate an accurate method.

A variation is to weight the more recent periods more heavily. The rationale is that more recent periods are better predictors. In producing

Figure 5.10
Sales forecasting using moving averages

Year	Sales volumes	2-year moving average	4-year moving average
2002	4830		
2003	4930		
2004	4870	4880	
2005	5210	4900	
2006	5330	5040	4960
2007	5660	5270	5085
2008	5440	5495	5267
2009		5550	5410

an estimate for year 2009 in Figure 5.10, one could weight the previous four years' sales performance by 0.4, 0.3, 0.2, and 0.1, respectively, to reach an estimate. This would generate a forecast of 5461. This approach is called exponential smoothing.

The decomposition method is applied when there is evidence of cyclical or seasonal patterns in the historical data. The method attempts to separate out four components of the time series: trend factor, cyclical factor, seasonal factor and random factor. The trend factor is the long-term direction of the trend after the other three elements are removed. The cyclical factor represents regular long-term recurrent influences on sales; seasonal influences generally occur within annual cycles.

It is sometimes possible to predict sales using leading indicators. A leading indicator is some contemporary activity or event that indicates that another activity or event will happen in the future. At a macro level, for example, housing starts are good predictors of future sales of kitchen furniture. At a micro level, when a credit card customer calls into a contact centre to ask about the current rate of interest, this is a strong indicator that the customer will switch to another supplier in the future.

Regression models work by employing data on a number of predictor variables to estimate future demand. The variable being predicted is called the dependent variable; the variables being used as predictors are called independent variables. For example, if you wanted to predict demand for cars (the dependent variable) you might use data on population size, average disposable income, average car price for the category being predicted and average fuel price (the independent variables). The regression equation can be tested and validated on historical data before being adopted. New predictor variables can be substituted or added to see if they improve the accuracy of the forecast. This can be a useful approach for predicting demand from a segment.

Activity-based costing

The third discipline that is useful for CPM is activity-based costing. Many companies, particularly those in a B2B context, can trace revenues to customers. In a B2C environment, it is usually only possible to trace revenues to identifiable customers if the company operates a billing system requiring customer details, or a membership scheme such as a customer club, store-card or a loyalty programme.

In a B2B context, revenues can be tracked in the sales and accounts databases. Costs are an entirely different matter. Because the goal of CPM is to cluster customers according to their strategic value, it is desirable to be able to identify which customers are, or will be, profitable. Clearly, if a company is to understand customer profitability, it has to be able to trace costs, as well as revenues, to customers.

Costs do vary from customer to customer. Some customers are very costly to acquire and serve, others are not. There can be considerable variance across the customer base within several categories of cost:

- **customer acquisition costs**: some customers require considerable sales effort to move them from prospect to first-time customer status: more sales calls, visits to reference customer sites, free samples, engineering advice, guarantees that switching costs will be met by the vendor
- **terms of trade**: price discounts, advertising and promotion support, slotting allowances (cash paid to retailers for shelf space), extended invoice due dates
- **customer service costs**: handling queries, claims and complaints, demands on salespeople and contact centre, small order sizes, high order frequency, just-in-time delivery, part load shipments, breaking bulk for delivery to multiple sites
- **working capital costs**: carrying inventory for the customer, cost of credit.

Traditional product-based or general ledger costing systems do not provide this type of detail, and do not enable companies to estimate customer profitability. Product costing systems track material, labour and energy costs to products, often comparing actual to standard costs. They do not, however, cover the customer-facing activities of marketing, sales and service. General ledger costing systems do track costs across all parts of the business, but are normally too highly aggregated to establish which customers or segments are responsible for generating those costs.

Activity-based costing (ABC) is an approach to costing that splits costs into two groups: volume-based costs and order-related costs. Volume-based (product-related) costs are variable against the size of the order, but fixed per unit for any order and any customer. Material and direct labour costs are examples. Order-related (customer-related) costs vary according to the product and process requirements of each particular customer.

Imagine two retail customers, each purchasing the same volumes of product from a manufacturer. Customer 1 makes no product or process demands. The sales revenue is $5000; the gross margin for the vendor is $1000. Customer 2 is a different story: customized product, special overprinted outer packaging, just-in-time delivery to three sites, provision of point-of-sale material, sale or return conditions and discounted price. Not only that, but Customer 2 spends a lot of time agreeing these terms and conditions with a salesperson who has had to call three times before closing the sale. The sales revenue is $5000, but after accounting for product and process costs to meet the demands of this particular customer, the margin retained by the vendor is $250. Other things being equal, Customer 1 is four times as valuable as Customer 2.

Whereas conventional cost accounting practices report what was spent, ABC reports what the money was spent doing. Whereas the conventional general ledger approach to costing identifies resource costs such as payroll, equipment and materials, the ABC approach shows what was being done when these costs were incurred. Figure 5.11 shows how an ABC view of costs in an insurance company's claims processing department gives an entirely different picture to the traditional view.[3]

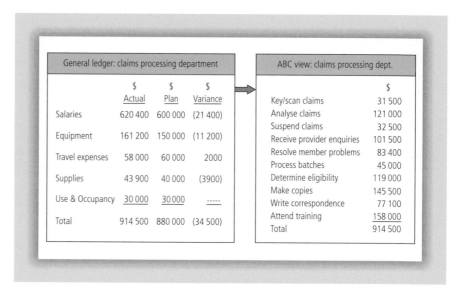

Figure 5.11
ABC in a claims processing department

ABC gives the manager of the claims-processing department a much clearer idea of which activities create cost. The next question from a CPM perspective is 'which customers create the activity?' Put another way, which customers are the cost drivers? If you were to examine the activity cost item 'Analyse claims: $121 000', and find that 80 per cent of the claims were made by drivers under the age of 20, you'd have a clear understanding of the customer group that was creating that activity cost for the business.

CRM needs ABC because of its overriding goal of generating profitable relationships with customers. Unless there is a costing system in place to trace costs to customers, CRM will find it very difficult to deliver on a promise of improved customer profitability. Overall, ABC serves customer portfolio management in a number of ways:

1. when combined with revenue figures, it tells you the absolute and relative levels of profit generated by each customer, segment or cohort

2. it guides you towards actions that can be taken to return customers to profit
3. it helps prioritize and direct customer acquisition, retention and development strategies
4. it helps establish whether customization and other forms of value creation for customers pay off.

ABC sometimes justifies management's confidence in the Pareto principle, otherwise known as the 80:20 rule. This rule suggests that 80 per cent of profits come from 20 per cent of customers. ABC tells you which customers fall into the important 20 per cent. Research generally supports the 80:20 rule. For example, one report from Coopers and Lybrand found that, in the retail industry, the top 4 per cent of customers account for 29 per cent of profits, the next 26 per cent of customers account for 55 per cent of profits and the remaining 70 per cent account for only 16 per cent of profits.

Lifetime value estimation

The fourth discipline that can be used for CPM is customer lifetime value (LTV) estimation, which was first introduced in Chapter 2. LTV is measured by computing the present day value of all net margins (gross margins less cost-to-serve) earned from a relationship with a customer, segment or cohort. LTV estimates provide important insights that guide companies in their customer management strategies. Clearly, companies want to protect and ring-fence their relationships with customers, segments or cohorts that will generate significant amounts of profit.

Sunil Gupta and Donald Lehmann suggest that customer lifetime value can be computed as follows:

$$LTV = m\left(\frac{r}{1+i-r}\right)$$

where
LTV = lifetime value
m = margin or profit from a customer per period (e.g. per year)
r = retention rate (e.g. 0.8 or 80%)
i = discount rate (e.g. 0.12 or 12%).[4]

This means that LTV is equal to the margin (m) multiplied by the factor $r/(1+i-r)$. This factor is referred to as the margin multiple, and is determined by both the customer retention rate (r) and the discount rate (i). For most companies the retention rate is in the region of 60 to 90 per cent. The weighted average cost of capital (WACC), which was discussed in Chapter 2, is generally used to determine the discount rate. The discount rate is applied to bring future margins back to today's value. Table 5.1 presents some sample margin multiples based on the two variables: customer retention rate and discount rate. For example, at a 12 per cent discount rate and 80 per cent retention rate the margin

Retention rate	Discount rate			
	10%	12%	14%	16%
60%	1.20	1.15	1.11	1.07
70%	1.75	1.67	1.59	1.52
80%	2.67	2.50	2.35	2.22
90%	4.50	4.09	3.75	3.46

Table 5.1 Margin multiples

multiple is 2.5. From this table, you can see that margin multiples for most companies, given a WACC of 10 to 16 per cent, and retention rates between 60 and 90 per cent, are between 1.07× and 4.5×. When the discount rate is high, the margin multiple is lower. When customer retention rates are higher, margin multiples are higher.

The table can be used to compute customer value in this way. If you have a customer retention rate of 90 per cent and your WACC is 12 per cent and your customer generates $100 margin in a year, the LTV of the customer is about $400 (or $409 to be precise; i.e. 4.09 times $100). The same mathematics can be applied to segments or cohorts of customers. Your company may serve two clusters of customers, A and B. Customers from cluster A each generate annual margin of $400; cluster B customers each generate $200 margin. Retention rates vary between clusters. Cluster A has a retention rate of 80 per cent; cluster B customers have a retention rate of 90 per cent. If the same WACC of 12 per cent is applied to both clusters, then the LTV of a customer from cohort A is $1000 ($400 × 2.50), and the LTV of a cohort B customer is $818 ($200 × 4.09). If you have 500 customers in cluster A, and 1000 customers in cluster B, the LTV of your customer base is $1 318 000, computed thus: ((500 × $1000) + (1000 × $818)).

Application of this formula means that you do not have to estimate customer tenure. As customer retention rate rises there is an automatic lift in customer tenure, as shown in Table 2.2 in Chapter 2. This formula can be adjusted to consider change in both future margins and retention rates either up or down, as described in Gupta and Lehmann's book *Managing Customers as Investments*.[5]

The table can be used to assess the impact of a number of customer management strategies: what would be the impact of reducing cost-to-serve by shifting customers to low-cost self-serve channels? What would be the result of cross-selling higher margin products? What would be the outcome of a loyalty programme designed to increase retention rate from 80 to 82 per cent?

An important additional benefit of this LTV calculation is that it enables you to estimate a company's value. For example, it has been computed that the LTV of the average US-based American Airlines customer is $166.94. American Airlines has 43.7 million such customers, yielding an estimated company value of $7.3 billion. Roland Rust and his co-researchers noted that, given the absence of international passengers and freight considerations from this computation, it was remarkably close to the company's market capitalization at the time their research was undertaken.[6]

Data mining

The fifth discipline that can be used for CPM is data mining. It has particular value when you are trying to find patterns or relationships in large volumes of data, as found in B2C contexts such as retailing, banking and home shopping.

An international retailing operation like Tesco, for example, has over 14 million Clubcard members in its UK customer base. Not only does the company have the demographic data that the customer provided on becoming a club member, but also the customer's transactional data. If ten million club members use Tesco in a week and purchase an average basket of 30 items, Tesco's database grows by 300 million pieces of data per week. This is certainly a huge cost, but potentially a major benefit.

Data mining can be thought of as the creation of intelligence from large quantities of data. Customer portfolio management needs intelligent answers to questions such as these:

1. How can we segment the market to identify potential customers?
2. How can we cluster our current customers?
3. Which customers offer the greatest potential for the future?
4. Which customers are most likely to switch?

Data mining can involve the use of statistically advanced techniques, but fortunately managers do not need to be technocrats. It is generally sufficient to understand what the tools can do, how to interpret the results, and how to perform data mining.

Two of the major vendors of data mining tools have developed models to guide users through the data mining process. SAS promotes a five-step data mining process called SEMMA (sample, explore, modify, model, assess) and SPSS opts for the 5As (assess, access, analyse, act and automate). These models, though different in detail, essentially promote a common step-wise approach. The first step involves defining the business problem (such as the examples listed above). Then you have to create a data mining database. Best practice involves extracting historical data from the data warehouse, creating a special mining data mart, and exploring that dataset for the patterns and relationships that can solve your business problem. The problem-solving step involves an iterative process of model-building, testing and refinement. Data miners often divide their dataset into two subsets. One is used for model training, i.e. estimating the model parameters, and the other is used for model validation. Once a model is developed that appears to solve the business problem, it can be adopted by management. As new data is loaded into the data warehouse, further subsets can be extracted to the data mining data mart and the model can be subjected to further refinement.

A number of different data mining tools are applicable to CPM problems: clustering, decision trees and neural networks.

Clustering

Clustering techniques are used to find naturally occurring groupings within a dataset. As applied to customer data, these techniques generally function as follows:

1. Each customer is allocated to just one group. The customer possesses attributes that are more closely associated with that group than any other group.
2. Each group is relatively homogenous.
3. The groups collectively are very different from each other.

In other words, clustering techniques generally try to maximize both within-group homogeneity and between-group heterogeneity. There are a number of clustering techniques, including CART (classification and regression trees) and CHAID (chi-square automatic interaction detection).[7] Once statistically homogenous clusters have been formed they need to be interpreted.

CRM strategists are often interested in the future behaviours of a customer: segment, cohort or individual. Customers' potential value is determined by their propensity to buy products in the future. Data miners can build predictive models by examining patterns and relationships within historic data. Predictive models can be generated to identify:

1. Which customer, segment or cohort is most likely to buy a given product?
2. Which customers are likely to default on payment?
3. Which customers are most likely to defect (churn)?

Data analysts scour historic data looking for predictor and outcome variables. Then a model is built and validated on these historic data. When the model seems to work well on the historic data, it is run on contemporary data, where the predictor data are known but the outcome data are not. This is known as 'scoring'. Scores are answers to questions such as the propensity-to-buy, default and churn questions listed above.

Predictive modelling is based on three assumptions, each of which may be true to a greater or lesser extent: [8]

1. The past is a good predictor of the future ... BUT this may not be true. Sales of many products are cyclical or seasonal. Others have fashion or fad lifecycles.
2. The data are available ... BUT this may not be true. Data used to train the model may no longer be collected. Data may be too costly to collect, or may be in the wrong format.

3. Customer-related databases contain what you want to predict ... BUT this may not be true. The data may not be available. If you want to predict which customers are most likely to buy mortgage protection insurance, and you only have data on life policies, you will not be able to answer the question.

Two tools that are used for predicting future behaviours are decision trees and neural networks.

Decision trees

Decision trees are so called because the graphical model output has the appearance of a branch structure. Decision trees work by analysing a dataset to find the independent variable that, when used to split the population, results in nodes that are most different from each other with respect to the variable you are tying to predict. Figure 5.12 contains a set of data about five customers and their credit risk profile.[9]

Name	Debt	Income	Married?	Risk
Joe	High	High	Yes	Good
Sue	Low	High	Yes	Good
John	Low	High	No	Poor
Mary	High	Low	Yes	Poor
Fred	Low	Low	Yes	Poor

Figure 5.12
Credit risk training set

We want to use the data in four of the five columns to predict the risk rating in the fifth column. A decision tree can be constructed for this purpose.

In decision tree analysis, Risk is in the 'dependent' column. This is also known as the target variable. The other four columns are independent columns. It is unlikely that the customer's name is a predictor of Risk, so we will use the three other pieces of data as independent variables: debt, income and marital status. In the example, each of these is a simple categorical item, each of which only has two possible values (high or low; yes or no). The data from Figure 5.12 are represented in a different form in Figure 5.13, in a way which lets you see which independent variable is best at predicting risk. As you examine the data, you will see that the best split is income (four instances highlighted in bold on the diagonal: two high income/good risk plus two low income/poor risk). Debt and marital status each score three on their diagonals.

Once a node is split, the same process is performed on each successive node, either until no further splits are possible or until you have reached a managerially useful model.

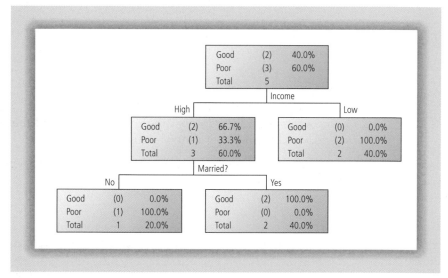

Predicted risk	High debt	Low debt	**High income**	**Low income**	Married	Not married
Good	1	1	2	0	2	0
Poor	1	2	1	2	2	1

Figure 5.13
Cross-tabulation of dependent and independent variables

The graphical output of this decision tree analysis is shown in Figure 5.14. Each box is a node. Nodes are linked by branches. The top node is the root node. The data from the root node is split into two groups based on income. The right-hand, low income box, does not split any further because both low income customers are classified as poor credit risks. The left-hand, high-income box does split further, into married and not married customers. Neither of these split further because the one unmarried customer is a poor credit risk and the two remaining married customers are good credit risks.

Figure 5.14
Decision tree output

As a result of this process the company knows that customers who have the lowest credit risk will be high income and married. They will also note that debt, one of the variables inserted into the training model, did not perform well. It is not a predictor of creditworthiness. Decision trees that work with categorical data such as these are known as classification trees. When decision trees are applied to continuous data they are known as regression trees.

Neural networks

Neural networks are another way of fitting a model to existing data for prediction purposes. The expression 'neural network' has its origins in the work of machine learning and artificial intelligence. Researchers in this field have tried to learn from the natural neural networks of living creatures.

Neural networks can produce excellent predictions from large and complex datasets containing hundreds of interactive predictor variables, but the neural networks are neither easy to understand nor straightforward to use. Neural networks represent complex mathematical equations, with many summations, exponential functions and parameters.[10]

Like decision trees and clustering techniques, neural networks need to be trained to recognize patterns on sample datasets. Once trained, they can be used to predict customer behaviour from new data. They work well when there are many potential predictor variables, some of which are redundant.

Customer portfolio management at Tesco

Tesco, the largest and most successful supermarket chain in the UK, has developed a CRM strategy that is the envy of many of its competitors. Principally a food retailer in a mature market that has grown little in the last 20 years, Tesco realized that the only route to growth was taking market share from competitors. Consequently, the development of a CRM strategy was seen as imperative.

In developing its CRM strategy, Tesco first analysed its customer base. It found that the top 100 customers were worth the same as the bottom 4000. It also found that the bottom 25 per cent of customers represented only 2 per cent of sales, and that the top 5 per cent of customers were responsible for 20 per cent of sales.

The results of this analysis were used to segment Tesco's customers and to develop its successful loyalty programmes.

CPM in the business-to-business context

Many B2B companies classify their customers into groups based on sales revenue. They believe that their best customers are their biggest customers. Some of these companies consciously apply the Pareto principle, recognizing that 80 per cent of sales are made to 20 per cent of customers, as shown in Figure 5.15.

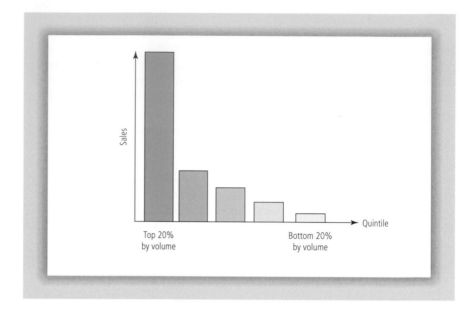

Figure 5.15
The Pareto principle, or 80:20 rule

Having clustered their customers by volume, they may then assign their best representatives, and offer the best service and terms of trade to these, the biggest and best customers. The assumption is often made in B2B contexts that large accounts are profitable accounts. Activity-based costing tells us that this is not necessarily so. It is not uncommon to find that small customers are unprofitable because their activity costs are greater than the margins they generate. Similarly, many companies find that their largest accounts are also unprofitable. Why? Large accounts create more work, more activity. The work of managing the account might require the services of a large number of people: a sales manager, a customer service executive and an applications engineer among others. The customer might demand customized product, delivery in less than container loads, just-in-time delivery, extended due dates for payment, and, ultimately, volume discounts on price. Very often it is the mid-range sales volume customers that are the most profitable. Figure 5.16 shows the profitability of customers who have been previously clustered according to volume. The chart shows that the top 20 per cent of customers by volume are unprofitable, just as are the bottom 20 per cent by volume.

When Kanthal, a Swedish manufacturer of electrical resistance heating elements, introduced ABC they found that only 40 per cent of their customers were profitable. Two of their top three sales volume customers were among the most unprofitable. The most profitable 5 per cent of customers generated 150 per cent of profits. The least profitable 10 per cent lost 120 per cent of profit. The challenge for Kanthal was deciding what to do with the unprofitable customers.[11] Their options

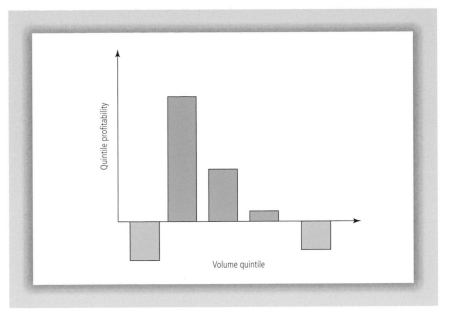

Figure 5.16
Customer
profitability by sales
volume quintile

included implementation of open book accounting so their customers could see how much it cost to serve them, negotiation of service levels with customers, introducing transparent rules for migrating customers up and down the service level ladder, simplifying and standardizing the order process, introducing a self-service portal, negotiating price increases, sorting product lines into those that could be delivered ex-stock and others for which advance orders were required, and rewarding account managers for customer profitability, both by per cent margin and total Krona (Crown) value.

Customer portfolio models

Since the early 1980s there have been a number of tools specifically designed for assessing B2B companies' customer portfolios.[12] They generally classify existing customers using a matrix and measurement approach. Many of these contributions have their origins in the work of the IMP (Industrial Marketing and Purchasing) group that you can read about in Chapter 2. CPM in B2B companies uses one or more variables to cluster customers; the most common single variable approach is to use sales revenue to cluster companies. You now know that this does not necessarily deliver a satisfactory profit outcome.

Bivariate models

Benson Shapiro and his colleagues developed a customer portfolio model that importantly incorporated the idea of cost-to-serve into the evaluation of customer value.[13] Figure 5.17 presents the matrix they developed.

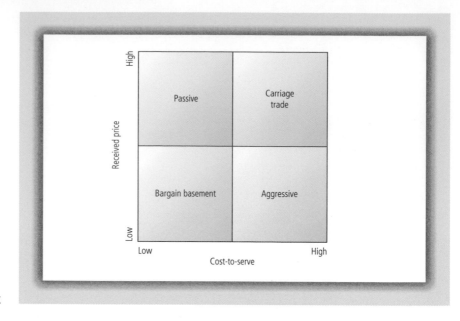

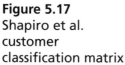

Figure 5.17
Shapiro et al.
customer
classification matrix

In this model customers are classified according to the price they pay and the costs incurred by the company to acquire and serve them. Four classes of customer are identified: carriage trade (often newly acquired customers who are costly to serve but pay a relatively high price), passive customers, aggressive customers and bargain basement customers. The important contribution of this model is that it recognizes that costs are not evenly distributed across the customer base. Some customers are more costly to win and serve and, if this is accompanied by a relatively low received price, the customer may be unprofitable. Table 5.2 shows how costs can vary before the sale, in production, in distribution and after the sale.

Pre-sale costs	Production costs	Distribution costs	Post-sale costs
Geographic location: close versus distant	Order size	Shipment consolidation	Training
Prospecting	Set-up time	Preferred transportation mode	Installation
Sampling	Scrap rate	Back-haul opportunity	Technical support
Human resource: management versus representatives	Customization	Location: close versus distant	Repairs and maintenance
Service: design support, applications engineering	Order timing	Logistics support, e.g. field inventory	

Table 5.2 How costs vary between customers

Renato Fiocca created an advance in customer portfolio modelling when he introduced his two-step approach.[14] At the first step customers are classified according to:

1. the strategic importance of the customer
2. the difficulty of managing the relationship with the customer.

The strategic importance of a customer is determined by:

- the value/volume of the customer's purchases
- the potential and prestige of the customer
- customer market leadership
- general desirability in terms of diversification of the supplier's markets, providing access to new markets, improving technological expertise and the impact on other relationships.

The difficulty of managing the customer relationship is related to:

- product characteristics, such as novelty and complexity
- account characteristics, such as the customer's needs and requirements, customer's buying behaviour, customer's power, customer's technical and commercial competence and the customer's preference to do business with a number of suppliers
- competition for the account, which is assessed by considering the number of competitors, the strength and weaknesses of competitors and the competitors' position vis à vis the customer.

On the basis of this information it is possible to construct a two-dimensional matrix as in Figure 5.18.

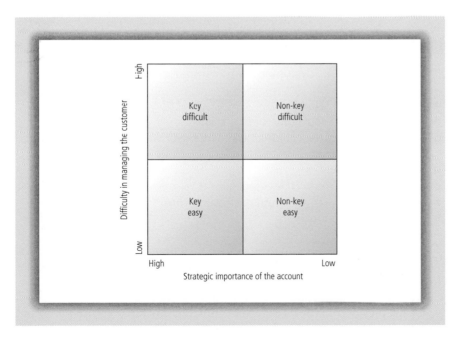

Figure 5.18
Fiocca's CPM model: step 1

The second step involves further analysis of the key accounts, shown in the left-hand cells of Figure 5.18. They are classified according to:

- the customer's business attractiveness
- the relative strength of the buyer/seller relationship.

The attractiveness of the customer's business is strongly influenced by conditions in the customer's served market. Fiocca identifies these as market factors, competition, financial and economic factors, technological factors and socio-political factors, as detailed in Table 5.3.

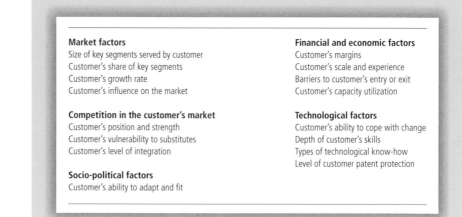

Table 5.3 Factors influencing the customer's attractiveness (Fiocca's model)

The strength of the customer relationship is determined by:

- the length of relationship
- the volume or dollar value of purchases
- the importance of the customer (percentage of supplier's sales accounted for by this customer)
- personal friendships
- cooperation in product development
- management distance (language and culture)
- geographical distance.

The data from this second step are then entered into a final nine-cell matrix, as shown in Figure 5.19, which point to three core customer management strategies: hold, withdraw or improve.

There have been a couple of published validations of this model,[15] but it has been criticized for its failure to consider customer profitability, and its rejection of non-key customers at step 1.

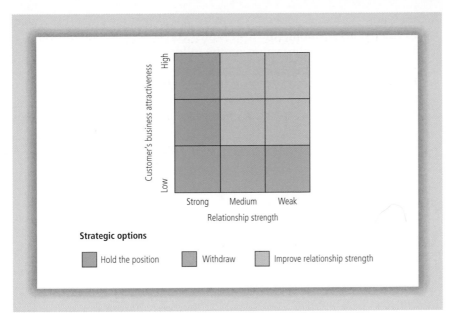

Figure 5.19
Fiocca's CPM model:
step 2

Trivariate CPM model

Peter Turnbull and Judy Zolkiewski have developed a three-dimensional CPM framework as shown in Figure 5.20.[16] The dimensions they propose are cost-to-serve, net price and relationship value. The first two variables are adopted from the Shapiro model. Relationship value, the third dimension, allows other strategic issues to be taken into account.

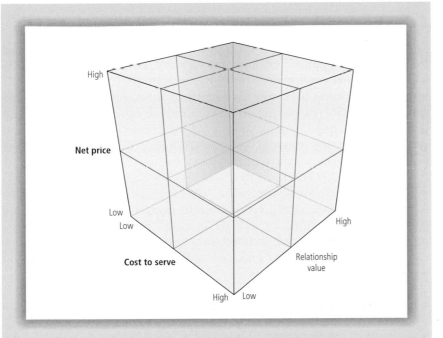

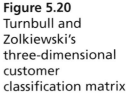

Figure 5.20
Turnbull and Zolkiewski's three-dimensional customer classification matrix

Relationship value is 'softer' or more judgemental than the other two dimensions. Among the questions considered when forming a judgement on relationship value are the following:

1. Are the goods or services critical to the customer?
2. Is the customer a major generator of volume for the supplier?
3. Would the customer be hard to replace if he switched to another supplier?
4. Does the customer generate cost savings for the supplier?

Additional customer portfolio management tools

In addition to specifically designed CPM tools there are a number of other tools in common use for strategic planning. These can also be very useful for CRM applications. These tools, however, operate at company-specific levels. This means that a CRM strategist would apply the tools to a specific customer to help in the assessment of that customer's future value. Among the tools are SWOT analysis, PESTE analysis, five-forces analysis and BCG matrix analysis.

We'll introduce them here briefly. For a fuller report you'd be well advised to refer to any basic corporate strategy or marketing strategy book.

SWOT and PESTE

SWOT is an acronym for strengths, weaknesses, opportunities and threats. SWOT analysis explores the internal environment (S and W) and the external environment (O and T) of a strategic business unit. The internal (SW) audit looks for strengths and weaknesses in the business functions of sales, marketing, manufacturing or operations, finance and people management. It then looks cross-functionally for strengths and weaknesses in, for example, cross-functional processes (such as new product development) and organizational culture.

The external (OT) audit analyses the macro- and micro-environments in which the customer operates. The macro-environment includes a number of broad conditions that might impact on a company. These conditions are identified by a PESTE analysis. PESTE is an acronym for political, economic, social, technological and environmental conditions. An analysis would try to pick out major conditions that impact on a business, as illustrated below:

- **political environment**: demand for international air travel contracted as worldwide political stability was reduced after September 11, 2001
- **economic environment**: demand for mortgages falls when the economy enters recession

- **social environment**: as a population ages, demand for healthcare and residential homes increase
- **technological environment**: as more households become owners of computers, demand for Internet banking increases
- **environmental conditions**: as customers become more concerned about environmental quality, demand for more energy efficient products increases.

The micro environmental part of the external (OT) audit examines relationships between a company and its immediate external stakeholders: customers, suppliers, business partners and investors.

A CRM-oriented SWOT analysis would be searching for customers or potential customers that emerge well from the analysis. These would be customers that:

1. possess relevant strengths to exploit the opportunities open to them
2. are overcoming weaknesses by partnering with other organizations to take advantage of opportunities
3. are investing in turning around the company to exploit the opportunities
4. are responding to external threats in their current markets by exploiting their strengths for diversification.

Five forces

The five-forces analysis was developed by Michael Porter.[17] He claimed that the profitability of an industry, as measured by its return on capital employed relative to its cost of capital, was determined by five sources of competitive pressure. These five sources include three horizontal and two vertical conditions. The horizontal conditions are:

- competition within the established businesses in the market
- competition from potential new entrants
- competition from potential substitutes.

The vertical conditions reflect supply and demand chain considerations:

- the bargaining power of buyers
- the bargaining power of suppliers.

Porter's basic premise is that competitors in an industry will be more profitable if these five conditions are benign. For example, if buyers are very powerful, they can demand high levels of service and low prices, thus negatively influencing the profitability of the supplier. However, if barriers to entry are high, say because of large capital requirements or dominance of the market by very powerful brands, then current players will be relatively immune from new entrants and enjoy the possibility of better profits.

Why would a CRM-strategist be interested in a five-forces evaluation of customers? Fundamentally, a financially healthy customer offers better potential for a supplier than a customer in financial distress. The analysis points to different CRM solutions:

1. Customers in a profitable industry are more likely to be stable for the near-term, and are better placed to invest in opportunities for the future. They therefore have stronger value potential. These are customers with whom a supplier would want to build an exclusive and well-protected relationship.
2. Customers in a stressed industry might be looking for reduced cost inputs from its suppliers, or for other ways that they can add value to their offer to their own customers. A CRM-oriented supplier would be trying to find ways to serve this customer more effectively, perhaps by stripping out elements of the value proposition that are not critical, or by adding elements that enable the customer to compete more strongly.

BCG matrix

The Boston Consulting Group matrix was designed to analyse a company's product portfolio with a view to drawing strategy prescriptions. The analysis takes into account two criteria, relative market share and market growth rate, to identify where profits and cash flow are earned. Figure 5.21 is a sample BCG matrix. The BCG claims that the best indicator of a market's attractiveness is its growth rate (hence the vertical axis of the matrix) and that the best indicator of competitive strength is relative market share (the horizontal axis). Relative market share, that is the market share of the business unit relative to its largest competitor, is claimed to improve the relative cost position due to the experience curve.

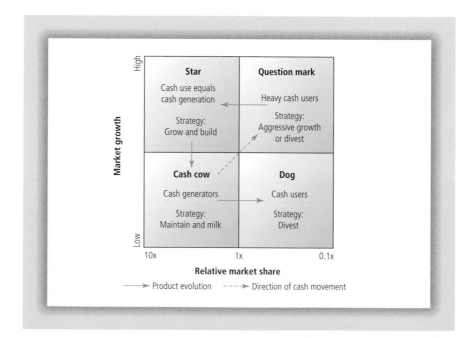

Figure 5.21
Boston Consulting Group matrix

The matrix categorizes products in a portfolio into one of four boxes and prescribes certain strategies: milk the cows, invest in the stars, ditch the dogs and then sort the question marks into those that you want to support as they become stars, and the remainder that you expect to convert into dogs.

A balanced portfolio of products contains question marks, stars and cash cows. Cash cows generate the cash flow that supports the question marks. As the question marks grow their relative market share, and become stars, they are establishing a position in the market that will eventually yield strong positive cash flows. This happens when a leading product maintains that position in a mature market.

From a CRM perspective, a customer with a balanced portfolio of products of its own has greater lifetime potential for a supplier than a customer with an unbalanced portfolio. A company with no new products in the pipeline will struggle to remain viable when the existing cash cows dry up. This happens as competitors fight to win market share and substitutes emerge.

Strategically significant customers

The goal of this entire analytical process is to cluster customers into groups so that differentiated value propositions and relationship management strategies can be applied. One outcome will be the identification of customers that will be strategically significant for the company's future. We call these strategically significant customers (SSCs). There are several classes of SSC, as follows:

1. **High future lifetime value customers**: these customers will contribute significantly to the company's profitability in the future.
2. **High volume customers**: these customers might not generate much profit, but they are strategically significant because of their absorption of fixed costs, and the economies of scale they generate to keep unit costs low.
3. **Benchmark customers**: these are customers that other customers follow. For example, Nippon Conlux supplies the hardware and software for Coca Cola's vending operation. While they might not make much margin from that relationship, it has allowed them to gain access to many other markets. 'If we are good enough for Coke, we are good enough for you', is the implied promise. Some IT companies create 'reference sites' at some of their more demanding customers.
4. **Inspirations**: these are customers who bring about improvement in the supplier's business. They may identify new applications for a product, product improvements, or opportunities for cost reductions. They may complain loudly and make unreasonable demands, but in doing so, force change for the better.

5. **Door openers**: these are customers that allow the supplier to gain access to a new market. This may be done for no initial profit, but with a view to proving credentials for further expansion. This may be particularly important if crossing cultural boundaries, say between west and east.

One company, a Scandinavian processor of timber, has identified five major customer groups that are strategically significant, as in Figure 5.22.

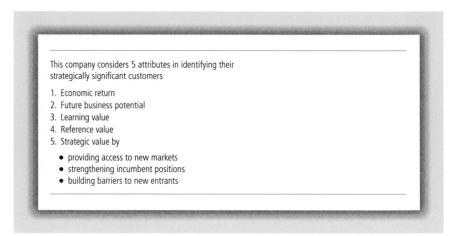

Figure 5.22
Strategically
significant
customers at a
Scandinavian timber
processor

The seven core customer management strategies

This sort of analysis pays off when it helps companies develop and implement differentiated CRM strategies for clusters of customers in the portfolio. There are several core customer management strategies:

1. **Protect the relationship**: this makes sense when the customer is strategically significant and attractive to competitors. We discuss the creation of exit barriers in our review of customer retention strategies in Chapter 9.
2. **Re-engineer the relationship**: in this case, the customer is currently unprofitable or less profitable than desired. However, the customer could be converted to profit if costs were trimmed from the relationship. This might mean reducing or automating service levels, or servicing customers through lower cost channels. In the banking industry, transaction processing costs, as a multiple of online processing costs are as follows. If Internet transaction processing has a unit cost of 1, an in-bank teller transaction costs 120 units, an ATM transaction costs 40, telephone costs 30 and PC banking costs 20. In other words, it is 120 times more expensive to conduct an in-bank transaction than the identical online transaction. Cost-reduction programmes have

motivated banks to migrate their customers, or at least some segments of customers, to other lower cost channels. An Australian electricity company has found that its average annual margin per customer is $60. It costs $13 to serve a customer who pays by credit card, but only 64 cents to service a direct debit customer. Each customer moved to the lower cost channel therefore produces a transaction cost saving of more than $12, which increases the average customer value by 20 per cent. Re-engineering a relationship requires a clear understanding of the activities that create costs in the relationship (see Case 5.3).

3. **Enhance the relationship**: like the strategy above, the goal is to migrate the customer up the value ladder. In this case it is done not by re-engineering the relationship, but by increasing your share of customer spend on the category, and by identifying up-selling and cross-selling opportunities.

4. **Harvest the relationship**: when your share of wallet is stable, and you do not want to invest more resources in customer development, you may feel that the customer has reached maximum value. Under these conditions you may wish to harvest, that is, optimize cash flow from the customer with a view to using the cash generated to develop other customers. This may be particularly appealing if the customer is in a declining market, has a high cost-to-serve or has a high propensity-to-switch to competitors.

5. **End the relationship**: sacking customers is generally anathema to sales and marketing people. However, when the customer shows no sign of making a significant contribution in the future it may be the best option. You can read about strategies for sacking customers in Chapter 9.

6. **Win back the customer**: sometimes customers take some or all of their business to other suppliers. If they are not strategically significant, it may make sense to let them go. However, when the customer is important, you may need to develop and implement win back strategies. The starting point must be to understand why they took their business away.

7. **Start a relationship**: you've identified a prospect as having potential strategic significance for the future. You need to develop an acquisition plan to recruit the customer onto the value ladder. You can read about customer acquisition strategies in Chapter 8.

Case 5.3

Sales support varies by segment at Syngenta

Syngenta, a leading global agribusiness organization, sought to segment the global market for crop protection products, such as herbicides and pesticides. Using qualitative and quantitative data Syngenta identified four segments among farmers.

1. 'Professionals': these are large spenders and keen to trial new technologies.
2. 'Progressives': these have large landholdings and are early adopters of new technologies.

3. 'Traditionalists': these are older and spend the least on crop protection products.
4. 'Operators': these are pessimistic about farming and have difficulty in keeping up to date with new technologies and farming practices.

Syngenta now uses these four segments to guide all of its marketing activities. Service levels vary between segments. Face-to-face communications are available to professionals and progressives, and direct mail is used for traditionalists and operators.

Summary

In this chapter you have learned about customer portfolio management. CPM is an essential component of strategic CRM. CPM is underpinned by analysis that clusters customers into groups that can then be treated to differentiated value propositions and customer management strategies. It strives to do this by estimating the current and future value of each group, taking into account the revenues each group will generate and the costs that will be incurred in acquiring and serving those customers. A number of basic disciplines underpin the CPM process: market segmentation, sales forecasting, activity-based costing, customer lifetime value estimation, and data mining. Market segmentation, which is widely practised by marketing management, needs to have a clear focus on customer value when used for CPM purposes. A number of sales forecasting techniques can also be used to estimate what customers are likely to buy in the future. Activity-based costing enables companies to understand the costs of marketing, selling and servicing customers, and consequently customer profitability. Customer lifetime value estimation models can be used to evaluate a customer's future worth to a company, and data mining techniques are particularly useful for detecting patterns and relationships within historic customer data.

The CPM processes tend to differ from business-to-consumer to business-to-business contexts. Not only have a number of portfolio analysis tools been developed specifically for B2B contexts, but activity-based costing is more easily applied in B2B contexts, whereas data mining is more visible in B2C contexts.

The purpose of all this analysis is to disaggregate potential and current customers into subsets so that different value propositions and relationship management strategies can be developed for each group. We close the chapter by identifying seven core customer management strategies that can be applied selectively across the customer portfolio.

References

1. Levitt, T. (1960) Marketing myopia. *Harvard Business Review*, July–August, pp. 45–56.
2. Day, G.S. (1986) *Analysis for strategic market decisions*. St Paul, MN: West Publishing.

3. Cokins, G. (1996) *Activity-based cost management: making it work.* London: McGraw-Hill.
4. Gupta, S. and Lehmann, D.R. (2005) *Managing customers as investments: the strategic value of customers in the long run.* Philadelphia: Wharton School Publishing.
5. Gupta, S. and Lehmann, D.R. (2005) *Managing customers as investments: the strategic value of customers in the long run.* Philadelphia: Wharton School Publishing.
6. Rust, R.T., Lemon, K.N. and Narayandas, D. (2005) *Customer equity management.* Upper Saddle River, NJ: Pearson Prentice Hall.
7. Saunders, J. (1994) Cluster analysis. In: G.J. Hooley and M.K. Hussey (eds). *Quantitative methods in marketing.* London: Dryden Press, pp. 13–28.
8. Berry, M.J.A. and Linoff, G.S. (2000) *Data mining: the art and science of customer relationship management.* New York: John Wiley.
9. The illustration is taken from Brand, E. and Gerritsen, R. *Decision Trees.* Available online at http://www.dbmsmag.com/9807m05.html
10. Berry, M.J.A. and Linoff, G.S. (2000) *Data mining: the art and science of customer relationship management.* New York: John Wiley.
11. Kanthal, A. Harvard Business School case study number 9-190-002. Robert S. Kaplan, author.
12. Reviewed by Zolkiewski, J. and Turnbull, P. (1999) *A review of customer relationships planning: does customer profitability and portfolio analysis provide the key to successful relationship management?* UMIST, Manchester, UK: MSM Working Paper Series. See also Zolkiewski, J. (2005) Customer portfolios. *Blackwell Encyclopaedia of Marketing,* pp. 1–87, and Johnson, M.D. and Selnes, F. (2004) Customer portfolio management: towards a dynamic theory of exchange relationships. *Journal of Marketing,* Vol. 68(2), pp. 1–17.
13. Shapiro, B.P., Rangan, K.V., Moriarty, R.T. and Ross, E.B. (1987) Manage customers for profits (not just sales). *Harvard Business Review,* September–October, pp. 101–108.
14. Fiocca, R. (1982) Account portfolio analysis for strategy development. *Industrial Marketing Management,* Vol. 11, pp. 53–62.
15. Turnbull, P.W. and Topcu, S. (1994) Customers' profitability in relationship life-cycles. Proceedings of the 10th IMP conference, Groningen, Netherlands; Yorke, D.A. and Droussiotis, G. (1994) The use of customer portfolio theory: an empirical survey. *Journal of Business and Industrial Marketing,* Vol. 9(3), pp. 6–18.
16. Turnbull, P. and Zolkiewski, J. (1997) Profitability in customer portfolio planning. In: D. Ford (ed.). *Understanding business markets,* 2nd edn. London: Dryden Press.
17. Porter, M.E. (1980) *Competitive strategy: techniques for analysing industries and competitors.* New York: Free Press.

Chapter 6

Customer relationship management and customer experience

By the end of this chapter, you will be aware of:

1. a definition of customer experience
2. the emergence and importance of the experience economy
3. the differences between goods, services and experiences
4. three key concepts in customer experience management: touchpoint, moment of truth and engagement
5. a number of methods for better understanding customer experience
6. a battery of experiential marketing strategies and tools
7. how customer experience is changed by CRM, sometimes for better and sometimes for worse
8. four features of CRM applications that have an impact on customer experience.

Introduction

The introduction of strategic CRM, or the implementation of CRM technology, has potentially major consequences for customer experience. In this chapter you'll find out more about customer experience and how CRM can change it: often for the better, but sometimes for the worse.

What is meant by customer experience?

These days, companies are becoming more interested in managing and improving customer experience. Amazon, for example, asserts that its mission is to deliver 'high quality end-to-end, order-to-delivery customer experience'. Customer experience has been described as 'the next competitive battleground'.[1]

In general terms an experience is an intrapersonal response to, or interpretation of, an external stimulus. But, what about **customer** experience? If you were to ask your customers, 'What is it like doing business with us?' their answers would be descriptions of their customer experience. More formally, customer experience can be defined as follows:

> Customer experience is the cognitive and affective outcome of the customer's exposure to, or interaction with, a company's people, processes, technologies, products, services and other outputs.

Let's pick apart this definition. When customers do business with a company they not only buy products, but they are also exposed to, or interact with, other types of company output. They might be exposed to your company's television commercials, they might interact with a customer service agent in a call centre or they might place an order at your company's sales portal. All these actions contribute to customer experience.

Based on their research in the e-commerce arena, Marian Petre and her colleagues wrote:

> 'A customer's experience with e-commerce extends beyond the interaction with the website. It includes finding the website, delivery of products, post-sales support, consumption of products and services, and so on. It is the "total customer experience" (TCE) that influences customers' perceptions of value and service quality, which consequently affects customer loyalty'.[2]

During all these exposures and interactions customers form both cognitive impressions (beliefs, thoughts) and affective impressions (feelings, attitudes) about value and quality, which in turn influence future buying and word-of-mouth intentions. One study in the hospitality industry, for example, found that 75 per cent of restaurant customers tell others about their poor service experiences but only 38 per cent tell others about their excellent experiences. Improving customer experience can therefore have two referral benefits. It can reduce negative word-of-mouth (WOM); it can also increase positive WOM.

The idea of customer experience has its origins in the work of Joseph Pine and James Gilmore.[3] They suggested that economies have shifted through four stages of economic development: extraction of commodities, manufacture of goods, delivery of services and staging of experiences, as shown in Figure 6.1. Customers have always had experiences, but Pine and Gilmore recognized a new form of value-adding economic activity that has previously been hidden or embedded in the service economy and they named this the experience economy.

Stages of economic development	Extract commodities	Make goods	Deliver services	Stage experiences
Degree of customization	Lowest			Highest
Interaction with customers	None			Co-production
Price strategy	Commodity pricing			Unique price
Value added	None			Massive

Figure 6.1
The experience economy

From service to experience

Services management experts have identified a number of special attributes that characterize services. Services are performances or acts that are:

- **Intangible–dominant**: services cannot be seen, tasted or sensed in other ways before consumption. A customer buying an office cleaning service cannot see the service outcome before it has been performed. Services are high in experience and credence attributes, but low on search attributes. Experience attributes are those attributes that can only be experienced by sampling a product. Your last vacation was high in experience attributes. You weren't able to judge fully what it would be like before you took the trip. Services like health, insurance and investment advice are high in credence attributes. Even when you have consumed these services you cannot be sure of the quality of the service delivered. How confident are you that your car is well serviced by your garage? Search attributes are attributes that can be checked out in advance of a purchase. Services are low in these because of their intangible–dominant character. Buyers therefore look for tangible clues to help them make sensible choices. Perhaps a buyer will look at the appearance of the equipment and personnel and view testimonials in a 'brag-book'. Service marketers therefore need to manage tangible evidence by 'tangibilizing the intangible'.
- **Inseparable**: unlike goods that can be manufactured in one time and location and consumed at a later time in another location, services are produced at the same time and place that they are consumed. Your dentist produces service at the same time you consume it. This means that service customers are involved in, and sometimes co-produce, the service. This co-production means that quality is more difficult to control and service outcomes are harder to guarantee. For example, a correct diagnosis by a doctor depends largely on the ability of the patient to recognize and describe his or her symptoms. Sometimes service providers' best intentions can be undone by customer behaviour. Promoters of rock concerts where there have been riots know only too well that customer behaviour can change the fundamental character of a concert experience. Sometimes, other customers participate in the service experience, making it more, or less, satisfying. In a bar, other customers create atmosphere, adding to the value of the experience. In a cinema, ringing mobile phones and talkative patrons can spoil an otherwise excellent movie experience.
- **Heterogeneous**: unlike goods that can be mechanically reproduced to exact specifications and tolerances, services cannot. Many services are produced by people. People do no always behave as scripted or trained. A band can perform brilliantly one weekend but 'die' the next. Sometimes the service outcome is co-produced by customer and service provider. All of these factors make it hard for companies to guarantee the content and quality of a service encounter. Many services, for example in the financial services sector, are becoming

increasingly automated in order to reduce the unacceptably variable level of quality that is associated with human interaction. Many customer service centres now script their service agents' interactions with customers to eliminate unacceptable customer experience.

● **Perishable**: services cannot be held in inventory for sale at a later time. A hotel room that is unoccupied on Monday night cannot be added to the inventory for Tuesday night. The opportunity to provide service and make a sale is gone forever. This presents marketers with the challenge of matching supply and demand.

You can remember these attributes using the mnemonic HIPI: heterogeneity, intangibility, perishability and inseparability.

Customers have always experienced services, but Pine and Gilmore suggest that the planned customer experience differs because management tries to engage the customer in a positive and memorable way. Using stage performance as their metaphor, they write: 'the newly identified offering of experience occurs whenever a company intentionally uses services as the stage and goods as props to engage a (customer)'.[4] This distinction points us towards two perspectives of customer experience: normative and positive.

● **Positive** customer experience describes customer experience as it is. It is a value free and objective statement of what it is like to be a customer.
● **Normative** customer experience describes customer experience as management or customers believe it should be. It is a value-based judgement of what the experience ought to be for a customer.

The planned customer experience

As noted above, customers have always undergone an experience whenever service is performed. Customers experience viewing a movie, going to a supermarket, or undergoing a Government tax audit. They also experience goods as they are consumed or used: driving a car, wearing a suit or operating a flight simulator.

Some customer experiences are commodity-like and purchased frequently; others are one-off experiences never to be experienced again. One experience of travelling to work on London Underground is much like another, but co-piloting a jet fighter to celebrate an important birthday would be, for most of us, a unique experience.

Customer experience may be the core product that customers buy or a differentiating value-add. Some companies are now in the business of staging and selling customer experiences as a core product.[5] You can buy experiences such as white water rafting, swimming with dolphins, feeding elephants, paragliding, bungee-jumping, driving a racing car, going on safari or climbing Sydney Harbour Bridge. Customers buy the experience: the bundle of cognitive and affective impressions that the purchase delivers (see Case 6.1).

Case 6.1

The Kiwi Experience

The Kiwi Experience is a company that takes customers, mostly backpackers, on bus tours around New Zealand. Unlike most bus tours customers can join, leave and rejoin the tour whenever they want. Kiwi Experience customers aren't buying a ticket from A to B; they buy an entire experience that incorporates accommodation, travel, entry to attractions, the company of other travellers and the leadership of the driver. Each customer's experience has the potential to be unique, even among those travelling on the same tour.

Source: Kiwi Experience[6]

However, many marketers try to add value to, and differentiate, their service by enhancing customer experience. You can see this when the variety of experiences in a service category differs substantially. Your experience on a charter flight differs from your experience on a scheduled flight; your experience at the Hard Rock Cafe differs from your experience at McCafé.

Sometimes these differentiated experiences are so singular that they become the embodiment of the brand. Branded customer experiences such as the Rainforest Café experience, the Dell online computer purchase experience or the IKEA shopping experience (Case 6.2) are all very distinct.

When companies plan customer experience they are attempting to influence the cognitive and affective responses of customers by carefully designing the elements that influence these responses.

Case 6.2

The IKEA shopping experience

IKEA is a global home furnishings retailer with a distinctive blue and yellow livery. Most IKEA stores offer free parking. The in-store experience directs shoppers on a one way route through room setups that allow IKEA merchandise to be displayed as it would be in use. On arrival at a store entrance customers can pick up pencils, paper, tape measure, store layout guides, catalogues, shopping carts, shopping bags and baby strollers. Shoppers can try out merchandise without being bothered by IKEA salespeople. Price tags contain details including item name, colours, materials, and sizes. Shoppers note the items they want and either collect them from the self-serve area or have a staff member arrange for it to be available at the furniture pick-up point. Since most IKEA furniture is flat packed, shoppers can take purchases home immediately, or IKEA will arrange home delivery. There are in-store restaurants. IKEA accepts cash, credit cards, debit cards and IKEA gift cards. IKEA offers a return and exchange solution to customers who are not fully satisfied. The entire in-store experience is very carefully planned, and periodically reviewed and improved.

Customer experience concepts

There are a number of core concepts that are associated with customer experience management. These include touchpoint, moment of truth, and engagement.

Touchpoints are found wherever your customer comes into virtual or actual contact with your company's products, services, communications, places, people, processes or technologies.

Touchpoints include websites, service centres, warehouses, contact centres, events, exhibitions, trade shows, seminars, Webinars, direct mail, e-mail, advertising, sales calls and retail stores. The variety and number of customer touchpoints varies across industries and between companies. The National Australia Bank, for example, has identified nine customer touchpoints: branch, e-mail, website, ATM, financial planner, Internet banking, personal banker, mobile mortgage specialist and customer contact centre. If you were undergoing hospital treatment your 'customer' experience would be made up of experiences at a number of touchpoints: during admission, in the ward, in the theatre, after surgery and during discharge.

An important challenge for managers is to ensure the customer's experience is consistent across all touchpoints. For example, if a campaign manager mails out a customer offer, all the sales representatives must be informed of the offer before they call on a customer to discuss pricing. Similarly, if the customer calls the contact centre for assistance, the offer should be on display in the centre so the customer service agent can treat the customer correctly.

The expression 'moment of truth' (MOT) was first introduced by Richard Normann, and popularized by Jan Carlzon, former President of the airline SAS.[7] Carlzon described a MOT as follows:

> 'Last year, each of our ten million customers came in contact with approximately five SAS employees, and this contact lasted an average of 15 seconds each time. Thus SAS is created 50 million times year, 15 seconds at a time. These 50 million "moments of truth" are the moments that ultimately determine whether SAS will succeed or fail as a business'.

Extending the metaphor beyond the importance of people, Carlzon's original focus, we can identify a MOT as any occasion the customer interacts with, or is exposed to, any organizational output which leads to the formation of an impression of the organization. Moments of truth occur during customer interactions at touchpoints. These are the moments when customers form evaluative judgements, positive or negative, about their experience. For example, when a customer calls a contact centre and interacts with an interactive voice response (IVR) robot, receives a visit from an account executive or enters a branch office, these are moments of truth. If a service technician arrives late for an appointment, this negative moment of truth might taint the entire experience, even though the service task was well performed. Customers generally have expectations of what should happen during moments of truth, and if those expectations are not met, dissatisfaction will result.

Engagement is a term that has become widely touted in the advertising industry in recent years. Agencies speak of engaging the consumer. Although there is no agreed definition of the term, in the present context, it can be thought of as the customer's emotional and rational response to a customer experience. Creating highly engaged customers – with strong levels of emotional or rational connection to a brand, experience or organization – presents a greater challenge than creating satisfied customers. Traditional measures of satisfaction do not perform well as measures of engagement, so managers need to develop new metrics.[8]

Companies that consciously design customer experience want to evoke strong, positive engagement. Such engagement might be expressed in a sense of confidence, integrity, pride, delight or passion.[9] Companies do this by carefully designing what happens during moments of truth at customer touchpoints. Customer experience can become stale over time, and stale experiences are not engaging. Repeat business from customers at Planet Hollywood and Rainforest Café is low for this reason. It is therefore necessary to constantly refresh the customer experience, provoking customer surprise by doing the unexpected.

How to understand customer experience

In order to improve customer experience, first it is necessary to understand it. Companies can use a number of methods for improving their insight into customer experience: mystery shopping, experience mapping, process mapping, plotting the customer activity cycle, performing ethnographies, and conducting participant and non-participant observation.

Mystery shopping

Mystery shopping involves the recruitment of paid shoppers to report on their customer experience with the company sponsoring the research. They might also perform a comparative shop during which they compare the sponsor's performance with competitors. A number of market research companies offer mystery shopping services. Mystery shopping is widely used in B2C environments such as retailing, banks, service stations, bars, restaurants and hotels. It is sometimes used in B2B environments. For example, an insurance company might use mystery shopping to assess the performance of its broker network.

Experience mapping

Experience mapping is a process that strives to understand, chart and improve what happens at customer touchpoints. Focus groups, face-to-face interviews or telephone interviews are conducted with a sample of customers who describe their experience at these touchpoints. The focus is on two important questions. What is the experience like? How can it be improved? The objective is to identify the gaps between actual and desired experience. Then the company can begin to focus on strategies to close the gaps. These strategies typically involve improvements to people and processes. Outcomes might be better training and reward schemes for people, or investment in IT to support process improvements. Figure 6.2 illustrates a hotel guest's experience map.

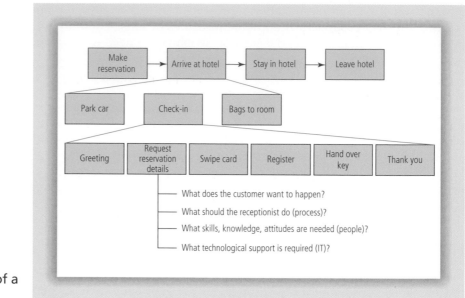

Figure 6.2
Experience map of a hotel guest

The map shows that the customer's experience occurs over four time periods. 'Arrival at hotel' is decomposed into three secondary episodes: parking the car, checking-in and taking bags to the room. The check-in episode is again decomposed, this time into six main components. It is at this level that the customer experiences the hotel's people and processes. This is where opportunities for improving people and processes can focus. Every customer experience can be decomposed and redesigned in this way. However, not all customer encounters contribute equally to the overall assessment of experience. For example, hospital patients are often prepared to tolerate food quality to a standard that would be utterly unacceptable because they need a surgical procedure. Companies are well advised to focus on the critical episodes and encounters that make up customer experience.

Process mapping

Process mapping is a form of blueprinting, a technique popularized by G. Lyn Shostack.[10] Blueprints are graphical representations of business processes. They are useful not only for developing ways to improve customer experience, but also for improving back-office internal customer–supplier relationships, setting service standards, identifying fail-points, training new people, and eliminating process redundancy and duplication.

The customer activity cycle (CAC)

The customer activity cycle (CAC) aims to depict the processes that customers go through in making and reviewing buying decisions.[11] Sandra Vandermerwe broke the process into three main stages:

1. deciding what to do
2. implementing the decision
3. reviewing what was done.

Sometimes, this process might be of very short duration but other times might last years. Consider at one extreme a ten-minute coffee break, and at the other, a multi-year relationship with a credit card vendor.

The CAC enables companies to break down a complex process into more basic elements and to collect data on the customer's experience at each point in the cycle. Then companies can look for ways to improve the experience. Figure 6.3 depicts the relationship between Citibank and a customer whose needs are changing as it begins to transact across borders. The basic CAC is shown as comprising four stages: opening a bank account, using banking facilities, expanding banking needs across borders and updating banking needs. The italicized box content shows what Citibank was able to do to improve the experience of the customer at each of these four stages.

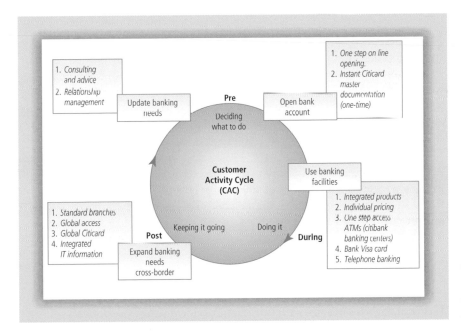

Figure 6.3 Citibank's understanding of the customer activity cycle

Ethnographic methods

Ethnographic methods can be used to gain a better understanding of the socio-cultural context of customer experience. Martyn Hammersley characterizes ethnography as participation, either overt or covert, in people's daily lives over a prolonged period of time, watching what happens, listening to what is said and asking questions.[12] Ethnography is a naturalistic form of investigation that reveals customer experience as it occurs in everyday life. Even mundane goods can be experienced in emotionally-charged ways. Eric Arnould, for example, shows how a table can be much more than just a piece of furniture. '(T)he table has become the "heart of the home" where meals, crafts, and study occur under mother's watchful eye'.[13] It has been well established that customers appropriate the values of upmarket brands such as Rolex or Chanel when they consume, but Jennifer Coupland's ethnography also shows how low-involvement, 'invisible', everyday products can serve an important social purpose, allowing families to create meanings that transcend the values that are associated with the brand name. She notes how families 'strive to erase brands … and create their own product value as if the brand never existed in the first place. Brands get in the way'.[14]

Participant observation

Companies can develop a better understanding of customer experience by participating in the customer experience at various touchpoints. Some companies require their senior management to learn about customer experience by providing front line customer service. This ensures that executives who are several hierarchical levels removed from customers understand what it is like to be a customer. For example, McDonald's periodically requires its senior managers to work as staff members in restaurants.

Non-participant observation

In preference to participant observation, other companies require their senior managers to observe customer interactions at customer touchpoints. This is particularly suitable when the primary customer touchpoint is a call centre or contact centre. Managers can listen in to customer calls to acquire a better understanding of customer experience, but not actually make or receive calls.[15]

Experiential marketing strategies and tactics

Managers wanting to improve customer experience will need answers to a number of questions, such as:

1. What sort of outcomes do our customers want to experience?
2. What is the current customer experience?
3. What tools and strategies are available to close any gap between current and desired experience?
4. How can we measure whether we have succeeded?

Len Berry writes that it is critical for companies to manage the experience clues which customers are exposed to or interact with. 'Anything that can be perceived or sensed – or recognized by its absence – is an experience clue'.[16] Bernd Schmitt identifies a number of experience clues that can be composed by customer management, whether in sales, marketing or service, to influence experiential outcomes. They include: communications, visual identity, product presence, co-branding, spatial environments, websites and electronic media, and people.[17]

Communications

Communications include company-generated messaging such as advertising, brochures, newsletters and annual reports. Increasingly, companies are also enabling customers to generate their own product or service-related messaging through user groups, chat sites and blogs. Much advertising, it must be said, is barely noticeable, and it takes an exceptional campaign to evoke a strong emotional response by rising above the noise generated by thousands of humdrum advertisements. You'll no doubt have your own short list of ads that evoke strong emotions.

Visual identity

Visual identity is communicated through brand names, logos and livery. BP, formerly British Petroleum, has been repositioning itself as a broadbased energy company rather than an oil refiner. BPs flower logo has helped in that repositioning, with the company name now signifying Beyond Petroleum.

Consumer brand names such as Jolt, a high caffeine and sugar cola, and business brands such as Accenture, have strong experiential value.

Product presence

Product presence comprises a number of product-related variables, such as product design, packaging, display, brand characteristics and point-of-sale. Innovative design can evoke strong emotional responses. James Dyson's dual cyclone vacuum cleaner completely revitalized the moribund vacuum cleaner market that had suffered the same low-tech industrial design values for the previous 80 years. Dyson's innovation excited the retail market, who found the new designs sexy, and consumers ditched their Hoovers and Electroluxes to buy Dyson's DC01 model at prices significantly above market norms.

Given that a large number of consumer brand choices are made at the supermarket shelf, packaging is very important, having only fractions of seconds to capture the attention and evoke a response from shoppers. Figure 6.4 shows an Australian packaging design innovation award winner: a supermarket package for a NESCAFÉ coffee line extension. The award citation read:

> 'This design expresses the very essence of "short black": neat, dark, concise. Here is a pack that is the personification of its promise. No-nonsense, pure, and pared back to basics: this is the essence of good

Figure 6.4
Packaging that evokes emotional response[18]

design. This diminutive jar has great "feel" in the hand, in fact it is very hard to resist picking it up'.

Brand characters such as Ronald McDonald (fast service food retail), Johnnie Walker (Scotch whisky) or Bertie Bassett (liquorice allsorts), can become important brand icons in their own right, which customers can become fiercely protective about when brand owners threaten change.

Co-branding

Co-branding includes a number of activities such as event marketing, sponsorship, alliances, partnerships, licensing, product placement, and cooperative campaigns of all kinds. Many companies have been associated with the fervour emanating from the Super Bowl, FIFA World Cup and the Olympics. Coca Cola knows the significance of event marketing, and has agreed to extend its sponsorship of the Olympics by remaining the 'Official Soft Drink' of the games until 2020. Ambush marketers attempt to capitalize on the audience size and event significance by feigning an 'official association' with events. This is often done in a jocular way, but official sponsors regard this as an infringement of their rights. Anheuser-Busch paid over US$50 million to become official sponsor of the 2002 Winter Olympics in Salt Lake City. The sponsorship agreement gave the brewery the rights to use the word Olympic and the five-ring logo. Schirf Brewery, a small local company, came up with an ambush marketing strategy. They marked their delivery trucks with 'Wasutch Beers. The Unofficial Beer. 2002 Winter Games'. Schirf technically didn't breach the sponsors' rights because they used neither the word Olympics nor the logo. Product placement in TV shows, movies, books and video games has become part of the marketer's armoury. There is little doubt that much of Aston Martin's brand cachet is linked to the James Bond movie franchise. There is a strong association between the brand and the context of its seen consumption. The 'Men in Black' movies have featured product placement for Ray-Ban, Mercedes Benz, Sprint and Burger King.

Spatial environments

Areas such as retail stores, office spaces, lobbies, car parks, buildings, gardens and public spaces can evoke strong cognitive and emotional responses. People in these spaces can be exposed a number of stimuli including noise, temperature, odour, colour, vibration, air characteristics (quality, movement, pressure, humidity), other people, architectural design, traffic, spatial arrangements, building size, space, complexity, signage and information load. Environmental psychologists study the impact of spatial environments on human behaviour. Albert Mehrabian and James Russell argued that all emotional responses to environmental stimuli could be reduced to three basic dimensions, pleasure, arousal and dominance, which, when moderated by the individual's personality is expressed as approach or avoidance behaviour towards the environment.[19] Environments that offer too little or too much arousal are unpleasant for most people and promote avoidance behaviours. Environments in which people feel they lack control are unattractive. Architects, interior designers and landscapers can construct environments that promote desired emotional or cognitive outcomes. Traditional bank branches feature classical architectural styles, oversized and heavy doors, solid timber furnishings, all carefully constructed to promote a sense of financial probity and conservatism.

Websites and electronic media

Websites and electronic media offer enormous opportunities to create customer experiences that are compelling. The use of sound, animation, audio and video clips, chat rooms, blogs, RSS feeds, and the capacity for site visitors to customize their own pages offers rich potential for emotional engagement. Figure 6.5 shows that online visitors are able to discriminate between good and bad experiences.

People

In many service contexts, people are absolutely critical. They can be the service (counsellor), produce the service (chef), sell the service (account manager), and represent tangible evidence of the service (consultant). The performance of people can evoke strong approach and avoidance behaviours in customers. Pushy salespeople may make one-off sales, but they don't build long-term relationships. Customers can become very attached to particular service providers. The significance of people to customer experience is recognized in the service–profit chain. This theory

Figure 6.5
Online customer
experience[20]

proposes that happy employees make happy customers make happy
shareholders. Research conducted in the USA indicates a clear connection
between employee experience, customer experience and business results.[21]

Customer experience and the role of CRM

The implementation of a CRM strategy, and the deployment of CRM
technologies, can have a significant impact on customer experience.
Strategic CRMs goal of winning and keeping profitable customers
through a customer-centric organizational culture implies that there will
be a dedicated focus on meeting the requirements of defined customer
groups. Customer experience should therefore satisfy targeted customer
expectations, while other potential customers or market segments
may not be served. The principles of customer portfolio management,
discussed in Chapter 5, suggest that companies will offer different
value propositions and service levels to different clusters of customers.
There will therefore be differentiated customer experiences across the
portfolio.

Operational CRM involves the application of technology in the
customer-facing functions of sales, marketing and service. CRM
practitioners want and expect CRM to influence customer experience in a
number of positive ways: customers will be recognized, their needs better
understood, order fulfilment will be more accurate, communications
will be more relevant and timely, and service will be more responsive
and reliable. However, CRM technology implementations are often
motivated by efficiency motives. For example, the implementation of
interactive voice response (IVR) technologies in call centres has allowed

routine customer interactions to be automated, reducing transaction costs by up to 60 per cent, and downsizing the number of service agents to those required for more complex calls. Customer response to IVR implementation is not always positive, particularly in more conservative segments of the customer base. That said, customers may not even be aware of several improvements that IVR can bring to customer experience: more accurate information (less human error), 24–7 access to information and enhanced data security and privacy.

Analytical CRM is the intelligent mining of customer-related data for strategic or tactical purposes. When analytical CRM works well, customers receive timely, relevant communications and offers. CRM practitioners are able to predict propensities to buy and detect opportune times to make offers, therefore ensuring that customers are not burdened with irrelevant communications. Analytical CRM can also be used to help customers in unexpected ways. Bank customers can be alerted when approaching a credit limit, thereby avoiding unwelcome fees, or telco customers can be migrated to a more suitable telephone contract, thereby reducing their operating costs. The CEO of CRM technology vendor RightNow Technologies uses a mining metaphor to describe how analytical CRM has been deployed historically.[22] He suggests that sales-focused CRM implementations have conventionally been used to strip-mine customers, rather than understand and meet their needs better. Strip-mining has compromised any efforts to deliver excellent customer experience. Rather than strip-mining, he suggests that it makes better sense to nurture customers as if they were renewable resources.

Features of CRM software applications that influence customer experience

CRM software applications that are difficult to navigate or configure or that are slow to respond leave the customer painfully aware of the limitations of a company's customer management expertise. Furthermore, once a CRM application is published on the web for customers and channel partners to use, performance and usability issues are experienced first-hand. Usability, performance, flexibility and scalability are key features of CRM solutions that deliver a favourable customer experience.[23]

Usability

Usability refers to the ease with which a CRM application can be navigated or used. High usability applications are intuitive and require very little effort to perform the required task, whether that is updating customer contact details, making an offer, or resolving a complaint. High usability applications require minimal user training prior to or at deployment, and are experienced as highly responsive by the customer. A highly responsive application is a necessary ingredient in delivering a highly responsive experience for the customer.

Older-style CRM applications traditionally used menu systems and function keys for navigation. Function keys can be very fast to use. However, they can only take the user through a flow that was originally conceived during system design. These approaches can be cumbersome in the front office and take time to arrive at the customer's desired outcome. Web technologies, on the other hand, incorporate hyperlinks and drill downs that support an intuitive, 'go where the customer wants' approach. If you want more information on something, you can click on the link. For this reason, a web-style interface has become the norm for CRM applications.

The only caveat to this is in the call centre, where high volumes of calls are handled in a largely predictable manner. In these situations, basic web-style technologies are not adequate and must be augmented by scripting or applets in order to deliver the required level of interactivity and performance.

Flexibility

Responsiveness can be 'hard wired' by pre-empting all of the processes that a customer may require and implementing these in the application in advance. The difficulty with this approach is that customers don't always follow the systems engineer's or workflow designer's script. An application's flexibility determines how many alternatives are available to the user at any given time; these alternatives are often implemented through hyperlinks, buttons or screen tabs. A highly flexible application will have many such links, and will not require specific processes to be followed. The customer does not want to be told by a call centre customer service representative 'I'm sorry, but I can't do A until I do B'.

High performance

The performance of a CRM system is often determined by its weakest link. All technologies must be aligned in order to create a high performance system. A CRM application running on an extremely fast network will still be slow if the database is overloaded. Even the best software application will be unresponsive if network performance, database performance or server performance are substandard. Most CRM applications separate the application server from the database server in order to improve performance.

Performance is also determined by integration and synchronization technologies. A CRM application will appear slow if the user has to wait for an automatic e-mail to be created and sent via the e-mail interface. Remote users will perceive the system as slow if they have to wait more than a few minutes for their daily synchronization to their laptop. The speed of these processes can have a dramatic effect on system acceptance and uptake.

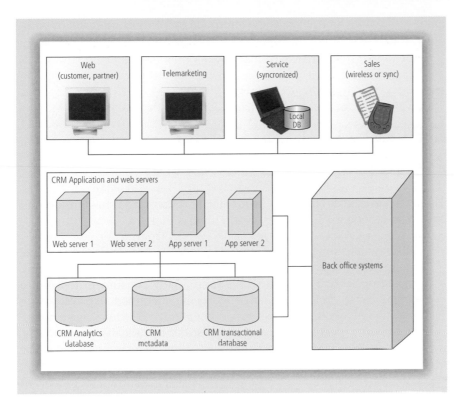

Figure 6.6
Typical CRM
architecture,
showing web, back-
office integration
and mobile. Note
the database tier
(bottom), the
application server
tier (middle) and
the user interface
tier (top)

An important characteristic of a high performing CRM system architecture is not only this ability to separate high load areas, such as the database and application servers, but also the ability to expand the application and web server tier by adding more servers as required. This is shown in the Figure 6.6.

Scalability

As the CRM system grows and is used by more internal and external people, the scalability of the system becomes important. Acceptable performance with 100 call centre users may become unacceptable once the customers are online and hitting the website, or field sales representatives start synchronizing across all territories at the same time. CRM applications should be evaluated based on proven numbers and types of users (concurrent on the web, synchronization, full load call centre, etc.) in order to assess their ability to scale. A system that is unable to scale will deliver inadequate customer experience as user numbers grow.

Finally, it should be recognized that high performance CRM systems require investment to keep up with changing customer expectations. It is most important that the CRM application be constantly monitored against predefined performance targets to ensure performance remains acceptable. This is particularly the case in high turnaround areas where the customer is involved, such as the call centre and website, and where high loads take place at the same time, such as the afternoon synchronization run or back-office integration run.

Researching the link between customer experience and CRM

There is very little research evidence of how CRM has influenced customer experience. The Meta Group reports that:

> 'business customers want to be identified for their appropriate requirements (e.g. resupply of goods and services that they already purchase), so that they can save time. Many consumers fall into a similar camp. But in exchange for being identified (e.g. providing information about themselves or having it collected), customers/ consumers expect to be treated as "special". This means free products, better service, useful information, etc. They also do not want to be bothered by endless phone calls or e-mails to sell them more "stuff" '.[24]

These comments do indicate that customer experience, following a CRM implementation, is not necessarily positive. Customers who are accustomed to receiving face-to-face calls from sales representatives might find they are expected to place orders and pay through a sales portal. Resistance, resentment and churn may result. Weary workers arriving home after a hard day's labour are confronted with cold calls selling products that aren't of the slightest interest. The avoidance of negative customer experience from ineptly implemented CRM is an important reason for ensuring the voice of the customer is heard during CRM project planning and implementation. It also signals the importance of monitoring customer response after a CRM implementation.

Despite these cautions, technology can fundamentally change customer experience for the better, because it reinvents what happens at customer touchpoints. Imagine a sales representative who has always carried hard copy brochures. Some are dog-eared; some are not current; some are missing. He is sitting in front of a qualified prospect with a product-related query who is ready to buy. The representative goes to his briefcase. The brochure is missing, and he cannot answer the query. 'I'll get back to you', he says. But he doesn't. He forgets and the opportunity is lost. Equipped with CRM, the interaction is very different. The representative carries a laptop with a current, searchable, product database. He answers the query successfully. The prospect asks for a firm quote. The representative activates the quotation engine. A quote is prepared and discussed. The representative requests the order. He wins the order. The order is entered into the laptop. The representative shares the screen information with the customer. An electronic signature is obtained. Order confirmation is sent to the buyer's e-mail address. That night the representative keys in his call report, synchronizes his laptop with the company's main computer, and the order fulfilment process begins.

Summary

In this chapter you've read about the links between CRM and customer experience. We defined customer experience as the cognitive and affective outcome of the customer's exposure to, or interaction with, a company's people, processes, technologies, products, services and other outputs. Customer experience is important because it influences future buying behaviour and word-of-mouth. Although customers have always had experiences in the purchase and consumption of goods and services, we have recently seen the emergence of the experience economy, in which companies have brought to market experiences such as open garden weekends, team-building exercises and canyoning. Three key concepts capture the essence of customer experience management: touchpoint, moment of truth and engagement. Customers are exposed to, or interact with, companies' people, processes and technologies at touchpoints such as call centres, shop fronts or automated kiosks. Some of these exposures or interactions are more significant than others, and become moments of truth that are important in the delivery of customer experience. Managers are keen to promote rational and emotional engagement with the company, brand or offer by delivering experiences that meet or exceed customer expectations. In order to improve customer experience it is important to understand current customer experience. A number of techniques are available to management for this purpose, including experience mapping, ethnographic research and participant observation. Having determined what the experience should be like, a number of tools and techniques can be deployed, including communications, visual identity, product presence, co-branding, spatial environments, websites and electronic media, and people. CRM practitioners want technology implementations to influence customer experience in a number of positive ways, such as more relevant and timely communications, and more responsive and reliable service, but customers do not always respond positively to change. Features of CRM solutions that influence customer experience include usability, flexibility, high performance and scalability.

References

1. Shaw, C. and Ivens, J. (2002) *Building great customer experiences.* Basingstoke, UK: Palgrave Macmillan.
2. Petre, M., Minocha, S. and Roberts, D. (2006) Usability beyond the website: an empirically grounded e-commerce evaluation instrument for the total customer experience. *Behaviour and Information Technology,* Vol. 25(2), pp. 189–203.
3. Pine, B.H. and Gilmore, J.H. (1998) Welcome to the experience economy. *Harvard Business Review,* July–August, pp. 97–105.

4. Pine, J.B. II and Gilmore, J. (1999) *The experience economy*. Boston, MA: Harvard Business School Press.

5. See for example http://www.redballoondays.com.au/

6. http://www.kiwiexperience.com/. Accessed 20 January 2008.

7. Normann, R. (2002) *Service management: strategy and leadership in service business*, 3rd edn. New York: John Wiley.

8. For more information refer to Bowden, J. (2007) The process of customer engagement: an examination of segment specific differences. Proceedings of the Academy of Marketing Conference, Kingston Business School, Egham, Surrey, July, CD-ROM.

9. McEwen, W. (2004) Why satisfaction isn't satisfying. *Gallup Management Journal Online*, November, pp. 1–4.

10. Shostack, G.L. (1987) Service positioning through structural change. *Journal of Marketing*, Vol. 51, pp. 34–43.

11. Vandermerwe, S. (1993) Jumping into the customer activity cycle: a new role for customer services in the 1990s. *Columbia Journal of World Business*, Vol. 28(2), Summer, pp. 46–66.

12. Hammersley, M. and Ackersley, P. (1995) *Ethnography: principles in practice*, 2nd edn. London: Routledge.

13. Arnould, E. and Proce, L. (2006) Market-oriented ethnography revisited. *Journal of Advertising Research*, September, pp. 251–262.

14. Coupland, J.C. (2005) Invisible brands: an ethnography of households and the brands in their kitchen pantries. *Journal of Consumer Research*, Vol. 32, pp. 106–118.

15. For an analysis of the listening tools that companies are using see McGuire, S., Koh, S.C.L. and Huang, C. (2007) Identifying the range of customer listening tools: a logical precursor to CRM? *Industrial Management and Data Systems*, Vol. 107(4), pp. 567–586.

16. Berry, L.L., Carbone, L.P. and Haeckel, S.H. (2002) Managing the total customer experience. *Sloan Management Review*, Spring, pp. 85–89.

17. Schmitt, B. (1999) *Experiential marketing*. New York: Free Press.

18. Image reprinted with the permission of Société des Produits Nestlé S.A., Vevey, Switzerland – trademark and design owners.

19. Mehrabian, A. and Russell, J.A. (1974) *An approach to environmental psychology*. Cambridge, MA: MIT Press.

20. Courtesy of Vividence Corporation. http://www.vividence.com. 2004.

21. Heskett, J.L., Sasser, W.E. and Schlesinger, L.A. (1997) *The service–profit chain*. New York: Free Press.

22. http://www.mycustomer.com/cgi-bin/item.cgi?id=132411. Accessed 27 September 2007.

23. This section is based on John Turnbull's contribution of Chapter 3 to Buttle, F. (2004). *Customer Relationship Management: Concepts and Tools*. Oxford: Elsevier.

24. http://www.ctiforum.com/technology/CRM/wp01/download/meta_tocrm.pdf. Accessed 28 September 2007.

Chapter 7
Creating value for customers

By the end of this chapter, you will understand:

1. the meaning of the term 'value'
2. how customers weigh up 'benefits' and 'sacrifices' in the value equation
3. three major forms of value delivery strategy adopted by successful companies
4. what is meant by the term 'value proposition'
5. how marketers create customer value by mixing together a number of variables known as the 7Ps.
6. the importance of customization in creating value
7. how the Internet is changing the way that customers receive value from communication and distribution.

Introduction

In this chapter you will learn about how companies create and deliver value to customers. You'll find out what customers mean when they talk about value, and the various elements that make up a company's value proposition.

Our definition of CRM, repeated below, stresses the centrality of value creation and delivery:

> CRM is the core business strategy that integrates internal processes and functions and external networks **to create and deliver value to targeted customers at a profit**. It is grounded on high-quality customer-related data and enabled by information technology.

Of the various forms of CRM that we have discussed, the task of directing the creation and delivery of value to targeted customers at a profit falls to strategic CRM.

Understanding value

Although the term 'value' is used in a number of different ways,[1] in a CRM sense it can be thought of as follows:

> Value is the customer's perception of the balance between benefits received from a product or service and the sacrifices made to experience those benefits.

It is possible to represent this definition in the form of an equation:

$$\text{Value} = \frac{\text{Benefits}}{\text{Sacrifices}}$$

The equation shows that you can increase the customer's perceived value in two main ways: increase the benefits they experience, or decrease the sacrifices they make.

Let's look at sacrifices. Customers make several types of sacrifice.

- **Money**: the price of the product or service, which may or may not be the listed price. There may be additional costs such as credit card surcharges, interest charges on extended payments or warranty costs. There may be discounts applied for relationship customers, early payment or volume purchases.
- **Search costs**: the purchasing process may include exhaustive pre-purchase work in searching for solutions and comparing alternatives. This can take considerable time. In a B2B context, a purchaser's time may have a real monetary cost. When purchasing involves several people these costs may be very high indeed. This is one of the reasons that customers are motivated to remain with existing suppliers and solutions. There may also be travel and accommodation costs as buyers visit reference customers to see solutions onsite. Transaction costs are normally lower when search costs are eliminated and purchasing processes are routinized. Some suppliers are prepared to take on the costs of managing inventory for important customers, so that they are less tempted to search for alternative solutions. Known as vendor managed inventory (VMI), it reduces search and reorder costs for customers.
- **Psychic costs**: purchasing can be a very stressful and frustrating experience. For some customers, holiday shopping at Christmas and other festivals means struggling to come up with gift ideas for relatives they rarely see, travelling on crowded public transport, pushing through throngs of shoppers, dealing with temporary sales staff who don't have enough product knowledge, paying inflated prices, carrying home arms full of heavy packages, and doing all these in bad weather! Psychic costs can be so great for some customers that they postpone purchases until a better time. Others cancel purchasing completely.

Perceived risk is also a consideration in assessing psychic cost. Perceived risk takes a variety of forms: performance, physical, financial, social and psychological. Performance risk occurs when the customer is not fully sure that the product will do what is required. Physical risk is when the customer feels that there may be some bodily harm done by the product. Financial risk is felt when there is danger of economic loss from the purchase. Social risk is felt when customers feel that their social standing or reputation is at risk. Psychological risk is felt when the customer's self-esteem or self-image is endangered by an act of purchase or consumption. When perceived risk is high, psychic cost is correspondingly high.

Customers often feel uncomfortable at higher levels of perceived risk and may try to reduce risk in a number of ways, as indicated in Figure 7.1. When customers try to reduce perceived risk, they are in effect trying to reduce the denominator of the value equation, thereby improving value. Suppliers can help customers reduce their levels of perceived risk in a number of ways. For example, performance risk is reduced by performance guarantees; financial risk is reduced by firm prices and interest-free payment plans.

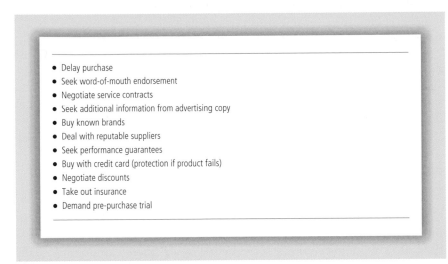

- Delay purchase
- Seek word-of-mouth endorsement
- Negotiate service contracts
- Seek additional information from advertising copy
- Buy known brands
- Deal with reputable suppliers
- Seek performance guarantees
- Buy with credit card (protection if product fails)
- Negotiate discounts
- Take out insurance
- Demand pre-purchase trial

Figure 7.1
How do customers reduce perceived risk?

Clearly there is more to the sacrifice component of the value equation than money alone. This explains why customers buy what appear to be suboptimal solutions to their problems. Why would a customer buy a printer for $300 when an identically specified machine is available for $100? Perhaps the answer lies in search and psychic costs. There is more to the benefit component than quality alone, although Bradley Gale has developed a value-based customer choice model that uses customer-perceived quality as the numerator and monetary price as the denominator. This assumes that customers will prefer the offer that delivers the best value ratio of quality against price.[2]

Total cost of ownership

There is a trend towards considering costs from the perspective of 'total cost of ownership' or TCO. TCO looks not only at the costs of acquiring products, but also at the full costs of using, and servicing the product throughout its life, and ultimately disposing of the product. What is thought of as 'consumption' can be broken down into a number of activities or stages, including search, purchase, ownership, use, consumption and disposal. TCO is an attempt to come up with meaningful estimates of lifetime costs across all these stages.

When customers take a TCO view of purchasing, suppliers can respond through a form of pricing called economic value to the customer (EVC). In a B2B context, EVC works by proving to customers that the value proposition being presented improves the profitability of the customer, by increasing sales, reducing costs or otherwise improving productivity. EVC computes for customers the value that the solution will deliver over the lifetime of ownership and use. Suppliers can apply EVC thinking to each stage of the 'consumption' process described above. For example, a computer supplier may agree to provide free service and to collect and dispose of unwanted machines after four years. Customers performing these tasks themselves would incur tangible costs. This is therefore the value that these activities have for customers.

EVC encourages suppliers to customize price for customers on the basis of their particular value requirements.

Customer value researchers have developed several typologies of customer-perceived value. Jag Sheth and colleagues have identified five types of value: functional, social, emotional, epistemic and conditional value.[3] In a B2B context, a distinction is made between economic value (satisfying economic needs at low transaction costs) and social value (satisfaction with the relationship with the supplier).[4]

How companies compete to create value for customers

Companies compete in a number of different ways, as indicated in Figure 7.2.[5] In a well-regulated economy, most companies compete by trying to deliver consistently better value than competitors. This means understanding customers' requirements fully and creating and delivering better solutions than competitors.

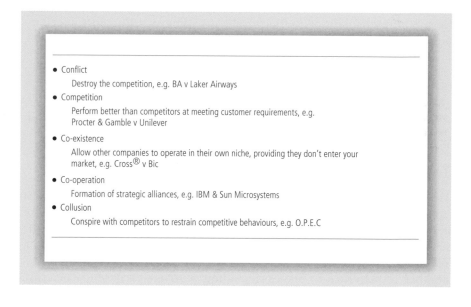

Figure 7.2
How companies compete
Source: Easton et al. (1993).

Value is contextualized rather than absolute. A solution that works in one context has value; that same solution, not working in another context, has no value. In a B2C context, McDonald's may have great value as a solution to the question, 'where shall I hold my 8-year-old daughter's birthday party?' It has less value as a solution to the question, 'where shall I take my fiancée for her 27th birthday?'

To create better value for customers, companies have to reinvent the numerator (benefits) and/or denominator (sacrifices) of the value equation. In a B2B context, this is often done in partnership with customers on a customer-by-customer basis. Unique solutions may be required. In B2C contexts, solutions are more often segment or niche specific, and are supported by market intelligence. To win and keep customers, companies have to constantly seek to improve the value they create. Given that this happens in a competitive environment, it is necessary not only to keep current with customer requirements, but also to stay up to date with competitors' efforts to serve these customers.

Sources of customer value

It is the job of professional marketers to develop the offers that create value for customers: the so-called value proposition. We can define value proposition as follows:

> A value proposition is the explicit or implicit promise made by a company to its customers that it will deliver a particular bundle of value-creating benefits.

Michael Treacey and Fred Wiersema have identified three fundamental types of value proposition that are delivered by successful companies. Indeed, these authors say that companies cannot be all things to all customers and need to concentrate on one of these three value delivery strategies. The strategies are characterized by product leadership, customer intimacy and operational excellence, and are summarized in Table 7.1.[6]

	Value delivery strategies		
	Operational excellence	**Product leadership**	**Customer intimacy**
Core business processes that …	Sharpen distribution systems and provide no hassle service	Nurture ideas, translate them into products and market them skilfully	Provide solutions and help customers run their businesses
Structure that …	Has strong, central authority and a finite level of empowerment	Acts in an ad hoc, organic, loosely knit and ever-changing way	Pushes empowerment close to customer contact
Management systems that …	Maintain standard operating procedures	Reward individuals' innovative capacity and new product success	Measure the cost of providing service and of maintaining customer loyalty
Culture that …	Acts predictably and believes 'one size fits all'	Experiments and thinks 'outside of the box'	Is flexible and thinks 'have it your way'

(Company traits)

Table 7.1 Three value disciplines

- **Operational excellence**: companies that pursue this strategy do a limited number of things very efficiently, at very low cost, and pass on those savings to customers. Companies renowned for this are Wal-Mart, Giordano and McDonald's. Unexpectedly, Toyota might also fit this strategy. If customers take a total cost of ownership view of price, then Toyota, with its reputation for reliability, durability and competitive service costs, fits the operational excellence model well. Operational excellence is underpinned by lean manufacturing and efficient supply chains, close cooperation with suppliers, rigorous quality and cost controls, process measurement and improvement, and management of customer expectations.
- **Product leadership**: companies aligning with this value discipline aim to provide the best products, services or solutions to customers. Continuous innovation underpins this strategy. Companies renowned for this are 3 M, Intel, GSK, LG and Singapore Airlines. Product leadership is reflected in a culture that encourages innovation, a risk-oriented management style, and investment in research and development.
- **Customer intimacy**: companies that pursue this strategy are able to adapt their offers to meet the needs of individual customers. Customer intimacy is based on customer insight. Companies renowned for customer intimacy include Saatchi and Saatchi, McKinsey and the US department store, Nordstrom. Adaptation and customization based on deep understanding of customer requirements underpin this strategy.

Value through the marketing mix

As mentioned above, it is the responsibility of marketing people to develop value propositions. They use a toolkit known as the marketing mix. The term 'marketing mix' is really a metaphor to describe the process of combining together various components to create value for customers. Eugene McCarthy grouped these components into a classification known as the 4Ps: product, price, promotion and place.[7] This approach is widely applied by goods manufacturers.

Services marketing experts in both B2B and B2C contexts have found this 4P taxonomy inadequate because it fails to take account of the special attributes of services (these were described in the last chapter). To recap, services are performances or acts that are, for the most part, intangible–dominant, inseparable (produced at the same time and place they are consumed), heterogeneous (of variable quality) and perishable.

Service marketers' response to these special characteristics has been to develop a new toolkit for creating customer value. It contains another 3Ps, making 7Ps in total.[8] The additional 3Ps are people, physical evidence and process, as shown in Figure 7.3. As we shall see later, though developed for services contexts, they can provide a useful framework for goods manufacturers too. Before we explore each of these sources of customer value, we'll look at the issue of customization.

Figure 7.3
Sources of customer value

Customization

CRM aims to build mutually beneficial relationships with customers at segment, cohort or individual level. A fundamental approach to achieving this goal is to customize the value proposition in order to attract and retain targeted customers. CRM aims to fit the offer to the requirements of the customer; it is not a one-size-fits-all approach.

Customization has both cost and revenue implications. It may make strategic sense because it generates competitive advantage and is appealing to customers, but there may be serious reservations because of the costs of customization. Companies need to ask whether investment in customization will generate a return higher than they could achieve through other strategies carrying a similar amount of risk. Customization may mean the loss of economies of scale, thus increasing unit costs. There may also be additional technology costs.

Case 7.1

Dell Computer customizes production using a product configurator

When Dell Computer's customers are online, they are able to design their own computers. Customers interface with the front end of a technology called a configurator. This is a rule-based system that enables or disables certain combinations of product features including chassis, hard disk capacity, memory, processor speed, software and connectivity. The technology is connected to back-office functions such as assembly and procurement. Each Dell Computer is made to order.

Customization means that companies have to be aware of, and responsive to, customers' differing requirements. Information systems designed to capture, store and distribute customer-related data also have a cost.

Configurator technologies can be quite sophisticated. In their simplest form they contain a set of rules (if the customer chooses chassis A, only allow one hard disk). At the other end of the spectrum are constraint-based optimization technologies. The constraints are applied in a systematic way to ensure the final configuration is optimum, for example, in producing least cost products.

Customization has been the norm in B2B markets for many years. Suppliers routinely make adaptations to suit the needs of customers. It is also true that customers make adaptations to suit suppliers. These adaptations serve as investments that make the relationship hard to break. As shown in Figure 7.4, suppliers can adapt, or customize, any of the 7Ps regardless of whether they manufacture goods or perform services. Although the additional 3Ps were developed for service companies, they also apply in the manufacturing context, as these examples show.

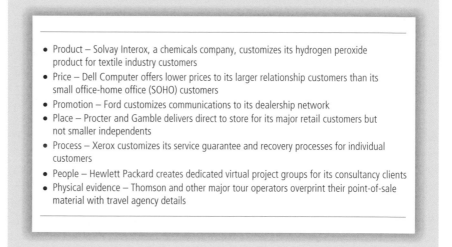

Figure 7.4
Customizing the 7Ps

- **Process**: important manufacturing industry processes are the order fulfilment process and the new product development process. Manufacturers can customize these to suit the requirements of different customers. Major FMCG manufacturers have evolved twin new product development processes. They have their own in-house processes, as well as customized processes in which they co-develop new products in partnership with major retailers.
- **People**: manufacturers can adjust the profile and membership of account teams to ensure that customers get the service they deserve and can afford. Kraft, for example, has customer teams for major retail accounts that consist of a customer business manager (c.f. key account manager), category planner, retail sales manager, sales information specialist, retail space management and supply chain specialist. This customer-facing team can then draw on additional company expertise if needed, including brand managers and logistics specialists. The

composition and membership of the team is agreed with each major retail account.

- **Physical evidence**: manufacturers use many different forms of physical evidence, such as scale models, cut-away models, product samples and collateral materials. Kitchen manufacturers provide customized swatches of worktop and cabinet colours to their major retail distributors.

Case 7.3

Tailored value propositions at Heineken Ireland

Heineken, a major beer exporter, has been very successful in the Irish beer market, with brands collectively capturing around 17 per cent of the total market. This success has been attributed to a deep understanding of the market, a strong portfolio of brands and a commitment to customer satisfaction. To sustain its position, Heineken sought to focus on delivering superior service to its 9000 commercial customers, namely pubs, hotels and wholesalers. To accomplish this Heineken implemented a Siebel CRM system.

For Heineken, one advantage of the Siebel software has been its ability to create single, comprehensive, profiles of customers which can be used to tailor product bundles and services, and to provide improved levels of customer service. Heineken believes that the CRM system provides the ability to build higher quality relationships with customers. For example, sales representatives are able to prioritize their interactions with key customers and instantly analyse historical data to identify sales trends and buying patterns of both individual customers and geographic areas, using their notebook computers while on the road.

Mass customization

A distinction can be made between 'craft customization' and 'mass customization'. The latter implies that an organization can communicate with target audiences at a mass or segment level, but is also able to offer customized value propositions for individual customers. Craft customization involves customized offers, but not at a mass market level.

Mass customization can be defined as follows:

> Mass customization is the use of flexible processes and organizational structures to create varied, and even individually tailored, value propositions, with neither a cost nor a lead time penalty.

This is not the same as offering customers more choice, customers certainly want their needs to be met; they do not necessarily want choice. Giving customers' choice has been the default strategy when companies have been unable to identify and meet customers' precise requirements. Choice means work for the customer in comparing offers; work adds to the cost of the consumption process.

A number of different types of mass customization have been identified, as shown in Table 7.2.[9] A relatively minor form of mass customization involves 'match to order'. This simply involves finding a match, from a range of standard products, to a particular customer's requirements. At the other extreme is 'engineer to order', which involves the co-design, in a joint enterprise between customer and supplier, of a unique solution to that customer's problem.

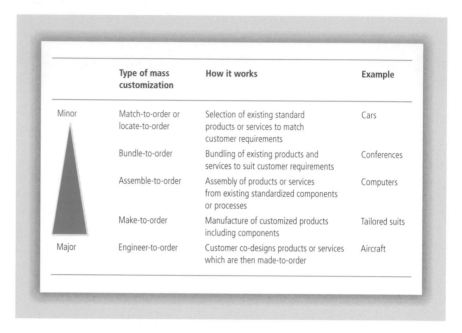

	Type of mass customization	How it works	Example
Minor	Match-to-order or locate-to-order	Selection of existing standard products or services to match customer requirements	Cars
	Bundle-to-order	Bundling of existing products and services to suit customer requirements	Conferences
	Assemble-to-order	Assembly of products or services from existing standardized components or processes	Computers
	Make-to-order	Manufacture of customized products including components	Tailored suits
Major	Engineer-to-order	Customer co-designs products or services which are then made-to-order	Aircraft

Table 7.2 Different forms of mass customization

It is in B2C markets that mass customization has lately become more widespread. Until recently, most B2C companies have either mass marketed standardized products or have developed product variants for particular niches. A growing number are now attempting to mass customize their offers. This is enabled by databases that store customer preferences, Internet-enabled interactivity that permits companies to learn about changing customer requirements through improved communication, modular product design, flexible manufacturing operations and supply chains, and mass customization technologies.

Mass customization is widespread in service industries serving end consumers. This is largely because of the inseparability of service production and consumption. The interaction between consumers and service producers during the service encounter lets customers influence both the service delivery process and the outcome.

Mass customization is also becoming more common in manufacturing companies. Dell Computer's mass customization model allows customers to design up to 14 000 different personal computer configurations. Ford was able to produce 27 million different Ford Fiestas, more than were actually sold.

Key issues for CRM strategists are these:

1. Do customers want customized products and services?
2. What degree of customization is desired?
3. Are customers willing to pay a premium for customization?

Frank Piller and Melanie Müller have reviewed the research on these questions, paying particular attention to the shoe manufacturing industry.[10] They found that consumers generally are aware of and value the benefits of mass customization (for shoe customers, better fit is the single most important benefit, followed at some distance by style and functionality), and the majority are willing to pay a premium – particularly women. Willingness to pay more varies across brands and customer segments. Adidas, for example, is able to command a 50 per cent price premium for customized sports shoes. Customization, however, does not universally mean that customers pay more. Some customized products eliminate features that have no value for customers, resulting in lower costs which are passed on in reduced prices.

Not all customer segments are willing to pay for mass customization. Levi Strauss has three different routes to market: jeans specialists, department stores and their own Original Levi Stores. Each channel reaches different market segments, and the company offers different product lines in each type of store. The Original Levi Store is the only channel where the company has offered mass customization. Customer measurements taken in-store are fed into the production system. A week or so later the customer receives a pair of customized Levi jeans. For Levi's, this differentiation allowed them to maintain a price premium in this one channel that has been impossible to achieve in their other channels. For customers there was the added value that the jeans fitted perfectly.

Amazon.com has become the world's largest and most successful online retailer, diversifying from books and CDs into other areas such as electronics and clothing. Much of Amazon's continued success has been related to its CRM strategy of retaining customers and growing share of wallet. Amazon utilizes CRM software to customize offerings to each customer. Based on information, such as previous purchases and products that have recently been browsed, Amazon's CRM software can predict a range of other products the customer is likely to be interested in. For example, a customer who purchases an Ernest Hemingway novel may receive a recommendation to purchase another novel by the author or a DVD documentary of Hemingway's life. Your author's customized Amazon.com webpage is presented in Figure 7.5.

Over the next few paragraphs we'll look at how value can be created by astute management of the marketing mix variables.

Value from products

Companies may make products, but customers do not buy products. Customers buy solutions to their problems. They buy benefits or, better said, they buy the expectation of benefits. Nobody ever buys a lawnmower because they want a lawnmower; people want attractive lawns. Products are means to ends.

Products that offer better solutions to problems create more value for customers. A better solution is one in which the balance between benefits and sacrifices of the value equation is enhanced for the customer.

Figure 7.5 Francis Buttle's Amazon.com customized webpage

Marketers often distinguish between different levels of the product, sometimes known as a customer value hierarchy.[11] The **core** product is the basic benefit that customers buy. Companies competing for customer demand must be able to meet the core benefit requirements. Let's consider the market for MBA-level education. MBA students typically are buying one or more of three basic benefits: salary enhancement, career development or personal growth. A second level is the **enabling** product. This consists of the physical goods and services that are necessary for the core benefit to be delivered. In the MBA case, this would comprise the buildings, classroom fixtures, faculty and educational technology. A third level, the **augmented** product consists of the factors that position and differentiate one competitor from another. In the MBA illustration this might be teaching method, for example, learning through real life projects, or an extensive international exchange programme, or a leafy out of town location.

Companies offering the same core benefit have to compete to deliver value to customers through enablers and augmentations. As Ted Levitt noted:

> … competition is not between what companies produce in their factories, but between what they add to their factory output in the form of packaging, services, advertising, customer advice, financing, delivery arrangements, warehousing and other things that people value.[12]

Product-based value is created for customers through product innovation, additional benefits, product–service bundling, branding and product synergies. We explore these below.

Product innovation

Most 'new' products are modifications of existing products, cost reductions or line extensions. Very few products are 'new to the world' or create new product categories. New products in all of these categories can improve customer value perceptions, but it is the dramatic ground-breaking inventions that create leaps in customer value. History is littered with them: Stephenson's locomotive, Edison's incandescent light bulb, Hargreaves's spinning jenny and Newcomen's steam engine. More recently we have had the Sony Walkman and Apple iPod.

Occasionally, old technologies provide value-creating modern day solutions. Trevor Bayliss invented the wind-up radio after seeing a programme about the spread of AIDS in Africa. The programme highlighted the difficulty that health professionals faced getting safe sex messages to rural and poor areas where there were no power sources for conventional radios. Thirtyfive per cent of the world has no access to electricity. Large-scale manufacturing of the Freeplay® wind-up radio began in 1995. The radio has two energy sources: dynamo power and solar cells. The product has created value for all concerned: the manufacturers, investors, resellers, employees, Bayliss and, of course, radio audiences. It has sold over two million units, and the technology has also been applied to lanterns and mobile phone chargers.

Additional benefits

Companies can create value for customers by attaching additional benefits to their products. A lawnmower operates more quietly. A car comes with a five-year warranty. A forklift truck is supplied with a free options package. Sometimes additional benefits are accompanied by repositioning the product in a different segment of the market. Lucozade had been a glucose drink for older people and was widely associated with illness. The brand owner, GlaxoSmithKline, repositioned this product as an energy drink in the rapidly growing sports drink market, where it has enjoyed considerable success (see Figure 7.6).

Low involvement product categories have low personal significance or relevance to customers. Customers feel very little sense of commitment to any brand and are therefore easily switched to competitors. Adding additional benefits helps brand owners to increase the level of customer involvement. There are two main approaches: product modification and product association. Product modification means changing the product in some way so that it ties in more closely to the customer's needs, values and interests. Detergent manufacturers, for example, have reformulated their brands so that they are more environmentally friendly. Diaper manufacturers have resegmented the market so that there are different products for boys and girls, day and night, babies of different weights and even 'swimmer' models. Product association means linking the brand to some issue or context that is of high importance to customers. PlayStation, for example, links a soccer computer game to the FIFA World Cup, while Mobil tied its brand to the Olympics, donating to sports funds for every gallon or litre purchased.

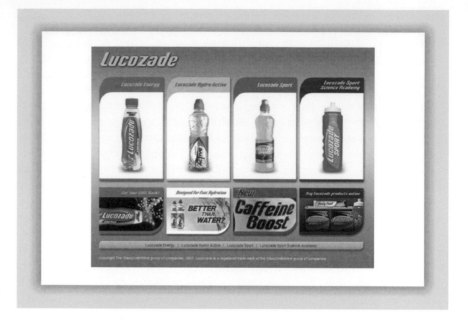

Figure 7.6
Repositioning
Lucozade as a sports
drink

Product–service bundling

Product–service bundling is the practice of offering customers a package of goods and services at a single price. Tour operators routinely bundle several elements of a vacation together: flights, transfers, accommodation and meal plans, for example. For the customer, bundling can reduce money, search and psychic costs. For the company, there are economies in selling and marketing.

Changing the composition of a bundle can increase customer perceived value; adding or removing elements from the bundle can both have this effect. Adding elements to the bundle increases the benefits side of the value equation. In a B2C context, for example, supermarket operators can offer a bagging service at the checkout at no extra cost to the customer. If the people performing this task are diverted from other tasks, then there may be no additional costs for the operator. Removing elements from the bundle enables the company to establish a new price point, therefore adjusting the value equation for customers. In a B2B context, companies often ask for elements to be removed from a bundle in return for a lower price. For example, a training college with its own IT department may ask the supplier of its IT equipment for a lower price in return for not using the supplier's help desk and IT support facilities. If the price is reduced by $5000 and the saving to the supplier is $6000, then both parties win.

Branding

A brand can be defined as follows:

> A brand is any name, design, style, word or symbol that distinguishes a product from its competitors.

Brands create value for customers in a number of ways, on both sides of the value equation. Brands reduce search costs by clearly identifying one product as different from others. Brands can also reduce psychic costs. Over time, customers assign meanings to brands. If you buy a Mercedes vehicle, it may be because you understand that the brand attributes are excellence in engineering, assured quality build and high resale value. A customer who understands what the brand means is less at risk than a customer who does not understand. Brand knowledge like this is acquired from experience, word-of-mouth or marketer-controlled communication. Brands also offer an implicit assurance of a particular customer experience. For example, when you buy any products carrying the Virgin brand it may be because you believe that Virgin's brand values are service excellence, innovation and good value.

Product synergies

Companies can create value for customers by finding synergies between products in the company's product portfolio. For example, if you take a Virgin flight you will be offered a Virgin cola. If you buy Microsoft software, the company will offer you complementary software for related applications. These synergies are also sometimes created from relationships within a company's network.

Disney is particularly good at exploiting synergies. Disney characters, such as Snow White and the Little Mermaid, are created in Disney's film division. The characters then appear in theme parks around the world, in the USA, Paris, Tokyo and Hong Kong, and in other service environments such as cruises, retail stores and on the Disney TV network. Finally, the characters are licensed for use in other applications. For example, you'll find Disney characters on lunch boxes and school bags, on clothing and shoes, and on McDonald's packaging for special movie-linked promotions.

Value from service

A service, as noted earlier, is a performance or act performed for a customer. Service is an important part of many companies' value propositions. In most developed economies, about 70 per cent of gross domestic product is created by service organizations. For these organizations, service is the core product. Even in manufacturing firms, service is often an important part of the enabling and augmented product. For example, carpet manufacturers make floor coverings to international standards. While there is some potential to compete through product innovation, many manufacturers believe the best way to compete is through offering better service to their distributors, and corporate and domestic customers. Typical services include stockholding, design, measurement, cutting to order, delivery and fitting. Companies need to understand that their efforts to improve service should be focused. Companies should find out what service elements are important to customers and where performance needs to be improved. If the customer's biggest problem is your failure to deliver on time, in full and with no errors, it makes little sense to invest in updating the livery of your vehicles and drivers.

In this section we look at a number of service-related methods for creating value: improving service quality, service guarantees, service level agreements and service recovery programmes.

Service quality

There are two major perspectives on service quality:

1. **Quality is conformance to specification**: this is consistent with Philip Crosby's view of quality.[13] Conformance to specification might mean:
   - producing error-free invoices
   - delivering on time, in full as promised to customers
   - acknowledging a customer complaint within 24 hours.
2. **Quality is fitness for purpose**: Joseph M. Juran advanced the point of view that quality means creating products that are well suited to customer requirements, and which therefore meet their expectations. It is the customer, not the company, who decides whether quality is right.[14] If you are a farmer, a Land Rover is the right quality vehicle. If you are an executive limousine company, a Mercedes is the right quality vehicle. In a services environment, fitness for purpose might mean
   - allowing the customer to select a preferred communication channel (phone, e-mail or postal service)
   - recruiting customer contact staff who are highly empathic and responsive
   - customizing service delivery for customers.

These perspectives on quality can happily coexist. Specifications for service performance can be based on customer expectations. If customers determine the standards, there need be no conflict between these two approaches.

Service quality theories

Two service quality theories have dominated management practice as companies try to improve their service performance: the SERVQUAL model and the Nordic model.

The Nordic model, originated by Christian Grönroos and developed by others, identifies three components of service quality:

- technical
- functional
- reputational (Table 7.3).[15]

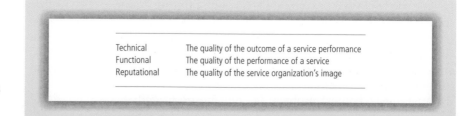

Technical	The quality of the outcome of a service performance
Functional	The quality of the performance of a service
Reputational	The quality of the service organization's image

Table 7.3 Grönroos model of service quality[16]

Technical quality can be thought of as the 'what' of service quality. Was the floor vacuumed thoroughly and surfaces dusted meticulously by the office cleaning contractor? Was the stock check performed professionally by the specialist audit firm? Functional quality can be thought of as the 'how' of service quality. Was the cleaner courteous? Was the stock-check team responsive? Reputational quality is both a product of technical and functional quality, in that reputation derives from performance, and it also produces a halo effect which can influence customer perceptions of quality, for better or worse. If I'm attending an opera at Teatro alla Scala (La Scala) in Milano then it must be good. If I'm receiving service from a state monopoly then it must be bad.

The significance of this model is that it stresses the importance of understanding customer expectations and of developing a service delivery system that performs well at meeting customers' technical and functional service quality expectations.

The SERVQUAL model, developed by A. 'Parsu' Parasuraman and colleagues in North America, identifies five core components of service quality: reliability, assurance, tangibles, empathy and responsiveness, as defined in Table 7.4.[17] You can remember them through the mnemonic RATER.

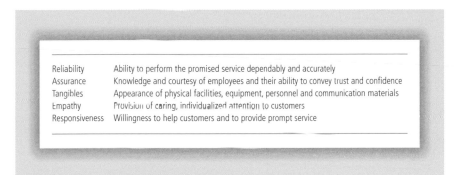

Reliability	Ability to perform the promised service dependably and accurately
Assurance	Knowledge and courtesy of employees and their ability to convey trust and confidence
Tangibles	Appearance of physical facilities, equipment, personnel and communication materials
Empathy	Provision of caring, individualized attention to customers
Responsiveness	Willingness to help customers and to provide prompt service

Table 7.4 SERVQUAL components[18]

The SERVQUAL authors have also developed a measurement and management model to accompany the conceptual model. The measurement model uses a 44-item questionnaire that measures customers' expectations and perceptions of the RATER variables.[19] The relative importance of these variables is also measured. This enables you to compute the relative importance of any gaps between expectation and perceptions. Management can then focus on strategies and tactics to close the important gaps.

The management model, reproduced in Figure 7.7, identifies the reasons for any gaps between customer expectations and perceptions (gap 5). Gap 5 is the product of gaps 1, 2, 3 and 4. If these four gaps, all of which are located below the line that separates the customer from the company, are closed then gap 5 will close. The gaps are as follows:

● Gap 1 is the gap between what the customer expects and what the company's management thinks customers expect.

- Gap 2 occurs when management fails to design service standards that meet customer expectations.
- Gap 3 occurs when the company's service delivery systems – people, processes and technologies – fail to deliver to the specified standard.
- Gap 4 occurs when the company's communications with customers promise a level of service performance that the service delivery system cannot provide.

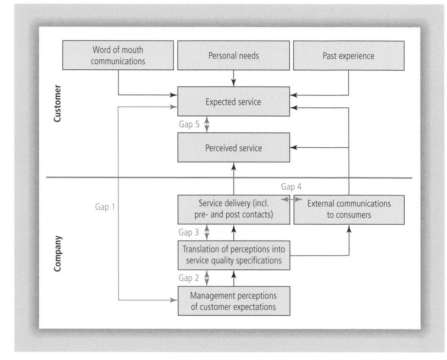

Figure 7.7
The SERVQUAL gaps model

The importance of SERVQUAL is that it offers managers a systematic approach to measuring and managing service quality. It emphasizes the importance of understanding customer expectations (see Figure 7.8), and of developing internal procedures that align company processes to customer expectations. Among the strategies and tactics that might be employed to close gaps 1–4 are the following:

1. To close gap 1 (between what customers expect and what managers think customers expect):
   - conduct primary research into customers' service quality expectations
   - learn from front-line customer contact staff
   - flatten the hierarchical structure
   - include expectations data in customer records.
2. To close gap 2 (between what managers think customers expect and service quality specifications):
   - commit to the development of service standards wherever possible
   - assess the feasibility of meeting customer expectations
   - develop a standards documentation process
   - automate processes where possible and desirable

- outsource activities where you lack the competencies
- develop service quality goals.
3. To close gap 3 (between service quality specifications and actual service delivery):
    - invest in people: recruitment, training and retention
    - invest in technology
    - redesign workflow
    - encourage self-organized teams
    - improve internal communication
    - write clear job specifications
    - reward service excellence.
4. To close gap 4 (between actual service delivery and the promises communicated to customers):
    - brief advertising agency on customer service expectations
    - train employees not to overpromise
    - penalize employees who overpromise
    - encourage customers to sample the service experience
    - excel at service recovery
    - encourage and manage customer complaints.

There is growing evidence that investment in service quality improvements pays off in enhanced customer satisfaction and customer retention, although like other investments there does appear to be a point at which diminishing returns set in.[20]

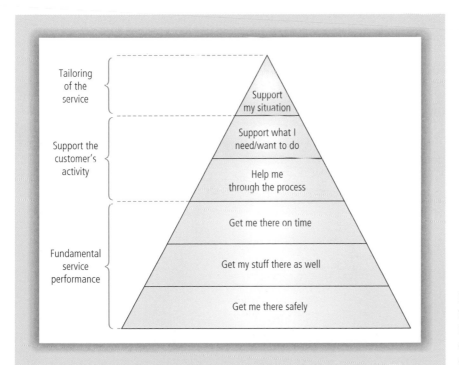

Figure 7.8
SAS airlines' understanding of customer expectations

The SERVQUAL model has been subject to much criticism, but it is still in widespread use in original and customized forms.[21] One criticism is that customers often do not have clearly formed expectations, and therefore that the disconfirmation approach is inappropriate. Some of these critics have developed an alternative, perceptions-only, model of service quality that they have dubbed SERVPERF.[22]

Service guarantees

From the customer's perspective, guarantees can be an effective way to reduce risk and thereby increase value. A service guarantee can be defined as follows:

> *A service guarantee is an explicit promise to the customer that a prescribed level of service will be delivered.*

Service guarantees can either be specific or general. Specific service guarantees apply to particular parts of the customer experience. For example:

> Sleep tight or it's a free night. We guarantee it (Howard Johnson's). PG&E will meet the agreed upon appointment time set with our customer during contact with our call centre or automatically credit your account with $30 (Pacific Gas and Electric).

General service guarantees apply to the entire customer experience (see Figure 7.9). For example:

> We guarantee to give perfect satisfaction in every way (LL Bean). Guaranteed. Period (Land's End).

Figure 7.9
ADT Money-Back Service Guarantee[23]

Although these examples are of guarantees offered to external customers, they can also be designed for internal customers. For example, the housekeeping supplies department at Embassy Suites guarantees that its internal customer, the housekeeping department, will get supplies on the day requested. If not, the department pays $5 to the housekeeper.

Service guarantees can be customized for individual customers or segments. An IT service centre guarantees a three hour service to priority one customers and 48 hour service to all others. Should the company fail to honour these guarantees it 'fines' itself by issuing a credit note to the customers.

Some guarantees, such as the Land's End example cited above, are unconditional. Others are conditional. For example, the PG&E guarantee above does not apply when a customer makes a same day appointment or when a service person misses the appointment to respond to an immediate emergency. If the guarantee is unconditional and the consequence of invoking the guarantee is that customer doesn't have to pay, there is effectively zero financial risk.

Service-level agreements

Service-level agreements (SLAs) can be defined as follows:

> A service level agreement is a contractual commitment between a service provider and a customer that specifies the mutual responsibilities of both parties with respect to the services that will be provided and the standards at which they will be performed.

SLAs can apply to both internal and external customer relationships. For example, it is not uncommon for utility companies to outsource their customer contact function to a third party. An external SLA is negotiated that carefully defines both parties' expectations of the services to be performed, the service processes to be followed, the service standards to be achieved and the price to be paid. The SLA may well form part of an enforceable legal contract. A number of metrics are used to measure performance of the supplier and compliance with SLA service standards. These include:

- **availability**: the percentage of time that the service is available over an agreed time period
- **usage**: the number of service users that can be served simultaneously.
- **reliability**: the percentage of time that the service is withdrawn or fails in the time period
- **responsiveness**: the speed with which a demand for service is fulfilled. This can be measured using turn-around time or cycle-time
- **user satisfaction:** this can be measured at the time the service is delivered or periodically throughout the agreed service period.

See Figure 7.10 for an example of a service level agreement scorecard.

Many companies also have internal SLAs between service departments and their internal customers. An IT services department, for example, may establish a number of different SLAs with different customer groups. It might undertake to process payroll for the human resource

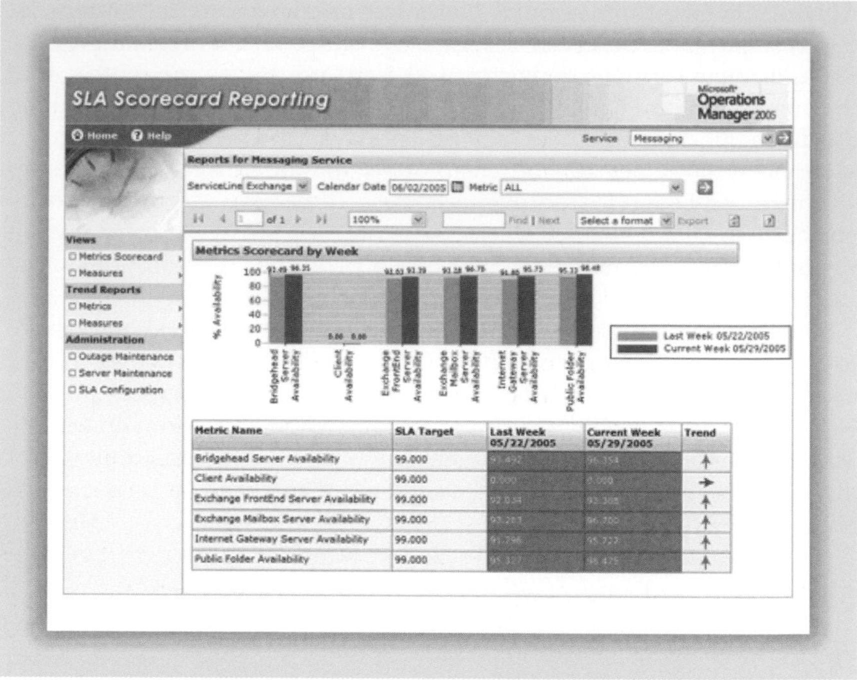

Figure 7.10
Service level
agreement
scorecard[24]

department or to maintain and service desktop devices for a contact centre. This is unlikely to be formalized in a contract.

SLAs create value for customers by reducing uncertainty about the services that will be delivered, their standards and costs. A successful SLA clarifies the boundaries and relative roles of customer and supplier. Each knows the other's responsibility. Service automation technologies discussed in Chapter 16 allow companies to manage service levels.

Service recovery programmes

Service recovery can be defined as follows:

> Service recovery includes all the actions taken by a company to resolve a service failure.

Services fail for many different reasons.[25] Sometimes technical service quality fails; at other times the failure is in functional service quality. Sometimes the fault lies with the company, sometimes with the customer and sometimes with a network member. Typically customers are not concerned with who is to blame; they just want the situation resolved.

Research shows that when companies resolve problems quickly and effectively there are positive consequences for customer satisfaction, customer retention and word-of-mouth.[26] It has even been found that customers who have been let down, then well recovered, are more satisfied than customers who have not been let down at all.[27] This can perhaps be explained in terms of the RATER dimensions of service quality. Getting service right first time demonstrates reliability, but recovering well after service failure shows empathy and responsiveness. Reliability can be programmed into a company's service production and delivery processes. Empathy and responsiveness demonstrate the human attributes of concern for others and flexibility. Conversely, customers who have been let down once, only to experience unsatisfactory recovery, can turn into 'terrorists' who actively look for opportunities to spread bad word-of-mouth.[28]

When customers experience service failure, they have the choice of doing nothing or voicing their displeasure. Customers who choose to voice their feelings can complain to the service provider, complain to associates and others in their personal network, or complain to a third party such as a consumer affairs organization or industry ombudsman.

Equity theory suggests that customers who complain are seeking justice and fairness. Equity theory explains that customers compare the sacrifices they make and the benefits they experience (as in the value equation) to other customers' sacrifices and benefits. When customers pay the same price, but experience an unsatisfactory level of service compared to other customers, they feel a sense on inequity or unfairness. When they complain, they want the company to fix the imbalance. They want justice.

Research suggests that there are different types of justice. Figure 7.11 highlights the three forms of justice that complainants seek: distributive justice, procedural justice and interactional justice.[29] Distributive justice is achieved if the customer gets the material outcome wanted after a complaint. Customers might be satisfied with an apology or a credit note against future purchases. Alternatively, a customer may want the service to be reperformed. If distributive justice is concerned with what is received, procedural justice is concerned with the customers' evaluation of the processes and systems that are encountered during the complaints handling episode. Customers generally do not want to complete forms, provide difficult-to-find proofs of purchase or write formal letters confirming the complaint. These requirements do not suggest that

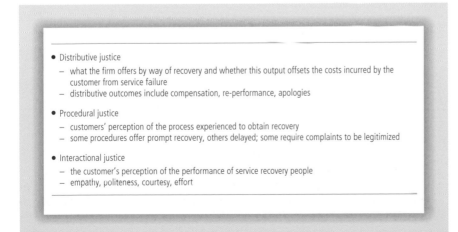

- Distributive justice
    - what the firm offers by way of recovery and whether this output offsets the costs incurred by the customer from service failure
    - distributive outcomes include compensation, re-performance, apologies

- Procedural justice
    - customers' perception of the process experienced to obtain recovery
    - some procedures offer prompt recovery, others delayed; some require complaints to be legitimized

- Interactional justice
    - the customer's perception of the performance of service recovery people
    - empathy, politeness, courtesy, effort

Figure 7.11
Service recovery and justice seeking

a company is organized and willing to resolve the problem quickly. Interactional justice is achieved if the customer judges that specific complaint-related interactions with the provider's people have been satisfactory. They want employees to be responsive and empathetic.

Value from processes

In the previous section we have described some business processes that help create customer perceived value: the service quality management process and the service recovery process. Elsewhere in the book we touch on additional processes that impact on customers: the order-to-cash cycle, the selling process, the campaign management process, the database development process and the innovation process, for example.

In Chapter 3 we defined a business process as a set of activities performed by people and/or technology in order to achieve a desired outcome. Business processes are how companies get things done. Companies are comprised of very large processes. IBM, for example, has identified 18 critical processes, Xerox 14 and Dow Chemical 9.[30] These big processes are in turn composed of smaller processes. For example, the manufacturing process takes a number of inputs – materials, technology, labour – and converts them into products. This big process is composed of several smaller processes, such as machining, assembly and packing processes. Companies have thousands of processes. But processes are more than simply workflow; they are also resources that can be used to compete more effectively, to create more value for both customers and company.[31] Xerox's 14 key business processes appear in Figure 7.12. Many of these macro-processes have an impact upon customer experience or value perceptions, including customer engagement, market management, product maintenance and product design and engineering processes.

1. Customer engagement
2. Inventory management and logistics
3. Product design and engineering
4. Product maintenance
5. Technology management
6. Production and operations management
7. Market management
8. Supplier management
9. Information management
10. Business management
11. Human resource management
12. Leased and capital asset management
13. Legal
14. Financial management

Figure 7.12
Xerox's 14 key business processes

Process innovation can create significant value for customers. For example, First Direct started out as a telephone bank with no branch network. Customer management was entirely IT enabled, with customer service being delivered from a number of call centres. The bank's customer satisfaction ratings have been consistently higher than competitors' branch operations. Daewoo established a direct-to-customer distribution channel that replaced the normal distributor arrangements of other automobile manufacturers. Customer experience was under better control and costs were reduced. easyJet speeded up customer service by improving plane turnaround times from 50 minutes to 33 through improved teamwork.

Case 7.3

Process innovation at SECOM

SECOM is the largest supplier of security services in Japan. Historically, service was very labour intensive as security guards were located at client sites. SECOM automated the detection of security breaches by combining crime detection sensors and telecommunications technology and moving its guards to a central location, from where they were despatched to deal with incidents. The business experienced high growth as a result. Subsequently, new technologies were added; remote sensing, image enhancement, geographical information systems and automated payment systems for clients.

In this section, we examine one additional process that impacts on the external customer's perception of value: the complaints management process.

The complaints management process

Customers complain when they experience one of two conditions: their expectations are under-performed to a degree that falls outside their zone of tolerance, or they sense they have been treated unfairly. Equity theory, described above, explains the customer's response to being treated unfairly. Customers also have a zone of tolerance for service and product performance. The range of tolerable performance will depend upon the importance of the product or the particular product attribute that is giving cause for complaint. Tolerances will be stricter for more important products and attributes. For unimportant products and attributes, customers tend to be less demanding. Where customer experience falls outside their zone of tolerance, there is cause for complaint.

Nobody likes receiving complaints, but they are unavoidable. Even the best companies sometimes fail customers and give cause for complaint. Therefore, it makes sense to implement a policy and process to receive, handle and resolve customer complaints. A positive view of customer complaints accepts that customers who complain are giving you a chance to win them back and retain their future value. Not only that, but complaints provide information that can help you identify, and correct, root causes of problems. Furthermore, the presence of a documented complaints-handling process has been shown to be strongly associated with excellent customer retention.[32] Worryingly, customers who don't complain may already have taken their business elsewhere.

A successful complaints handling process enables companies to capture customer complaints before customers start spreading negative word-of-mouth or take their business elsewhere. Research suggests that negative word-of-mouth can be very influential.[33] Up to two-thirds of customers who are dissatisfied do not complain to the organization.[34] They may, however, complain to their social networks. Unhappy customers are likely to tell twice as many people about their experience as customers with a positive experience.[35]

Many customers who are unhappy don't complain. Why? There are a number of possible reasons:

- They feel the company doesn't care. Perhaps the company or the industry has a reputation for treating customers poorly.
- It takes too much time and effort.
- They fear retribution. Many people are reluctant to complain about the police, for example.
- They don't know how to complain.

Companies can address all of these issues by making their customers aware of their complaints policy and processes. A complaints management process that is simple and easy to access should facilitate the capture of complaints. Some companies use dedicated freephone and fax lines. Some reward complainants. Stew Leonard's, the Connecticut retailer, rewards in-store complainants with an ice-cream.

Complaints enter companies at many different customer touchpoints – accounts receivable, order processing, sales engineering, logistics, customer contact centre – and so on. A well-designed complaints-handling process will capture complaints from various touchpoints and then aggregate and analyse them to identify root causes. Ultimately this should enable the company to achieve a higher level of first-time reliability, reduce the amount of rework, and lift levels of customer satisfaction and

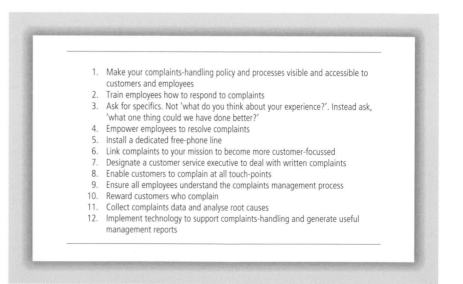

Figure 7.13 Improving the complaints management process

1. Make your complaints-handling policy and processes visible and accessible to customers and employees
2. Train employees how to respond to complaints
3. Ask for specifics. Not 'what do you think about your experience?'. Instead ask, 'what one thing could we have done better?'
4. Empower employees to resolve complaints
5. Install a dedicated free-phone line
6. Link complaints to your mission to become more customer-focussed
7. Designate a customer service executive to deal with written complaints
8. Enable customers to complain at all touch-points
9. Ensure all employees understand the complaints management process
10. Reward customers who complain
11. Collect complaints data and analyse root causes
12. Implement technology to support complaints-handling and generate useful management reports

retention. An international standard, ISO 10002, has been released to help companies identify and implement best practice in complaints policy and process. Software is available to help companies improve their complaints-handling expertise.[36] Figure 7.13 details some ideas for improving complaints management processes.

Value from people

Many companies claim that people are their key differentiators, and a major source of customer value. This is especially so in professional services such as counselling, consulting and coaching where people are the product. The UK-based home improvement retailer B&Q has also added value to the shopping experience by recruiting former building tradesmen such as carpenters, electricians and plumbers to help customers diagnose their problems and choose the right products in-store. Even in the high-tech arena, people can be regarded as strengths that deliver value to customers. Nortel, for example, claims:

'At Nortel we believe that our people are our strength. Their knowledge, commitment and talents drive our success'.

There are many important roles that need to be filled for CRM to deliver its promise of enhanced customer retention and company profitability. We examine these in greater detail in Chapter 17.

One of the more important jobs in CRM is the customer contact role. The customer contact role is a boundary-spanning role. That is, the role occupant sits in the space between an organization and its external customers. They are paid by the company, but work closely with customers. Boundary spanners have two fundamental and interdependent roles: information management and relationship management. Boundary spanners are accountable for collecting information about customers. What are the customer's requirements, expectations and preferences? What are the customer's future plans? Who is involved in the customer's buying decisions? The boundary spanner may have responsibility for maintaining the accuracy of the customer data records. This information enables the role occupant to perform the second role, managing the customer relationship. This might involve winning, growing and maintaining the customer's business, handling customer queries and complaints, representing the customer's interests to his employer and ensuring the customer's satisfaction.

There is a trend towards key account management that is driven by a number of trends: global customers, consolidated purchasing, vendor reduction programmes and customers who want better service and closer relationships with their suppliers. The role of key account manager, national account manager or global account manager is extremely important. Occupants need an advanced, and rare, skill, knowledge and attitude profile including selling skills, negotiating skills, communication skills, analytical skills, problem-solving skills, customer knowledge, market knowledge, competitor knowledge, customer orientation, as well as a detailed understanding of what their own company's network can deliver.

Value from physical evidence

Some companies create value for customers by managing physical evidence. This is especially important for service companies with intangible–dominant outputs. In the absence of physical evidence, customers may find it very hard to determine whether or not they are receiving value. Physical evidence can be defined as follows:

> Physical evidence consists of the tangible facilities, equipment and materials that companies use to communicate value to customers.

Physical evidence includes a company's premises and their internal and external environments, print materials, websites, corporate uniforms and vehicle livery.

It makes sense for companies to audit and create an inventory of the physical evidence that can influence customers' perceptions of value. Banks, for example, generally occupy traditional buildings with columns, porticoes, steps and large, heavy doors. This is designed to communicate conservative values, security and probity. McDonald's uses primary colours, bright lights and the ubiquitous golden arches in the form of the letter 'M'. Hospitals convey impressions of good hygiene and care through white uniforms, immaculately clean premises and well-maintained gardens. You only need to reflect on the traditional clothing, livery and appearance of funeral services to understand the significance of physical evidence.

Web portals also act as physical evidence. The only physical evidence that remotely located customers who don't receive visits from sales representatives might have of a supplier is their web portal. Many companies have developed portals for their customers and partners. Users generally obtain access through a secure sign-on procedure and then have access to information relevant to their own role, for example as customer or partner. Managers of the portal can push information out to users on a segment or individual basis. Users can transact, communicate and enquire online in a secure environment. A web portal can be defined as follows:

> A web portal is a website that serves as a gateway to a range of subject-related resources.

In addition to corporate portals, there are general consumer portals, such as Yahoo! (www.yahoo.com) and MSN (www.msn.com), and specialized or niche portals. There are many niche portals for special interest groups such as gardeners (www.garden.com), cricket fans (www.cricinfo.com), investors (www.fool.com) and chief executives (www.ceoexpress.com). Portals act as gateways to the rest of the Internet, and often include features such as search engines, directories, customizable homepages and e-mail.

General portals provide customer value by bringing together related content from different sources, providing convenient access for users. For example, the website www.buzgate.org (see Figure 7.14) is a portal that provides access to a comprehensive array of online public and private sector resources for small- and medium-sized businesses (SMB).

Figure 7.14 Information availability online at www.buzgate.org[37]

Portals like these function in much the same way as a high street retailer, in that they act as repositories for many different products (resources).

Value from customer communication

Companies are now able to create value for customers from communication practices that were impossible in earlier years. A significant change is that companies are now able to facilitate multilateral communication: company-to-customer, customer-to-company and even customer-to-customer. Traditionally customer communication has been one way: from companies to customers. The conventional tools for company-to-customer communication are unilateral: advertising, sales promotion, publicity, public relations and personal selling. With the exception of selling, these communication channels are non-interactive. Customer-company communication is enabled through e-mail, web forms, instant messaging, phone, fax, web collaboration, as well as old-fashioned correspondence. Companies can also facilitate customer-to-customer (peer-to-peer) communication by web logs (better known as blogs), chat rooms, newsgroups and online communities. Collectively, these are known as customer generated media (CGM). Southwest Airlines, for example, has established a blog intended to 'give our readers the opportunity to take a look inside Southwest Airlines and to interact with us. This is as much your blog as it is ours.

Three processes are responsible for the enhanced power of communication to create value for customers: disintermediation, personalization and interactivity.

Disintermediation

Today, the development of new technologies has lead to the emergence of many direct-to-customer (DTC) communication tools including e-mail, direct mail and SMS messaging to cell-phones. Companies are now able to get their message direct to customers. Equally, customers can get their messages direct to companies and to other customers in the ways described above.

Personalization

High-quality customer-related data, CRM technologies and DTC channels, in combination, enable companies to tailor offers and communications to individual customers. This is what Don Peppers and Martha Rogers have called one-to-one marketing.[38] Data on customers' buying history and propensities-to-buy can be used to develop offers that meet with a much higher response rate and conversion rate than conventional mailings. The content, timing and delivery channels for communications can be based on customer preferences.

Another form of personalization is found online. CRM technologies are available that allow customers to personalize their own corporate web pages. Customers of www.lastminute.com can personalize their home page (mylastminute.com) using technology that stores their preferences. This enables the company to refine its messaging to the customer base. It claims to achieve click-through rates that are 30 per cent higher than non-targeted messaging.[39] You can also create your own daily newspaper at www.ft.com, based on your personal interests and preferences. This can then be used as your homepage.

Case 7.2

Customized communication at Mercedes-Benz

Mercedes-Benz decided to launch its new M-Class off-road vehicle in the USA knowing that it was already a crowded market. However, they accessed publicly available and corporate data to obtain details of all current owners of off-road and Mercedes vehicles. Mercedes then undertook a series of personalized direct mailings to the database, with the objective of raising awareness about the vehicle. The pretext for the communication was to ask for help in the process of designing the vehicle. There was an overwhelming response and the respondents were sent questionnaires which asked for guidance on design issues.

Two months later Mercedes pre-sold its first year sales target of 35 000 vehicles. It had been expecting to spend some US$70 million marketing the car, but by using this CRM-based approach it only needed to spend US$48 million, saving US$22 million. The programme was so successful that Mercedes is looking to use the same approach in the future with other model launches.

Personalization can also be performed on communications between customers and employees, such as customer service agents. For example, scripts can be tailored to enable agents unfamiliar with a product or customer segment to perform competently in telephone interactions.

Interactivity

Interactive technologies have been around since the advent of the telephone. Recently, the Internet has revolutionized the scope for interactivity through three major technologies: e-mail, instant messaging and the World Wide Web (WWW). E-mail enables customers and companies to interact effectively. For example, customers can e-mail for information that is unavailable on the frequently asked questions (FAQ) pages of corporate websites. E-mail gives customers access to a specific named person or work group, such as help@ or info@. Contact with a name gives customers the sense that there is an individual who is taking care of them. Instant messaging enables communications to take place in real-time, which is not always possible with e-mail.

The WWW is an Internet-enabled service that allows computer users to communicate globally with each other. A company can upload a website and anticipate huge reach. Websites come in a variety of forms: some are simply electronic brochures; others enable transactions to be made; another group of sites are highly interactive. Some excellent websites offer an experience similar to human dialogue. Configuration engines allow the most appropriate products to be offered based on an analysis of the customer's specific needs. Problem resolution logic allows customers to find the best solution to a problem, and web chat windows allow human dialogue over the web, if all else fails.

Value from channels

The traditional task of the distribution function is to provide time and place utilities to customers. Effectively this means getting products and services to customers when and where they want. Consumer goods companies have usually constructed channels using intermediaries such as wholesalers and retailers. B2B companies usually sell direct or employ industrial distributors. The location of service providers may be critical or irrelevant to the creation of value for customers. Customers want their grocery retailers to be conveniently located, but don't care where their Internet service provider is located.

An emerging task for intermediaries in the B2B environment is value augmentation. Channel partners in technology industries add services and complementary products that are not available from the core product manufacturer. The purchase of an ERP system, for example, may require implementation services, technical services, business process re-engineering, change management, customization of software or specialized hardware, such as radio frequency (RF) handheld units in the warehouse. Channel partners not only distribute the ERP product, they also provide or coordinate others to provide these additional products and services.

Internet-enabled disintermediation has allowed many companies to replace or supplement their traditional bricks-and-mortar channels. Many companies have elected to develop transactional websites so that they can sell direct. Others have developed brochureware sites that direct interested prospects to traditional channel members. One major benefit attached to this latter option is that it reduces the level of channel conflict that can be extremely high if an intermediary believes that a supplier is attempting to sell direct to the intermediaries' customers. Additional routes to market include:

- portal directories such as Yahoo! and Excite
- search engines such as AltaVista and Infoseek
- electronic shopping malls such as www.eMall.sg and www.emallroad. com
- virtual resellers such as Amazon and CDNow.[40]

Customers may find that it is too costly and inefficient to deal with a large number of potential disintermediated suppliers. This has created opportunities for reintermediation. Reintermediation adds an electronic intermediary to the distribution channel. Illustrations include:

www.netbuydirect.com for a wide range of factory-direct products
www.lastminute.com for holidays, flights, accommodation, car hire and gifts
www.laterooms.com for discounted hotel rooms
www.moneyworld.com for mortgages, credit cards, bank loans, insurances and pensions.

Ultimately, companies face four options when creating value for customers from electronic channels.[41]

1. **No Internet sales**: this might be the best option for small businesses with a local clientele. Companies on the Internet access an international audience. If they are unable to fill the demand that might arise, they are perhaps better off using traditional channels.
2. **Internet sales by reseller only**: a reseller, selling on behalf of many producers, may be big enough in terms of customer numbers and revenues to invest in online transactional capability. Fulfilment of orders may be performed by the reseller or producer.
3. **Internet sales by producer only**: it would be unusual for a company selling through bricks-and-mortar channels to establish a web presence that is in direct competition to those channel members. This would generate significant channel conflict.
4. **Internet sales by all**: both reseller and producer sell online.

Which of these strategies will add value for customers depends upon whether customers enjoy additional time and place utility from online purchasing.

Summary

This chapter has stressed the importance of creating value for customers. Value creation and delivery is a role for strategic CRM. Value can be thought of as the relationship between the benefits experienced from a product or service and the sacrifices made to enjoy those benefits. Value is therefore enhanced when sacrifices are reduced or benefits increased. Three major types of sacrifice have been identified: money, search and psychic costs. Companies can offer improved value to customers by creating and delivering better solutions to customers' problems.

Researchers have identified three major value delivery strategies that successful companies have adopted: operational excellence, product leadership and customer intimacy. Marketers are generally responsible for designing customer value propositions. Value propositions are constructed by mixing together a number of variables that will appeal to customers. These variables are known as the marketing mix. For goods manufacturers they comprise the 4Ps: product, price, promotion and place. In the services environment, the 4Ps are supplemented by three additional Ps: process, physical evidence and people. In the B2B environment, value propositions have long been customized. Customization is now emerging as a powerful force in the B2C environment too. Any of the 7Cs can be customized.

Management can create additional value by their management of the 7Ps. For example, product innovation, branding and product–service bundling are ways to create additional value. Similarly, service quality improvement programmes, service guarantees, service level agreements and service recovery programmes may be seen as value adding.

The Internet, customer-related databases and CRM technologies are allowing companies to tailor their customer communication strategies at segment or, often, unique customer level. Messages can be communicated directly to customers, side-stepping the media long used for broadcast advertising. They can also be personalized, not only in the form of address, but also in content and timing. Unlike traditional media, the newer channels, including the Internet, are interactive. Companies can get instant feedback from their customers.

References

1. Zeithaml, V.A. (1988) Consumer perceptions of price, quality and value: a means-end model and synthesis of evidence. *Journal of Marketing*, Vol. Vol. 52, pp. 2–22, July.
2. Gale, B.T. (1994) *Managing customer value: creating quality and service that customers can see*. New York: Free Press, This book presents a view that quality and monetary price are the basis of value computation by customers.
3. Sheth, J.N., Newman, B.I. and Gross, B.L. (1991) *Consumption Values and Market Choices: Theory and Applications*. Cincinnati: South-Western Publishing Company.
4. Gassenheimer, J.B., Houston, F.S. and Davis, J.C. (1998) The role of economic value, social value, and perceptions of fairness in inter-organizational relationship retention decisions. *Journal of the Academy of Marketing Science*, Vol. Vol. 26, pp. 322–337, (Fall).
5. Easton, G., Burrell, G., Shearman, C. and Rothschild, R. (1993) *Managers and competition*. Oxford: Blackwell.

6. Treacey, M. and Wiersema, F. (1995) *The discipline of market leaders*. London: Harper Collins.
7. McCarthy, E.J. (1996) *Basic Marketing*, 12th edn. Homewood, IL: RD Irwin.
8. Booms, B.H. and Bitner, M.-J. (1981) Marketing strategies and organizational structures for service firms. In: J. Donnelly and W.R. George (eds.). *Marketing of Services*. Chicago: American Marketing Association, pp. 47–51.
9. The table is based on Piller, F.T., Moeslein, K. and Stotko, C.M. (2004) Does mass customization pay? An economic approach to evaluate customer integration. *Production Planning and Control*, Vol. 15(4), pp. 435–444.
10. Piller, F.T. and Müller, M. (2004) A new marketing approach to mass customization. *International Journal of Computer Integrated Manufacturing*, Vol. Vol. 17(7), pp. 583–593.
11. See, for example, Kotler, P. (2000) *Marketing management: the millennium edition*. Saddle River, HJ: Prentice Hall and Levitt, T. (1980) Marketing success – through differentiation of anything. *Harvard Business Review*, January–February, pp. 83–91.
12. Levitt, T. (1969) *The marketing mode*. New York: McGraw-Hill, p.2..
13. Crosby, P.B. (1979) *Quality is free*. New York: McGraw-Hill.
14. Juran, J.M. (1964) *Managerial breakthrough*. New York: McGraw-Hill.
15. Grönroos, C. (1984) A service quality model and its marketing implications. *European Journal of Marketing*, Vol. Vol. 18, pp. 36–44.
16. Grönroos, C. (1984) *Strategic Management and Marketing in the Service Sector*. London: Chartwell-Bratt Ltd..
17. Parasuraman, A., Zeithaml, V.A. and Berry, L.L. (1985) A conceptual model of service quality and its implications for future research. *Journal of Marketing*, Vol. 49, Fall, pp. 41–50; Parasuraman, A., Zeithaml, V.A. and Berry, L.L. (1988) SERVQUAL: a multiple-item scale for measuring consumers' perceptions of service quality. *Journal of Retailing*, Vol. 64(1), pp. 22–37; Parasuraman, A., Zeithaml, V.A. and Berry, L.L. (1991) Refinement and reassessment of the SERVQUAL scale. *Journal of Retailing*, Vol. 64, pp. 12–40; Parasuraman, A., Zeithaml, V.A. and Berry, L.L. (1994) Reassessment of expectations as a comparison standard in measuring service quality: implications for future research. *Journal of Marketing*, Vol. 58(1), pp. 111–132.
18. Parasuraman, A., Zeithaml, V.A. and Berry, L.L. (1988) SERVQUAL: a multi-item scale for measuring consumer perceptions of service quality. *Journal of Retailing*, Vol. Vol. 64, pp. 12–40.
19. Parasuraman, A., Zeithaml, V.A. and Berry, L.L. (1988) SERVQUAL: a multiple-item scale for measuring consumers' perceptions of service quality. *Journal of Retailing*, Vol. 64(1), pp. 22–37; Parasuraman, A., Zeithaml, V.A. and Berry, L.L. (1991) Refinement and reassessment of the SERVQUAL scale. *Journal of Retailing*, Vol. 64, pp. 12–40.
20. Buttle, F. (1996) SERVQUAL: review, critique and research agenda. *European Journal of Marketing*, Vol. 30(1), pp. 8–32; Rust, R.T. (1995) Return on quality (ROQ): making service quality financially accountable. *Journal of Marketing*, Vol. 59(2), April, pp. 58–71.

21. Buttle, F. (1996) SERVQUAL: review, critique and research agenda. *European Journal of Marketing*, Vol. Vol. 30(1), pp. 8–32.

22. Cronin, J.J. and Taylor, S.A. (1992) Measuring service quality: a re-examination and extension. *Journal of Marketing*, Vol. 56, July, pp. 55–68; Cronin, J. J and Taylor, S.A. (1994) SERVPERF versus SERVQUAL: reconciling performance-based and perceptions-minus expectations measurement of service quality. *Journal of Marketing*, Vol. 58, January, pp. 125–131.

23. Copyright © 2008. ADT Security Services, Inc., Boca Raton, FL, USA. Used with permission.

24. http://technet.microsoft.com/en-us/library/Aa996021.67ad4a0d-8784–4988-be36-70b3a8a3dce2(en-us,TechNet.10).gif. Accessed 21 January 2008.

25. Keaveney, S.M. (1995) Customer switching behaviour in service industries: an exploratory study. *Journal of Marketing*, Vol. Vol. 59, pp. 71–82, (April).

26. Tax, S.W., Brown, S.W. and Chandrashekaran, M. (1998) Customer evaluations of service complaint experiences: implications for relationship marketing. *Journal of Marketing*, Vol. Vol. 62, pp. 60–76, April.

27. Hart, C.W., Heskett, J.L. and Sasser, W.E. Jr. (1990) The profitable art of service recovery. *Harvard Business Review*, Vol. Vol. 68, pp. 148–156, July–August.

28. Tax, S.S. and Brown, S.W. (1998) Recovering and learning from service failure. *Sloan Management Review*, Vol. Fall, pp. 75–88.

29. Sparks, B. and McColl-Kennedy, J.R. (2001) Justice strategy options for increased customer satisfaction in a service recovery setting. *Journal of Business Research*, Vol. Vol. 54, pp. 209–218.

30. Davenport, T.H. (1993) *Process innovation: reengineering work through information technology*. Boston, MA: Harvard Business School Press.

31. Process engineering is a complex topic that is beyond the scope of this book. Interested readers can find out more in Hammer, M. and Champy, J. (1993) *Re-engineeering the corporation*. New York: Harper Business; Davenport, T.H. (1993) *Process innovation: reengineering work through information technology*. Boston, MA: Harvard Business School Press; Keen, P.G.W. (1997) *The process edge: creating value where it counts*. Boston, MA: Harvard Business School Press.

32. Buttle, F. and Ang, L. (2006) Customer retention management processes: a quantitative study. *European Journal of Marketing*, Vol. Vol. 40(1–2), pp. 83–99.

33. Buttle, F.A. (1998) Word-of-mouth: understanding and managing referral marketing. *Journal of Strategic Marketing*, Vol. Vol. 6, pp. 241–254.

34. Richins, M. (1983) Negative word-of-mouth by dissatisfied customers: a pilot study. *Journal of Marketing*, Vol. Vol. 68, pp. 105–111.

35. TARP. (1995) American Express – SOCAP study of complaint handling in Australia. Society of Consumer Affairs Professionals.

36. http://www.listeningpost.com.au/Services/LPReviewcheckyour10002conformance/tabid/57/Default.aspx. Accessed 11 October 2007.

37. Courtesy of BUZGate.org™. BUZGate.org is a public service resource and referral network serving small business start-up, growth and sustainability by facilitating connections between public and private resource providers and resource users in a non-commercial, educationally focused portal environment.

38. Peppers, D. and Rogers, M. (1993) *The one-to-one future*. London: Piatkus; Peppers, D. and Rogers, M. (1997) *Enterprise one-to-one (1997)*. London: Piatkus; Peppers, D., Rogers, M. and Dorf, B. (1999) *The one-to-one fieldbook*. Oxford: Capstone; Peppers, D. and Rogers, M. (2000) *The one-to-one manager*. Oxford: Capstone.

39. Lastminute.com. (2001) Annual report.

40. Sarkar, M., Butler, B. and Steinfeld, C. (1996) Exploiting the virtual value chain. *Journal of Computer Mediated Communication*, Vol. Vol. 1(3).

41. Kumar, N. (1999) Internet distribution strategies: dilemmas for the incumbent. *Financial Times*, special issue on mastering information management, 7. www.ftmastering.com

Chapter 8
Managing the customer lifecycle: customer acquisition

By the end of this chapter, you will understand:

1. the meaning of the terms 'customer lifecycle' and 'new customer'
2. the strategies that can be used to recruit new customers
3. how companies can decide which potential customers to target
4. how to communicate with potential customers
5. what offers can be made to attract new customers.

Introduction

Over this and the next chapter you will be introduced to the idea of a customer lifecycle and its management. The core customer lifecycle management processes are the customer acquisition, customer development and customer retention processes. These three processes determine how companies identify and acquire new customers, grow their value to the business and retain them for the long term. We also review the key metrics or key performance indicators (KPIs) which companies can use to assess their customer lifecycle performance. We examine customer development and retention processes in the next chapter.

In this chapter you will learn about the important issue of customer acquisition, the first stage of the customer lifecycle. New customers have to be acquired to build companies. Even in well-managed companies there can be a significant level of customer attrition. These lost customers need to be replaced. We look at several important matters for CRM practitioners: which potential new customers to target, how to approach them and what to offer them.

Customer lifecycles are presented in different ways by different authorities, but basically they all attempt to do the same thing. They attempt to depict the development of a customer relationship over time. Because we are taking a management view of customer relationships, we have collapsed the customer lifecycle into three major management activities:

- acquiring new customers
- retaining existing customers
- developing customer value.

The first task in managing the customer lifecycle is to acquire customers. Customer retention is a pointless exercise if there are no customers to retain. Customer acquisition is always the most important goal during new product launches and with new business start-ups. For small businesses with ambitions to grow, customer acquisition is often as important as customer retention. A one-customer company, such as

BICC, which supplies copper cable to a single customer, British Telecom (BT), can double its customer base by acquiring one more customer. On the other hand, the loss of that single customer could spell bankruptcy.

Even with well-developed and implemented customer retention plans, customers still need replacing, sometimes at a rate of 25 per cent or more a year. In a B2C context, customers may shift out of a targeted demographic as they age and progress through the family lifecycle; their personal circumstances may change and they may no longer need or find value in your product; they may even die. In a B2B context, you may lose corporate customers because they have been acquired by another company with established buying practices and supplier preferences; they may have stopped producing the goods and services for which your company provided input; they may have ceased trading. Customers lost to these uncontrollable causes indicate that customer acquisition will always be needed to replace natural attrition.

Several important questions have to be answered when a company puts together a customer acquisition plan. These questions concern targets, channels and offers:

1. Which prospects (potential new customers) will be targeted?
2. How will these prospects be approached?
3. What offer will be made?

These issues need to be carefully considered and programmed into a properly resourced customer acquisition plan. Most marketing plans do not distinguish between customer acquisition and customer retention. They are not separately funded or plotted strategies. We recommend that companies think about these as separate but related issues, and develop appropriate strategies.

What is a new customer?

A customer can be new in one of two senses:

1. new to the product category
2. new to the company.

New-to-category

New-to-category customers are customers who have either identified a new need or have found a new category of solution for an existing need. Consider the B2C context. When a couple has their first child they have a completely new set of needs connected to the growth and nurturing of their child. This includes baby clothes, food and toys, for example. As the child grows, the parents are faced with additional new-to-category decisions, such as preschool and elementary education. Sometimes, customers also become new-to-category because they find a new category to replace an existing solution. Mobile phones have now significantly replaced card or cash-operated pay-phones in many countries. Environmentally friendlier detergents and diapers are growing their share of market, as customers switch from current products.

Sometimes, customers beat marketers to the punch by adopting established products for new uses. Marketers then catch on and begin to promote the new use. Arm and Hammer baking soda was used by customers to deodorize fridges and rubbish bins, and as a mild abrasive for whitening teeth. The manufacturer, Church and Dwight, responded to this revelation and began promoting a variety of different applications. It is now an ingredient in toothpaste. Their website, www.armhammer. com, provides visitors with many other tips for baking soda applications including cleaning, deodorizing, personal care and baking. The website encourages visitors to write in describing novel applications for the product. Automobile manufacturers noticed that many utility vehicles were not being bought by tradesmen, but as fun vehicles for weekend use. They began promoting this use, while at the same time trying to innovate in product design to meet the requirements of that market segment. The result has been the emergence of a completely new market segment: the market for sports utility vehicles (SUVs). Several websites serve this market, for example, www.suvoa.com, the site for Sports Utility Vehicle Owners of America.

The same distinction between new needs and new solutions also exists in the B2B marketplace. A customer can be new-to-category if they begin an activity that requires resources that are new to the business. For example, when McDonald's entered the coffee shop market, they needed to develop a new set of supplier relationships. New-to-category customers may also be customers who find a new solution for an existing problem. For example, some clothing manufacturers now use computer-operated sewing machines to perform tasks that were previously performed by skilled labour using traditional sewing machines.

New-to-company

The second category of new customers is customers that are new to the company. New-to-company customers are won from competitors. They might switch to your company because they feel you offer a better solution or because they value variety. Generally, new-to-company customers are the only option for growing customer numbers in mature markets where there are very few new-to-category customers. In developed economies, new players in grocery retail can only succeed by winning customers from established operators. They would not expect to convert those customers completely, but to win a share of their spending by offering better value in one or more important categories. Once the customer is in-store, the retailer will use merchandising techniques such as point-of-sale signs and displays to increase spending.

New-to-category customers may or may not be expensive to recruit. For example, when children leave home for university banks compete vigorously for their patronage. They advertise heavily in mass media, communicate direct to students, offer free gifts and low or zero-cost banking for the duration of the studentship. On the other hand, supermarket retailers incur no direct costs in attracting these same students to their local stores.

New-to-company customers can be very expensive to acquire, particularly if they are strongly committed to their current supplier. Commitment is reflected in a strong positive attitude to, or high levels of investment in, the current supplier. These both represent high switching costs. A powerful commitment to a current supplier can be difficult, and often too expensive, to break. High potential value customers are not always the most attractive prospects, because of this commitment and investment. A lower value customer with a weaker commitment to the current supplier may be a better prospect.

Portfolio purchasing

New customers can be difficult to identify in markets where customers exhibit portfolio purchasing behaviours. Customers buy on a portfolio basis when they buy from a choice set of several more or less equivalent alternatives. A customer who has not bought from one of the portfolio suppliers for a matter of months, or even years, may still regard the unchosen supplier as part of the portfolio. The supplier, on the other hand, may have a business rule that says: 'If a customer has not bought for three months, mail out a special offer'. In the UK many grocery customers shop at both Tesco and Sainsbury's. These retailers do not simply compete to acquire and retain customers. Instead they compete for a larger share of the customer's spending, that is, to grow share of wallet (SOW).

Strategic switching

You may encounter evidence of strategic switching by customers. These are customers who shift their allegiances from one supplier to another in pursuit of a better deal. Banks know that their promotional pricing stimulates hot money. This is money that is moved from account to account across the banking industry in search of a better rate of interest. Sometimes the money may only be in an account overnight.

MCI, the telecoms company, discovered that about 70 per cent of customers newly acquired from competitors stayed for four months or less. These customers had been acquired when MCI mailed a cheque valued at $25, $75 or more to competitors' customers. When the cheque was banked, this automatically triggered the transfer of service to MCI. A few months later these customers again switched suppliers when another deal was offered and the cheque was already cashed. MCI fixed the problem by adjusting the promotion. Instead of mailing an immediately cashable cheque, its promotion was relaunched as a 'staged rebate' promotion. The accounts of new customers who stayed for three, nine and 13 months were credited with sums equivalent to the cheque value that would previously have been sent.[1]

Sometimes, a customer may have been regained a second or further time as a new customer. For example, if the new parents mentioned previously were to have a second child after four years, they would most likely have been removed from mother and baby databases. A new customer record would have to be created. The customer would need to be targeted afresh. In portfolio markets, a customer who has not purchased in quarter 1 may be treated as a new customer for promotional purposes in quarter 2, as the company attempts to reactivate the customer.

Customer value estimates

Companies must choose which of several potential customers or customer segments to target for acquisition. Not all prospects have similar potential. The final choice will depend on a number of considerations.

1. What is the estimated value of the customer? This depends on the margins earned from the customer's purchases over a given time period.
2. If that customer switches from his current supplier(s), what proportion of category spending will your company earn?
3. What is the probability that the customer will switch from current supplier(s)?

Imagine a competitor's customer who will spend $5000, $6000, $7000 and $8000 with that supplier over the next four years at gross margins of 40 per cent. Without discounting those future margins, the customer is worth $10400 ($2000 + $2400 + $2800 + $3200). Let's assume that your intelligence, based on customer satisfaction and loyalty scores, suggests that you have a 40 per cent chance of converting the customer and that, once converted, you will win a 50 per cent share of the customer's available spending in that category.

The value of this customer can now be computed as follows: gross margins, multiplied by share of the customer's spending, multiplied by the probability of winning the customer's business. Using the numbers above, this customer is worth $10 400 × 0.50 × 0.40 or $2080. The question now becomes: can you recruit this customer and maintain a relationship over the next four years for less than $2080? If you can, then the customer will make a net contribution to your business. This simple algorithm allows you to compare different customer acquisition opportunities. Other things being equal, a customer that shows a higher potential contribution is a better prospect. The approach can be adjusted customer by customer and can take account of a number of additional factors such as: discounting future margins, producing differently costed approaches to customer acquisition, re-estimating future margins to take account of cross-selling opportunities, and estimating the annualized costs of customer retention.

The Conversion Model™

Jan Hofmeyr has developed the Conversion Model™. This contains a battery of questions designed to assess whether or not a customer is likely to switch. His basic premise is that customers who are not committed are more likely to be available to switch to another provider. Commitment, in turn, is a function of satisfaction with the brand or offer, attractiveness of the alternatives and involvement in the brand or offer. Involvement is low if the product or its usage context is relatively unimportant to customers. The Conversion Model™ allows customers to be segmented into four subsets according to their level of commitment: entrenched, average, shallow or convertible. There are two clusters of committed customers and two of uncommitted customers:

- **committed customers**
  - **entrenched** customers are unlikely to switch in the foreseeable future
  - **average** customers are unlikely to change in the short term, but may switch in the medium term.
- **uncommitted customers**
  - **shallow** customers have a lower commitment than average, and some of them are already considering alternatives
  - **convertible** customers are most likely to defect.

Hofmeyr suggest that companies can measure customer commitment by asking just four questions:

1. How happy are you with (whatever it is)?
2. Is this relationship something that you care about?
3. Is there any other (whatever it is) that appeals to you?
4. If so, how different is the one (whatever) from the other?

Non-customers are also segmented according to commitment scores into four availability subsets: available, ambivalent, weakly unavailable and strongly unavailable. There are two clusters that are open and two that are unavailable:

- **open non-customers**
  - **available** non-customers prefer the alternative to their current offer though they have not yet switched, and are ready to switch
  - **ambivalent** non-customers are as attracted to the alternative as they are to their current brand.
- **unavailable non-customers**
  - **weakly unavailable** non-customers prefer their current brands
  - **strongly unavailable** non-customers have a strong preference for their current brands.

Hofmeyr claims that these profiles can be used to guide both acquisition and retention strategies.[2] He suggests that where the number of open non-customers is greater than the number of uncommitted customers, companies should focus strongly on customer acquisition.

Companies need to nurture their relationships with committed customers, reassuring them that their decision is wise, and find ways to enrich and enhance their customers' experience. The strategy for uncommitted customers is to investigate why there is a low level of commitment and address the causes. Maybe it is a low-involvement category, or maybe customers are dissatisfied with their experience. Whether companies should appeal to open non-customers depends upon the value they can generate. Finally there are many potential reasons why some market segments are composed of unavailable non-customers. They may have tried your offer, and didn't find it satisfying, they may be committed to their current brand or supplier, they may be aware of your offer but find it unappealing, or they may simply be unaware of your offer. You might be able to fix this last problem with advertising or other forms of customer communication, shifting these non-customers from the unavailable cluster to the open cluster. Customer experience research might reveal what customers do not like about your offer or doing business with you, and give you some clues about how to make their experience more satisfying.

A core principle of CRM is that market or customer-related data is used to target acquisition efforts accurately. By contrast, poorly targeted acquisition efforts waste marketing budget and may alienate more prospects than they gain through irrelevant or inappropriate messaging. We now turn to the practice of new customer prospecting.

Prospecting

Prospecting is, of course, a mining term. In that context it means searching an area thought likely to yield a valuable mineral deposit. In CRM, it means searching for opportunities that might generate additional value for the company.

Prospecting is an outcome of the segmenting and targeting process described in Chapter 5. Prospects are endproducts of that process. Segmentation divides a heterogenous market into homogenous subsets, even down to the level of the unique customer. Targeting is the process of choosing which market segments, clusters or individuals, to approach with an offer. In Chapter 5, we identified several characteristics of the strategically significant customer that companies would find most attractive in a prospect. We'll now look at prospecting from the business-to-business perspective.

Business-to-business prospecting

In the B2B environment it is very often the task of marketers to generate leads for the salesperson to follow up. Leads are individuals or companies that might be worth approaching. The lead then needs to be qualified. The qualification process submits all leads to a series of questions, such as:

- Does the lead have a need for my company's products?
- Does the lead have the ability to pay?
- Is the lead authorized to buy?

If the answers are yes, yes and yes, the lead becomes a genuine prospect. Ability to pay covers both cash and credit. The ability to pay of prospective customers can be assessed by subscribing to credit rating services, such as Dun & Bradstreet or Standard & Poor's. Being a well-known name is no guarantee that a prospect is credit-worthy, as suppliers to Enron Corporation found out. Enron was one of the world's leading energy companies, employing 21 000 people, before it became bankrupt in 2001. Authority to buy may be invested in a named individual, a decision-making unit composed of a group of employees, a group composed of internal employees and external advisor(s) or, in some rare cases, an external individual or group. Andersen Consulting (now Accenture) was appointed by Chrysler to act as systems integrator for a new robotics system. Recommendations were developed by Andersen employees only, but Chrysler retained the power to veto any choice.

Once leads are qualified, companies need to decide the best channels for initiating contact. A distinction can be made between direct to customer (DTC) channels, such as salespeople, direct mail, e-mail and telemarketing, and channels that are indirect, either because they use partners or other intermediaries or because they use bought time and space in media. The improved quality of databases has meant that direct channels allow access to specific named leads in target businesses.

Sources of B2B leads

Leads come from a variety of sources. In a B2B context this includes the sources identified in Figure 8.1. Many companies are turning to satisfied customers who may be willing to generate personal referrals. Customer-related data enables many companies to identify which customers are very satisfied. These special customers can then be proactively approached for a referral. They may be prepared to write a letter or e-mail of introduction, provide a testimonial or receive a call to verify the credentials of a salesperson.

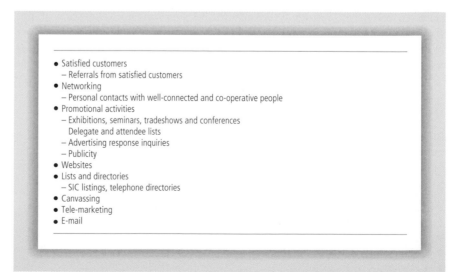

- Satisfied customers
  - Referrals from satisfied customers
- Networking
  - Personal contacts with well-connected and co-operative people
- Promotional activities
  - Exhibitions, seminars, tradeshows and conferences
    Delegate and attendee lists
  - Advertising response inquiries
  - Publicity
- Websites
- Lists and directories
  - SIC listings, telephone directories
- Canvassing
- Tele-marketing
- E-mail

Figure 8.1
Sources of business-to-business leads

Networking can be defined as follows:

> Networking is the process of establishing and maintaining business-related personal relationships.

A network might include members of a business association, friends from university or professional colleagues in other companies. In some countries it is essential to build and maintain personal networks. In China, for example, the practice of guanxi, covered in Chapter 2, means that it is well nigh impossible to do business without some personal connections already in place.

Referral networks are common in professional services. Accountants, banks, lawyers, auditors, tax consultants, estate agents will join together into a referral network in which they undertake to refer clients to other members of the network.

Promotional activities can also generate useful leads. Exhibitions, seminars, trade shows and conferences can be productive sources. Companies that pay to participate in these events may either be able to obtain privileged access to delegate and attendee lists, or to generate lists of their own, such as a list of visitors to their own stand at a trade show.

B2B marketers generally do little advertising, even though this can generate leads. B2B advertising is generally placed in highly-targeted specialist media such as trade magazines.

An important activity for some B2B companies is publicity. Publicity is an outcome of public relations (PR) activity. Publicity can be defined as follows:

> Publicity is the generation of free editorial content relevant to a company's interests.

Successful PR can generate publicity for your product or company in appropriate media. This coverage, unlike advertising, is unpaid. Though unpaid, publicity does create costs. Someone has to be paid to write the story and submit it to the media. Many magazines, trade papers and online communities are run on a shoestring. They employ very few staff and rely heavily on stories submitted by companies and their PR staff to generate editorial matter. Editors are looking for newsworthy items, such as stories about product innovation, original customer applications or human-interest stories about inventors and entrepreneurs. Editorial staff generally will edit copy to eliminate deceptive or brazen claims.

Prospecting on the Internet

Company websites can also be fruitful sources of new customers. Anyone with access to the Internet is a prospective customer. The Internet enables potential customers to search globally for products and suppliers. To be effective in new customer generation, websites must take into account the way prospects search for information. There are four main ways:[3]

1. keying in a page's URL
2. using search engines

3. exploring directories, web catalogues or portals
4. surfing.

A URL is a website address. URL stands for uniform (or universal) resource locator. By typing it into a web browser's address window, you move straight to the website. Even if you didn't know IBMs URL you could reasonably guess that it is www.ibm.com. URLs can be saved as favourites once you are sure of the address.

Search engines provide an indexed guide to websites. Users searching for information type keywords into a web-based form. The engine then reports the number of hits, that is, webpages that feature the keyed word or words. Users can then click on a hyperlink to take them to the relevant pages. To ensure that your site is hit when a prospect is searching, your website needs to be registered with appropriate search engines. There are hundreds of search engines, but among the most well-known are Google, Infoseek, Netscape, Webcrawler, AltaVista and Lycos. Sites such as www.searchenginewatch.com offer tips of how to benefit from website registration. There are also meta search engines. These are engines that search for keywords on other search engines. Among them are www.metacrawler.com and www.37.com which lets users search through 37 other search engines.

Directories or web catalogues such as Yahoo! provide a structured hierarchical listing of websites, grouped into categories such as business, entertainment and sport. Companies choose under which category to register. For example, Rolls Royce aero engine division (www.rolls-royce.com) and four other manufacturers can be accessed from Business_and_Economy > Business_to_Business > Aerospace_and_Defense > Engines > Manufacturers on the Yahoo! directory.

Portals, which were introduced in Chapter 7, are websites that act as gateways to the rest of the Internet. Portals tend to be focused on particular industries or user groups and offer facilities such as search engines, directories, customizable home pages and e-mail. For example, the portal www.CEOExpress.com provides a wealth of information and access to other sites that may be of use to busy Chief Executives (Figure 8.2).

Surfing is a term used to describe a more intuitive and less structured approach to website searching.

When prospective customers reach your site they need to be able to do what they want. This may mean searching for a product, registering for information (effectively enabling permission-based prospecting by supplying their name, alias or e-mail address), requesting a quotation, describing their requirements and preferences.

Lists of prospects can be developed from many sources such as telephone directories, business lists, chamber of commerce memberships, professional and trade association memberships, and magazine circulation data. Lists can also be bought readymade from list compilers and brokers. Lists of prospects, organized by their Standard Industrial Classification code are widely used (see Chapter 5 for more detail). Some lists are of poor quality: out-of-date, containing duplications, omissions, and other errors. High quality lists with full contact details, including phone and e-mail address tend to be more expensive. Lists can support direct marketing efforts by phone, mail, e-mail, fax or face-to-face.

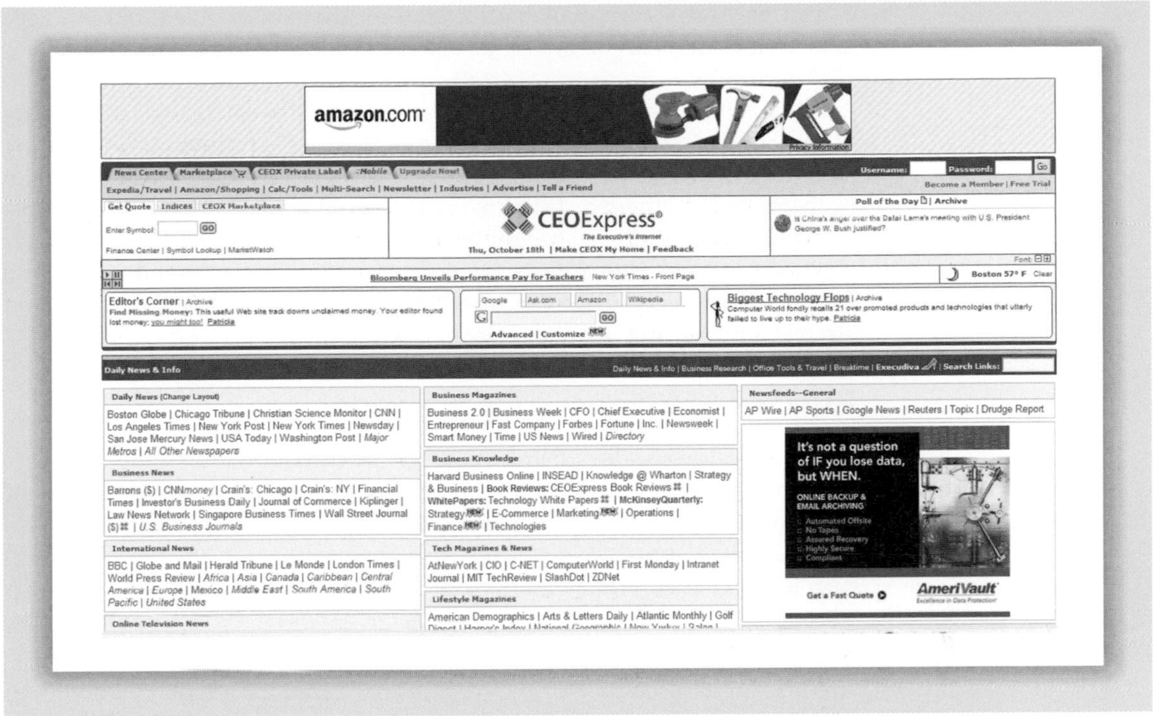

Figure 8.2 The portal CEOExpress

Canvassing involves making unsolicited calls, sometimes known as cold calls. This can be a very wasteful use of an expensive asset: the salesperson. Some companies have banned their salespeople from cold calling. Others outsource this activity to third parties. Some hotel chains, for example, use hospitality students to conduct a sales blitz that is essentially a telephone-based cold calling campaign.

Telemarketing is widely used as a more cost-effective way of prospecting than use of a salesperson. Telemarketing, sometimes called telesales, is a systematic approach to prospecting using the telephone, and, sometimes, other electronic media such as fax and e-mail. Telemarketing is usually performed by staff of customer contact centres. These are either in-house or outsourced. Outbound telemarketers make outgoing calls to identify and qualify leads. Inbound telemarketers receive calls from prospective customers. In addition to prospecting, telemarketing can be used to manage other parts of the customer lifecycle: cross-selling, handling complaints and winning back at-risk or lost customers, for example.

A growing number of companies are using e-mail for new customer acquisition. E-mail offers several clear advantages. A very large proportion of business decision makers have e-mail, although this does vary by country and industry. It is very cheap, costing about the same to send one thousand e-mails as it does to send a single e-mail. It is quick and simple for recipients to respond. Content can be personalized. Production values can be matched to audience preferences: you can use richly graphical or simple textual content. It is an asynchronous prospecting tool, in other words it is not tied to a particular timeframe like a sales call.

E-mail messages sit in mailboxes until they are read or deleted. It is a very flexible tool that can be linked to telesales follow-up, 'call-me' buttons or click-throughs.

When e-mail is permission-based, response rates can be extraordinarily high.[4] However, there is growing resistance to spam e-mail. E-mails are spammed when they are sent to large numbers of recipients who have not been properly screened. What is spam to one recipient may be valuable information to another. An important ingredient in e-mail marketing is a process by which prospects are encouraged or incentivized to provide e-mail addresses for future contact. We examine both telemarketing and e-mail campaigning in greater detail in Chapter 15.

Business-to-consumer prospecting

In B2C contexts, the distribution of customer acquisition effort is different. More emphasis is put on advertising, sales promotion, buzz or word-of-mouth and merchandising. However, all of the techniques you have just read about are also used, but generally in a different way. We'll turn to them later. First, we'll look at advertising.

Advertising

Advertising is used as a prime method for generating new customers in B2C environments. It can be defined as follows:

> Advertising is the creation and delivery of messages to targeted audiences through the purchase of time or space in media owned by others.

Advertising can be successful at achieving two different classes of communication objective: cognitive and affective. Cognition is concerned with what audiences know; affect is concerned with what they feel. Advertising alone is often insufficient to generate behavioural outcomes, such as trial purchasing. It can, however, predispose audiences to make an intention-to-buy based on what they learned about and felt towards the advertised product.

Cognitive advertising objectives include: raising awareness, developing understanding, and generating knowledge. New customers generally need to be made aware of the product and to understand what benefits it can deliver. Affective advertising objectives include developing a liking for the product and generating preference.

In high involvement purchasing contexts, where products or their usage context are personally significant and relevant, prospects will normally progress through a learn–feel–do process when making their first purchase. In other words, before they buy they acquire information that helps them learn about and compare alternatives, thus reducing perceived risk. They then develop a preference for, and intention to buy, a particular offer. Customers are essentially conducting a complex problem-solving process. Advertising is one of the sources they can use in the learn–feel part of that process. It is, however, not the only source of information, nor is it necessarily the most powerful.

High-involvement advertising can employ long copy because prospects use advertising to learn about alternatives. Comparison advertising and copy featuring endorsements by opinion formers may be influential. Media that help prospects to acquire and process information are those that have a long dwell-time, such as magazines and newspapers.

Advertising can also evoke powerful emotional responses in audiences. The type of response that advertisers seek in prospects is 'I like the look of that. I really must try it'. This is an affective response linked to a buying intention. Advertisements for fashion items, jewellery and vacation destinations often aim for an emotional response. Television advertisements evoke emotions by their clever mix of voice, music, images and sound effects. Advertisers can pre-test different executions to ensure that the right sort of emotional response is evoked.

In low-involvement contexts, where the product category or its usage context is relatively unimportant, prospects are very unlikely to go through a complex and demanding learn–feel–do process. Rather, there will be little or no prepurchase comparison of alternatives. The prospect is much more likely to simply become aware of the product and buy it. There may not even be a postpurchase evaluation of the experience, except in the most elementary of forms. Post-purchase evaluation may only take place if the product fails to deliver the benefits expected. The purchase model is therefore learn–do. The role of advertising for low-involvement products is to build and maintain brand awareness and recognition. Copy needs to be kept short: prospects won't read long advertising copy. Recognition can be achieved with the use of simple visual cues. Repetition of the ad in low involvement media such as television and radio will be needed to build awareness and recognition.

Advertisers are concerned with two major issues as they attempt to generate new customers: message and media issues. Which messages will generate most new customers, and which media are most cost-effective at customer acquisition?

Message

Although precise measurement has not been conducted, it has been suggested that heavy media users are exposed to over one thousand advertisements per week.[5] Yet how many can a person recall? In an increasingly communicated world, it is a first requirement that an advertisement must stand out from the background clutter and claim the audience's attention. Advertisers call this 'cut-through'. Without it, no cognitive, affective or behavioural outcomes can be achieved. An advertisement that stands out is one that differs from the many advertisements and other stimuli that compete for the prospect's attention. 'Standing out' is a matter of message creativity, execution and media selection. What stands out? Here are some examples:

- black and white advertisements in colour magazines
- image-based advertisements in text-dominated media
- loud advertisements in quiet media
- advertisements that leave you wondering 'what was that all about?'
- advertisements that challenge your comprehension and emotions.

Message execution is an important issue in gaining an audience's attention. Messages can be executed in many different ways. Execution describes the way in which a basic copy strategy is delivered. Basic copy strategy is the core message or theme of the campaign. Execution styles can be classified in a number of ways: rational or emotional, factual or fanciful, funny or serious. Individual forms of execution include slice of life (product being used in a recognizable context), aspirational (associates the product with a desirable outcome or lifestyle), testimonial (the product is endorsed by an opinion influencer), and comparative (the advertisement compares one or more alternatives with the advertised product).

Advertisements often close with a 'call to action', such as a suggestion that the audience clip a coupon, call a number or register online. These actions generate useful sources of prospects that can then be followed up.

Pre-testing messages on a sample of potential new customers is a way to improve the chances of an ad achieving its objectives. Among the criteria you can assess are the following:

- **recall:** how much of the advertisement can the sample recall?
- **comprehension:** does the sample understand the advertisement?
- **credibility:** is the message believable?
- **feelings evoked:** how does the sample feel about the advertisement?
- **intention to buy:** how likely is it that the sample will buy?

If you buy space or time in media that have local or regional editions, you can conduct post-tests to assess the effectiveness of different executions in achieving the desired outcomes.

Media

Media selection for new customer acquisition is sometimes quite straightforward. For example, there are print publications such as *What Digital Camera?* and *Which Mortgage?* that are targeted specifically at new-to-category prospects and are suitable for high-involvement products. An uninvolved prospect will only learn passively about your product because there is no active search for and processing of information. Consequently, for low involvement prospects, frequency is a more important media consideration than reach. These are defined as follows:

> **reach** is the total number of a targeted audience that is exposed at least once to a particular advertisement or campaign

> **frequency** is the average number of times that a targeted audience member is exposed to an advertisement or campaign.

The total number of exposures is therefore computed by multiplying reach by frequency. If your advertisement reaches two million people an average of four times, the total number of impressions or exposures is eight million. For high-involvement products lower levels of frequency are generally sufficient. Advertising agencies should be able to offer advice on how many exposures (frequency) it takes to evoke a particular response in an audience member.[6]

You can compute various media efficiency statistics to help you get better value for money from your customer acquisition budget. These include response rates and conversion rates.

Response rates provide a first-level indicator of advertisement effectiveness. Examples include the number of coupons clipped and returned or calls requesting information (RFI) made to a contact centre. Conversion rates offer a second-level indicator of advertisement effectiveness. Examples include sales made as a percentage of coupons returned or proposals submitted as a percentage of RFIs.

Table 8.1 gives you an idea of the types of statistics that can be used to evaluate and guide customer acquisition strategies. The table contains a number of descriptive and analytical statistics for four different print advertising vehicles: cost-per-thousand (column 5: how may dollars does it cost to reach 1000 of the advertising vehicle's audience), coupons returned, coupons returned as a percentage of audience reached, orders received from new customers, coupon conversion rate, total order value received, average order value and advertising effectiveness ratio (column 12: how many dollars of orders were received per dollar spent on advertising in the vehicle).

The Daily News is most cost-efficient at delivering an audience since its cost-per-thousand (CPM) is lowest (column 5). The Supermarket Tabloid returns most coupons (column 6), but runs second to the Consumer Colour Magazine in terms of coupon response rate (the percentage of the delivered audience that return a coupon – column 7). The coupon conversion rate tells you how many coupon enquiries convert into first-time customers (column 9). The Daily News generates most orders from new customers (column 8), but the Consumer Colour Magazine generates the highest total order value (column 10), highest average order value (column 11) and the best advertisement cost to total sales ratio (column 12). The Sunday News turns out to perform worse than the other vehicles in all categories. It does, however, generate a relatively large number of lower value customers quite cost effectively. It generated 175 customers spending an average of $60, and for every dollar spent on advertising it yielded revenues of $17.50.

Critics of the use of advertising for customer acquisition claim that advertisements are ineffective at customer acquisition. They argue that advertisements work on current and past customers and therefore impact more on retention.[7] Others point to the ineffectiveness of advertising at influencing sales at all. Len Lodish, for example, concluded that 'there is no simple correspondence between increased television advertising weight and increased sales'.[8] In one study he found that the sales of only 49 per cent of advertised products responded positively to increases in advertising weight.[9]

Sales promotion

Sales promotion can be defined as follows:

> any behaviour-triggering temporary incentive aimed at prospects, customers, channel partners or salespeople.

Although sales promotions can be directed at salespeople and channel members, our concern here is only with sales promotions aimed at prospects. As the definition makes clear, sales promotions offer a temporary and immediate inducement to buy a product. They are not

1	2	3	4	5	6	7	8	9	10	11	12
Vehicle	Date	Readership	Ad space cost $	Cost per thousand $	Coupons returned	Coupon response rate	Orders received from new customers	Coupon conversion rate	Total order value $	Average order value $	Ratio: Ad cost to total order value
Daily News	15/3	300 000	$ 500	$ 1.67	655	0.0022%	200	30.53%	$10 000	$ 50	1:20
Supermarket tabloid	20/3	500 000	$1000	$ 2.00	1205	0.0024%	80	6.64%	$ 3 200	$ 40	1:3.2
Sunday News	25/3	200 000	$ 600	$ 3.00	350	0.00175%	175	50.00%	$10 500	$ 60	1:17.5
Consumer colour magazine	30/3	30 000	$1000	$33.33	120	0.004%	100	83.33%	$22 000	$220	1:22

Table 8.1 Customer acquisition report

part of the normal value proposition. There are many forms of consumer sales promotion:

- **Sampling:** this is the provision of a free sample of the product. This can be delivered in a number of ways: mailed or dropped door-to-door, or bound or packed with a related item. Sampling is expensive, not only because of distribution costs, but also because it may be necessary to set up a special production run with unique promotional packaging. However, sampling is highly effective at generating a trial, especially if the sample is accompanied with a voucher offering a discount on the first regular purchase. Sampling has been used for coffee, breakfast cereal and moisturizer products. It has also been used in the online context. Charles Schwab, the execution-only broker, offered free e-trading to new customers. It signed up 8500 new customers, over 6000 of who remained active once the three month trial period ended.
- **Free trials:** some companies offer products to customers on an approval basis. If they like the product they keep it and pay. Automobile dealers offer test drives to prospective purchasers. One bedding retailer offers beds on a free trial basis to customers. They deliver the bed to the customer's home and let them try it for a month. If they don't like it the company collects the bed.
- **Discounts:** these are temporary price reductions. This reduces perceived risk and improves value for a first time purchaser. Discounts can be promoted on-pack, at point-of-sale or in the media.
- **Coupons:** these act like money. They are redeemable on purchase, at the point-of-sale.
- **Rebates or cash back:** in consumer goods markets, these are often offered on-pack and require collection of proofs of purchase. Their use has extended into automobile and mortgage markets. Take out a loan to buy a car, and get $500 in cash back from the dealer.
- **Bonus packs:** a bonus pack is a promotion in which the customer gets more volume at an unchanged price. A customer might get 2.5 litres of juice for the price of a 2 litre pack.
- **Banded packs:** a banded pack promotion offers two, or rarely three, products banded together at a bundled price. A customer might be offered a banded pack of shaving gel and aftershave balm.
- **Free premiums:** a free premium is a gift to the customer. The gift may be offered at the point-of-purchase, in packaging, or require the customer to mail, e-mail, text or phone in a request.
- **Cross-promotions:** these occur when two or more non-competing brands create a mutual promotion. A proof of purchase from a theatre entitles the patron to a 25 per cent discount on a restaurant meal, and vice versa.
- **Lotteries:** a lottery is a game of chance, not involving skill. Consumers are invited to purchase the product and be entered into a draw for a prize. Prizes are highly variable. They range from low value items to high value prizes such as personal makeovers, exotic vacations and even fully furnished houses.
- **Competitions:** unlike a lottery, a competition requires skill or knowledge. The prizes are varied, as in the case of lotteries.

Buzz or word-of-mouth

A growing number of companies are trying to attract new customers through word-of-mouth (WOM) influence, also known as buzz. Word-of-mouth can be defined as follows:

> Word-of-mouth is interpersonal communication about a product or organization in which the receiver assumes the communicator to be independent of commercial influence.

Word-of-mouth has been shown to influence receivers' knowledge, emotions, intentions and behaviours, and because of its apparent separation from commercial influence it is regarded as independent and trustworthy.[10] Brands such as Body Shop, Amazon.com, YouTube.com and Krispy Kreme owe much of their success to word-of-mouth. Marketers can promote word-of-mouth by identifying and sponsoring opinion formers, such as radio show hosts. Giving people something to talk about is a high priority for buzz marketers; this includes advertisements, slogans and product innovations that are high in conversational value and capture people's attention and interest. An example is Budweiser's use of 'Whassup?' in its TV commercials: the expression caught on in everyday communication.

Buzz marketing can be supported by online discussion groups or user forums. Viral marketing is a more carefully programmed way of enabling customers to pass on information about, or links to, products and organizations that they use or support. For example, if you buy an eBook produced in the .DNL format, each page has a 'send to a friend' button so that you can share the book with a friend. The friend has access to a certain number of free pages before a payment gateway is encountered, at which the new reader has to pay by credit card to progress.

Merchandising

Merchandising can be defined as follows:

> Merchandising is any behaviour-triggering stimulus or pattern of stimuli other than personal selling that takes place at retail or other points-of-sale.

Merchandising is designed to influence behaviour in-store or at other points of sale such as restaurants, banks or gas stations. Merchandisers have a large number of techniques available. These include retail floor plans, shelf-space positioning, special displays, window displays and point-of-sale print. Some forms of merchandising are particularly useful for generating new customers, for example money-off signs, 'as used by' and 'as advertised' signs. Related item displays place two or more related items together, for example toppings next to ice-cream or dressings next to salads. Sales of one category assist sales of the other, for example, a new type of topping or dressing. Eye-level positions on shelves are generally more productive than 'reach' or 'stoop' positions. If merchandisers can position new products in these preferred positions sales will be positively influenced (Figure 8.3).

Figure 8.3
Western Australian
meat merchandised
in Korea

Other tools for customer acquisition

As mentioned earlier in the section on B2B customer acquisition, B2C companies can also use referral schemes, promotions such as consumer exhibitions, publicity, telemarketing, e-mail and canvassing to generate new customers.

Companies believe that delighted, or even completely satisfied customers will naturally speak well of the company. Eismann, the German frozen food manufacturer, estimates that 30 per cent of its new customers are recruited by **referrals** from satisfied customers.[11] In spite of high levels of naturally-occurring referrals companies may still choose to develop a customer referral scheme (CRS). CRSs are also known as member-get-member (MGM) and recommend-a-friend (RAF) schemes. These work by inviting existing customers to recommend a friend and rewarding the recommender with a gift. It is important to choose the right customer and the right time to invite a referral. Broadly, schemes are more effective when targeted at a relevant section of the customer base, for example customers who are satisfied or customers who have just experienced excellent service. For example, companies offering roadside assistance to stranded motorists will ask for a referral when the vehicle is repaired and the customer's anxiety levels have been reduced.[12]

Case 8.1

Customer referrals at NTL

NTL is a leading Internet, telephone and pay television provider in the UK. The organization has grown both organically and through acquisition. It now has a customer base of over one million households.

To achieve further growth, NTL started to use its current customers to help with prospecting. The company developed profiles of customers who had previously referred others. This profile was mapped onto the entire database, and current customers matching the profile were contacted. NTL offered one month's free subscription to existing customers who introduced a new customer. This proved to be hugely successful, with 34 per cent of existing customers in the consumer broadband market referring at least one potential customer. After the two month promotion was complete, 29 per cent of those referred had signed up for a service with NTL.

Lexus, the automobile manufacturer, invites up to 300 potential buyers to stylish **events** such as dinner and theatre shows or dinner and concert performances. The Lexus vehicles are on display. Also invited are current Lexus owners who sit among the prospects and talk to them. Lexus knows from customer satisfaction surveys which customers to invite. It is a very soft sell. Current owners receive no direct reward for participation, other than the opportunity to enjoy the event itself.

Fashion retailers will organize fashion **shows** for current customers who are invited to bring along a friend who might be interested. Party plans have been popular for many years. Distributors of products such as Tupperware and Anne Summers sex aids organize parties in their own homes. They invite friends and neighbours along. Refreshments are offered and products are exhibited and demonstrated.

Free **publicity** such as that obtained by Richard Branson, founder of the Virgin Group of companies, enables many companies to spend less than major competitors on advertising. Branson excels at gaining publicity. When Virgin cola was launched in the USA, he hired a tank to roll into Times Square and take a 'shot' at Coca Cola's illuminated advertising sign. All the television networks were invited to film the stunt, as were representatives of the press. A huge amount of free publicity was achieved as the brand sought to build its customer base.

Telemarketing and **cold-canvassing** to people's homes is a contentious issue. Many customers feel that these methods are too intrusive, and privacy regulations may prevent companies from engaging in these practices. For example, in Australia people can register their landline and mobile telephone numbers on a 'Do Not Call' register. In some other countries, regulation is less restrictive and some industries, for example telecommunications and utilities, still use both telemarketing and door-to-door canvassing for lead generation. Outbound telemarketing can then be used for lead qualification. Selling door-to-door to well-targeted prospects is a different matter. Fuller Brushes, Avon Cosmetics, Collier's Encyclopaedias and Prudential Insurance have a long tradition of door-to-door selling.

SMS messaging can also be used for customer acquisition. Because it is text and not voice, it does not have to be 'answered' in the traditional sense. SMS has been used very successfully for local bar and club promotions among adolescent consumers. As the medium is so immediate, offers can be switched on at the last minute for highly perishable cinema and retail offers. As personal communication devices become more popular, so will the distribution of messaging in text and video formats, which will be increasingly targeted to the prospects' known profiles.

E-mail is also useful for B2C customer acquisition programmes (Figure 8.4). Over 95 per cent of people having Internet access at home use it for e-mail, often on a daily basis.[13] In the UK, organizations such as Dell Computers, Barclays Bank, Comic Relief and Epson Printers have used e-mail to acquire new customers. The same benefits and reservations outlined in the earlier discussion of e-mail also apply in the B2C context.

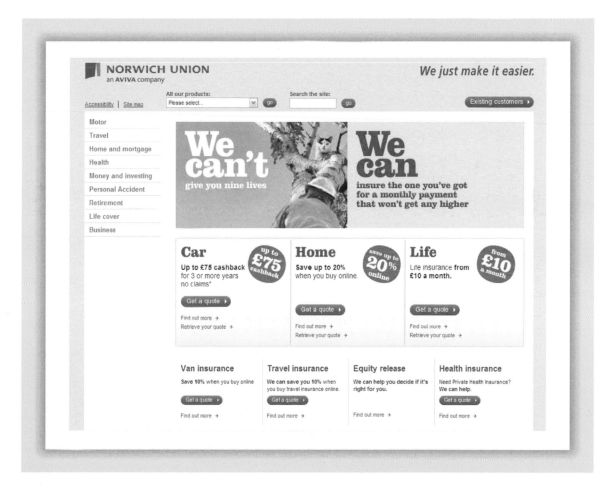

Figure 8.4 Landing page from an e-mail customer acquisition campaign[14]

Recent innovations in new customer acquisition tactics are **product placement** and product integration. Product placement involves arranging for products to be shown on display or in use in television shows, movies, videogames and web-cast productions. There is no explicit promotion of the product. It is simply seen in the production. Actors may use the product or it may be used as a background prop. There are three different compensation models for product placement. First, a company can pay for placement. Secondly, the product is donated in exchange for its appearance in the production: a form of barter. Thirdly, the product is donated to the production company to strengthen the storyline or build character, but is returned afterwards. A particular form of placement is **product integration**. This occurs where a product is integral to the storyline. Companies can pay considerable sums for their products to appear in movies. It is estimated that the product placement market was growing at a compound rate of over 16 per cent per annum, to a value of over US$3.5 billion in 2004. Researchers expect product placement to be worth US$7 billion in 2009. Over half product placements are food and beverage, health and beauty or household brands.[15]

Pitchers or pitchmen approach prospective customers and ask them to buy a product. Pitching is a well-known practice in street trading, but has now been extended into other forms of retail. For example, pitchers will approach dancers in a club and ask them if they've tried a new drink, then suggest that they buy some. Pitchers generally are expected to act as if they are unpaid advocates, therefore simulating genuine word-of-mouth.

Key performance indicators of customer acquisition programmes

CRM practitioners are concerned with three key performance indicators (KPIs) for these customer acquisition activities:

1. How many customers are acquired?
2. What is the cost per acquired customer?
3. What is the value of the acquired customer?

The ideal result would be a low cost programme that generates lots of highly valuable customers.

Some customer acquisition programmes may require major capital investment, as well as incurring marketing expenses. A supermarket operator may build new stores to increase geographic coverage. A financial services institution may invest in IT infrastructure for a new Internet-based channel. A manufacturer of automotive parts may build a new factory close to prospective customers.

Customer referral schemes are very cost effective methods for acquiring customers. They cost little to operate, but they also generate few new customers. However, the customers generated by these schemes tend to be more loyal (less likely to churn) and higher spenders. Advertising can generate a lot of enquiries, but these may be very poor quality prospects, with low conversion rates into first-time customers and, ultimately, low customer value. This is particularly true if the advertising is poorly targeted. Customers won by a sales promotion may be deal-prone. In other words, they are not acquired for the long-term, but switch whenever there is a better opportunity.

Companies can compare the relative costs of customer acquisition per channel before deciding how to spend their acquisition dollars. For example, a motoring membership organization knows that its member-get-member scheme has a direct cost per new customer of £22, compared to £100 for direct response television and £70 for door drops. The average is £35. A telecommunications company reports that it costs £52 to win a new customer through its recommend-a-friend programme, compared to an average of £100 and an advertising-generated cost of £200.[16] The costs of acquiring new customers online are variable over time and across categories. In 1999, Amazon.com claimed it was costing $29 to acquire each new customer;[17] credit card operators thought it cost $50 to $75, and mortgage customers cost $100 to $250 to acquire.[18]

Companies have a choice of acquiring new customers through relatively costly but fast-acting marketing investments, or through slower but low or zero-cost word-of-mouth processes. Julian Villanueva and colleagues have researched the effects of marketing-induced versus word-of-mouth customer acquisition on firm performance. Using data from an Internet firm that provided free web hosting to registered users during a 70-week-long observation period, they found that customers acquired through word-of-mouth were themselves productive at generating new customers through their own word-of-mouth. They also generated more word-of-mouth activity than those acquired by marketing-induced channels. Each customer acquired through marketing is expected to bring around 1.59 new customers throughout his or her lifetime, while a customer acquired through word-of-mouth is expected to bring 3.23 customers (including him or herself).[19]

Costs of customer acquisition are one-off costs that are not encountered again at any stage in a customer's tenure. The costs might include prospecting costs, advertising costs, commissions to salespeople, collateral materials, sales promotion costs, credit referencing, supplying tangibles (e.g. credit cards) and database costs. Many sales managers incentivize their salespeople to find new customers. These incentives whether cash, merchandise or some other reward, are a cost of acquisition.

Making the right offer

In addition to carefully targeting new customers for acquisition, companies need to consider what offer they will make to the target. Some industries are consistent in their use of entry-level products for customer acquisition.

Insurance companies use automobile insurance to acquire new customers. Developed countries require drivers to be insured to at least third-party level. Since insurance expires annually, it offers the prospect of repeat purchase. Generally premiums are highly discounted and offer little or no margin to the insurer. However, automobile insurance does give the company at least one year in which to cross-sell additional insurance products: home and contents insurance, travel insurance, health insurance, mortgage protection insurance and so on. Churn rates on automobile insurance can be as high as 50 per cent, giving average customer tenure of only two years. During this period insurers have to make the cross-sales.

Banks use relatively high interest rates on deposit accounts or relatively low charges on credit-cards. The world's largest pure-play Internet bank is the Citibank-owned, UK-based brand 'Egg'. The bank has used incentive rates to win new credit card customers. Nearly nine out of ten newly acquired customers stayed with the bank when the incentive rates were withdrawn. Although only launched in 1998, Egg has been able to cross-sell additional products and services into the customer base, growing from a cross-holding ratio of 1.36 average products owned in 2001 to 2.95 in 2007.

Supermarkets price high demand, frequently purchased items, such as bread, as loss leaders in order to build store traffic.

Operational CRM tools that help customer acquisition

CRM software provides a number of operational tools that help in the customer acquisition process, including lead management, campaign management and event-based marketing. We cover these in more detail in Capters 14 and 15, but introduce them here.

Lead management

Sales-force automation (SFA) software helps B2B companies to manage the selling process. An important part of that process is lead management. There are hundreds of different lead management software vendors, some installed and some on-demand. Many of these enable the recommended lead management approaches of published sales methodologies to be implemented, among them the Customer-Centric Selling, Miller Heiman and Solution Selling methodologies.

The lead management process includes a number of subprocesses, including lead generation, lead qualification, lead allocation and lead tracking. These need to operate effectively and efficiently. Lead allocation processes ensure that leads are routed to the right salesperson. Lead tracking processes trace the conversion of prospects into customers. Lead management software generally allows salespeople to customize their interactions by applying selling workflow rules that vary according to prospect attributes, such as company size and level of qualification. Sales representatives may want to reject leads, further qualify them, redefine them as opportunities, or take other actions as required.

Successful lead management programmes are supported by analytics. Sales managers want to know which lead generation programmes generate high conversion rates and/or high revenues, which leads are costly to convert and which territories have the greatest success at lead generation and conversion.

Campaign management

Campaign management software is widely deployed in B2C environments for new customer acquisition. Campaign managers design, execute and measure marketing campaigns with the support of CRM technologies. Sometimes these are multimedia campaigns across direct mail, e-mail, fax, outbound telephony and SMS platforms. The technology assists in selecting and grouping potential customer targets, tracking contacts, measuring campaign results and learning from the results how to produce more effective and efficient campaigns in the future.

Campaign management software not only enables companies to manage and execute automated and personalized campaigns, generating leads for sales follow-up, but also enables them to generate and manage contact lists, while simultaneously complying with anti-spam legislation.

Experimentation is a common feature of campaign management. Experiments can be performed on subsets of the current customer database. For example, different cells of the recency–frequency–monetary value (RFM) matrix can be treated to different offers in order to develop an understanding of the propensities to buy of different customer groups. If the results were to show that women aged 15–25 were particularly responsive to a health and beauty bundled offer, you could search for prospects matching that profile, or buy additional lists to target.

Event-based marketing

Event-based marketing (EBM) is also used to generate new customers. EBM provides companies with opportunities to approach prospects at times which have a higher probability of leading to a sale.

In retail banking, an event such as a large deposit into a savings account might trigger an approach from the bank's investment division. A name change might trigger an approach from a financial planner. A call from a customer enquiring about rates of interest on a credit card might trigger a call from a customer retention specialist.

Many B2C companies can link purchasing to life stage events. For example, finance companies target mortgages at newlyweds and empty nesters whose children have left home. Clothing retailers target different offerings at customers as they age: branded fashion clothing at single employed females; baby clothes for new mothers and so on. If you can associate purchasing with particular life stage events you'll be well placed to target your customer acquisition efforts.

Public events, such as interest rate falls or hikes, tax law changes and weather events or competitive events, such as new product launches, might signal an EBM opportunity. For example, an insurance company might launch a health insurance campaign following announcements in the press of an upcoming influenza epidemic.

Support from CRM analytics

Clearly, these operational CRM tools have to be supported by sound analytics to ensure that the right offer is made to the right prospect through the right channel at the right time.

It is often possible to query current customer-related databases for clues to guide customer acquisition. Supermarket operators can mine transactional data to provide insight into the baskets of goods that customers buy. If you were to find that 60 per cent of customers buying frozen apple pies also bought premixed custard, you might think it worthwhile targeting the other 40 per cent with an offer. A bank wanting to generate new customers for its savings account can develop a model predicting propensity to buy based on current product ownership. In the B2B environment, salespeople may have entered data about prospects' satisfaction with competitors' offerings into their sales call records. Those who are less satisfied will probably show a higher propensity to switch, and may be worth targeting with an offer.

Affiliation data can also be used to guide customer acquisition. Customers may be members of, or otherwise associated with, a number of organizations: a university, a sports club or a charity. Affinity marketers recognize membership as an opportunity. Banks like MBNA have led the way in affinity marketing of credit cards. MBNA, the organization and the member all benefit from the arrangement. MBNA offers a credit card to members of the organization. The organization receives a fee for allowing the bank access to its member data. Members enjoy a specially branded card and excellent customer experience from the bank. Affinity groups include members of the World Wildlife Fund, fans of Manchester United and congregations of the Uniting Church.

Case 8.2

How Standard Life used predictive analytics for customer acquisition

Standard Life used the SPSS data mining product, Clementine, to understand the characteristics of its mortgage clients better, so it could more accurately search for potential new clients. Also, the bank now has the capability to profile incoming prospects quickly and personalize their web experiences accordingly. As a result of its data mining efforts, Standard Life was able to build a propensity-to-buy model for the Standard Life bank mortgage, discover the key drivers for purchasing a remortgage product, achieve a nine-times greater response to its campaigning to the profiled group than a control group, and generate $47 million of additional mortgage business.

Source: SPSS[20]

Summary

Customer acquisition is the first issue that managers face as they attempt to build a valuable customer base. There are three major decisions to be made: which prospects to target; how to communicate with them; and what offer to communicate to them. New customers are of two kinds. They are either new to the product category or new to the company. In principle, the best prospects are those that have potential to become strategically significant customers, but any customer that generates value over and above their acquisition cost is a net contributor. You will certainly want to recruit new customers that generate more profit than they consume in acquisition and retention costs.

Business-to-business prospects are generated in a number of ways, including referrals, interpersonal networks, promotional activities such as exhibitions, trade shows and conferences, advertising, publicity and public relations, canvassing, telemarketing and e-mail.

New customers for consumer companies can be generated from much the same sources as B2B prospects, but much greater effort is put into advertising, sales promotion, buzz or word-of-mouth and merchandising.

Operational CRM applications such as lead management, campaign management and event-based marketing are useful disciplines for customer acquisition. CRM analytics underpin the success of these applications. The transactional histories of current customers can be analysed and the cost-effectiveness of different customer acquisition strategies can be computed. By analysing customer data, companies are better informed about which prospects are most promising and which offers to make. Predictive modelling can determine relationship-starter products, such as automotive insurance which is used to acquire customers in the personal insurance market. When sales have been made and the customer's permission to use their information has been obtained, other products can be cross-sold, turning acquisition into repeat purchase and subsequently into customer retention.

References

1. Peppers, D. and Rogers, M. (1997) *Enterprise one-to-one*. London: Piatkus.
2. Hofmeyr, J. and Rice, B. (2000) *Commitment-led marketing: the key to brand profits is in the customer's mind*. Chichester: John Wiley.
3. Chaffey, D., Mayer, R., Johnston, K. and Ellis-Chadwick, F. (2000) *Internet marketing*. London: Financial Times/Prentice Hall.
4. Godin, S. (1999) *Permission marketing: turning strangers into friends and friends into customers*. New York: Simon and Schuster.
5. See discussion at http://www.frankwbaker.com/adsinaday.htm
6. Herbert Krugman claimed that three exposures were enough. See Krugman, H.E. (1975) What makes advertising effective? *Harvard Business Review*, March–April, p. 98.

7. Ehrenberg, A.S.C. (1974) Repetitive advertising and the consumer. *Journal of Advertising Research*, Vol. 14, pp. 25–34; Barnard, N. and Ehrenberg, A.S.C. (1997) Advertising: strongly persuasive or just nudging? *Journal of Advertising Research*, Vol. 37(1), pp. 21–31.

8. Lodish, L., Abraham, M., Kalmenson, S., Livelsberger, J., Lubetkin, B., Richardson, B. and Stevens, M.E. (1995) How TV advertising works: a meta-analysis of 389 real-world split cable TV advertising experiments. *Journal of Marketing Research*, Vol. 32, May–June, pp. 125–139.

9. Abraham, M.M. and Lodish, L. (1990) Getting the most out of advertising and promotion. *Harvard Business Review*, Vol. 68(3), pp. 50–56.

10. Buttle, F. (1998) Word-of-mouth: understanding and managing referral marketing. *Journal of Strategic Marketing*, Vol. 6, pp. 241–254.

11. Naumann, E. (1995) *Creating customer value: the path to sustainable competitive advantage*. Cincinnati, OH: International Thomson Press.

12. Buttle, F. and Kay, S. (2000) RAFs, MGMs and CRSs: Is £10 enough? Proceedings of the Academy of Marketing Annual Conference.

13. LBM Internet, UK. Personal communication.

14. Courtesy of Norwich Union. http://www.norwichunion.com/

15. http://www.pqmedia.com/ppsm2005-es.pdf. Accessed 20 October 2007.

16. Buttle, F. and Kay, S. (2000) RAFs, MGMs and CRSs: Is £10 enough? Proceedings of the Academy of Marketing Annual Conference.

17. Lee, J. (1999) Net stock frenzy. *Fortune*, Vol. 39(2), 1 February, pp. 148–151.

18. Gurley, J.W. (1998) The soaring cost of e-commerce. *Fortune*, Vol. 138(2), 3 August, pp. 226–228.

19. Villanueva, J., Yoo, S. and Hanssens, D.M. (2006) The impact of marketing-induced versus word-of-mouth customer acquisition on customer equity. Marketing Science Institute working paper 06–119.

20. http://www.spss.com/success/template_view.cfm?Story_ID=78. Accessed 25 July 2007.

Chapter 9

Managing the customer lifecycle: customer retention and development

By the end of this chapter, you will understand:

1. what is meant by the term 'customer retention'
2. the economics of customer retention
3. how to select which customers to target for retention
4. the distinction between positive and negative customer retention
5. several strategies for improving customer retention performance
6. several strategies for growing customer value
7. why and how customers are 'sacked'.

Introduction

The customer lifecycle is made up of three core customer management processes: customer acquisition, customer retention and customer development. The processes of customer retention and development are the focus of this chapter. Customer acquisition is covered in Chapter 8.

The major strategic purpose of CRM is to manage, for profit, a company's relationships with customers through three stages of the customer lifecycle: customer acquisition, customer retention and customer development.

A customer retention strategy aims to keep a high proportion of valuable customers by reducing customer defections (churn), and a customer development strategy aims to increase the value of those retained customers to the company. Just as customer acquisition is focused on particular prospects, retention and development also focus on particular customers. Focus is necessary because not all customers are worth retaining and not all customers have potential for development.

We will deal with the issue of retention first, before turning to development.

A number of important questions have to be answered when a company puts together a customer retention strategy.

- Which customers will be targeted for retention?
- What customer retention strategies will be used?
- How will the customer retention performance be measured?

We believe that these issues need to be carefully considered and programmed into a properly resourced customer retention plan. Many companies, perhaps as many as six out of ten, have no explicit customer retention plan in place.[1] Most companies spend a majority of their time, energy and resources chasing new business, with 75 per cent or more of marketing budgets being earmarked for customer acquisition.[2]

What is customer retention?

Customer retention is the maintenance of continuous trading relationships with customers over the long term. Customer retention is the mirror image of customer defection or churn. High retention is equivalent to low defection.[3]

Conventionally, customer retention is defined as:[4]

> Customer retention is the number of customers doing business with a firm at the end of a financial year, expressed as percentage of those who were active customers at the beginning of the year.

However, the appropriate interval over which retention rate should be measured is not always one year. Rather, it depends on the customer repurchase cycle. Car insurance and magazine subscriptions are bought on an annual basis. Carpet tiles and hi-fis are not. If the normal hi-fi replacement cycle is four years, then retention rate is more meaningful if it is measured over four years instead of twelve months. Additional complexity is added when companies sell a range of products and services, each with different repurchase cycles. Automobile dealers might sell cars, parts, fuel and service to a single customer. These products have different repurchase cycles which make it very difficult for the dealer to have a whole of customer perspective on retention.

Sometimes companies are not clear about whether an individual customer has defected. This is because of the location of customer-related data, which might be retained in product silos, channel silos or functional silos.

- **Product silos:** consider personal insurance. Insurance companies often have product-based information systems. Effectively, they regard an insurance policy as a customer. If the policy is renewed, the customer is regarded as retained. However, take a customer who shops around for a better price and, after the policy has expired, returns to the original insurer. The insurer may take the new policy to mean a new customer has been gained, and an old customer has churned. They would be wrong.
- **Channel silos:** in the B2B context, independent office equipment dealers have formed into cooperative buying groups to purchase goods at lower prices and benefit from other economies of scale in marketing. When a dealer stops buying direct from Brother Electronics and joins a buying group, Brother's customer data may report a defection, but all that has happened is that the dealer has begun to buy through a different channel.[5] Telecommunications companies acquire customers through many channels. Consider a customer who buys a 12 month mobile phone contract from a Vodafone-owned retail outlet. Part way through the year Vodafone launches a new pay-as-you-go product with no contractual obligation. The customer allows her current contract to expire and then buys the new pay-as-you-go product, not from a Vodafone outlet but from a supermarket.

Vodafone regards her as a lost customer because the contract was not renewed. They would be wrong.

● **Functional silos:** customer-related data are often kept in functional silos that are not integrated to provide a whole of customer perspective. A customer might not have made a product purchase for several years, and is therefore regarded as a churned customer on the sales database. However, the same customer might have several open queries or issues on the customer service database, and is therefore regarded as still active.

The use of aggregates and averages in calculating customer retention rates can mask a true understanding of retention and defection. This is because customers differ in their sales, costs-to-serve and buying behaviours. It is not unusual for a small number of customers to account for a large proportion of company revenue. If you have 100 customers and lose ten in the course of a year, your raw defection rate is 10 per cent. But what if these customers account for 25 per cent your company's sales? Is the true defection rate 25 per cent? Consideration of profit makes the computation even more complex. If the 10 per cent of customers that defected produce 50 per cent of your company's profits, is the true defection rate 50 per cent?

What happens if the 10 per cent of lost customers are at the other end of the sales and profit spectrum? In other words what if they buy very little and/or have a high cost-to-serve? It could be that they contribute less than 5 per cent to sales and actually generate a negative profit, i.e. they cost more to serve than they generate in margin. The loss of some customers might improve the company's profit performance. It is not inconceivable that a company could retain 90 per cent of its customers, 95 per cent of its sales and 105 per cent of its profit!

A solution to this problem is to consider three measures of customer retention:

1. **Raw customer retention rate:** this is the number of customers doing business with a firm at the end of a trading period, expressed as percentage of those who were active customers at the beginning of the period.
2. **Sales-adjusted retention rate:** this is the value of sales achieved from the retained customers, expressed as a percentage of the sales achieved from all customers who were active at the beginning of the period.
3. **Profit-adjusted retention rate:** this is the profit earned from the retained customers, expressed as a percentage of the profit earned from all customers who were active at the beginning of the period.

A high raw customer retention rate does not always signal excellent customer retention performance. This is because customer defection rates vary across cohorts of customers. Defection rates tend to be much higher for newer customers than longer tenure customers. Over time, as seller and buyer demonstrate commitment, trust grows and it becomes progressively more difficult to break the relationship.[6] Successful customer acquisition programmes could produce the effect of a high customer defection rate, simply because new customers are more likely to defect.

A high sales-adjusted customer retention rate might also need some qualification. Consider a corporate customer purchasing office equipment. The customer's business is expanding fast. It purchased 30 personal computers (PCs) last year, 20 of which were sourced from Apex Office Supplies. This year it bought 50 PCs, of which 30 were from Apex. From Apex's point of view it has grown customer value by 50 per cent (from 20 to 30 machines), which it might regard as an excellent achievement. However, in a relative sense, Apex's share of customer has fallen from 67 per cent (20/30) to 60 per cent (30/50). How should Apex regard this customer? The customer is clearly a retained customer in a 'raw' sense, has grown in absolute value, but has fallen in relative value. Consider also a retail bank customer who maintains a savings account, but during the course of a year transfers all but a few dollars of her savings to a different institution in pursuit of a better interest rate. This customer is technically still active, but significantly less valuable to the bank.

Manage customer retention or value retention?

This discussion indicates that companies should focus on retaining customers that contribute value. Sometimes this will mean that the focus is not on retention of customers, *per se*, but on retention of share of wallet. In the banking industry, for example, it may be more important for companies to focus on managing the overall downward migration of customer spending than managing customer retention. Many customers simply change their buying behaviour rather than defect. Changes in buying behaviour may be responsible for greater changes in customer value than defection. One bank, for example, lost 3 per cent of its total balances when 5 per cent of checking account customers defected in a year, but lost 24 per cent of its total balances when 35 per cent of customers reduced the amounts deposited in their checking accounts. The need to manage migration, rather than defection, is particularly important when customers engage in portfolio purchasing by transacting with more than one supplier.[7]

Improving customer retention is an important objective for many CRM implementations. Its definition and measurement need to be sensitive to the sales, profitability and value issues discussed previously. It is important to remember that the fundamental purpose of focusing CRM efforts on customer retention is to ensure that the company maintains relationships with value-adding customers. It may not be beneficial to maintain relationships with all customers; some may be too costly to serve, others may be strategic switchers constantly in search of a better deal. These can be value-destroyers, not value-adders.

Economics of customer retention

There is a strong economic argument in favour of customer retention, which was first introduced in Chapter 2. The argument goes as follows:[8]

1. **Increasing purchases as tenure grows:** over time, customers come to know their suppliers. Providing the relationship is satisfactory, trust grows while risk and uncertainty are reduced. Therefore, customers commit more of their spending to those suppliers with whom they have a proven and satisfactory relationship. Also, because suppliers develop deeper customer intimacy over time, they can enjoy better yields from their cross-selling efforts.

2. **Lower customer management costs over time:** the relationship start-up costs that are incurred when a customer is acquired can be quite high. It may take several years for enough profit to be earned from the relationship to recover those acquisition costs. For example, it can take six years to recover the costs of winning a new retail bank customer.[9] In the B2B context in particular, ongoing relationship maintenance costs such as selling and service costs can be low relative to the costs of winning the account. Therefore, there is a high probability that the account will become more profitable on a period-by-period basis as tenure lengthens. These relationship maintenance costs may eventually be significantly reduced or even eliminated as the parties become closer over time. In the B2B context, once automated processes are in place, transaction costs are effectively eliminated. Portals largely transfer account service costs to the customer. In the B2C context, especially in retailing, the assertion that acquisition costs generally exceed retention costs is hard to prove. This is in part because it is very difficult to isolate and measure customer acquisition costs.[10]

3. **Customer referrals:** customers who willingly commit more of their purchases to a preferred supplier are generally more satisfied than customers who do not. They are therefore more likely to utter positive word-of-mouth and influence the beliefs, feelings and behaviours of others. Research shows that customers who are frequent buyers are heavier referrers. For example, online clothing customers who have bought once refer three other people; after ten purchases they will have referred seven. In consumer electronics, the one-time customer refers four; the ten times customer refers 13. The referred customers spend about 50 to 75 per cent of the referrer's spending over the first three years of their relationship.[11] However, it is also likely that newly acquired customers, freshly enthused by their experience, would be powerful word-of-mouth advocates, perhaps more than longer-term customers who are more habituated.[12]

4. **Premium prices:** customers who are satisfied in their relationship may reward their suppliers by paying higher prices. This is because they get their sense of value from more than price alone. Customers

in an established relationship are also likely to be less responsive to price appeals offered by competitors.

These conditions mean that retained customers are generally more profitable than newly acquired customers. Drawing from their consulting experience, Dawkins and Reichheld report that a 5 per cent increase in customer retention rate leads to an increase in the net present value of customers by between 25 and 95 per cent across a wide range of industries, including credit cards, insurance brokerage, automobile services and office building management.[13] In short, customer retention drives up customer lifetime value.

Which customers to retain?

Simply, the customers who have greatest strategic value to your company are prime candidates for your retention efforts. These are the customers we defined as having high lifetime value or who are otherwise strategically significant as high volume customers, benchmarks, inspirations or door openers, as described in Chapter 5.

You need to bear in mind that the cost of customer retention may be considerable. Your most valued customers are also likely to be very attractive to your competitors. If the costs of retaining customers become too great then they might lose their status as strategically significant.

The level of commitment between your customer and you will figure in the decision about which customers to retain. If the customer is highly committed, they will be impervious to the appeals of competitors, and you will not need to invest so much in their retention. However, if you have highly significant customers who are not committed, you may want to invest considerable sums in their retention.

Some companies prefer to focus their retention efforts on their recently acquired customers. They often have greater future lifetime value potential than longer tenure customers. There is some evidence that retention rates rise over time, so if defections can be prevented in the early stages of a relationship, there will be a pay-off in future revenue streams.[14] A further justification for focusing on recently acquired customers comes from research into service failures. When customers experience service failure, they may be more forgiving if they have a history of good service with the service provider. In other words, customers who have been recently acquired and let down are more likely to defect or reduce their spending than customers who have a satisfactory history with the supplier.[15]

Retention efforts where there is portfolio purchasing can be very difficult. Should effort be directed at retaining the high-share customer with whom you have a profitable relationship, the medium-share customer from whom you might lose additional share to competitors or the low-share customer from whom there is considerable lifetime value potential? The answer will depend on the current value of the customer, the potential for growing that value, and the cost of maintaining and developing the relationship.

Strategies for customer retention

Positive and negative retention strategies

An important distinction can be made between strategies that lock the customer in by penalizing their exit from a relationship, and strategies that reward a customer for remaining in a relationship. The former are generally considered negative, and the latter positive, customer retention strategies. Negative customer retention strategies impose high switching costs on customers, discouraging their defection.

In a B2C context, mortgage companies have commonly recruited new customers with attractive discounted interest rates. When the honeymoon period is over, these customers may want to switch to another provider, only to discover that they will be hit with early redemption and exit penalties. Customers wishing to switch retail banks find that it is less simple than anticipated: direct debits and standing orders have to be reorganized. In a B2B context, a customer may have agreed a deal to purchase a given volume of raw material at a quoted price. Some way through the contract a lower cost supplier makes a better offer. The customer wants to switch, but finds that there are penalty clauses in the contract. The new supplier is unwilling to buy the customer out of the contract by paying the penalties.

Some customers find these switching costs are so high that they remain customers, though unwillingly. The danger for CRM practitioners is that negative customer retention strategies produce customers who feel trapped. They are likely to agitate to be freed from their obligations, taking up much management time. Also, they may utter negative word-of-mouth. They are unlikely to do further business with that supplier. Companies that pursue these strategies argue that customers need to be aware of what they are buying and the contracts they sign. The total cost of ownership (TCO) of a mortgage should, and does, include early redemption costs.

When presented with dissatisfied customers complaining about high relationship exit (switching) costs, companies have a choice. They can either enforce the terms and conditions, or not. The latter path is more attractive when the customer is strategically significant, particularly if the company can make an offer that matches that of the prospective new supplier.

Positive customer retention strategies

In the following sections we look at a number of positive customer retention strategies, including creating customer delight, adding customer-perceived value, creating social and structural bonds and building customer engagement.

Customer delight

It is very difficult to build long-term relationships with customers if their needs and expectations are not understood and well met. It is a fundamental precept of modern customer management that companies should understand customers, and then acquire and deploy resources to ensure their satisfaction and retention. This is why CRM is grounded on detailed customer-related knowledge. Customers that you are not able to serve well may be better served by your competitors.

Delighting customers, or exceeding customer expectations, means going beyond what would normally satisfy the customer. This does not necessarily mean being world-class or best-in-class. It does mean being aware of what it usually takes to satisfy the customer and what it might take to delight or pleasantly surprise the customer. You cannot really strategize to delight the customer if you do not understand the customer's fundamental expectations. You may stumble onto attributes of your performance that do delight the customer, but you cannot consistently expect to do so unless you have deep customer insight. Consistent efforts to delight customers show your commitment to the relationship. Commitment builds trust. Trust begets relationship longevity.

Customer delight occurs when the customer's perception of their experience of doing business with you exceeds their expectation. In formulaic terms:

$$CD = P > E$$

where CD = customer delight, P = perception and E = expectation.

This formula implies that customer delight can be influenced in two ways: by managing expectations or by managing performance. In most commercial contexts customer expectations exceed customer perceptions of performance. In other words, customers can generally find cause for dissatisfaction. You might think that this would encourage companies to attempt to manage customer expectations down to levels that can be delivered. However, competitors may well be improving their performance in an attempt to meet customer expectations. If your strategy is to manage expectations down, you may well lose customers to the better performing company. This is particularly likely if you fail to meet customer expectations on important attributes.

Customers have expectations of many attributes, for example product quality, service responsiveness, price stability and the physical appearance of your people and vehicles. These are unlikely to be equally important. It is critical to meet customer expectations on attributes that are important to the customer. Online customers, for example, look for rapid and accurate order fulfilment, good price, high levels of customer service and website functionality. Online retailers must meet these basic requirements.

Dell Computers believes that customer retention is the outcome of their performance against three variables: order fulfilment (on-time, in full, no error (OTIFNE)), product performance (frequency of problems encountered by customers) and after-sales service (percentage of problems fixed first time by technicians). The comments in parentheses are the metrics that Dell uses.

Figure 9.1 identifies a number of priorities for improvement (PFIs) for a restaurant company. The PFIs are the attributes where customer satisfaction scores are low, but the attributes are important to customers. In the example, the PFIs are food quality and toilet cleanliness. There would be no advantage in investing in speedier service or more helpful staff.

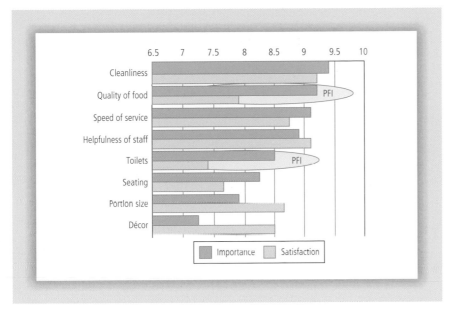

Figure 9.1
Using customer satisfaction and importance data to identify priorities for improvement

Kano's customer delight model

Noriaki Kano has developed a product quality model that distinguishes between three forms of quality. Basic qualities are those that the customer routinely expects in the product. These expectations are often unexpressed until the product fails. For example, a car's engine should start first time every time, and the sunroof should not leak. The second form is linear quality. These are attributes of which the customer wants more or less; for example, better comfort, better fuel economy and reduced noise levels. Marketing research can usually identify these requirements. Better performance on these attributes generates better customer satisfaction. The third form is attractive quality. These are attributes that surprise, delight and excite customers. They are answers to latent, unarticulated, needs and are often difficult to identify in marketing research. As shown in Figure 9.2, Kano's analysis suggests that customers can be delighted in two ways: by enhancing linear qualities beyond expectations and by creating innovative attractive qualities.[16]

Exceeding expectations need not be costly. For example, a sales representative could do a number of simple things such as:

● volunteer to collect and replace a faulty product from a customer rather than issuing a credit note and waiting for the normal call cycle to schedule a call on the customer

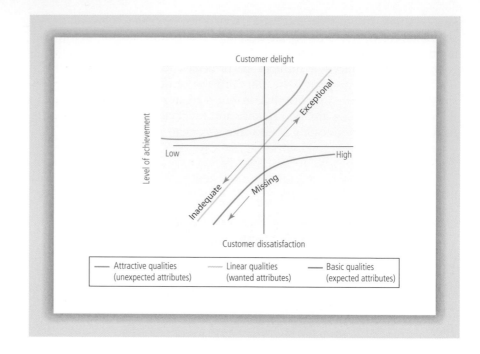

Figure 9.2
Customer delight
through product
quality.
Source: Kano 1995

- offer better, lower cost solutions to the customer, even though that might reduce profit margin
- provide information about the customer's served market. A packaging company, for example, might alert a fast-moving consumer goods manufacturer customer to competitive initiatives in their served markets.

Some efforts to delight customers can go wrong. For example, sooner is not necessarily better: if a retail store customer has requested delivery between 1 pm and 3 pm, and the driver arrives an hour early, the truck may clog up goods inwards and interfere with a carefully scheduled unload plan. Many contact centres play music while callers are waiting online. This is to divert the caller's attention and to create the illusion of faster passage of time. However, the cycle time of the selected music must not be too fast, otherwise callers will be exposed to the same songs repeatedly. Also, the music needs to be appropriate to the context. Customers may not appreciate '(I Can't Get No) Satisfaction' by the Rolling Stones if they are waiting online to complain.

A number of companies have adopted 'Customer Delight' as their mission, including Cisco, American Express and Kwik Fit, the auto service chain. Others pay homage to the goal but do not organize to achieve it. In the service industries, customer delight requires frontline employees to be trained, empowered and rewarded for doing what it takes to delight customers. It is in the interaction with customers that contact employees have the opportunity to understand and exceed their expectations. The service quality attributes of empathy and responsiveness are on show when employees successfully delight customers.

Companies sometimes complain that investing in customer delight is unproductive. As noted earlier, expectations generally increase as competitors strive to offer better value to customers. Over time, as customers experience delight, their expectations change. What was exceptional becomes the norm. In Kano's terms, what used to be an attractive attribute becomes a linear or basic attribute. It no longer delights. Delight decays into normal expectation, and companies have to look for new ways to pleasantly surprise customers. In a competitive environment, it seems to make little sense to resist the quest for customer delight because competitors will simply drive up expectations anyway.

Add customer-perceived value

The second major positive customer retention strategy is to add customer-perceived value. Companies can explore ways to create additional value for customers. The ideal is to add value for customers without creating additional costs for the company. If costs are incurred then the value-adds may be expected to recover those costs. For example, a customer club may be expected to generate a revenue stream from its membership.

There are three common forms of value-adding programme: loyalty schemes, customer clubs and sales promotions.

Loyalty schemes

Loyalty schemes reward customers for their patronage. Loyalty schemes or programmes can be defined as follows:

> A loyalty programme is a scheme that offers delayed or immediate incremental rewards to customers for their cumulative patronage.

The more a customer spends, the higher the reward. Loyalty schemes have a long history. In 1844, in the UK, the Rochdale Pioneers developed a cooperative retailing operation that distributed surpluses back to members in the form of a dividend. The surpluses were proportionate to customer spend. S&H Pink Stamps and Green Shield stamps were collected in the 1950s and 1960s, and redeemed for gifts selected from catalogues. In the 1970s, Southwest Airlines ran a 'Sweetheart Stamps' programme that enabled travellers to collect proofs of purchase and surrender them for a free flight for their partner.[17]

Today's CRM-enabled loyalty schemes owe their structure to the frequent flier programmes (FFP) that started with American Airlines' Advantage programme in 1981. The airline made a strategic decision to use its spare capacity as a resource to generate customer loyalty. Airlines are high fixed-cost businesses. Costs do not change much, regardless of whether the load factor is 25 per cent or 95 per cent. American knew that filling the empty seats would have little impact on costs, but could impact significantly on future demand. The airline searched its reservation system, SABRE, for details of frequent fliers in order to offer them the reward of free flights.

This basic model has migrated from airlines into many other B2C sectors: hotels, restaurants, retail, car hire, gas stations and bookstores, for example. It has also transferred into B2B contexts with many suppliers offering loyalty rewards to long-term customers.

The mechanics of these schemes have changed over time. Initially, stamps were collected. The first card-based schemes were anonymous, i.e. they carried no personal data, not even the name of the participant. Then magnetic stripe cards were introduced, followed by chip-embedded cards that carried a lot of personal and transactional data. Innovators developed their own individual schemes. Eventually, these transformed into linked schemes, in which, for example, it was possible to collect air miles from various participating companies such as gas stations, credit cards and food retailers. Current schemes are massively different from the early programmes. For example, Nectar is a consortium loyalty scheme operating in the UK managed not by the participants, but by an independent third party. Its core retail participants are all number one or two in their respective markets: Sainsbury's, Barclaycard, Debenhams and BP. Shoppers register with the scheme, then carry a single magnetic stripe card and collect points that are converted into vouchers redeemable in a wide range of retailers, including supermarkets, liquor stores, catalogue retailers, restaurants, hotels, cinemas, travel outlets and tourist attractions. Each of the major retail participants had been a member of another loyalty programme, and customers were able to convert their existing credits to Nectar points (see Figure 9.3).

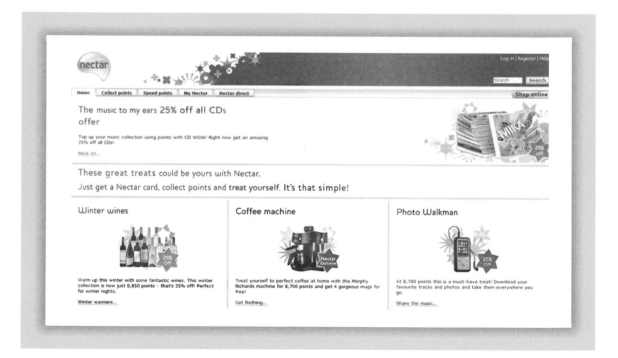

Figure 9.3 Nectar loyalty program

Loyalty programmes provide added value to consumers at two points, during credit acquisition and at redemption. Although the credits have no material value until they are redeemed, they may deliver some pre-redemption psychological benefits to customers, such as a sense of belonging and of being valued, and an enjoyable anticipation of desirable future events. At the redemption stage, customers receive both psychological and material benefits. The reward acts to positively reinforce purchase behavior. It also demonstrates that the company appreciates its customers. This sense of being recognized as valued and important can enhance customers' overall sense of well-being and emotional attachment to the firm. However, customers can become loyal to the scheme, rather than to the company or brand behind the scheme.[18]

Loyalty schemes are not without critics. Critics question their cost and effectiveness. Certainly, they can be very expensive to establish and manage. In respect of operating costs, retail schemes typically reward customers with a cash rebate or vouchers equivalent to 1 per cent of purchases. This comes straight out of the bottom line so a retailer that is making 5 per cent margin loses one-fifth or 20 per cent of its profit to fund the scheme. There may also be a significant investment in technology to support the scheme, and marketing to launch and sustain the scheme. Supermarket operator Safeway dropped its UK loyalty programme, which had been costing about £30 million annually. Shell is reported to have spent up to £40 million to develop its smart card scheme.[19] Unredeemed credits represent liabilities for scheme operators. For example, it has been suggested that if all the unused air miles were redeemed on the same day it would take 600 000 Boeing 747s to meet the demand.[20]

Case 9.1

Loyalty programme at Boots the Chemist

Boots the Chemist is the UK's leading health and beauty retailer. Ninety per cent of the UKs 60 million plus population visits a Boots store at least once a year. The company has an annual turnover of around £3 billion from a network of some 1500 stores in the UK and Irish Republic.

Boots launched their CRM strategy in 1999. It was built around the 'Advantage Card', a loyalty programme enabled by a chip-embedded smart card. The standard reward for purchases is four points for every £1 spent, equivalent to a 4 per cent discount or rebate. This is a very generous rate of reward compared to the other retail sectors, where the major supermarket loyalty schemes represent a 1 per cent saving for customers.

After an initial investment in excess of £30 million, the programme has become the third largest retail loyalty scheme in the UK. Boots reported that it took three years to achieve the programme's revenue objectives, and there have been many other benefits such as higher levels of customer retention, increased in-store spending and overall increased profitability.

Boots took its time to introduce the scheme, rather than rapidly following the trend to loyalty schemes in the early 1990s. It conducted extensive market research to determine which customer segments to target, how to differentiate their programme and how to ensure that it fitted the organization's image. The market research discovered that 83 per cent of Boots' customers were female, aged 20–45, who on 55 per cent of their visits to a store purchased a non-essential 'indulgent' item. Considering the results from the market research, the 'Advantage Card' was targeted towards female customers, rewarding them with indulgent items instead of reducing the cost of their normal shopping.

Since inception the card has become the largest smart card-based retail loyalty card scheme in the world. It currently has over 13 million cardholders, and more than 40 per cent of transactions in-store are now linked to the card.

Schemes are also criticized for their effectiveness. Critics claim that schemes have become less distinctive and value-adding as many competitors now operate me-too programmes. Indeed, it is very hard to find any hotel chain that does not have a loyalty programme. Customers now expect to accumulate credits as part of the standard hotel value proposition. Many UK supermarket shoppers carry loyalty cards from more than one supermarket.[21] The customer's choice set when grocery shopping might include all suppliers with whom they have a card-based relationship.

One major concern is that loyalty schemes may not be creating loyalty at all. Loyalty takes two forms: attitudinal and behavioural loyalty. Attitudinal loyalty is reflected in positive affect towards the brand or supplier. Behavioural loyalty is reflected in purchasing behaviour.[22] There is very little longitudinal evidence about shifts in customer behaviours after joining a loyalty scheme. One retailing study, however, using longitudinal data from a convenience store franchise, found that shoppers who were heavy buyers at the beginning of a loyalty programme did not change their patronage behaviour after joining. However, shoppers whose initial patronage levels were low or moderate gradually became more behaviourally loyal to the firm, increasing their shopping spend at the franchise. For light buyers, the loyalty programme encouraged shoppers to buy from additional categories, thus deepening their relationship with the franchise.[23]

Whether or not they develop loyalty, these schemes certainly reward buying behaviour. Accumulated credits represent investments that the customer has made in the scheme or the brands behind the scheme. When customers get no return from this investment, they can be deeply distressed. Members of at least five airline schemes, Braniff, Midway, MGM Grand, Legend and Ansett, lost their air miles when their airlines folded. Members of Pan Am's FFP were fortunate to have their credits transferred into Delta Airlines when Pan Am stopped flying. Frequent fliers of Australia-based Ansett forfeited their miles after the airline stopped flying in 2001. Passengers organized themselves into a group to lobby, ultimately unsuccessfully, for their loyalty to be recognized and rewarded by the company administrators, or prospective purchasers of the airline.

Additionally, loyalty schemes are successful enablers of customer insight. Personalized cards are obtained only after registering personal data. Then it becomes possible to monitor transactional behaviour. Chip-embedded smart cards carry the information on the card itself. A huge amount of data is generated that can be warehoused and subjected to data mining for insights into purchasing behaviour. These insights can be used to guide marketing campaigns and offer development. Boots, for example, ran a series controlled experiments mailing health and beauty offers to select groups of carefully profiled customers. It achieved 40 per cent response rates, in comparison to 5 per cent from the control group.[24]

The loyalty scheme concept has been migrated into the online environment. One of the innovators, beenz, which was established in 1998, has not survived. Other scheme brands include iPoints (see Figure 9.4) and MyPoints.

Figure 9.4
www.ipoints.co.uk
website

Customer clubs

Customer clubs have been established by many organizations. A customer club can be defined as follows:

> A customer club is a company-run membership organization that offers a range of value-adding benefits exclusively to members.

The initial costs of establishing a club can be quite high, but thereafter most clubs are expected to cover their operating expenses and, preferably, return a profit. Research suggests that customer clubs are successful at promoting customer retention.[25]

To become a member and obtain benefits, clubs require customers to register. With these personal details, the company is able to begin interaction with customers, learn more about them, and develop offers and services for them. Clubs can only succeed if members experience benefits they value. Club managers can assemble and offer a range of value-adding services and products that, given the availability of customer data, can be personalized to segment or individual level. Among the more common benefits of club membership are access to member-only products and services, alerts about upcoming new and improved products, discounts, magazines and special offers. For example, IKEA FAMILY, the home furnishing retailer's club, offers members discounts on selected IKEA products, a free home furnishing magazine quarterly, news updates via e-mail and discounts on exclusive IKEA FAMILY products.

There are a huge number of customer clubs. One report estimates that there are 'several hundreds' in Germany alone.[26] B2C clubs include:

- Swatch the Club (see www.swatch.com)
- The Pampers Parenting Institute (see http://us.pampers.com/en_US/ppi.do)
- The Harley Owners' Group (HOG) (see http://www.harley-davidson.com/wcm/Content/Pages/HOG/hog_selector.jsp?locale=en_US)
- The Volkswagen Club (see http://www.vw-club.de/).

There are over a million paid-up members of the Harley Owners' Group (see Figure 9.5), which was established in 1983. They choose from two levels of membership, full and associate, and a variable membership

Figure 9.5
Harley Owners' Group

length, from one year to lifetime. Among the many benefits are roadside assistance, a membership manual, a touring handbook, a dedicated website, magazines, a mileage programme, a selection of pins and patches, membership in over 1000 chapters, invitations to events and rallies, and a lot more.

Sales promotions

Whereas loyalty schemes and clubs are relatively durable, sales promotions offer only temporary enhancements to customer value. Sales promotions, as we saw in the last chapter can also be used for customer acquisition. Retention-oriented sales promotions encourage the customer to repeat purchase, so the form they take is different. Here are some examples.

- **In-pack or on-pack voucher:** customers buy the product and receive a voucher entitling them to a discount off one or more additional purchases.

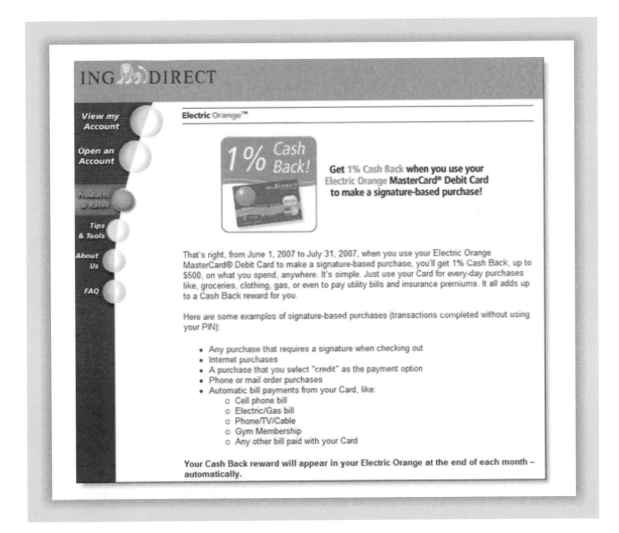

Figure 9.6 Cash-back sales promotion

- **Rebate or cash back:** rebates are refunds that the customer receives after purchase. The value of the rebate can be adjusted in line with the quantity purchased, in order to reward customers who meet high volume targets.
- **Patronage awards:** customers collect proofs of purchase, such as store receipts or barcodes from packaging, which are surrendered for cash or gifts. The greater the volume purchased the bigger the award.
- **Free premium for continuous purchase:** the customer collects several proofs of purchase and mails them in, or surrenders them at retail outlets to obtain a free gift. Sometimes the gift might be part of a collectable series. For example, a manufacturer of preserves and jams developed a range of collectable enamel badges. Customers collected proofs of purchase and mailed them in to receive a badge. There were 20 different badges in the series. This promotion was so popular that a secondary market was established so that collectors could trade and swap badges to obtain the full set.
- **Collection schemes:** these are long-running schemes where the customer collects items with every purchase. Kellogg's ran a promotion in which they inserted picture cards of carefully chosen sports stars into packets of cereals. Customers didn't know which card they had until they bought and opened the pack. These became collectable items.
- **Self-liquidating premium:** a self-liquidating promotion is one that recovers its own direct costs. Typically, consumers are invited to collect proofs of purchase, and mail them in with a personal cheque or money order. This entitles the customer to buy a product at a discounted premium, such as a camera or gardening equipment. The promoter will have reached a deal with the suppliers of the products to buy in bulk at a highly discounted rate, perhaps on a sale or return basis. Margins earned from the sale of product, plus the value of the cheque or money order cover the costs of running the promotion which, as a consequence, becomes self-liquidating.

Bonding

The next positive customer retention strategy is customer bonding. B2B researchers have identified many different forms of bond between customers and suppliers. These include interpersonal bonds, technology bonds (as in EDI), legal bonds and process bonds. These different forms can be split into two major categories: social and structural.[27]

Social bonds

Social bonds are found in positive interpersonal relationships between people on both sides of the customer-supplier dyad. Positive interpersonal relationships are characterized by high levels of trust and commitment. Successful interpersonal relationships may take time to evolve, as uncertainty and distance are reduced. As the number of episodes linking customer and supplier grow, there is greater opportunity for social bonds to develop. Suppliers should understand that if they act opportunistically or fail to align themselves to customer preferences, trust and confidence will be eroded.

Strong social bonds can emerge between employees in companies having similar sizes, cultures and locations. For example, small and medium-sized businesses generally prefer to do business with similar sized companies, and Japanese companies prefer to do business with other Japanese companies. Geographic bonds emerge when companies in a trading area cooperate to support each other.

Social relationships between buyer and seller can be single or multi-level. A single-level relationship might exist between the supplier's account manager and the customer's procurement officer. The more interpersonal links there are between the dyad, the more resistant the relationship is to breakdown. For example, technical, quality and operations people talk to their equivalents on the other side.

Social bonds characterized by trust generally precede the development of structural bonds. Mutual investments in business relationships serve as structural bonds. These structural bonds can be formally recognized in an alliance or joint venture having legal status. Companies are unlikely to commit resources if there is a low level of trust in the partner's integrity and competence.

Structural bonds

Structural bonds are established when companies and customers commit resources to a relationship. Generally, these resources yield mutual benefits for the participants. For example, a joint customer-supplier quality team can work improving quality compliance, benefiting both companies. Resources committed to a relationship may or may not be recoverable if the relationship breaks down. For example, investments made in training a customer's operatives are non-returnable. On the other hand, a chilled products manufacturer that has installed refrigerated space at a distributor's warehouse may be able to dismantle and retrieve it if the relationship dissolves.

A key feature of structural bonding is investment in adaptations to suit the other party. Suppliers can adapt any element of the offer – product, process, price and inventory levels, for example – to suit the customer. Customers, on the other hand, also make adaptations. For example, they can adapt their manufacturing processes to accommodate a supplier's product or technology.

Power imbalances in relationships can produce asymmetric adaptations. A major multiple retailer might force adaptations from small suppliers, while making no concessions itself. For example, it could insist on a reduction in product costs, co-branding of point-of-sale material, or even attempt to coerce the supplier not to supply competitors.

Different types of structural bond can be identified. All are characterized by an investment of one or both parties in the other:

- **Financial:** where the seller offers a financial inducement to retain the customer. Insurance companies form financial bonds with customers by offering no-claims discounts, tenure related discounts and multi-policy discounts.
- **Legal:** when there is a contract or common ownership linking the relational partners.

- **Equity:** where both parties invest in order to develop an offer for customers. For example, the owners of airports invest in the shells of the duty-free retail outlets. The retailer invests in the internal fixtures and fittings.
- **Knowledge-based:** when each party grows to know and understand the other's processes and structures, strengths and weaknesses.
- **Technological:** when the technologies of the relational partners are aligned, for example, with EDI, just-in-time logistics and manufacturing.
- **Process:** when processes of the two organizations are aligned. For example, the quality assurance programme on the supplier side and the quality inspection programme on the customer side. Some suppliers manage inventory levels for their customers, ensuring inventory levels are optimized. This is known as vendor managed inventory (VMI). The chemicals company, Solvay Interox, uses telemetry systems to perform VMI for its customers.
- **Values-based:** some companies are renowned for their strong values. Co-operative Bank is known for its pro-environment, ethical stance. It bonds closely with other companies, such as investment houses, that adopt the same position. It refuses to invest in companies that have poor environmental records.
- **Geographic:** these bonds exist when companies in a trading area (street, city region or country) create a buyer–seller–referral network that supports all members of their group. In the UK, retailers in downtown Leamington Spa have combated out of town developments by creating a loyalty programme in which customers can collect and redeem loyalty credits at any member store.
- **Project:** when the partners are engaged in some special activity outside of their normal commercial arrangements, for example, a new product development project. There may be an exchange of resources to enable the desired outcome to be achieved, for example, an exchange of engineers and technologists between the companies.
- **Multi-product:** when a customer buys several products from a supplier, the bond is more difficult to break. There are economies for customers when they deal with fewer suppliers. When a relationship with a supplier of several products is dissolved, the customer may incur significant money, search and psychic costs in identifying one or more replacements. Further, the level of perceived risk attached to a new relationship may become uncomfortable.

Case 9.2

Customer retention at Korea Telecom

Korea Telecom places a high level of importance on creating valuable relationships with customers, both business and consumer, in the telecommunications markets of South Korea and South East Asia.

The organization places significant emphasis on maintaining high retention rates in markets which are becoming increasingly competitive. Korea Telecom estimates that it costs around

US$185 to gain a consumer for its broadband Internet service, and about two years for the organization to recover the cost. Consequently the organization undertakes a number of activities as part of its CRM strategy to retain customers, for example bundling together of a number of services such as Internet, mobile and home phone at a discount to customers who enter into service contracts for at least two years.

Social bonds are generally easier to break than structural bonds. Structural bonds link organizations. Social bonds link people. If the account manager and procurement officer do not grow to trust each other, they may fall out, but this is unlikely to bring down a joint venture.

Build customer engagement

The final positive strategy for building customer retention is to build customer engagement. Various studies have indicated that customer satisfaction is not enough to ensure customer longevity. For example, Reichheld reports that 65 to 85 per cent of recently defected customers claimed to be satisfied with their previous suppliers.[28] Another study reports that one in ten customers who said they were completely satisfied, scoring ten out of ten on a customer satisfaction scale, defected to a rival brand the following year.[29] Having satisfied customers is, increasingly, no more than a basic requirement of being in the game.

Highly engaged customers have levels of emotional or rational attachment or commitment to a brand, experience or organization that are so strong that they are highly resistant to competitive influence. The terms engagement, attachment and commitment tend to be used interchangeably to describe this phenomenon. The topic of customer engagement was introduced in Chapter 6.

Learning from research into customer commitment

A number of authorities have urged companies to work on developing customer commitment so that they develop a strong attachment to, or engagement with, a brand or company.[30]

Three different forms of commitment have been identified: instrumental, relational, and values-based.[31]

1. **Instrumental commitment:** this occurs when customers are convinced that no other offer or company could do a better job of meeting their needs. They are not just very satisfied, but unbeatably satisfied. All expressed and latent needs have been met. When a customer feels that his or her bank has the best products, the best access, the best processes, the lowest interest rates on loans and the best reputation, he or she is committed.

2. **Relational commitment:** customers can become highly attached to a company's people. An emotional tie may be formed with an individual person, a work group or the generalized company as a whole. Customers who talk about 'my banker' or 'my mechanic' or 'my builder' are expressing this attachment. They feel a sense of personal identification with that individual. Often, these are employees who 'break the rules' or 'go the extra mile' to completely satisfy customers. They are reliable, competent, empathic and responsive. When these employees recover an at-risk customer, they create a friend. Customer-focused organizations make heroes out of these individuals. They are feted and celebrated. For example, American Express tells the story of a customer service agent who responded to a call from a customer who had been robbed, by arranging to have replacement travellers checks delivered personally to the customer. The CSA also confirmed the customer's hotel reservation, arranged for a car to collect the customer from the phone booth and notified the police, all above and beyond the call of duty. Customers can also become attached to a work group. In banking, for example, some customers are highly committed to a specific branch and prefer not to transact elsewhere. Finally, customers can become attached to an organization as a whole, believing its people to be better than competitors on dimensions that are important to the customer. They may provide 'the best service' or be 'the friendliest people'.

3. **Values-based commitment:** customers become committed when their values are aligned with those of the company. Values can be defined as follows:

> Values are core beliefs that transcend context and serve to organize and direct attitudes and behaviours

Customers have many and varied core beliefs, such as environmental consciousness, honesty, child protection, independence, family-centredness and so on. Many of these reflect cultural norms. Where these values coincide with those of an organization, the customer may become committed to the organization. Companies that are accused of using child labour, damaging the environment or otherwise acting unethically place themselves at risk. Nestlé had been accused of marketing infant formula in African countries where the infrastructure made its use dangerous. Many babies died as mothers used unclean water and unsterilized equipment. This is estimated to have cost the company $40 million.[32] Sales of Shell fuel were estimated to have fallen between 20 and 50 per cent during the Brent Spar boycott.[33] The company had planned to decommission the 4000 tonne Brent Spar oil platform by dumping it into the North Sea. Just as customers can take action against companies that they feel are in beach of their values, they can also commit to companies that mirror with their values. Research supports the claim that there is a hierarchical relationship from values, to attitudes, to purchase intention, and ultimately to purchase.[34]

A number of companies benefit from values-based commitment: Body Shop, John Lewis, Harley Davidson, Co-operative Bank and Virgin.

- **Body Shop International**, the health and beauty retailer, was founded by Anita and Gordon Roddick. The company's values include a refusal to source products tested on animals, and support for community trade, human rights and the environment. A successful and influential business was developed on the back of these values. Body Shop influenced other retailers to become more sensitive to these issues.
- **The John Lewis Partnership** is a UK-based department store with a 140-year history. It is a mutual organization, owned by its staff and incorporated as a trust. Profits are not distributed to external shareholders; they are shared with employees who are regarded as partners. The company is reputed to look after these partners very well including, for example, having a final salary pension scheme.
- **Harley Davidson**, the US motorcycle manufacturer, has a phenomenally committed customer base. When Harley riders replace their bikes, 95 per cent buy another Harley. The bike is a central part of a lifestyle that is grounded on fraternity, independence and rebellion. Image is critical to the Harley rider. In the US, the average age of a Harley rider is 47 (up from 38 a decade ago), the median income is US$83 000 and the typical cruiser bike costs $17 000. The challenge of Harley is to develop value propositions that appeal to a younger customer.[35]
- **Co-operative Bank** is positioned in the UK retail banking market as the ethical bank. The mutually-owned bank believes its ethical stance is directly responsible for about 20 per cent of pre-tax profits. One-third of the bank's customers moved to the bank because of its ethical and eco-friendly policies.[36]
- **The Virgin Group** is a family of over 200 privately owned strategic business units ranging from airline to rail, cosmetics, cola, telecommunications, music and financial services. In 2006 group sales reached £10 billion. The values of the Virgin brand are integrity, value for money, quality and fun. Virgin Group is chaired by its founder, the renegade but highly visible Sir Richard Branson. Customers are attracted to the brand because of its reputation for fairness, simplicity and transparency. Customers trust the brand and rely on it in markets that are new to them. For example, Virgin was a late mover into the UKs indexed linked mutual fund marketplace. It still managed to become market leader in 12 months, despite having no history as a financial institution.

Highly engaged customers are more involved with your brand or company. This not only implies frequent purchasing, but also other attributes of what might be called 'corporate citizenship', such as being an unpaid advocate by uttering positive word-of-mouth, providing frequent feedback on their experiences, participating in company research, contributing to new product or service development, being more forgiving if the company makes a mistake or service fails, and participating in online communities and user groups.

The outcome of higher levels of engagement, it is claimed, is a more durable customer relationship. One report, for example, indicates that the rate of account closures at a bank were 37 per cent lower for emotionally engaged customers than for rationally satisfied customers.[37]

Context makes a difference

Context makes a difference to customer retention in two ways. First, there are some circumstances when customer acquisition makes more, indeed the only, sense as a strategic goal. Secondly, customer retention strategies will vary according to the environment in which the company competes.

When launching a new product or opening up a new market a company's focus has to be on customer acquisition. In contexts where there are one-off purchases such as funerals, infrequent purchases such as heart surgery, or unique conditions such as gave rise to the demand for Y2K compliance software, customer retention is subordinate to acquisition.

The impact of contextual conditions on the choice and timing of customer retention practices has not been thoroughly researched. However, we can see that a number of contextual considerations impact on customer retention practices:

- **Number of competitors:** in some industries there is a notable lack of competitors, meaning that companies do not suffer badly from customer churn. This typically applies in state-provided services such as education and utilities such as gas, electricity, rail and telecommunications, whether deregulated or not. When customers are dissatisfied they have no competitor to turn to. They may also believe that the competitors in the market are not truly differentiated by their service standards. In other words, each supplier is as bad as the others. The result is inertia.
- **Corporate culture:** in corporate banking, the short-term profit requirement of both management and shareholders has resulted in a lack of genuine commitment to relationship banking. Banks have been very opportunistic in their preference for transactional credit-based relationships with customers.[38]
- **Channel configuration:** sellers may not have the opportunity to maintain direct relationships with the ultimate buyers and users of their products. Instead, they may rely on their intermediaries. Caterpillar, for example, does not have a relationship with the contractors who use their equipment. Instead, it works in partnership with about 1500 independent dealers around the world to provide customer service, training, field support and inventories of spare parts.
- **Purchasing practices:** the purchasing procedures adopted by buyers can also make the practice of customer retention futile. Customers do not always want relationships with their suppliers. For example, towards the end of the 1990s, government departments in the UK and elsewhere adopted compulsory competitive tendering (CCT) as their mechanism for making purchasing decisions. The process is designed to prevent corrupt relationships developing and to ensure that tax-payers get good value for money, i.e. pay a low price for the services rendered. Every year or so, current suppliers and other

vendors are invited to pitch for the business. Price is often the primary consideration for the choice of supplier.

- **Ownership expectations:** the demands of business owners can subordinate customer retention to other goals. For example, Korean office equipment manufacturers are very focused on sales volumes. They require their wholly-owned overseas distributors to buy quotas of product from Korea and sell them in the served market, regardless of whether the products are well-matched to local market conditions and customer requirements. The distributors are put in a position of having to create demand against competitors that do a better job of understanding and meeting customer requirements.[39]
- **Ethical concerns:** public sector medical service providers cannot simply focus on their most profitable customers or products. This would result in the neglect of some patients and a failure to address other areas of disease management. Private sector providers do not necessarily face this problem. The Shouldice Hospital in Ontario specializes in hernia repairs. Their website, www.shouldice.com, reports that they have repaired 300 000 hernias over a 60 year period, with a 99 per cent success rate. They even organize annual reunions. Recently, these events have been attended by 1000 satisfied patients.

Key performance indicators of customer retention programmes

CRM practitioners are concerned with achieving a number of key performance indicators (KPIs) for these customer retention activities, among them:

- raw customer retention rate
- raw customer retention rate in each customer segment
- sales-adjusted retention rate
- sales-adjusted retention rate in each customer segment
- profit-adjusted retention rate
- profit-adjusted retention rate in each customer segment
- cost of customer retention
- share of wallet of the retained customers
- customer churn rate per product category, sales region or channel
- cost-effectiveness of customer retention tactics.

The choice of KPI will vary according to context. Some companies do not have enough data to compute raw retention rate per segment. Others may not know their share of wallet (share of customer spending on the category).

The role of research

Companies can reduce levels of customer churn by researching a number of questions:

1. Why are customers churning?
2. Are there any lead indicators of impending defection?
3. What can be done to address the root causes?

The first question can be answered by contacting and investigating a sample of former customers to find out why they took their business elsewhere.

Customers defect for all sort of reasons, not all of which can be foreseen, prevented or managed by a company. For example, Susan Keaveney identified eight causes of switching behaviours in service industries generally: price, inconvenience, core service failures, failed employee responses to service failure, ethical problems, involuntary factors, competitive issues and service encounter failures. Only six of these eight causes of switching behaviours can be influenced by the service provider.[40] Another industry-specific study found that between 20 per cent and 25 per cent of supermarket shoppers changed their primary store in a 12 month period. Twenty-four per cent of switchers changed allegiance because a new competitive store had opened, 14 per cent because they had moved house, 11 per cent for better quality and 10 per cent for better choice.[41]

The second question attempts to find out if customers give any early warning signals of impending defection. If these were identified the company could take pre-emptive action. Signals might include the following:

- reduced RFM scores (recency–frequency–monetary value)
- non-response to a carefully targeted offer
- reduced levels of customer satisfaction
- dissatisfaction with complaint handling
- reduced share of customer (e.g. customer only flies one leg of an international flight on your airline)
- inbound calls for technical or product-related information
- late payment of an invoice
- querying an invoice
- customer touchpoints are changed, e.g. store closes, change of website address
- customer change of address.

Customer researchers are also advised to analyse the reasons for customer defection, and to identify the root causes.[42] Sometimes these can be remedied by management. For example, if you lose customers because of the time taken to deal with a complaint, management can audit and overhaul the complaints management process. This might involve identifying the channels and touchpoints through which complaints enter the business, updating complaints database management, or training and empowering frontline staff. Root causes can be analysed by customer segment, channel and product. The 80:20 rule may be applicable. In other words, it may be possible to eliminate 80 per cent of the causes of customer defections with relative ease.

Strategies for customer development

Customer development is the process of growing the value of retained customers. Companies generally attempt to cross-sell and up-sell products into the customer base while still having regard for the satisfaction of the customer. Cross-selling, which aims to grow share of wallet can be defined as follows:

> Cross-selling is selling additional products and services to an existing customer.

Up-selling can be defined as follows:

> Up-selling is selling higher priced or higher margin products and services to an existing customer.

Customers generally do not respond positively to persistent and repeated efforts to sell additional products and services that are not related to their requirements. Indeed, there is an argument that companies should seek to down-sell where appropriate. This means identifying and providing lower cost solutions to the customers' problems, even if it means making a lower margin. Customers may regard up-selling as opportunistic and exploitative, thereby reducing the level of trust they have in the supplier, and putting the relationship at risk. However, multi-product ownership creates a structural bond that decreases the risk of relationship dissolution. There are a number of CRM technologies that are useful for customer development purposes.

- **Campaign management** software is used to create up-sell and cross-sell customer development campaigns and track their effectiveness, particularly in terms of sales and incremental margin.
- **Event-based marketing:** campaigns are often associated with events. For example, a bank will offer a customer an investment product if deposits in a savings account reach a trigger point.
- **Data mining:** offers are based on intelligent data mining. Transactional histories record what customers have already bought. Data mining can tell you the probability of a customer buying any other products (propensity to buy), based on their transactional history or demographic/psychographic profile. First Direct, the Internet and telephone bank, uses propensity to buy scores to run targeted, event-driven cross-sell campaigns through direct mail and call centres. They aim at high conversion rates through follow-up calls.

- **Customization:** offers are customized at segment or unique customer level. Also personalized is the communication to the customer and the channel of communication: e-mail, surface mail, SMS or phone call, for example.
- **Channel integration:** customer development activities are integrated across channels. It is regarded as bad customer management practice to have different channels making different offers to the same customer. In retail, channel integration is observed when channels such as stores, web and direct to consumer channels act in an integrated, customer-centric manner. For this to happen, customer information and customer development plans need to be shared across channels.
- **Integrated customer communications:** the messages communicated to customers are consistent across all channels.
- **Marketing optimization:** optimization software is available from CRM analytics organizations such as SAS. Optimization enables marketers to enjoy optimal returns from up-sell and cross-sell campaigns across multiple channels and customer segments, taking account of issues such as budget constraints, communication costs, contact policies (e.g. no more than two offers to be communicated to any customer in any quarter), customers' transactional histories and propensities to buy.

In professional services, the client audit is often the foundation for cross-selling and up-selling of clients. In B2B environments, sales representatives need to be alert to opportunities for cross- and up-selling. This means understanding customers' manufacturing processes, and knowing their product innovation plans.

In mature markets, where customer acquisition is difficult or expensive, the development of retained customers is an important source of additional revenues. For example, in the mature mobile telecommunications market, the penetration of handsets is at a very high level. Winning new-to-market customers is regarded as too difficult, since these are the laggards and expensive to convert. Network operators have begun to focus on selling additional services to their existing customer bases, including data applications.

Strategies for terminating customer relationships

Companies rarely hesitate to terminate employee positions that serve no useful purpose. In a similar vein, a review of customer value might identify customers that are candidates for dismissal, including customers who will never be profitable or who serve no other useful strategic purpose. More specifically, these include fraudsters, persistent late payers, serial complainants, those who are capricious and change their minds with cost consequences for the supplier, and switchers who are constantly searching for a better deal. This certainly happens in reverse; customers sack suppliers when they switch vendors.

Relationships dissolve when one partner no longer views the relationship as worth continuing investment. In a B2B context, activity links, resource ties and actor bonds would be severed. However, even if there is no strategic value in a customer, dissolution of the relationship is not always an attractive option because of contractual obligations, expectations of mutuality, word-of-mouth risks and network relationships.

McKinsey reports that 30 to 40 per cent of a typical company's revenues are generated by customers who, on a fully costed, standalone, basis would be unprofitable.[43] It is therefore important to conduct regular reviews of the customer base to identify potential candidates for dismissal. If this is not done sales, marketing and service resources will continue to be suboptimally deployed. Nypro, a large plastic injection moulder, had 800 customers and sales of $50 million in 1987 when it decided to move out of low value-add manufacturing. Many of these customers served no useful strategic purpose and, by 1997, the company had only 65 customers, all of whom were large and required value-added solutions rather than cheap moulded products. However, sales revenues were $450 million.

Sacking customers needs to be conducted with sensitivity. Customers may be well connected and spread negative word-of-mouth about their treatment. In the year 2000, UK banks began a programme of branch closures in geographic areas that were unprofitable. Effectively, they were sacking low-value customers in working-class and rural areas. There was considerable bad publicity, the government intervened and the closure strategy was reviewed.

Case 9.3

Sacking unprofitable customers at the CBA

The Commonwealth Bank of Australia (CBA), like many other banks, has been criticized in the media for adopting a strategy of sacking unprofitable customers.

In recent years the bank has closed branches in many areas that were considered unprofitable, particularly in less populated areas of rural and regional Australia. The bank believes customers are unprofitable if their balance is less than $500. For these customers the bank has introduced higher bank fees. The bank has also introduced transaction fees of up to $3 when customers withdraw their money over the counter in a branch.

The media has widely speculated that actions such as these by many banks will continue to occur as banks and other financial institutions attempt to shift customers to electronic banking channels, where the cost to the bank of performing a simple deposit or withdrawal transaction can be just a few cents as opposed to a few dollars for similar over-the-counter service in a branch.

There are a number of strategies for sacking customers:

- **Raise prices:** customers can choose to pay the higher price. If not, they effectively remove themselves from the customer base. Where price is customized this is a feasible option. When banks introduced transaction fees for unprofitable customers many left in search of a better deal.
- **Unbundle the offer:** you could take a bundled value proposition, unbundle it, reprice the components and reoffer it to the customer. This makes the value in the offer transparent, and enables customers to make informed choices about whether they want to pay the unbundled price.
- **Respecify the product:** this involves redesigning the product so that it no longer appeals to the customer(s) you want to sack. For example, the airline BA made a strategic decision to target frequent-flying business travellers who they regarded as high value. They redesigned the cabins in their fleet, reducing the number of seats allocated to economy travellers.
- **Reorganize sales, marketing and service departments** so that they no longer focus on the sackable segments or customers. You would stop running marketing campaigns targeted at these customers, prevent salespeople calling on them and discontinue servicing their queries.
- **Introduce ABC class service:** you could migrate customers down the service ladder from high quality face-to-face service from account teams, to sales representatives, or even further to contact centre or web-based self-service. This eliminates cost from the relationship and may convert an unprofitable customer into profit. In a B2C context, this equates to shifting customers from a high-cost to a low-cost service channel. Frontier Bank, for example, introduced a no-frills telephone account for business customers who needed no cash processing facilities. A minimum balance was needed for the bank to cover its operating costs. Customers who did not maintain the targeted credit balance in their account were invited to switch to other products in other channels. If they refused, the bank asked them to close their account.[44]

Empirical evidence on how companies terminate customer relationships is sparse. However, one study of German engineering companies reports that very few firms have a systematic approach to managing unprofitable customers. Most respondents confirm that unprofitable relationships are commonplace; indeed, a fifth of firms have a customer base more than half of which is not, or not yet, profitable. Companies fall into three clusters in respect of the customer-sacking behaviours:[45]

1. **Hardliners** take an active and rigorous stance in terminating unprofitable relationships, including the regular clearance of their customer portfolio. More qualitative implications, such as a potential loss of trust in relationships with other customers or negative word-of-mouth, do not seem to hinder their willingness to sack unprofitable customers.

2. **Appeasers** take a more cautious approach concerning the termination of unprofitable relationships, above all due to strategic considerations such as not playing customers into competitors' hands.
3. The **undecided** are reluctant to terminate unprofitable relationships, mainly because they fear the costs of attracting new customers.

Summary

In this chapter we have looked at the important issues of how companies can retain, develop and, if necessary, sack customers. The economic argument for focusing on customer retention is based on four claims about what happens as customer tenure lengthens: the volume and value of purchasing increases, customer management costs fall, referrals increase and customers become less price sensitive. Measures of customer retention vary across industry because of the length of the customer repurchase cycle. There are three possible measures of customer retention. Raw customer retention is the number of customers doing business with a firm at the end of a trading period, expressed as percentage of those who were active customers at the beginning of the same period. This raw figure can be adjusted for sales and profit. Customer retention efforts are generally directed at customers who are strategically valuable. These same customers may be very attractive to competitors and may be costly to retain.

A number of alternative strategies can be used to retain customers. A distinction can be made between positive and negative retention strategies. Negative retention strategies impose switching costs on customers if they defect. Positive retention strategies reward customers for staying. There are four main forms of positive retention strategy. These are meeting and exceeding customer expectations, finding ways to add value, creating social and structural bonds and building customer engagement. Companies have a number of methods for adding value, including loyalty schemes, customer clubs and sales promotions. What is an appropriate customer retention strategy will be contextually defined. Not all strategies work in all circumstances. In addition to customer retention, two other customer management activities were discussed in this chapter. These are developing and sacking customers. Customer development aims to increase the value of the customer by cross-selling or up-selling products and services to existing customers. The termination of customer relationships aims to improve the profitability of the customer base by divesting customers who show no signs of ever becoming profitable or strategically significant.

References

1. Research conducted in Australia indicates that less than 40 per cent of companies had a customer retention plan in place. See Ang, L. and Buttle, F. (2006) Customer retention management processes: a quantitative study. *European Journal of Marketing*, Vol. 40(1–2), pp. 83–99.

2. Weinstein, A. (2002) Customer retention: a usage segmentation and customer value approach. *Journal of Targeting, Measurement and Analysis for Marketing*, Vol. 10(3), pp. 259–68; Payne, A.F.T. and Frow, P. (1999) Developing a segmented service strategy: improving measurement in relationship marketing. *Journal of Marketing Management*, Vol. 15(8), pp. 797–818.

3. This section is based on Ahmad, R. and Buttle F. (2001) Customer retention: a potentially potent marketing management strategy. *Journal of Strategic Marketing*, Vol. 9, pp. 29–45.

4. Dawkins, P.M. and Reichheld, F.F. (1990) Customer retention as a competitive weapon, Directors & Board, Summer, pp. 42–47.

5. Ahmad, R. and Buttle, F. (2002) Customer retention management, a reflection on theory and practice. *Marketing Intelligence and Planning*, Vol. 20(3), pp. 149–161.

6. Reichheld, F.F. (1996) *The loyalty effect: the hidden force behind growth, profits, and lasting value*. Boston MA: Harvard Business School Press.

7. Coyles, S. and Gorkey, T.C. (2002) Customer retention is not enough. *McKinsey Quarterly*, No 2, pp. 80–89.

8. Based on Reichheld, F.F. and Sasser, W.E. Jr (1990) Zero defections: quality comes to services. *Harvard Business Review*, September–October, pp. 105–111; Reichheld, F.F. (1996) *The loyalty effect*. Boston: Harvard Business School Press.

9. Murphy, J.A. (1996) Retail Banking. In: Buttle F. (ed.) *Relationship marketing: theory and practice*. London: Paul Chapman Publishing, pp. 74–90.

10. East, R. and Hammond, K. (2000) Fact and fallacy in retention marketing, Working paper. Kingston Business School: UK.

11. Bain & Co/Mainline. (1999) Consumer spending online. Bain & Co.

12. East, R. and Hammond, K. (2000) Fact and fallacy in retention marketing. Working paper, Kingston Business School, UK. Reichheld (1996, op.cit.) shows profit from customer referrals grows as tenure lengthens.

13. Dawkins, P. M. and Reichheld, F. F. (1990) Customer retention as a competitive weapon, *Directors & Board*, Summer, pp. 42–47.

14. Reichheld, F.F. (1996) *The loyalty effect: the hidden force behind growth, profits, and lasting value*. Boston MA: Harvard Business School Press.

15. Bolton, R.N. (1998) A dynamic model of the duration of the customer's relationship with a continuous service provider: the role of satisfaction. *Marketing Science*, Vol. 17(1), pp. 45–65.

16. Kano, N. (1995) Upsizing the organization by attractive quality creation. In: G.H. Kanji (ed.). *Total Quality Management: Proceedings of the First World Congress*. London: Chapman & Hall.

17. Gilbert, D. (1996) Airlines. In: Buttle F. (ed.) *Relationship marketing, theory and practice*. London: Paul Chapman Publishing, pp. 31–144.

18. Dowling, G. and Uncles, M. (1997) Do customer loyalty programs really work? *Sloan Management Review, Summer*, Vol. 38(4), pp. 71–82.

19. Dignam, C. (1996) Being smart is not the only redeeming feature. *Marketing Direct*, September, pp. 51–56.

20. Quoted in Gilbert, D. (1996) Airlines. In: Buttle F. (ed.) *Relationship marketing: theory and practice*. London: Paul Chapman Publishing, pp. 31–144.
21. Reed, D. (1995) Many happy returns. *Marketing Week,* November, 17, pp. 7–11.
22. Dick, A.S. and Basu, K. (1994) Customer loyalty: towards an integrated framework. *Journal of the Academy of Marketing Science*, Vol. 22(2), pp. 99–113.
23. Liu, Y. (2007) The long-term impact of loyalty programs on consumer purchase behaviour and loyalty. *Journal of Marketing*, Vol. 71, *October*, pp. 19–35.
24. For more information on the history and development of these schemes see Worthington, S. (2000) A classic example of a misnomer: the loyalty card. *Journal of Targeting, Measurement and Analysis for Marketing*, Vol. 8(3), pp. 222–234.
25. Stauss, B., Chojnacki, K., Decker, A. and Hoffmann, F. (2001) Retention effects of a customer club. *International Journal of Service Industry Management*, Vol. 12(1), pp. 7–19.
26. Stauss, B., Chojnacki, K., Decker, A. and Hoffmann, F. (2001) Retention effects of a customer club. *International Journal of Service Industry Management*, Vol. 12(1), pp. 7–19.
27. Buttle, F., Ahmad, R. and Aldlaigan, A. (2002) The theory and practice of customer bonding. *Journal of Business-to-Business Marketing*, Vol. 9(2), pp. 3–27.
28. Reichheld, F.F. (1993) Loyalty-based management. *Harvard Business Review,* March–April, pp. 63–73.
29. Mitchell, A. (1998) Loyal yes, staying no. *Management Today,* May, pp. 104–105.
30. Hofmeyr, N. and Rice, B. (2000) *Commitment-led marketing*. New York: John Wiley; Ulrich, D. (1989) Tie the corporate knot: gaining complete customer commitment. *Sloan Management Review,* Summer, pp. 19–27.
31. Aldlaigan, A. (2000) Service quality, organizational attachment and relational intention in retail banking. Unpublished PhD thesis. Manchester Business School, UK.
32. Nelson-Horchler, J. (1984) Fighting a boycott, image rebuilding, Swiss style. *Industry Week*, Vol. 220, pp. 54–56.
33. Klein, N. (2000) *No Logo*. Harper Collins: London.
34. Follows, S.B. and Jobber, D. (2000) Environmentally responsible purchase behaviour a test of a consumer model. *European Journal of Marketing*, Vol. 34(5–6), pp. 723–746.
35. Helyar, J. (2002) Will Harley-Davidson hit the wall? *Fortune,* Vol. 146(3), August 12, pp. 120–124.
36. Croft, J. (2002) Ethics proves big draw for Co-op Bank. *Financial Times London*, May 15, p. 20.
37. Fleming, J.H. and Asplund, J. (2007) *Human Sigma, managing the employee-customer encounter*. New York: Gallup Press.
38. Schell, C. (1996) Corporate banking. In: Buttle F. (ed.) *Relationship marketing theory and practice*. London: Paul Chapman Publishing, pp. 91–103.

39. Ahmad, R. and Buttle, F. (2002) Customer retention management, a reflection on theory and practice. *Marketing Intelligence and Planning*, Vol. 20(3), pp. 149–161.

40. Keaveney, S.M. (1995) Customer switching behaviour in service industries: an exploratory study. *Journal of Marketing*, Vol. 59, pp. 71–82.

41. East, R., Harris, P., Lomax, W., Willson, G. and Hammond, K. (1998) Customer defection from supermarkets. *Advances in Consumer Research*, Vol. 25(1), pp. 507–512.

42. Hart, C.W.L., Heskett, J.L. and Sasser, W.E. Jr (1990) The profitable art of service recovery. *Harvard Business Review,* July–August, pp. 148–156.

43. Leszinski, R., Weber, F.A., Paganoni, R. and Baumgartner, T. (1995) Profits in your backyard. *The McKinsey Quarterly*, No. 4, p. 118.

44. Ahmad, R. and Buttle, F. (2002) Retaining telephone banking customers at Frontier Bank. *International Journal of Bank Marketing*, Vol. 20(1), pp. 5–16.

45. Helm, S., Rolfes, L. and Günter, B. (2006) Suppliers' willingness to end unprofitable customer relationships: an exploratory investigation in the German mechanical engineering sector. *European Journal of Marketing*, Vol. 40(3–4), pp. 366–383.

Chapter 10

Managing networks for customer relationship management performance

By the end of this chapter, you will understand:

1. the meaning and composition of a business network
2. how networks contribute to the achievement of CRM objectives
3. the meaning of network position and network competence
4. the SCOPE network model of CRM
5. that network management is about both managing in networks and management of networks

Introduction

This chapter focuses on networks and their influence on CRM. Companies do not exist in splendid isolation. They are positioned within a network, and it is the performance of that network which determines whether companies achieve their goals. CRM performance is more assured when the resources of the network are aligned and coordinated to contribute to the creation and delivery of value to the focal company's customers.

Our definition of CRM, repeated below, recognizes the role of the business network in the achievement of CRM outcomes.

> CRM is the core business strategy that integrates internal processes and functions and **external networks** to create and deliver value to targeted customers at a profit. It is grounded on high-quality customer-related data and enabled by information technology.

Competition for the customer's spend is changing. In the past, competition has been head to head between independent companies. Today, competition is increasingly between networks. A good illustration of this is the motor industry. In the 1920s Ford not only assembled cars, they also owned steel mills, coal mines, iron ore mines, steam ships, rubber plantations, sheep farms and railroads. It was standard practice for companies to own and manage as many factors of production that they could. Today it is different. In the year 2000, Ford only produced about 50 per cent of the value of their cars. The rest was outsourced to members of their supplier network. In Ford's strategic group, General Motors produces 70 per cent of the value of its cars, Chrysler 30 per cent and Toyota only 20 per cent.

Conventionally it has been the manufacturer or service provider that dominates business networks through their brand power. Companies like IBM, GE (General Electric), UPS (United Parcel Service) and AMP (Australian Mutual Provident) are examples. This is changing. Sometimes the members of the supply chain can be so powerful that they call the shots. Intel and Microsoft carry so much weight that computer manufacturers such as Dell, Toshiba and Compaq take great risks if these components are not part of the finished product.

Members of the demand chain can also wield significant power and influence. A high percentage of sales in some retail categories are retailer brands (own brands). Wal-Mart and Tesco both specify precisely what they require from their own brand manufacturers. Sometimes manufacturers have a role in helping determine the specification, but ultimately it is clear where the final decision rests: with the retailer. Multiple retailers also have sufficient power to expect compliance from manufacturers of major brands. Even Procter and Gamble, Unilever and General Foods are not exempt from their influence. Wal-Mart, however, does claim to want closer relationships based on open dialogue and information exchange with key vendors (see Case 10.1).

Case 10.1

Wal-Mart's commitments to key vendors

Wal-Mart makes a number of commitments to major suppliers with whom it wants to develop partner-like relationships.

- Wal-Mart looks for a very close relationship and strong commitment from its key vendors. Highly valued qualities are trust and integrity.
- Wal-Mart is willing to listen to new solutions, opinions and ideas. Don't be afraid to contribute.
- Analytical skills are essential when dealing with Wal-Mart. We will give you access to all kinds of data. Use the data to build a win–win relationship.
- Wal-Mart is hungry for consumer insight. We place great value on any information that can improve our understanding of the people who shop in Wal-Mart stores.
- Prepare to engage management. Wal-Mart management is as keen as anyone to hear what business partners have to say. Don't feel bound by hierarchy or categories.

What is a network?

The term 'network' can, in general terms, be thought of as a structure made up of nodes that are related to each other by threads. Figure 10.1 shows the nodes and threads of a simplified social network, that is, a group of friends and acquaintances. The nodes are the ovals and the lines joining them are the threads. The nodes are people (lettered A to L) and the threads are the social links between them. This network has been drawn from the perspective of person A. She is a very well-connected person. Persons B to I are all connected to A by direct threads. One step removed from person A is person K. A does not know K personally, but she knows persons I and J, both of whom know K. K knows L, who is two steps removed from A. Where does A's network finish? Clearly, the answer is 'not at the edge of the diagram'. Each of the people with whom A is directly connected has relationships with other people, many of whom are not shown on this diagram. They in turn have connections with others, and so on. Person A's network, in principle, contains all her direct connections, their direct connections, and their direct connections, and their direct connections, and their ... *ad infinitum*. Network analysts tend to draw boundaries around networks to make them more visible and amendable to analysis.

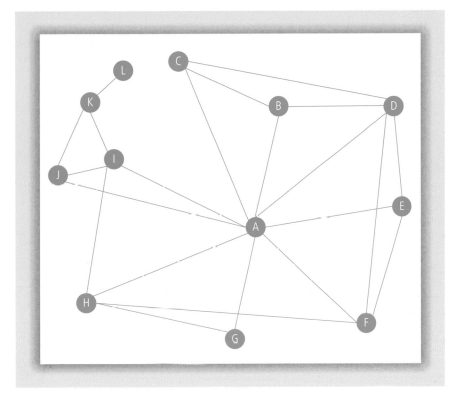

Figure 10.1
A network

Business networks

Business networks exist. They are unavoidable. They are a fact of business life whether they are actively coordinated or not. A business network can be defined as follows:

> A business network is made up of nodal companies, organizations and individuals, and the relationships between them.

In the context of business markets, these nodes are business units such as suppliers, producers, distributors, partners, regulators, contractors, customers and other companies, organizations and individuals. The relationships between these business units are expressed in actor bonds, activity links and resource ties. To recap material that was introduced in Chapter 2, actor bonds are interpersonal contacts between people in network-related firms; activity links are the commercial, legal, administrative and other connections that form between companies as they interact; resources are the human, financial, legal, physical, managerial, intellectual and other strengths or weaknesses of firms in the network.

Intercompany and interpersonal relationships within a network form a complex social structure. This happens in many ways. Equity stakes in companies make for complex patterns of ownership and influence. Company A has a stake in company B; company B has a stake in companies A and C. Company C has stakes in companies A and D. Directors have multiple memberships of network companies' boards. Marketers meet up at branch meetings of their professional organizations. Salespeople organize social events for their key account holders. Personal relationships contribute to the atmosphere of a business relationship, making it close or distant, friendly or antagonistic, open or closed. Established interpersonal relationships both enable and constrain the development of other interpersonal relationships.

Any firm participates in a host of different relationships, and the firms with which it has relationships also have relationships with other firms. Therefore, any one firm occupies a position within a network of other firms. Each firm in a network is likely to have its own picture of the network, which may be very different from other firms in the same network. Each firm tries to exert some influence over significant parts of its network, for example to ensure that manufacturing inputs are available and customer demand is constant. Some research has suggested that the average firm has ten such strategically important network relationships.[1]

Network position

Every company occupies a network position. Network positions are the products of an organization's past and present operations. They result from relationships and interactions that were, or are, needed for the firm to do what it was set up to do. Every company in every network occupies a particular position in relationship to other network members. Network position can be defined as follows:

> A company's network position is the sum total of a company's network relationships and all the activity links, resource ties and actor bonds that these relationships contain.

These relationships both constrain and enable what that firm can do in the future. A company that has all the relationships in place to be a successful shipbuilder cannot become a financial institution without creating new relationships that provide the necessary skills and resources. Relationships can have more advantageous consequences. A supplier might introduce a firm to one of its customers, enabling them to work on a project of shared interest. Alternatively, a supplier might choose to withdraw from a relationship with a customer in order not to endanger a relationship with a bigger, more profitable customer.

A company's network position is a resource that can create competitive advantage. Networks supply the resources and perform the activities that enable companies to create and deliver value to their customers. Network positions are dynamic. Members adapt their network positions to ensure their survival and prosperity. They look for opportunities to exploit. For example, they seek out relationships that can be used to lift sales or reduce costs. Avon Rubber, for example, manufactures engine mounts for the car industry and counts Ford as one of its strategically significant customers. It leveraged its relationship with this reference customer to win business from Saab, and to enable it to present its credentials to other car manufacturers.

Clearly, some network positions are more influential than others. For example, a network member might be positioned as a gatekeeper to opportunities that are highly sought after by other network members. The supplier of a subassembly, such as a braking system for a car, has considerable network power in enabling or disabling access of component suppliers to the car manufacturer.

Whether a desired network position is achieved is determined at least in part by the firm's network competence. This is the firm's ability to accrue and/or utilize the necessary knowledge, skills, qualifications and experience to successfully manage network interactions.[2] Skilful management of the company's network position can realize several benefits. Toyota uses its network position to enhance their cars' reliability, economy and design. Toyota works with and through its network members to keep costs low, while ensuring product quality is high. Every company's network position is subject to a set of relational obligations and restraints among network members. For example, in the Toyota scenario (see Figure 10.3) the company expects tier one suppliers to develop and strengthen their relationships with tier two suppliers to ensure that Toyota gets the quality they require. Tier two suppliers expect tier one suppliers to maintain a good relationship with Toyota to ensure that they have ongoing access to a strategically significant customer.

It is unlikely that all the potential for competitive advantage that is contained in a network is presently exploited. Focal companies may not be fully aware of the opportunities that exist for cooperation and rationalization between network members. For example, there may be opportunities to bring together the innovative competencies of one network member, the manufacturing expertise of another and the marketing know-how of a third company, to create and launch successful new products. Or there may be opportunities to develop joint purchasing arrangements. Perhaps it might be possible to eliminate some processes that are duplicated. For example, a supplier may have a quality assurance programme in place; the supplier's customer may not need a quality control programme based on inspection of that supplier's products.

What is meant by 'focal firm?'

We've already used the expression 'focal firm' in this chapter. The focal firm is the firm whose network is being considered. If you are examining Delta Plastics' network, Delta Plastics is the focal firm. Sometimes the threads linking a focal firm to its network are loosely connected; at other times they are contractually defined and tightly controlled, as in the relationship between Dell Computers and its component suppliers.

There is growing recognition that the resources within networks need to be actively coordinated and managed. A focal organization must take responsibility for managing its network so that it creates and delivers sustainable value to customers. Failure by a network member to provide the necessary resources or perform the required activities could threaten the performance of the focal organization. Although firms do try to exert influence within their immediate network neighbours, actions elsewhere in the network – though several steps removed from the focal firm – might make a considerable difference to that firm's performance. For example, the collapse of an agricultural chemical firm in Brazil might lead to a dramatic rise in the cost of coffee beans, which in turn drives up the retail price of coffee in overseas markets, in turn fuelling consumer demand for an alternative hot beverage, tea.

Business networks and CRM

Networks are important from a strategic CRM perspective, because network members supply the material inputs, services, funding, people, technology and knowledge that are used to create value propositions for the focal firm's customers. They also provide services such as advertising, logistics and distribution that help raise and satisfy customer demand.

Consider, for example, that some retailers have developed relationships with banks to offer financial services products to the retailer's customers. You can find this arrangement in the UK, where Tesco and Royal Bank of Scotland are partners, and in Australia where Woolworths and Commonwealth Bank partner. This is an arrangement that blurs the conventional customer-perceived distinctions between retailer and bank. For partnerships like these to succeed, each partner needs to understand the other party's competences, to share customer-related information, to align their technologies and to be clear about the goals of the partnership. If the relationship between the retailer and the bank is poorly managed, value will not be delivered to customers or created for the partners. Liberating the potential value in customer relationships also hinges on companies effectively managing their non-customer network relationships, that is, relationships with alliance partners, suppliers, distributors, financiers and so on.

The need to manage business networks is recognized in modern CRM systems, with the move towards extra-enterprise, or collaborative, CRM. CRM systems now include applications for managing relationships with partners (PRM), the integration of websites for investor relations, the management of relationships with employees (ERM) and, through integration with enterprise resource planning (ERP), the management of suppliers.

The SCOPE of CRM

There are four main constituencies of a focal organization's network. As illustrated in Figure 10.2, they are suppliers, owners/investors, partners and employees. This figure shows the focal firm's customers at the heart of the network and the four constituencies rotating around them. You can use the mnemonic SCOPE to remember the constituencies in the network: S = suppliers, C = the focal firm's customers who are at the hub of the network, O = owners/investors, P = partners and E = employees. The direction of the arrowhead in the outer wheel is meant to indicate that they are all aligned to the common goal of helping the focal firm create and deliver value for, and from, their chosen customers. Three of these constituencies are external to the company: suppliers, owners/investors and partners. One is internal: employees. We can even think of this internal constituency as being a network in its own right. Individuals within firms have formal relationships with colleagues, for example in a reporting hierarchy or cross-functional teams. They also have informal relationships that are not task oriented. We examine relationships with suppliers, partners and employees in subsequent chapters.

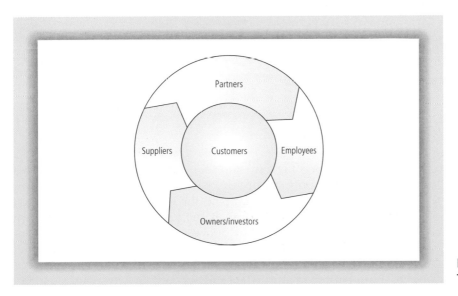

Figure 10.2
The SCOPE of CRM

Most companies operate within and through two major network constituencies: supplier networks and distribution networks. We introduce these in the following sections.

Supplier networks

As you read earlier, Toyota only manufactures about 20 per cent of the value of its cars. It relies on a network of approximately 50 000 supplier relationships to create and supply the inputs required for car manufacture. This is not to say that Toyota tries to manage 50 000 relationships. The company has a number of critical relationships with tier one suppliers (see Figure 10.3); these in turn have a number of important relationships that enable them to create and deliver what Toyota wants. They have relationships with third tier companies that enable them to meet their customers' requirements, and on.[3]

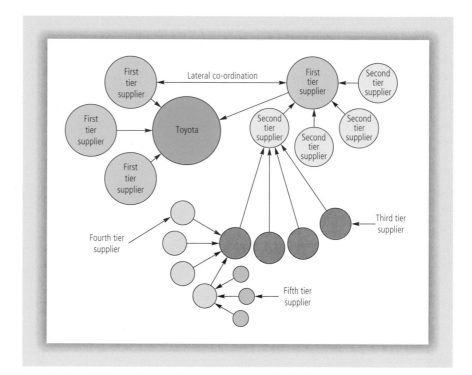

Figure 10.3
Toyota's supplier network

Toyota regards these tier one suppliers as 'systems suppliers'. This means that they not only supply the parts that they manufacture, but they are also responsible for managing the contributions of a network of lower tier suppliers. This is much the same idea as the 'category captain'. Some large supermarket operators have appointed category captains to work cooperatively with them to create profitable product categories. A category is a class of product, such as men's shaving supplies, hosiery or ice-cream. The category captain is responsible to the retailer for assembling a network of complementary lower tier suppliers that contribute to the category performance.

This illustrates a number of features of networks. Unlike single supplier–customer relationships, networks consist of a large number of indirect relationships. They also demand careful coordination. Toyota needs to work closely with tier one suppliers, so that they know exactly what Toyota wants and when. Many of these tier one suppliers will have their own CRM systems to manage their relationships with Toyota. Tier one, in turn, needs to coordinate with tier two suppliers. There might also need to be lateral coordination between suppliers at any tier. For example, this might be needed when Toyota's tier one suspension subassembly manufacturer needs to coordinate with Toyota's tier one braking system subassembly manufacturer.

Large companies within networks can exert considerable influence on the overall structure and performance of the network. Toyota might, for example, insist on specific product quality standards, not only from tier one suppliers, but also from tier two, three or four suppliers. It might also require a tier three supplier to stop purchasing from a tier four supplier, if that supplier also supplies a competitor. Toyota does, in fact, try to influence suppliers up to three tiers away.

Networks may be global. With increased concentration of manufacturing and globalization of brands, companies are faced with the challenge of sourcing inputs that are of a universal standard, whether the end customer is in America or Azerbaijan, Sydney or Shanghai. Kodak has addressed this problem by classifying its suppliers into three groups, world source suppliers, preferred suppliers and niche suppliers, as shown in Figure 10.4. This enables Kodak managers to purchase with confidence.

- World-source supplier
    - Required sources of specified products. Global suppliers. Prices negotiated centrally. Formal variance approval required for purchasing from other sources.

- Preferred supplier
    - Kodak identifies a few specific sources for a specific input. Purchasing from these sources is encouraged though not mandated. May have global or regional pricing agreements.

- Niche supplier
    - Specific suppliers of input for specific applications.

Figure 10.4
Kodak's supplier classification

Distribution networks

All companies have distribution networks. Some commentators prefer to use the term 'demand chain' to describe the linear arrangement of customers of the focal firm, their customers, and the customers of these customers, until the end user is reached. However, closer examination shows these to be network arrangements, not linear chains. Figure 10.5 shows how IBMs demand network moves computers so they reach end users in Italy.[4]

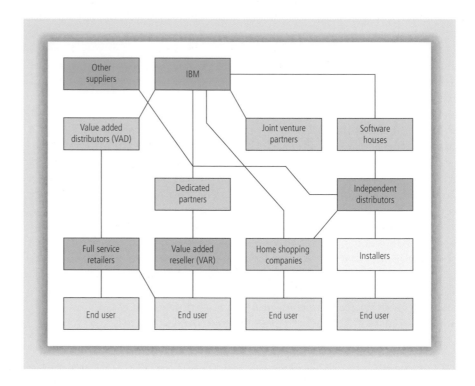

Figure 10.5
IBM's distribution network in Italy

This network illustrates a number of other features of business networks. Networks comprise a variety of organizations that contribute in different ways to the performance of a focal organization. Companies bring different competencies, resources, relationships, management styles and histories to the network. Quite possibly, each company will have been established and developed for different purposes, and may be working towards objectives that are in conflict with those of the focal firm. There is often potential for conflict in the relationships of customers and the focal firm. In this illustration, IBM supplies home shopping companies directly, thus denying its other first tier customers the opportunity to develop their own relationships with these catalogue companies. Managing network relationships can be very demanding. Customers will probably require different forms of contact with the focal company. Some might want the support of a key account management team; others might want to self-manage their purchasing through a portal. The focal company may or may not be willing to accommodate these requirements, depending upon the profit potential of the customer, or other considerations.

Principles of network management

In this section we set out a number of principles of network management.[5]

Networks are not controlled by single companies. There is no senior management team directing the operation of any network. All networks are complex, adaptive, self-regulating systems. Networks evolve as companies interact with each other over time, each member jostling for position, acting and reacting as they see fit.

However, there are circumstances where single companies do have significant influence, though not absolute control, over business networks. It is also true that all companies, whether they are bit players or star performers, want to exert influence over important network relationships in order to enhance and protect their competitive positions.

The degree of interdependence between network members plays a big role in determining the extent to which any party can influence, or be influenced by, others. If company A is highly dependent on company B, company B has the power to manage the relationship as it sees fit. If company A is also dependent on B, in other words the parties are mutually dependent, the power balance is likely to tend towards equilibrium and the relationship is likely to be managed as a partnership. If neither party is dependent on the other, then there may be no relationship to manage. It is clear that network management can be as much about being manageable, as about managing.[6]

Thomas Ritter and his colleagues have developed the idea of 'network competence' to describe the proficiency of companies in the twin tasks of managing both networks and individual relationships within networks. A company that is high in network competence not only has the necessary knowledge, skills, and qualifications, but also uses them effectively to manage relationships at both the network level and the individual level.[7] This suggests an important distinction that can be made between management of networks and management in networks.

Management of networks

Single companies, particularly in highly concentrated industries, can exert significant influence over business networks. You have already read about the Toyota case, for example. There are other contexts where this influence is found. Grocery supply-networks are dominated by retail multiples such as Wal-Mart and Tesco. Franchise operations are run by franchisors that typically specify and control every detail of their franchisees' operations. In these situations senior managers of the focal firm might think of themselves as being the network hub or channel captain. Their strategic orientation is towards the performance of the entire network.

New business start-ups are typically faced with the challenge of designing their networks from scratch. They have no relationships *in situ*, so they have to create the relationships that will enable them to create and deliver the desired value proposition and customer experience, in effect facing the same challenges as those charged with responsibility for strategic CRM. These challenges fall into three major categories: identify network requirements, acquire network expertise and manage network performance.

1. **Identify network requirements**: companies need to identify the business activities that must be performed by network members to create and deliver value for and from their chosen customers. These activities may be performed by suppliers, distributors, franchisees, contractors or business partners, for example. Some of these will be critical to value creation and delivery, others will not.

2. **Acquire network expertise**: companies will need to evaluate their current network position to identify current network members and assess whether they have the resources and commitment to perform the activities required. If the present network is inadequate, companies will need to extend their network to find the resources to perform the activities that are required. Effectively, they will be leveraging existing or developing new actor bonds at the organizational or interpersonal level to improve network performance. The resource constellation of the network is the sum of resources that are invested in interfirm relationships across the network as a whole. In a complex network, there is almost certain to be both underemployed resources and resource shortages. Are there ways in which the resources of the network could be better deployed? For example, does the focal company need to run its own fleet of vehicles when a network member has spare capacity in logistics? Must the focal company set up a retail sales-force if another network member can perform the same function on a commission basis?

   New network members are critical for winning a higher share of customer wallet. Tesco, for example, has created partnerships with a number of organizations, including a travel agency, insurance company and car manufacturer, as shown in Case 10.2. It has developed a number of other joint ventures where it does not have the competencies itself to exploit opportunities.

Case 10.2

Network partners at Tesco

Tesco has actively sought to create partnering programmes with other organizations. Partners have included:

- Lunn Poly, one of the UKs multiple travel agencies, to offer a discounted travel service
- B&Q, a major home improvement chain to offer discounted 'do-it-yourself' and homeware products
- Royal Bank of Scotland to offer banking and other financial services

- Direct Line to offer household insurance products
- General Motors to enable customers to buy cars at discounted prices.

The objective of all these programmes has been to win a greater share of customer spend.

3. **Manage network performance**: companies will need to brief network members so that they understand the focal company's customers and their role in creating value for them. This may mean writing specifications, implementing common CRM applications, setting and monitoring quality standards or designating people to take an oversight or coaching role. Companies will need to monitor how well the existing network is performing and look for ways to improve performance. Improvements can take two forms: more effective contributions or more efficient contributions from the network. Network members can contribute to CRM performance in a number of ways, including the following:

   - **Offering new customer insight**: they may be able to improve the focal company's understanding of its customers. In Australia when Commonwealth Bank and Woolworth's, the food retailer, created a joint venture to launch Ezi-Bank, the bank learned a lot more about their customers from access to Woolworth's transactional data.
   - **Creating value-adds** for the focal company or its customers as a result of better cost performance at meeting specifications, improved product quality or identifying new opportunities.

There is a clear danger in overspecifying network relationships. Marks & Spencer, for example, had very tight control over its supplier relationships. It established specifications and controlled design and quality rigorously. One effect was to stifle innovation. Suppliers did what they were told and failed to contribute to their full potential.

A number of different managerial roles have been identified in the management of business networks.[8]

- The **network architect** designs a network for a given purpose. This might, for example, be the leader of a joint venture across international borders, involving several companies. Typically, network architects are senior management with strategic responsibility. For example, when companies decide that they want to implement a CRM system, a senior manager often acts as network architect, specifying the various network tasks that need performing as the CRM project takes shape. The architect (we called this person the CRM programme director in Chapter 3) may identify a number of roles for network partners: systems integrators, CRM software vendors, data analytics companies and so on, as outlined in Figure 10.6.
- The **lead operator** introduces particular businesses or individuals into the network.

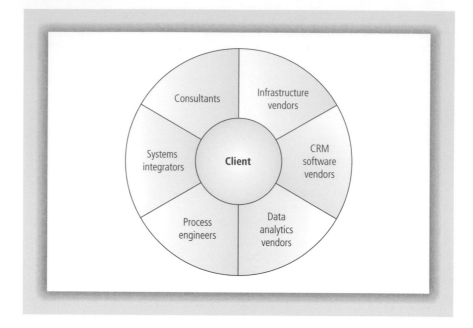

Figure 10.6
Technology
partners for CRM
implementations

- The **caretaker** takes an overview of the performance of the network, perhaps suggesting ways in which the network resources could be better deployed.

Management in networks

Not all network relationships are alike. The challenge of managing network relationships is all the more apparent when you consider how much variety exists. Network relationships vary in terms of their importance, intensity, closeness, strength, adaptation, commitment and power distribution.[9]

Not all relationships are equally important. Some assume more importance because of their implications for value creation or value destruction. A relationship that is difficult and costly to manage may be important because it is a value destroyer. On the other hand a relationship with a strategically significant customer assumes importance because of the value it produces. Relationship intensity is expressed in the number, frequency and level of contacts between the companies. In a close relationship there would be sharing of information, joint problem solving and commitment of resources by both partners, and trust would evolve over time. Closeness does not necessarily imply a lack of conflict. Conflict and cooperation can coexist in strong relationships; they are not necessarily mutually exclusive. Stronger relationships are more able to withstand challenges to the social and structural bonds that tie them. The power distribution between network members, as you read above, can also have a significant impact on how network relationships are managed.

Management in networks is both about managing individual relationships and managing clusters of relationships. For example, consumer goods manufacturers commonly cluster their customers into two groups: retail multiples and independents. Each is managed in very different ways. Retail multiples are treated as important individual customers and may have dedicated account managers, category specialists, merchandising teams and logistics specialists assigned to them, whereas independents are treated as a homogenous cluster and serviced through independent wholesalers.

Research into network competence

Thomas Ritter and his colleagues have begun to research the influence of network competence on the performance of focal organizations.[10] Using data collected from 308 German mechanical and electrical engineering companies, they found that network competence has a strong positive influence on the focal firm's product and process innovation success. Another study examined the performance of 149 university spin-offs, formed to commercialize technologies originating from publicly funded research institutions. They found that several performance variables, including sales growth, sales per employee, profit, perceived customer relationship quality and long-term survival, are influenced by the spin-off's network competence. Research is in an early stage of development, but it promises to deliver results of use to managers.

Summary

In this chapter you have learned about the importance of business networks to CRM performance. Networks are an inescapable feature of the business landscape. They are complex, interactive systems that are always undergoing change. Every company occupies a network position which is really no more than the sum total of its network relationships and all the activity links, resource ties and actor bonds that these relationships contain. Network constituents can be remembered through the mnemonic SCOPE: suppliers, customers, owners, partners and employees. Two of these are particularly important to CRM. Network members supply the material inputs, services, funding, people, technology and knowledge that are used to create value propositions for the focal firm's customers, and network members play demand chain roles in communicating and distributing products and services to customers. No networks are subject to the absolute control of any single company, though all organizations strive to enhance their network position by exerting influence over other network members. Senior managers need to master two network management competences: managing of networks, and managing in networks. Management of networks involves identifying the activities that need to be performed in order for companies to create and deliver value for and from customers, and to recognize, then coordinate and manage, the actors and resources that are best suited to perform those activities. Sometimes these will be internal to an organization; often they will be external. Management in networks involves managing both clusters of network members, such as segments of customers, and managing individual network members, such as advertising agencies or logistics partners.

References

1. Håkansson, H. and Henders, B. (1992) International co-operative relationships in technological development. In: M. Forsgren, J. Johanson, et al. (eds.) *Managing networks in international business.* Philadelphia: Gordon and Breach, pp. 32–46.
2. Ritter, T. and Germunden, H.G. (2003) Network competence: its impact on innovation success and its antecedents. *Journal of Business Research*, Vol. 56, pp. 745–755.
3. Blenkhorn, D. and Noori, A.H. (1999) What it takes to supply Japanese OEMs. *Industrial Marketing Management*, Vol. 19(1), pp. 21–31.
4. Ford, D. (2001) *Understanding business markets and purchasing.* London: Thompson Learning.
5. This section is largely derived from the work of the IMP (Industrial Marketing and Purchasing) group of researchers. Some relevant IMP publications, which were used to put together this part of the chapter are: Ford, D., Berthon, P., Gadde, L-E., Håkansson, H., Naudé, P., Ritter, T. and Snehota, I. (2002) *The business marketing course: managing in complex networks.* Chichester: John Wiley; Ford, D., Gadde, L-E., Håkansson, H., Lundgren, A., Snehota, I., Turnbull, P. and Wilson, D. (1998) *Managing business relationships.* Chichester: John Wiley; Gemünden, H-G., Ritter, T. and Walter, A. (1997) *Relationships and networks in international markets.* Oxford: Pergamon; Håkansson, H. and Snehota, I. (1995) *Developing relationships in business networks.* London: International Thompson Press; Naudé, P. and Turnbull, P. (1998) *Network dynamics in international marketing.* Oxford: Pergamon. See also the IMP Group's website www.impgroup.org.
6. Ritter, T., Wilkinson, I.F. and Johnston, W.J. (2004) Managing in complex business networks. *Industrial Marketing Management*, Vol. 33, pp. 175–183.
7. Ritter, T. and Gemünden, H.G. (2003) Network competence: its impact on innovation success and its antecedents. *Journal of Business Research*, Vol. 56, pp. 745–755.
8. Snow, C.C., Miles, R.E. and Coleman, H.J. Jr. (1992) Managing 21st century network organizations. *Organizational Dynamics*, Winter, pp. 5–19.

9. Cheung, M.Y.S. and Turnbull, P.W. (1998) A review of the nature and development of inter-organisational relationships: a network perspective. In: P. Naudé and P.W. Turnbull (eds). *Network dynamics in international marketing*. Oxford: Pergamon, pp. 42–69.

10. Ritter, T. and Gemünden, H-G. (2003) Network competence: its impact on innovation success and its antecedents. *Journal of Business Research*, Vol. 56(9), September, pp. 745–755; Ritter, T. and Gemünden, H-G. (2004) The impact of a company's business strategy on its technological competence, network competence and innovation success. *Journal of Business Research*, Vol. 57(5), May, pp. 548–558; Achim, W., Auer, M. and Ritter. T. (2006) The impact of network capabilities and entrepreneurial orientation on university spin-off performance. *Journal of Business Venturing*, Vol. 21(4), July, pp. 541–567; Ritter, T. and Gemünden, H-G. (2003) Inter-organizational relationships and networks: an overview. *Journal of Business Research*, Vol. 56(9), September, pp. 691–697.

Chapter 11
Managing supplier and partner relationships

By the end of this chapter, you will understand:

1. the role that suppliers and partners play in the achievement of CRM outcomes
2. the many types of supplier and partner
3. trends in supplier relationship management.

Introduction

This chapter examines the important role that suppliers and partners play in the achievement of CRM outcomes. As was made clear in the last chapter, every company is located in a network of other companies, organizations, groups and individuals, the performance of which significantly determines that company's success or failure. Among two of the more important network constituencies are suppliers and partners, who sit at different positions in the value chain.

The value chain (Figure 11.1) is a framework developed by Michael Porter that identifies ways companies create value.[1] The nine value-creating activities are clustered into primary and secondary activities. The primary activities listed along the bottom of the value chain are inbound logistics, operations, outbound logistics, marketing and sales, and service. The support activities are listed vertically at the top of the value chain and are procurement, technology development, human resource management and firm infrastructure. Value can be created by companies by managing each component of the value chain more efficiently and effectively, and by improving coordination of these activities across the business. In this chapter we are concerned with the

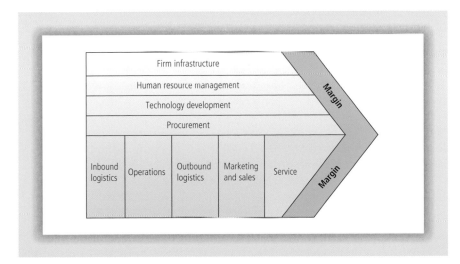

Figure 11.1
Michael Porter's
value chain model

relationships that companies establish with suppliers as they procure input goods and services (a secondary activity, according to Porter) and with partners in other parts of the value chain, for example, operations, outbound logistics, marketing, selling and service.

In the sections that follow we will first look at relationships with suppliers, and then partners.

Supplier relationships

Suppliers are the 'S' in the SCOPE model that was introduced in Chapter 10. Many people think that supplier relationship management is quite distinct from CRM. In IT terms this may be so. Supplier relationship management is a back-office function managed through enterprise resource planning (ERP), supply chain management (SCM) or specialist supplier relationship management (SRM) applications. CRM is a front-office function managed through a different set of software applications, though these can be seamlessly integrated with ERP, SCM and SRM. For example, SAP Business Suite offers a comprehensive family of industry-specific software applications including ERP, SRM, SCM and CRM that allow for complete integration.

We discuss supplier relationships here because we believe that suppliers can and should be aligned and synchronized to contribute significantly to the achievement of value for both the focal company and its customers. At the very least, suppliers need to be briefed and managed so that they provide the right inputs, at the right time and at the right price to enable the focal company to serve its customers well.

Case 11.1

Synchronizing customer and supplier management at SEAT

Supply chain management is synchronized with customer purchasing at Spanish auto manufacturer, SEAT.

EXEL is a global leader in providing supply chain solutions to the automotive industry. EXEL works closely with SEAT providing an all in one solution for the car manufacturer and its suppliers. Essentially EXEL manages the logistics for the just-in-time assembly line, linking the manufacturer with a network of more than 120 component suppliers. To achieve this EXEL manages the supply of 95 500 components every day and nearly 6500 components every hour, from the suppliers to the assembly line where 2335 cars per day are manufactured. It takes only 105 minutes between a part being ordered by SEAT and that part being assembled in the car. To build 2335 cars per day, EXEL receives an order for a new car every 35 seconds.

Relationships with suppliers are critical to the delivery of value to both the focal company and its customers. In 2006 General Motors spent US$164 billion and General Electric spent US$74 billion on purchasing input goods and services. For many companies, purchasing costs are 50 per cent or more of the total costs of running the business. There are variations between industries: in electricity and gas utilities, input goods and services represent 10 to 15 per cent of sales. In electronics it is 30 to 60 per cent; in chemicals it is 40 to 85 per cent. In 2006, Toyota spent a total of ¥16 335 billion on input goods and services. A 1 per cent saving in procurement costs would lead to a direct improvement in Toyota's bottom line over ¥163 billion, undoubtedly thrilling shareholders!

The relationship between suppliers and their customers has often been portrayed as a conflicted, adversarial power struggle in which each player manoeuvres to secure a bigger share of profit. While there is still clear evidence of short-term, opportunistic behaviours on both the supplier and customer side, in recent years there has been a trend towards a more relational approach to supplier management. This is characterized as a shift from a win–lose approach to supplier management to a win–win approach.

Improvements in supply network management offer much more than the simple prospect of reductions in direct input costs.[2] Many companies now cooperate closely with their suppliers in a number of activities, such as product development, supplier accreditation and process alignment.

Product development

Suppliers may have ideas for product improvements or new products. A leading machine tool manufacturer, Mazak Corporation, is often in a position to advise customers of ways to make manufacturing operations more cost-effective. One study of the South African textile industry has found that collaboration between clothing manufacturers and clothing retailers accelerates the product development process, and enables fashion items to be brought to market more quickly than those of competitors.[3] Sometimes product development costs and risks are shared between customer and supplier.

Supplier accreditation programmes

Some companies have introduced supplier accreditation programmes, under which certified or preferred supplier status is granted to suppliers that meet certain quality standards. If you are not accredited you are not shortlisted to supply, and without accreditation you cannot begin to establish a relationship. There are three main supplier accreditation options: requiring suppliers to be certified as ISO 9000 compliant; requiring suppliers to monitor and improve their operations against an external business excellence standard or developing and implementing your own accreditation programme.

One common approach to supplier accreditation is to require suppliers to be accredited against the international standard, ISO 9000. The ISO

9000 series is an international quality standard in which quality is defined as:

> 'the totality of features and characteristics of a product or service that bear on its ability to satisfy stated or implied needs'.

The ISO 9000 series is a family of related standards that have been developed to help organizations design, implement and operate effective quality management systems.

- ISO 9000 describes the fundamentals of quality management systems and sets out the terminology that is used in quality management systems.
- ISO 9001 specifies the requirements of a quality management system when organizations need to demonstrate their ability to provide products and services that meet customer or regulatory requirements.
- ISO 9004 provides guidelines for both the effectiveness and efficiency of quality management systems.
- ISO 19011 provides guidance on auditing quality management systems.

When a company is certified to ISO 9000 standards, this means that the company has documented its quality system to the satisfaction of an approved third party. ISO 9000 is administered by the International Organization for Standardization, based in Geneva, and is subject to periodic change.

Other companies insist that their suppliers apply for the Malcolm Baldrige National Quality Award, the European Quality Award or some other acknowledged business excellence model. The European Quality Award (see Figure 11.2), which is administered by the European Foundation for Quality Management, assesses company performance against a non-prescriptive framework. The model's framework contains nine criteria. Five of these are 'enablers' (leadership, policy and strategy, people, partnerships and resources) and four are 'results' (customer

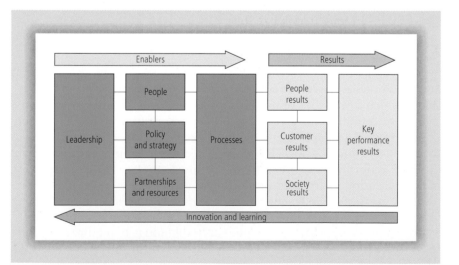

Figure 11.2
EFQM excellence model[4]

results, people results, society results and key performance results). The 'enabler' criteria describe what an organization does. The 'results' criteria describe what an organization achieves. 'Results' are explicitly linked to 'enablers'.[5]

Other companies operate their own supplier accreditation programmes: Ford, Motorola and Body Shop for example. Motorola have said:

> 'If you're a Motorola supplier, an ISO 9000 certification won't even buy you a cup of coffee. We would never stop auditing a company with ISO 9000. It's just a fraction of what we are looking for'.[6]

The Body Shop rates its suppliers for their adherence to Body Shop's published ethical standards.

Process alignment

Once customers and suppliers make a commitment to each other, they may begin to look for opportunities to align their processes. Process alignment has the objective of reducing the costs of maintaining the relationship. Two processes are widely aligned: quality processes and the order fulfilment processes.

Aligning quality processes

Failure to comply with quality standards can be a huge cost for some companies. It has been suggested that the poor quality of incoming goods accounts for up to 70 per cent of total non-quality costs.[7] Despite W. Edwards Deming's injunction that companies should 'cease dependence on inspection to achieve quality',[8] many companies still use inspection for that purpose. An alternative is for the supplier and customer to determine jointly how to improve quality performance, thereby reducing, for both companies, the cost of nonconformance, and improving their competitive position. Process alignment on both sides of the relationship might look like this:

- the customer establishes best in class quality standards
- the supplier benchmarks quality conformance against best-in-class and identifies opportunities for improvement
- supplier and customer agree strategy for quality improvement, involving kaizen (continuous improvement by all people involved in the process), information sharing and ongoing benchmarking
- supplier introduces a quality assurance programme (quality inspection programme abandoned by customer!).

Figure 11.3 shows how NCR changed its purchasing processes as it became more relationally oriented.[9] Important changes were that the company ceased the practice of inviting suppliers to tender annually and developed a number of key supplier relationships. The quality of bought in parts improved materially.

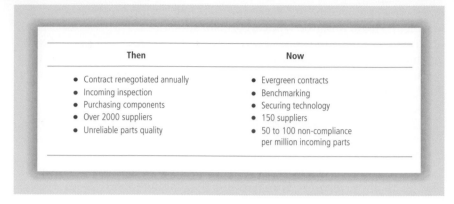

Then	Now
• Contract renegotiated annually	• Evergreen contracts
• Incoming inspection	• Benchmarking
• Purchasing components	• Securing technology
• Over 2000 suppliers	• 150 suppliers
• Unreliable parts quality	• 50 to 100 non-compliance per million incoming parts

Figure 11.3
How NCR's purchasing policies changed

Aligning the order fulfilment process

A second process that is often redesigned as companies become closer is the order-to-cash cycle, or the order fulfilment process. This process involves the customer establishing an acceptable inventory level and issuing an order for inventory replenishment when that limit is approached. The supplier fills the order and invoices the customer. The customer pays the invoice. Costs are removed and accuracy improved by the application of two different technology-based solutions: electronic data interchange and portals.

Electronic data interchange (EDI) enables suppliers and customers to trade electronically. EDI involves the interchange of unambiguously structured inventory, order and invoice data between computers according to agreed message standards. It eliminates the labour-intensive paper trail that is characteristic of many order processing systems. Large manufacturers, such as automobile companies, require their suppliers to implement EDI.

EDI delivers a number of strategic and operational benefits to companies. Strategic benefits from EDI include the following:

● EDI acts as a structural bond that not only symbolizes the commitment of the participants, but also acts as barrier to exiting the relationship
● EDI provides convenient access to accurate customer purchasing and payment histories and to detailed customer management costs that can be useful when conducting customer portfolio analysis
● EDI ensures improved customer service (more accurate and timely fulfilment)
● EDI records allow suppliers to produce more accurate demand forecasts
● EDI creates the possibility to developing new business processes such as just-in-time operations.

Operational benefits from EDI include cost savings, improved accuracy, better fulfilment performance, and improved cash flow and working capital positions.

● EDI eliminates the need to re-enter data from paper documents, thus preventing clerical errors. It has been suggested that 70 per cent of all computer input has previously been output from another computer. Each re-entry of data is a potential source of error.

- Electronic processing of orders costs a fraction of paper-based systems, perhaps as little as one-tenth. This is partly because EDI reduces the need for people to be involved in order processing.
- EDI systems can reduce inventory costs. When customers submit their delivery requirements with order data, suppliers can plan production with more confidence, thus reducing inventories. Reduction in inventory can result in major savings.
- Use of EDI to transmit invoice data and payments can improve cash flow and working capital, as invoices are routinely dealt with according to rules built into the system.

One study of EDI in the automotive industry finds that although component suppliers are compelled to implement EDI by their assembler customers, they derive significant benefits including improved productivity, clerical staff savings, increased data accuracy, enhanced customer service and reduction in administrative costs. Suppliers who integrate EDI into their other systems enjoy even more dramatic results.[10]

Portals are becoming more common as companies try to reduce transaction costs and improve customer service. Extranets provide the infrastructure that enable customers to access a supplier's portal. A portal acts as a storefront. It is a company's electronic shop window. It has on display a number of products and services that are customizable for different portal visitors. The extranet enables customers and other visitors to get access to parts of the 'store' behind the portal 'storefront' from outside the company. Visitors gain access by password or security certificate. Customers can use a supplier's portal to place orders, track order progress, download training manuals, obtain price lists, access FAQ pages, and obtain invoices, brochures and collateral materials. Suppliers can use portals to service the requirements of some or all of their customers. One of the major benefits is that it reduces service costs by eliminating the use of more expensive communication channels, such as sales representatives, couriers, fax and telephone. Effectively, portals facilitate customer self-service. Whether this enhances or detracts from customer satisfaction is a moot point.

One company that has segmented its customer base, offering EDI to one segment and portal service to another, is Flymo, a manufacturer of lawnmowers available both through retail multiples and independent retailers. As shown in Case 11.2, Flymo services its large superstore customers by EDI. Smaller customers transact with Flymo though a portal.

Case 11.2

Flymo's electronic customer service

Flymo is a leading UK brand of lawnmower, targeted principally at the household market. The brand is distributed through two major channels: large do-it-yourself superstores and smaller, often independent, distributors. Flymo introduced parallel technologies to service these two segments. In collaboration and with the full support of the DIY superstores, it introduced an EDI system. Smaller distributors were serviced by Flymo through a portal. Co-developed with IBM, and connected to IBMs global network for security purposes, the portal was introduced in 1998. It cost £100 000 to develop and implement, generating payback in less than one year. Flymo's smaller customers use it for online ordering, accounts and invoicing. It has eased communication between Flymo and dealers and raised customer satisfaction, although not all smaller customers responded positively to its introduction. It has also freed staff from routine order processing activity to deliver better customer service.

Trends in supplier relationship management

A number of trends in supplier relationship management are helping companies improve the value they create for themselves and their customers. Important among these are vendor reduction programmes, category management, product development alliances and electronic procurement.

Vendor reduction programmes

The tradition has been for companies to have many suppliers competing to supply inputs. These would be played off against each other to obtain the best deal on any particular transaction. This short-term focus is now being replaced by a relational approach to supplier management known as strategic sourcing or supplier partnering. A main driver of this change has been recognition of the high fixed costs of supplier management.

Purchasing costs can be divided into fixed and variable. Variable costs are those that are associated with a particular transaction. These include the costs of the purchased product and other item costs such as insurance and transportation.

Fixed costs are all the other costs of creating and maintaining a relationship with a supplier. These costs include:

1. The costs of raising and processing each order. The UKs Chartered Institute of Purchasing and Supply estimates these average about £50, regardless of the value of the items purchased.[11]
2. The time of management and staff, as they check supplier credentials and credit ratings, communicate with suppliers, audit conformance to order specification and identify the best deal on a transaction-by-transaction basis.
3. Accommodation, heating, lighting, technology and so on.

These costs are fixed regardless of the value of the items purchased, and could possible be greater than the invoiced value of the purchased items.

Purchasers customarily try to reduce variable costs by negotiating better prices or by outsourcing specialist services, such as logistics, to third parties. Often, however, there may be greater gains to be enjoyed from controlling fixed costs, and this generally means reducing the number of vendors with whom you transact.

Companies engaged in vendor reduction programmes are pursuing a number of benefits:

1. **Reduced transaction costs**: the fixed costs of purchasing are reduced when the number of vendors is reduced. This is complemented by reduced search costs. If you deal with a few regular suppliers, you spend less time and money searching for new suppliers to add to your list.
2. **Additional volume discounts**: by consolidating purchases that had previously been distributed among a number of suppliers, customers place themselves in a stronger negotiating position. Dun & Bradstreet, for example, consolidated their purchasing of tele-communications, IT and travel to yield annual savings of $10 million.
3. **Performance compliance**: closer relationships with fewer suppliers, supported by shared information about future requirements and enabled by IT, produces better order fulfilment. Given closer relationships with fewer suppliers, customers expect their logistics and quality standards to be met. For example, many companies have adopted an OTIFNE logistics performance standard that requires suppliers to deliver on time (OT), in full (IF) and with no error (NE). If your supplier achieves on time compliance of 80 per cent, in full compliance of 90 per cent and no error compliance of 70 per cent, overall performance compliance computes at $90 \times 80 \times 70$ per cent, or only 50 per cent.
4. **Increased technical cooperation**: suppliers and customers can share customer and technical information to reduce risk, share costs and improve the probability of new product success.

Figure 11.4 sets out the benefits that retailer Tesco believes they enjoy from their strategic sourcing programme, and Figure 11.5 names a number of American, European and Australian retailers and manufacturers that have pursued vendor reduction programmes. You will see the results that some companies, like British Home Stores, Ford, SEAT, Shell Retail

Tesco claims several advantages:
- Lower costs
- Improved investment climate
- Better product quality
- Improved logistics
- Better product development

... and one danger:
- Supplier complacency

Figure 11.4
Tesco benefits from vendor reduction programmes

Figure 11.5
Vendor reduction
programmes from
around the world

British Home Stores (UK)	-	from 1,000 product suppliers to 80, of whom 35 supply 80% of BHS's retail assortment
Shell Retail (UK)	-	from 50 product suppliers to 30
Laura Ashley (UK)	-	from 8 logistics vendors to 1
Xerox (USA)	-	from 5000 suppliers to 400 in 5 years
Compaq (USA)	-	from 35 logistics vendors to 5
Ford (USA)	-	from 3200 suppliers to 2100 in 6 years
SEAT (Spain)	-	from 1500 suppliers to 300 in 2 years
Woolworths (Australia)	-	from 2000 product suppliers to 300
Wattyl (Australia)	-	from 100 suppliers to 10

and Xerox, have achieved by applying vendor reduction across the entire organization. The data on Compaq and Laura Ashley indicate the economies that are feasible within a particular area, such as logistics.

Category management

In recent years a number of retailers have introduced category management, in collaboration with brand manufacturers, as a means of improving business performance. Traditionally, retailers have bought brands from manufacturers, very often on deals, and then merchandised and promoted furiously to reduce inventory levels. Category management differs from this brand-centric procurement model, and can be defined as follows:

> Category management is the management of a group of related or substitutable products as a single strategic business unit.

The focus is not on brands, but on categories such as shampoos, cereals, women's underwear and children's shoes. Category management has been described as:

> 'a management system (that) aims to reduce the distance from supplier to customer by defining and managing product categories, rather than individual brands, in an environment of enhanced mutual trust and cooperation between manufacturer and retailer'.[12]

Category managers are responsible for integrating procurement, pricing and merchandising of all brands in a category and jointly developing and implementing category-based plans with manufacturers, to enhance the outcomes for both parties.[13] The retailer will often work with a 'category captain', usually a brand leader in the category, to create the category plan. The captain will be responsible for assembling a network of co-suppliers to contribute to the category. Jointly, the category captain and retailer decide upon product assortment, promotions, pricing, placement and space allocation, and new product development. Category plans strive to meet the needs of the retailer, suppliers and customers alike.

Category management requires the retailer and supplier to establish close links that enable them to agree category objectives, optimize the category assortment, introduce new products, de-list brands or items that do not contribute to category performance and plot category or brand promotions. Category management is enabled by IT applications such as EDI, electronic funds transfer and activity-based costing.

Category management is sometimes cited as a win–win strategy for both retailer and manufacturer, potentially capable of generating a number of benefits, as shown in Figure 11.6[14] However, the consultants McKinsey & Company warn that most of the benefits from category management are skewed in favour of the retailer.[15] Indeed, research confirms that retailers enjoy higher prices and higher profits under category management than do competitors with traditional brand procurement strategies. Higher retailer profits are only achieved under certain conditions, particularly when interbrand competition is high and consumer store switching is low. Few economic benefits exist for the retailer when these conditions are absent.[16]

Benefits for supplier	Benefits for retailer
Increased profitability	**Financial:**
Increased business knowledge	Increased sales
Improved relationships with retailers	Increased margins
	Reduced costs
	Improved efficiency
	Increased market share
	Non-financial:
	Organizational learning
	More effective strategy implementation
	Better customer service
	Improved customer knowledge
	Understanding cost structures
	More open communications with suppliers
	Improved personal relationships
	Stability of best practice

Figure 11.6
Category management benefits

Product development alliances

It is becoming more common for companies to cooperate with their suppliers in product improvement and new product development programmes. Supplier competencies can be used to reduce development costs and accelerate time to market. For example, suppliers may be able to advise on cheaper or better specifications for the product. They may share some of the cost burden if they are assured of being a key supplier when the product is eventually brought to market. Suppliers may even be the original source of new product ideas for their customers. Technical Felts, a manufacturer of air filtration felts, membranes and fabrics, partners with significant customers to develop application-specific solutions to those customers' air quality problems.

Collaboration platforms provide a set of technological tools and an information environment for collaboration between businesses developing new products. These platforms enable the alignment and integration of processes or work from geographically-separated network members. For example, Boeing has established virtual design teams with its suppliers to work on aircraft design projects. Technology companies working on systems integration projects for clients that have multinational sites are also linked by these collaborative platforms.

Case 11.3

Cooperation between electronics components suppliers and OEMs in the automobile industry

Significant cooperation between electronics components suppliers and OEMs, such as Toyota and BMW, underpins brand success. Innovations in automotive electronics have become increasingly complex, resulting in high-end vehicles containing more than 70 electronic control units and offering a variety of functions to the driver. In-vehicle telematics and infotainment systems provide services like digital radio, broadcast services, television, global positioning systems and MP3 audio. Future applications and services will integrate information sources available outside and inside the car, requiring vehicle systems connecting invehicle consumer electronics devices with the outside world in order to realize the vision of an intelligent networked car, connected with the environment and providing the driver with information according to his demands. There is now very close cooperation between automobile brand owners and components suppliers. Automobile manufacturers do not have the inhouse competencies to develop these electronics applications independently.

Source: Bosch GmbH[17]

Electronic procurement

Another trend in supplier relationship management is the development of electronic procurement. There is a strong economic incentive for companies to transact with suppliers online, and equally for suppliers to offer online procurement to their customers. For customers, online purchasing offers the prospect of reduced procurement costs and immediate order placement. One significant feature of online procurement is disintermediation (the elimination of one or more intermediaries from the supply chain). In other words, buyers can interact directly with suppliers and enjoy cost savings and communication direct to suppliers.

Suppliers, in turn, are motivated to sell direct to customers because it offers the prospect of three benefits: reduced customer management costs, enhanced control over the customer experience and enhanced cash flow due to immediate payment. Banks have found that transaction costs are dramatically reduced. Transaction costs over the Internet are one-tenth of branch-based costs. Even telephone-based transactions are less than one-half the cost of branch transactions. In the travel business, distribution costs for a $1000 package holiday are $150 if sold on commission through a travel agent, but $20 if sold direct over the Internet. These lower costs can be passed on to customers in the form of lower prices. The investment company Fidelity, for example, charges 3.25 per cent of the value of a purchase when a retail customer uses a standard paper-based application form to buy shares in mutual funds; when the purchase is made online the charge is only 1 per cent.

The trend towards electronic procurement is found in both business-to-business and business-to-consumer contexts.

Business-to-consumer e-commerce

Although the volume of consumer purchasing made online varies from country to country, and from product to product, the USA is still the marketplace in which online purchasing is at its most advanced. According to the US Census Bureau, in 2003 70 million American households (62 per cent of households) had one or more computers, up from 56 per cent in 2001, and sixty-two million households (55 per cent of households) had Internet access, up from 50 per cent in 2001. The Internet has become an integral part of the US economy. Eighteen per cent of adults conducted banking online in 2003. Twelve per cent of adults used the Internet to search for a job. Nearly half the adult population (47 per cent) used the Internet to find information on products or services. About one-third of adults (32 per cent) actually purchased a product or service online, compared with 2.1 per cent of adults who used the Internet for shopping in 1997.[18] The trend is upward as consumers become more confident in their remote shopping behaviours.

Forecasting consumer spending on the Internet is a dangerous occupation. In 1998, for example, it was forecast that 7 per cent of consumer expenditure would be online by the end of the century.[19] That did not happen. In 2006, US business-to-consumer e-commerce accounted for just 2.8 per cent of total retail sales, up from 2.4 per cent in 2005.[20] The categories that dominate consumer spending are computer hardware, movie and event tickets, automotive, office supplies, consumer electronics and child and baby products.[21]

Companies manage their customer interface on the Internet in different ways. Some companies only take orders online. Others also receive payment online. A few also deliver their product online, for example, software companies. Generally, shoppers like the convenience and speed of online purchasing and they expect to enjoy a price advantage over their bricks-and-mortar shopping.

Business-to-business e-commerce

B2B e-commerce is a much more significant phenomenon than B2C e-commerce. The US Census Bureau reports that in 2005 business-to-business e-commerce, which they define as transactions by manufacturers and merchant wholesalers, accounted for 92 per cent of all e-commerce. Evidence indicates that B2B e-commerce relies overwhelmingly on proprietary electronic data interchange (EDI) systems.[22] Experts generally agree that the value of transactions in B2B e-commerce is about ten times the value of B2C e-commerce.

In the USA 27 per cent of the total shipments by value of manufactured output was sold online. The industries with the largest percentage of online sales were transport equipment manufacturing (53 per cent) and beverage and tobacco manufacturing (49 per cent). Eighteen per cent of merchant wholesaler trade sales were completed online in the same year.[23] The trend for both manufacturer and merchant wholesaler online sales is upward.

B2B e-commerce is growing quickly because entry costs are very low. It can cost as little as $1000 to design a brochure-type website, with ongoing annual costs of web-hosting and site maintenance of only a few hundred dollars. In addition, for companies that choose not to use EDI, web-based trading employs open networks and standards delivering a much higher degree of interactivity and flexibility. The Internet is ubiquitous, accessible and cheap.

Timmers has provided a useful taxonomy of business models in B2B e-commerce.[24] Among the B2B models he recognizes are e-shops, e-procurement, e-malls, e-auctions and third-party marketplaces.

- **E-shops** we normally associate with B2C e-commerce, but some B2B enterprises also enable customers to purchase online. Customers anticipate lower prices, better information and greater convenience. Site operators expect enhanced revenues from reduced cost, increased sales and possibly the sale of advertising space, such as banner ads. Hewlett Packard's small and medium-sized business customers can buy direct online.[25] Some company websites, such as www.dell.com devote sections of their websites to corporate purchasing, as distinct from the household section.
- **E-procurement** involves the electronic tendering and procurement of goods and services. Japan Airlines, for example, procures some of its supplies through its web presence. For the customer, anticipated benefits include wider choice of suppliers, lower input costs and reduced transaction costs due to automation of the process. E-procurement may be accompanied by electronic negotiation and contracting. Customers and suppliers might also perform collaborative specification. Suppliers hope they will have the opportunity to submit more tenders, perhaps globally and experience lower tendering costs.
- An **e-mall** is a collection of e-shops on a single site. PTplace.com is an e-mall established by industrial components distributors for industrial components distributors. Distributors of Barden, Cooper, Dodge/Reliance, Drives Inc., FAG, Gates, INA, MRC, SKF or Timken products can shop for components at the one location, placing orders electronically, checking order status, availability and obtaining customized pricing. Each brand has its own shop at the site.
- **E-auctions** are electronic versions of conventional auctions. They feature electronic bidding, sometimes linked with payment and delivery. Some are enhanced by multimedia presentations of the

goods being auctioned. Benefits for suppliers and customers include increased efficiency in buying and selling. Websites such as www. liquidation.com, www.graysonline.com.au and even eBay conduct auctions of commercial and industrial equipment and supplies.

- **Third-party marketplaces** are buyer–seller websites that are operated by third parties. Microsoft has a third party marketplace for companies whose products and services may suit Microsoft's small business customers.[26] Sometimes, an entrepreneurial third party forms a strategic alliance with key partners to establish the marketplace. This was the case with Hospitalitybex which was established in Singapore in 2000 to serve as an electronic marketplace for the hospitality industry. Hospitalitybex was initially set up with a small number of industry partners, with the primary objective of streamlining the procurement process. It provides a one-stop destination for product and service sourcing, negotiation, selection, ordering, fulfilment, payment and reporting for the now 4000 organizational members.[27]

Not all of these e-commerce options are necessarily relational in character. E-auctions, for example, are compatible with a very transactional view of supplier relationships. Each auction can be viewed as a unique event in which participants buy and sell as if there were no history linking them. However, we are seeing evidence of co-opetition, that is, cooperation between competitors, to secure better deals on input raw materials and goods. For example, keen rivals Unilever and Procter and Gamble cooperate in the procurement of raw materials for manufacturing.

Partners

Relationships with business partners also need to be managed so that they can contribute to the achievement of CRM goals. We are not using the term 'partner' in this section in the same way that some CRM technology firms use it. Many technology firms offer what they call partner relationship management (PRM) applications. These applications help vendors manage their relationships with channel members, such as retailers and value added resellers (VAR). PRM is best thought of as the deployment of CRM tools for the management of relationships with a particular segment, that is, the channel member or partner. We examine PRM later in the book.

In this chapter we define the main function of partners as helping companies create and deliver value to their customers. They are the 'P' in the SCOPE model that was introduced in Chapter 10. Figure 11.7 identifies a number of different types of partners, divided into groups focused either on value creation or on value delivery.

Partners in value creation

We can identify a number of different types of partner in value creation: joint venture or alliance partners, category teams, benchmarking groups, regulators, customer advocacy groups and sponsors.

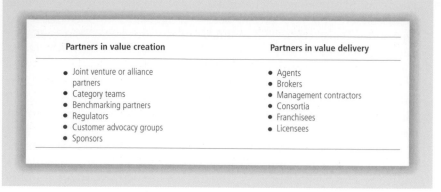

Figure 11.7
Partners in the
SCOPE model of
CRM

Strategic alliances

The terms 'joint venture', 'strategic alliance' and 'business partnership' tend to be used interchangeably. Indeed there is no clear consensus on the differences, if any, between these terms. They all feature interfirm cooperation. Partners in joint ventures or alliances maintain their own strategic autonomy while simultaneously establishing activity links, resource ties and actor bonds between the partner organizations for particular purposes. When British Airways and American Airlines agreed to coordinate routes, schedules and reservation systems, this was an alliance. It was neither a merger nor an acquisition. Both retained their autonomy. Alliances may involve two or more companies, two or more nations and two or more jurisdictions. They can be highly complex entities with no clear legal status. Equally they can be very simple arrangements.

Not all alliances are strategic. To be so they must contribute to the strategic goals of both organizations. You would expect to find a more balanced contribution and participation in a strategic alliance. Historically, many joint ventures (JV) have been initiated to enable a dominant partner to enter a minor partner's market. Essentially, the JV served as an export channel and there was little strategic value for the minor player. More recently, however, many JVs have featured bilateral or multilateral cooperation between partners in the development of new products for sale in the partners' and other markets.

Case 11.4

The STAR Alliance

The STAR Alliance is an alliance between 17 international and 3 regional airlines serving 855 destinations in 155 countries. The international members are Air Canada, Air New Zealand, All Nippon Airways, Asiana Airways, Austrian Airlines, BMI, LOT, Lufthansa, SAS, Singapore Airlines, South African Airways, Spanair, Swiss, TAP Portugal, Thai Airways International, United Airlines and US Airways.

The Star Alliance network was established in 1997 as the first global airline alliance to offer customers worldwide reach and a seamless travel experience. In 2006 the alliance flew 405 million passengers, 859 billion passenger kilometers, on 16 000 daily departures with a fleet of 2777 aircraft, generating US$115 billion. Passengers who are members of one of the Star Alliance airline frequent flyer programmes are able to earn miles or points on all qualifying flights across the Star Alliance network. Star Alliance Silver and Star Alliance Gold status are additional benefits that passengers become entitled to when they reach a higher status in an individual airline frequent flyer programme. Start Alliance Gold benefits include priority wait-listing, priority airport standby (where allowed by law), priority check-in, priority boarding (where available), extra baggage allowance and worldwide lounge access. Other member benefits include reduced waiting times and faster connections, because member airlines are located close to each other or share positions. Not only do passengers benefit, but so do the airlines. They experience economies of scale in purchasing everything from toilet paper to aircraft, shared costs estimated at over US$1.5 billion, shared technology and shared airport positions.

There are a number of different types of alliances. Broadly they can be classified into alliances between non-competing firms and alliances between competitors (known as co-opetition).

Alliances between non-competing firms

There are three main strategic motives behind alliances between non-competing firms: market expansion, vertical integration or diversification.[28]

Market expansion

Companies may enter into JVs to develop new domestic or international markets. Renault formed a JV with DINA (Diesel Nacional, SA) in order to enter the Mexican market. When Procter and Gamble decided to enter the Chinese market, they formed a JV with Guanzhou Lonkey Industrial Company (GLIC). P&G brought its technology and manufacturing expertise to the table. GLIC brought its distribution network and local knowledge. In the USA, medical clinics are establishing partnerships with retailers such as Wal-Mart, Target and the drug-store chain CVS to offer convenient and low-cost treatment for minor illnesses and injuries. In Brazil, Bradesco Bank has grown its credit portfolio through partnerships with retail chains that offer loans to poorer consumers.

Vertical integration

Vertical partnerships bring together neighbours in the supply or demand chain. Aerospatiale and Thomson set up a vertical partnership called

Sextant Avionique. Thomson manufactures avionics and electronic equipment used by Aerospatiale in its aircraft and helicopters. They formed a 50:50 JV to manufacture and design new forms of equipment for the aerospace industry. Pepsi acquired part of Pizza Hut, KFC and Taco Bell to secure access to the restaurant market segment.

Diversification

Alliances aimed at diversification feature cross-industry agreements. BMW and Rolls Royce got together to establish a JV to enable BMW to enter the aircraft engine market. JVs may be initiated when technologies begin to converge. Philips and DuPont have cooperated in the development of an optical disk system for data storage.

Alliances between competing firms

Alliances between competitors seem paradoxical. How can competitors cooperate? Research suggests that perhaps 70 per cent of alliances are between competitors.[29] There are, again, three main types of alliances between competitors: shared supply alliances, quasi-concentration alliances and complementary alliances.

Shared supply alliances

This happens when competitors get together to experience economies of scale on the manufacture of some component or some stage of the manufacturing process. Volkswagen and Renault jointly manufacture automatic gearboxes. The European market for automatic transmission cars is only 8 per cent of the overall car market. Together, because of the volumes, they generate economies that they could not enjoy independently, as they cooperate in research and development and manufacturing.

Quasi-concentration alliances

In a quasi-concentration alliance the parties collaborate for the creation of a product that the consortium then offers to the market. In other non-consortium activities the parties compete as usual. An example is the development of the Tornado fighter plane by BAe, DASA and Alenia. Given the huge capital costs it made little sense for the three to compete in the market independently. Quite possibly none of them would have made a return on their investment in the project. Collectively they were able to pool their resources and develop a product, the manufacture of which was shared among the three partners.

Complementary alliances

In a complementary alliance, partners bring different competencies to the alliance. Commonly, one partner has developed a new product that is distributed through the other party's distribution network. Ford sold rebadged Mazda cars, and Chrysler sold Mitsubishi cars in the USA. Chrysler only sold those models that filled gaps in Chrysler's product line.

Category teams

You read earlier in this chapter about the trend towards category management. A category team consists of the network of brand principals that contribute to a category offer by a retailer. The retailer, in partnership with the category captain, decides which brands and lines to stock. The UKs count line confectionary market contains a number of 'must-have' brands manufactured by Mars, Nestlé and Cadbury. Whoever serves as category captain, these three manufacturers must be offered shelf space.

Benchmarking partners

Benchmarking is defined as follows:

> Benchmarking is a business improvement discipline involving the continuous, systematic evaluation of products, services and processes against organizations that are recognized as representing best practice.

Xerox, the copier company, is reputed to have originated benchmarking. Xerox's patents expired towards the end of the 1970s. As that happened, Japanese competitors like Canon introduced their products to the US market. To Xerox's alarm, they did so at a retail price that was lower than Xerox's manufacturing costs. Xerox began a benchmarking programme to find out what they could do to match and better the Japanese.

One of the key components of the benchmarking process is the selection of benchmarking partners (see Figure 11.8). A common misunderstanding about benchmarking is that it is simply a matter of identifying and learning from best in class companies. It is not so. Benchmark groups are networks of companies who expect mutual gain from their participation.

The benchmarking group may be internal to a company, intra or trans-industry. Each has their value, depending upon the benchmarking objective. For example, if you are a bank wanting to identify the practices which generate the highest average deposits per account, you would want to create an internal benchmarking group.

An intra-industry benchmarking group has been established by 18 corporations in the telecommunications industry, including AT&T, Nynex, MCI and GTE. They are learning from each other by sharing

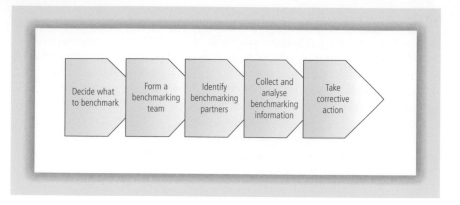

Figure 11.8
The benchmarking
process

their knowledge of customer satisfaction, new product development and customer service.

A trans-industry group of benchmarking participants from FedEx, Caterpillar, Westinghouse and DuPont was established to learn from each other about best practices in the area of financial management. The London Benchmarking Group (LBG) is a group of over 100 companies working together to measure corporate community investment (CCI).

Participants usually have concerns about disclosure of competitively sensitive information to their benchmarking partners. For this reason, codes of practice have been developed. These include the Benchmarking Code of Conduct of the American Productivity and Quality Centre, and the European Benchmarking Code of Conduct.[30]

Benchmarking groups can have significant impact on the creation of customer value. GPT Payphone Systems manufactures payphones, phonecards and payphone management systems for customers in 80 countries. It set up a benchmarking programme to identify best practice in receiving and managing customer returns. As a result it set up and rolled out a barcode booking-in system for returns that also served to track repairs, and a buffer stock system for replacing returned goods. The result was a 99.7 per cent success rate in next day replacement, and a considerable increase in customer satisfaction.[31]

Case 11.5

Benchmarking at Avon Cosmetics

In the USA, Avon Cosmetics' immediate customers are the 450 000 sales representatives that sell Avon products to the end consumer. Fifteen per cent of this sales-force generates 50 per cent of sales. Avon established an internal benchmarking study to identify and share best practice within and across the company's five geographic sales regions. The objective was to improve branch productivity through a range of process improvements. Among the outcomes were changes to the way managers were trained in the use of the company's IT system, an improved call management system and regular meetings between customer service supervisors to share ideas and experiences.

Regulators

Many industries are regulated, particularly those in which consumers are thought to be at risk either because of deregulation or because of monopolistic competition. These include financial services, telecommunications, rail, gas, electricity and airlines.

In the UK, Ofcom is the regulator for the communications industries, with responsibilities across television, radio, telecommunications and wireless communications services. Under the Communications Act 2003, Ofcom's statutory duties are:

> 'to further the interests of citizens in relation to communications matters; and to further the interests of consumers in relevant markets, where appropriate by promoting competition'.

A close relationship with regulators allows communications companies to ensure that they are not in breach of regulations or legislation, and have early knowledge of, and perhaps influence, forthcoming regulations or legislation. The regulator's office is also a source of useful insight into the issues that are worrying customers. Ofcom, for example, operates a complaints-handling process and conducts consumer research. Ofcom's investigation of the consumer experience of the fixed and mobile, Internet and digital broadcasting markets aimed at measuring how well consumers are faring in respect of choice, price and range; availability and take-up; awareness, comparing and switching; protection and concerns.

Customer advocacy groups

Customer advocacy groups (CAGs) promote and protect the interests of consumers. CAGs operate within many countries. There is the Consumers' Association of Canada, the Consumers' Association of Singapore and the Consumers' Association of Iceland, for example.

In the UK, the Consumers' Association, publishers of *Which?* magazines and books, is a not-for-profit organization which has been researching and campaigning on behalf of consumers since it was founded in 1957. With over 650 000 members, it is the largest consumer organization in Europe. Its mission is to 'make individuals as powerful as the organizations they have to deal with in their daily lives'.[32]

There are some international consumer advocacy groups too. Consumers International (CI) is a federation of national consumer associations that 'defends the rights of all consumers, particularly the poor and marginalized, through empowering national consumer groups and campaigning at the international level'.[33] CI represents over 220 member organizations in 115 countries. It focuses on issues such as food distribution, health care and globalization.

CAGs can have direct influence on corporate behaviour, and indirect influence through lobbying activity. During the 1970s the UKs Consumers' Association (CA) developed its role as a campaigning body and lobby group. In 1972 it was instrumental in the establishment of the Office of Consumer Unions (BEUC) which lobbies consumer issues to the EC in Brussels. The CA claims responsibility for several important Acts of Parliament which have improved the position of consumers, including the Unfair Contract Terms Act 1977, the Consumer Agreements Arbitration Act 1988, the Property Misdescriptions Act 1991, the Cheques Act 1992 and the Sale and Supply of Goods Act 1994. The CA has recently campaigned to curtail the marketing of low quality food to children, to lift safety in the cosmetic surgery industry and to reduce bank charges.

Individual activists may also be worth considering as part of the 'P' constituency of SCOPE. For example Ralph Nader, the American lawyer and consumer activist, wields considerable influence. His 1965 book, *Unsafe at Any Speed*, detailed the carelessness of the American automobile industry in producing unsafe vehicles. A particular target was General Motors with its fragile Corvair. Nader wrote:

> 'A great problem of contemporary life is how to control the power of economic interests which ignore the harmful effects of their applied science and technology'.[34]

The book led to congressional hearings and a series of automobile safety laws were passed in 1966. Since 1966, Nader has agitated for the introduction of at least eight major federal consumer protection laws, including the motor vehicle safety laws and the Safe Drinking Water Act. He has been involved in the launching of federal regulatory agencies, such as the Occupational Safety and Health Administration (OSHA), the Environment Protection Agency (EPA) and the Consumer Product Safety Administration. Nader had input into the recall of millions of defective motor vehicles and also improved access to government through the Freedom of Information Act of 1974.[35]

Some consumer advocacy groups concentrate on single industries, for example the Timeshare Consumers' Association which aims to 'help make timeshare an enjoyable, value-for-money form of holidaying for consumers'.[36] Pharmaceutical companies work with and through patient advocacy groups (PAGs) to achieve the aims of both the advocacy group and themselves (see Case 11.6). PAGs are established to represent the interests of sufferers from disease, their families and carers. In the UK, for example, there are the National Schizophrenia Fellowship (NSF), Depression Alliance, SANE, Parkinson's Disease Society, British Diabetic Association, National Osteoporosis Society, Amarant Trust, Terence Higgins Trust, Women Health Concern, Aids Treatment Project, Wellbeing, Macmillan Cancer Relief, the British Heart Foundation and many others. The relationship between the pharmaceutical company and PAG can be mutually beneficial.[37]

Case 11.6

Hoechst-Roussel aligns with patient advocacy groups

When Hoechst-Roussel Pharmaceutical launched Trental (pentoxifylline) for the treatment of intermittent claudication, an early form of peripheral arterial disease, its marketing management tried to reach senior citizens, the primary market for Trental, by launching an educational programme. Most older people did not view the major symptom of this condition – leg cramps or pain while walking – as a disease; rather they interpreted the symptoms as a normal part of ageing and, therefore, they did not seek treatment or even tell their physicians about the problem. The programme was unsuccessful until Hoechst decided to reach the senior population in a more effective and credible way through the development of a relationship with the National Council on Ageing (NCOA), a non-profit American resource of information, training, advocacy, and research on all aspects of ageing. The result was a national NCOA-sponsored public service education programme called 'Leg Alert'. At its core, Leg Alert was a medical screening programme. In the programme's first year, local Leg Alert screening events were held in communities across the national; local co-sponsors typically were an NCOA member centre, a local television station, and a local shopping mall, which also hosted the screening. Local physicians directed each event and served as programme spokespersons. The programme's first-year success – measured by such criteria as number of persons screened, media impressions achieved and product sales – was so great that Leg Alert 'how-to' screening handbooks now have been developed and distributed to senior centres and hospitals.

Sponsors

Although sponsors are generally insignificant in the for-profit context, they play a much more important role in the not-for-profit (NFP) context. Indeed, sponsors may be the principal source of income for the NFP.

Sponsorship can be defined as follows:

> Sponsorship is the material or financial support of some property, normally sports, arts or causes, with which an organization is not normally associated in the course of its everyday business.

The relationship between sponsor and sponsored is one in which the sponsor pays a cash or in-kind fee in return for access to the exploitable commercial potential associated with the property. Overall, in 2006, global expenditure on sponsorship hit US$34 billion.[38] There has been significant growth in sponsorship in recent years. This has been attributed to several conditions: the perceived ineffectiveness and inefficiency of advertising; government restrictions on tobacco and alcohol advertising; reduced government assistance to the arts; increased popularity and commercialism of sports and arts; the increasing trend to globalization of corporate/brand entities; and the progress of relationship marketing.[39]

Sponsors are looking for a number of commercial gains from sponsorship including:

1. Increasing awareness and visibility for the product or company
2. Influencing consumer attitudes
3. Influencing consumer behaviour
4. Associating the product or company with a lifestyle
5. Entertaining key clients
6. Rewarding employees
7. Finding opportunities to launch new products
8. Differentiating the product or company from competitors.

For example, the cigarette manufacturer Rothmans sponsored the Williams Formula 1 motor racing team. Their objectives in sponsoring motorsport were to: increase awareness of their brands, encourage consumer trial and purchase of brands and maintain loyalty towards their more established products.[40]

Organizations that enjoy the support of sponsors are common in the arts, sports or causes. However, trends indicate that such organizations are becoming more professional in seeking revenue streams from other sources. They are finding that they compete for limited sponsorship funds and that they must make a business case and deliver to the sponsors objectives in order to maintain the relationship.

Partners in value delivery

We identify a number of different types of partners in value delivery: agents, brokers, management contractors, consortia, franchisees and licensees. These might be thought of as customers under the 'C' of SCOPE. However, what sets this group apart from customers is that they do not take title to the products they sell. They do not therefore generate direct revenue streams for the focal company.[41] Partners in value delivery are an integral part of many CRM implementations. In many cases, end customers regard them as the suppliers of the goods, rather than the manufacturer.

Agents

Agents are commonly used when a business is small or geographically separated from the markets served and it doesn't want or cannot afford to recruit and operate its own sales team. Agents do not purchase and resell; they simply represent the principals whose products they sell. They are order providers, offering business owners the opportunity to access their established networks. Agents generally work on a commission basis. Agencies are common in the fashion industry. Apparel manufacturers broadly split into two groups. Large international, national or regional brands such as Bennetton, Nike and Giordano tend to operate at the high-volume end of the fashion market. Brands such as

Sass and Bide, Michelle Jank and Tea Rose tend to operate at the other extreme, selling through few outlets, known as 'destination outlets' at higher prices. Whereas the former have their own sales teams, the latter tend to operate through agencies.

Agents representing manufacturers fall into two major categories.

1. Manufacturer's agents represent one or more principals that produce non-competing lines. They provide an outsourced selling function. Generally they agree contractual terms covering lines sold, territorial rights, prices, commissions, order processing routines and returns policy.
2. A selling agent is contracted to sell a manufacturer's entire output. Very often these are found in primary and production-oriented businesses such as mining, forestry and industrial equipment.

CRM systems can assist the manufacturer–agent relationship in several ways. They can provide a portal through which product information is published, marketing funds are approved and order progress is tracked. Furthermore, agents themselves are users of CRM systems, as they communicate and sell to their clients.

Brokers

The role of the broker is to bring together buyer and seller. Brokers can be hired by either party. They assume no risk. Common examples are food brokers, real estate brokers and insurance brokers.

Management contractors

Management contractors are companies that undertake to manage some important part of a business, even the customer interface, on behalf of a principal. They are common in the hospitality industry, where the ownership and operation of hotels are separated. It is not unusual for hotels to be owned by an insurance or investment company, and for the operation of the hotel to be contracted out to a hotel management company. Contractors manage properties for well-known brand owners such as Holiday Inn, Marriott, Sheraton and Hilton. The contractor pays all the operating expenses and retains a management fee, normally between 3 per cent and 5 per cent of gross income, remitting the surplus to the owner. The owner provides the property, fixtures, working capital and assumes full legal responsibility. The contractor may undertake to manage the hotel under the operating standards of their own brand, or manage to the standards of another hotel brand. Sometimes hotel management companies are brought in to turn around a struggling property.

Where a contractor is brought in to manage the customer interface, it is in a position to influence customer experience, either positively or negatively. It is critical that the contractor understands the experience that the principal wants its customers to enjoy. CRM systems allow principals to access detailed information about customer interactions, therefore enabling them to manage their contractor relationships more effectively.

Consortia

A consortium is a group of organizations that act cooperatively for mutual benefit. Often the organizations are independent of each other, as in the Best Western and Flag Hotel consortia, and the members of the SPAR group of independent grocery retailers.

Sometimes they are not independent. Keiretsu and chaebols are Asian examples. Some Japanese companies have formed into keiretsu. The keiretsu is a family of interlocked organizations, connected by common memberships on boards of directors, shared banking arrangements and close personal relationships. Sumitomo and Mitsubishi are examples. In Korea, some companies have formed into chaebols. These consortia are similar to the keiretsu, but are reliant on close government connections for financial support: Daewoo and Samsung are examples.

Consortia are generally not-for-profit organizations, built to generate economies of scale for their members. There are economies to be found in purchasing, marketing, training and development, and operations. Whereas a single hotel could not afford to develop and promote itself internationally, as a member of a consortium in which all members pay an advertising appropriation, it could create an international presence. Similarly, consortia can afford to invest in a centralized reservation system, which would be unaffordable to an individual member. Consortia members also operate as a cross-referral network.

Consortia managements generally establish standards that members must meet in their operations. Best Western hotels reject 90 per cent of applicants. The consortium's objective is to create and deliver a consistent customer experience wherever they encounter a consortium member. Leading Hotels of the World, for example, is a consortium of hotels, spas and resorts which stress excellence in service, physical structure, cuisine and guest comforts. Failure to meet the required standards may result in exclusion.

Franchisees

Franchising is a rapidly growing form of business. A franchise is a license to operate a business format for a prescribed time format within a defined geographic area. Franchisees receive training in the operational and managerial processes for running the format successfully. They get access to a proven customer value proposition and a turnkey business operation. Typically, a franchise or investment fee is paid up front, as well as an ongoing royalty on sales. Franchise operations are among the best known in many industries: McDonald's, Holiday Inn, Century 21, Dunkin' Donuts, Midas, H&R Block, for example.

The relationship between franchisor and franchisee can be conflicted. Sources of conflict are generally connected to the asymmetry of the power relationship: the sharing of revenues from the franchisee's operation, the level of franchisor support and the degree of franchisor control. The franchisor typically demands that franchisees do not depart from the approved format. They want customers to have a standard experience wherever they encounter the brand. Franchisees, in turn, may feel that they, the entrepreneurs, know more about the strengths and weaknesses of the business format than the principal. After all, they come into contact with customers and they have to run the operation. If franchisees were found to be changing the product offer and modifying processes, the franchisor would most likely terminate the contract.

There is a growing recognition that the franchisor and franchisees together can create a mutually beneficial network through closer cooperation. Mature franchising operations, such as Domino's Pizza, are now committed to learning from their franchisees' experiences. They no longer believe that headquarters is the source of all innovation and knowledge about their business.

Licensees

Licenses are rights granted to a business partner to exploit intangible assets, such as technology, skills, designs or knowledge, in exchange for remuneration such as fees or royalties. The value of licensing arrangements is estimated to exceed US$150 billion annually.

Licensing is commonly linked to the movie industry. Disney characters such as Mickey Mouse and Donald Duck have a long history of being licensed. Their images appear on a huge range of merchandise, from pyjamas to lunch boxes and breakfast cereals. Technology is also widely licensed. When Kodak invented the disc camera, it licensed the technology to a large number of competitors in order to speed up its access to world markets and inhibit competitors' investments in substitute technologies. Toshiba licenses its technology to Chartered Semiconductor Manufacturing. IBM makes over US$2 billion annually from licensing its patents.

Licensing has spread into the packaged goods market. Allied Domecq has licensed the use of the Kahlua brand to the company Herbal Enterprise, who are introducing Kahlua Iced Coffee into supermarkets. You can also smoke Kahlua cigars. Jack Daniels, the bourbon brand, is licensed for use in Jack Daniel's Grilling Sauces. Licensors seem increasingly enthusiastic about these licensing deals, which pay royalties of 1 to 7 per cent of retail sales, because they generate out of category exposure for their brands and yield additional revenues for relatively little risk.

As with franchising, licensing arrangements can be fraught with difficulties. From the focal company's perspective it is important to ensure that licensees understand the brand values of the property they are licensed to exploit. The contract is designed to protect the property and ensure that it is used in appropriate applications. Disney would not license Donald Duck for use in a pornographic website.

CRM technologies play an important role in ensuring current standards, marketing material, product specifications and regulations are communicated to partners. This relies on technologies for content management that allow companies to manage the release of information. Network members can then be advised when a product specification is changed or an advertising campaign is about to be released.

Summary

In this chapter you have learned about the importance of two constituencies in the business network: suppliers and partners. Both help focal firms create value for themselves and their customers. Whereas suppliers provide the input goods and services that companies convert into marketable value propositions, partners cooperate with focal companies in other ways to create and deliver value for and from the company's customers. Relationships between suppliers and their customers are becoming increasingly cooperative and less conflicted. Many companies now collaborate closely with their suppliers in a number of activities, such as product development, supplier accreditation and process alignment. Electronic data interchange (EDI) and portals are widely employed to help manage the vendor–customer relationships. The trend towards electronic procurement is found in both business-to-business and business-to-consumer contexts. B2B electronic procurement, which has ten times the value of B2C online purchasing, takes a number of forms, including e-shops, e-procurement, e-malls, e-auctions and third party marketplaces. Relationships with business partners also need to be managed so that they can contribute to the achievement of CRM goals. Companies have a number of different types of partners in value creation: joint venture or alliance partners, category teams, benchmarking groups, regulators, customer advocacy groups and sponsors. There are also a number of different types of partners in value delivery: agents, brokers, management contractors, consortia, franchisees and licensees.

References

1. Porter, M. (1985) *Competitive advantage: creating and sustaining superior performance.* New York: Free Press. The value chain is rather outdated in some respects. It imagines marketing as something that is done after products are made (operations), rather than having a role in determining what should be made. It also shows that the endpoint of managing the activities in the value chain is improved margin. CRM practitioners prefer to think in terms of customer profitability over the longer-term, rather than margins on individual transactions. For an alternative value chain (introduced in Chapter 1) that reflects this CRM focus see Buttle, F. (2003) *Customer relationship management: concepts and tools.* Oxford: Elsevier.
2. We prefer the term 'supply network management' to the more conventional term 'supply chain management', because it clearly acknowledges its systemic rather than linear nature.
3. Parker, H. (2000) Inter-firm collaboration and the new product development process. *Industrial Management & Data Systems*, Vol. 100(6), pp. 255–260.
4. Copyright © 2008. European Foundation for Quality Management. Used with permission.

5. For more information, go to http://www.efqm.org/
6. Henkoff, R. (1993) The hot new seal of quality. *Fortune*, June 28 pp. 68–71 .
7. Bergman, B. and Klefsjö, B. (1994) *Quality: from customer needs to customer satisfaction*. McGraw-Hill: London.
8. Deming, W.E. (1986) *Out of crisis*. Cambridge, MA: Cambridge University Press.
9. Cali, J.F. (1993) *TQM for purchasing management*. McGraw-Hill: New York.
10. MacKay, D. and Rosier, M. (1996) Measuring organizational benefits of EDI diffusion: a case of the Australian automotive industry. *International Journal of Physical Distribution & Logistics Management*, Vol. 26(10), pp. 60–78.
11. http://www.cips.org/professionalpractice/faqs/detail.asp?record= 73. Accessed 6 November 2007.
12. Hutchins, R. (1997) Category management in the food industry: a research agenda. *British Food Journal*, Vol. 99(5), pp. 177–180.
13. Basuroy, S., Mantrala, M.K. and Walters, R.G. (2001) The impact of category management on retailer prices and performance: theory and evidence. *Journal of Marketing*, Vol. 65, October, pp. 16–32.
14. Hogarth-Scott, S. (1995) Shifting category management relationships in the food distribution channels in the UK and Australia. *Management Decision*, Vol. 35(4), pp. 310–318.
15. Freedman, P.M., Reyner, M. and Tochtermann, T. (1997) European category management: look before you leap. *The McKinsey Quarterly*, Vol. 1, pp. 156–164.
16. Basuroy, S., Mantrala, M.K. and Walters, R.G. (2001) The impact of category management on retailer prices and performance: theory and evidence. *Journal of Marketing*, Vol. 65, October, pp. 16–32.
17. http://drops.dagstuhl.de/opus/volltexte/2005/379. Accessed 24 December 2008.
18. http://www.census.gov/prod/2005pubs/p23-208.pdf. Accessed 11 November 2007.
19. Phillips Traffica Limited. (1998) The net effect report. London.
20. http://www.census.gov/mrts/www/data/html/06Q4.html. Accessed 11 November 2007.
21. http://www.itfacts.biz/index.php?id=P3375. Accessed 11 November 2007.
22. US Census Bureau. (2007) E-stats www.census.gov/estats. Accessed 11 November 2007.
23. US Census Bureau. (2007) E-stats www.census.gov/estats. Accessed 11 November 2007.
24. Timmers, P. (2000) *Electronic commerce: strategies and models for business-to-business trading*. Chichester: John Wiley.
25. http://h71016.www7.hp.com/home.asp?oi=E9CED&BEID=19701& SBLID=
26. http://office.microsoft.com/en-us/officelive/FX102267171033.aspx
27. http://www1.hospitalitybex.com/hbex/hbex.asp
28. This section is derived largely from Dussuage, P. and Garrette, B. (1999) *Cooperative strategy: competing successfully through strategic alliances*. Chichester: John Wiley.

29. Morris, D. and Hergert, M. (1987) Trends in international collaborative agreements. *Columbia Journal of World Business*, Vol. 22(2), pp. 15–21.

30. Bendell, T., Boulter, L. and Goodstadt, P. (1998) *Benchmarking for Competitive Advantage*. London: Financial Times Pitman Publishing.

31. Bendell, T., Boulter, L. and Goodstadt, P. (1998) *Benchmarking for Competitive Advantage*. London: Financial Times Pitman Publishing.

32. *Which?* Annual Report of the Consumers' Association, 2005–6.

33. For more details refer to http://www.consumersinternational.org

34. Nader, R. (1965) *Unsafe at any speed: the designed in dangers of the American automobile*. New York: Grossman Publishers (out of print).

35. For more details refer to http://www.nader.org

36. For more details refer to http://www.timeshare.org.uk

37. Buttle, F.A. and Boldrini, J. (2001) Customer relationship management in the pharmaceutical industry: the role of the patient advocacy group. *International Journal of Medical Marketing*, Vol. 1(3), February, pp. 203–214.

38. http://www.sponsorship.com/Resources/Sponsorship-Spending.aspx. Accessed 11 November 2007.

39. Quester, P.G. and Thompson, B. (2001) Advertising and promotion leverage on arts sponsorship effectiveness. *Journal of Advertising Research*, Vol. 41(1), January–February, pp. 33–47.

40. Andrews, S. and Tucker, E. (1996) Rothmans International: the role of sponsorship as a promotional tool. The European Case Clearing House, Bedford, Case no 596–004–1.

41. Although this is generally true, franchisees often pay a fee up-front for rights to use the business format, periodic marketing levies and training fees.

Chapter 12
Managing investor and employee relationships

By the end of this chapter, you will understand:

1. why investors should understand what is involved in a CRM implementation
2. that the return from an investment in CRM can vary from immediate to long-term
3. how to respond to high levels of investor churn
4. the importance of people to the successful roll-out and operation of CRM technology
5. the concepts of internal marketing, empowerment and service profit chain.

Introduction

In the last chapter we looked at the role of suppliers and partners in the achievement of CRM outcomes. In this chapter we examine two other constituencies and their contribution to CRM success: owners or investors and employees in the business.

Owners and investors can be an important source of capital, in return for which they expect growth in shareholder value. Given that CRM does not always yield an immediate return, their expectations may need to be managed. Employees are critical to the successful deployment of CRM. People design and implement the CRM strategy, and they use technology tactically. CRM cannot succeed without the ongoing commitment of people to the CRM vision, strategy and objectives, and their willingness to use the CRM toolkit.

Owner/investor relationships

Owners and investors are significant stakeholders in businesses. They are an important source of capital that allows businesses to be established, to operate and grow, and in return they expect the value of that capital to grow. In other words, they want shareholder value to be created. Shareholder value can only be created if the business makes a return on investment that is greater than the weighted average cost of the capital invested in the business (WACC). If the WACC (determined by the relative weight and cost of equity and borrowings) is 10 per cent, and that capital is invested in the business earning a return of 20 per cent, there has been a significant increase in shareholder value. On the world's stock markets, shareholder value is measured by dividends and increases in the company's share price. If you buy a share at $40, and in the course of the year the share rises in price to $50, and you receive a dividend of $5, there has been a $15 increase in shareholder value.

Peter Doyle points out that managers are agents whose task is to act in the interests of the principals, the shareholders with financial rights over the business. Managers, he suggests, have a primary responsibility to maximize shareholder value over time.[1]

What, then, is the link between CRM and shareholder value? The value of a business is the present day value of all margins that will be earned from sales to customers in the future. In earlier chapters, we have discussed the idea of customer lifetime value (LTV). The value of a business is equal to the LTV generated by its customers. CRM, therefore, can have a huge impact on shareholder value. It does so by creating and retaining profitable relationships with customers. A number of specific CRM competences influence shareholder value:

1. **Target market selection**: target markets vary in their attractiveness. Where demand is falling or static, or there is intense competition, margins come under pressure, with negative consequences for shareholder value. Shareholders prefer markets that show signs of both margin and market growth.
2. **Customer acquisition**: effective and efficient customer acquisition reduces the costs of acquisition, but grows the numbers of new customers acquired.
3. **Customer retention**: focused and effective customer retention means that strategically-significant customers are retained, as is their lifetime value.
4. **Customer development**: effective cross-selling and up-selling grows share of wallet and the value of retained customers.
5. **Value proposition development**: a key component of strategic CRM is the development of value propositions that customers prefer over competitors and want to buy.
6. **Technology implementation**: CRM systems enable companies to manage the customer lifecycle more effectively and efficiently. Sales-force automation ensures that opportunities are identified, tracked and moved to closure. Marketing automation ensures that campaigns and events are more effective. Service automation ensures that customers' service requirements are satisfied cost-effectively.
7. **Database management**: customer-related data is an important intangible asset that can be exploited to grow customer value and therefore shareholder value. CRM applications need appropriately high-quality data to be effective.
8. **Network management**: successful companies are excellent at identifying and building relationships with partners who can help create and deliver customer value.

Shareholder value, as delivered by CRM expertise, works as shown in Figure 12.1. The basic CRM disciplines of managing the value of current and new customers are shown to the left and centre of the diagram. At the right is a third source of growth that can power shareholder value: the creation of new businesses.

The two fundamental approaches to growing shareholder value through current customers are to sell more and/or reduce the cost-to-serve. Unless

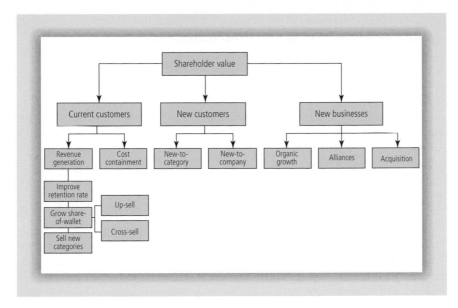

Figure 12.1
Shareholder value
through CRM

there is a massive re-engineering of sales and service channels (e.g. moving from a branch network to an online presence), cost containment is unlikely to add significantly to shareholder value. Revenue generation through current customers offers greater potential. There are three core strategies: increase customer retention rate, grow share of category spending (share of wallet) by up-selling or cross-selling, and introduce new product categories to current customers. New customer acquisition offers another route for revenue growth. Customers can be new in two senses: either they are new to the category or they are new to the company, having been won from competitors. The third CRM-related strategy for growing shareholder value is to develop new businesses – either by growing them organically, by forming alliances with other organizations or by acquiring new businesses.

As already noted, investors and owners expect to experience enhanced shareholder value though dividend receipts or rising share price. Generally, Western investors, whether institutional or individual, take a rather short-term view of their investments. They expect to see a speedy, if not immediate, return. This short-termism is responsible for hot investment money racing from one money-making opportunity to another.

The period of time that it can take for CRM to show a return on investment varies according to the type of CRM that is being implemented.

A strategic CRM implementation demands investments in technology, processes and people. These projects often involve major changes in corporate culture and restructuring of the business around customer groups, and may take three to five years to return a profit. Even then, the evidence of a return may differ from the financial indicators normally preferred by investors. Success at strategic CRM may be reflected in higher levels of customer satisfaction and customer retention or in a greater share of customer spend. You might also find that employees' attitudes to customers have changed, or that the business acquires, shares and uses customer information more intelligently.

Over a three to five year term it may be impossible to prove that any shift in sales or profit is due to CRM or, for that matter, any other type of programme. Business performance is influenced by many conditions, a large number of which are beyond the control of any single enterprise, for example, business cycles, exchange rates, international relations, government regulations, competitor action and technological advances. Changes in these conditions over a three to five year term may serve to promote, counterbalance or reduce the impact of a CRM programme.

An operational CRM project, such as sales-force automation, might yield a return within 12 to 24 months. Computer infrastructure and software has to be installed, the selling process modelled, and current data transferred onto the new system. Then salespeople need to be trained to work the new system. The returns on such an investment might include higher levels of salesperson productivity, such as calls made, proposals written or enquiries handled. An operational CRM project for 3Com, the company behind Palm handheld computers, involved shifting customer service from call centre to web self-service. 3Com enjoyed $16.8 million savings over a two year period as fewer calls entered the call centre, talk times fell, call transfers fell and training costs fell. It is not reported whether customer satisfaction was influenced.

An analytical CRM implementation can show results almost immediately, as long as the right type of customer-related data is available to be able to run campaigns. Even a more complex project, in which internal data from several databases is integrated and enhanced with bought-in data, can show a return within a year. However, if a data warehouse needs to be created from scratch, the time-to-return can be much lengthier. Figure 12.2 shows how a UK-based business-to-business catalogue company used CRM analytics to target more precisely prospects for a particular mailing. The company ran an experiment in which their conventional approach to direct marketing was contrasted with a CRM-enabled approach. The numbers show that under the CRM

	CRM	Traditional
Number of catalogues mailed	1000	5000
Mailing cost	£3,000	£15,000
New customers obtained 2003	65	45
Conversion rate new customers	6.5%	0.09%
Initial sales per new customer	£180	£120
Total new initial sales revenues	£11,700	£5,400
Acquisition cost per customer	£46.15	£333.33
Average customer sales 2003–2006	£7,500	£2,200
2 year gross margin (40%)	£3,000	£880
2003 customers still active in 2006	80%	35%

Figure 12.2
Analytical CRM at
Business Direct

approach fewer catalogues were mailed, conversion rates and initial sales per new customer were higher, customer acquisition costs were lower and two-year sales and margins were higher.

It is possible to conduct many such experiments on subsets of customers, to generate evidence that there is a return on CRM investment. You can prove CRMs value by reference to specific data, such as customer acquisition costs, sales per customer, customer retention rates and customer tenure.

A collaborative CRM project might take two or more years to reap benefits. A manufacturer that wants to introduce portal-based self-service to its customers faces the challenge of raising customer enthusiasm for the change. There might be significant levels of resistance from customers who prefer the current service model, whether that is face-to-face sales representation or telesales. Collaborative CRM implementations align the people, processes and/or technologies of two or more organizations and therefore have the potential for major delays.

Fred Reichheld claims that 'just as there are customers and employees who are right for your business there are investors who are right'.[2] The typical investor, focused on the short-term, is not the right investor for companies that are in pursuit of high levels of customer retention, which generates long-term increases in shareholder value. He suggests that even if you are a publicly-owned company you can pursue one or more of four ways to create a stable group of long-term oriented investors: educate current investors; shift the investor mix to institutions that avoid investor churn; attract the right kind of core owner and operate as a privately owned company.

Educate current investors

Investors are justifiably sceptical of new business models. In recent years they have been promised improved profitability from BPR, ERP and TQM (business process re-engineering, enterprise resource planning and total quality management). Many investors have been disappointed. Why should their response be any different to another three letter acronym, CRM, particularly when various reports suggest that upwards of 60 per cent, and perhaps as many as 90 per cent, of CRM implementations have failed?[3]

Investors need to understand that CRM, well implemented, does have an influence on shareholder value. Many vendors provide case illustrations for cautious or sceptical investors. One notable success story is the Royal Bank of Canada (RBC), which won the first international award for CRM excellence in large corporations. RBC started their CRM initiative in 1995. They have invested well over $100 million in their transition to being a CRM-driven company. The bank's vice president for CRM claims:

> 'we no longer view CRM as a programme … (It) is our core strategy. We absolutely conclude that CRM is paying us back in spades. It has

enabled us to grow both top of the house revenue line and at the same time achieve huge cost savings'.

Revenue growth is running at 10–15 per cent per annum and profit growth at 25 per cent.

Investors need to understand that CRM, when well implemented, influences both sides of the profit equation: costs and revenues. CRM is very much about recruiting and retaining the right customers. These are customers who generate long-term value for the business. The long term may be several years, particularly if the repurchase cycle is extended. General Motors reckons its customers are worth $276 000 over a lifetime of being GM customers, during which time they purchase 11 GM vehicles.[4]

Finally, investors need to understand that CRM yields long-term benefits. There may be short-term results, but the true benefits may take years to deliver. Failure at CRM is indeed still an option … but it is not a requirement.

Shift the investor mix towards institutions that avoid investment churn

Most investors routinely churn their portfolios in search of a better return. However, some institutions are more stable investors than others, preferring to buy and hold for the long-term. Low churn investing appeals to a limited number of investment houses. Once you have identified them, it is suggested that you market your stock to them in much the same way as you market your products and service to your customers. This means segmenting the institutional investor market, targeting particular investors and positioning your stock against other stocks competing for the buying power of those chosen investors. Nike is one company that has pursued this strategy in order to maintain a stable shareholder base.

Attract the right kind of core owner

This approach is based on finding an institutional or individual investor who understands your CRM goals and is prepared to take a controlling position, and be patient for the long-term benefits. Reichheld cites Warren Buffett as the archetypal controlling investor. Buffett runs the investment company Berkshire Hathaway, where portfolio turnover is below 10 per cent. He has bought stock in very few companies over the last twenty years, and has remained loyal to those companies. He looks for companies that show high return on equity, a strong customer base, a simple business idea and an undervalued market position. Buffett is not the only investor taking the long view. Japanese and German investors typically take a much longer term view of their investments than most of their Western counterparts.

Go private

Companies that are privately owned do not need to dance to the tune of the stock market. They can take a long-term view of investments in customer management. However, private ownership is not for everybody. The level of debt that is needed to fund a CRM-based approach to business development can be very high. In fact it may be too high a risk for most private business owners to bear.

The entrepreneur Richard Branson floated the Virgin Group on the London stock market in 1986. By October 1988 he had bought back all the distributed shares, at huge personal cost. He had been unable to run the businesses under the Virgin umbrella in the way he wanted. His entrepreneurial approach to management, he felt, was incompatible with the institutional demands for immediate returns on investment. The institutions would not have tolerated the results achieved by his airline, Virgin Atlantic. Established in 1984, it was in only 1995 that the airline showed a return on capital employed that would have been positive enough to please an institutional investor, 27 per cent. Just three years previously, the airline recorded a negative 29.7 per cent return. Branson was able to keep to his strategy of 'happy employees + customer value = business performance'.

Investor relations portals

Just as web technologies have allowed customers, suppliers and channel partners to operate as an extension of an organization's CRM system, so too have investor portals led to unprecedented levels of access for investors (see Figure 12.3 for an example of an investor portal). Many organizations today operate an investor website, allowing access to important information, such as company overviews, mission and vision, strategy, financial reports, publications and presentations, statutory filings, analyst views and market assessments. Investors are able to register with the website, request information, sign up for mailing lists and provide feedback. Sometimes the website offers search engine enabled access to an investor-relevant knowledge base.

Employees

It is hard to overestimate the importance of people to the success of CRM. People design and implement the CRM strategy, they use CRM software to help them run campaigns and events, and to sell to and service customers. Further, basic human skills such as showing empathy and responding are vital to delivering excellent experience in interaction with customers.

Figure 12.3
General Electric's
investor portal

Many companies intuitively recognize the importance of their people in creating value for customers and company alike. Some explicitly acknowledge the importance of people. The PepsiCo 2006 annual report, for example, says:

> Our people represent PepsiCo's ultimate competitive advantage … Our 'ownership culture' empowers our associates. We are a big company that thinks like a small enterprise. Our associates fundamentally see their jobs as finding solutions for customers and consumers and doing what it takes to exceed their expectations.[5]

Companies need to be able to identify, recruit, develop and retain high-quality employees who can contribute effectively to the achievement of the company's CRM goals. Employee turnover is a huge cost in some industries. In food service, for example, frontline staff can turnover at 200 per cent or more each year. Turnover in senior positions can also be high. Nearly 20 per cent of managing directors change position each year. When an employee departs companies incur the direct costs of replacing that person: search costs, interviewing costs, relocation costs and so on. There may also be indirect costs, such as business lost when customer accounts are not properly serviced. In extreme cases, employees may take customers with them when they depart. This is common in the advertising industry. When creative staff leaves an established agency to set up on their own, they very often take clients with them.

Companies need to define the competencies that are needed to work successfully in defined CRM roles. Employees who are responsible for managing an important strategic alliance will need different competencies from employees working on the analysis of customer data using data mining tools. They in turn will need different competencies from those who work in the frontline, interfacing with customers, perhaps in a call centre. We review some important CRM roles in Chapter 17.

Whatever their role, it is important that employees buy into the CRM mission and vision, understand their role, and appreciate what the company is trying to achieve in its served markets. The importance of obtaining employee buy-in to the CRM vision was emphasized in Chapter 3. It is often necessary to market the CRM project's vision, strategy and objectives to employees to achieve initial buy-in and ongoing commitment. This deployment of marketing strategies and tactics to the workforce is known as internal marketing.

Internal marketing

The concept of internal marketing has been in existence since the 1980s, when Len Berry suggested that it made sense to apply marketing-like strategies to people management.[6] Winning and keeping good employees was thought to be much like winning and keeping good customers. Furthermore, to win employees' commitment to your CRM strategy, you were advised to market that strategy to them as if it were a product they were expected to buy. Internal marketing can be defined as follows:

> Internal marketing is a planned effort to overcome organizational resistance to change and to align, motivate and integrate employees towards the effective implementation of corporate and functional strategies.[7]

There isn't much evidence of companies writing internal marketing plans along the same lines as their external marketing plans, but it is possible to employ the same architecture to think in a structured way about how you would win your colleagues' commitment to your CRM strategy. Most marketing plans address a number of core issues: marketing objectives, market segmentation and targeting, market positioning and marketing mix. We'll explain each of these briefly in the context of internal marketing of your CRM strategy.

- **Marketing objectives**: these might include broad qualitative goals, such as winning commitment to the CRM strategy, motivating employees to adopt new work practices or developing a culture in which the customer's voice is central. Equally, objectives might be readily quantifiable, for example, training 100 per cent of employees to understand the concept of customer lifetime value.
- **Market segmentation and targeting**: segmentation involves dividing the internal market into homogenous subsets so that you can target each group with a different marketing mix. You might, for example,

segment by the employee's degree of customer contact.[8] This has been done by a European Train Operating company, as shown in Figure 12.4. They identified four segments of employees, varying in levels of customer contact and therefore with varying levels of influence on customer experience.

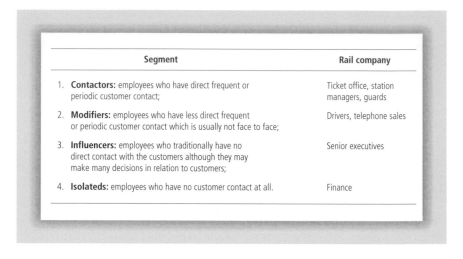

Segment	Rail company
1. **Contactors:** employees who have direct frequent or periodic customer contact;	Ticket office, station managers, guards
2. **Modifiers:** employees who have less direct frequent or periodic customer contact which is usually not face to face;	Drivers, telephone sales
3. **Influencers:** employees who traditionally have no direct contact with the customers although they may make many decisions in relation to customers;	Senior executives
4. **Isolateds:** employees who have no customer contact at all.	Finance

Figure 12.4
Segmenting the internal market by level of customer contact

- **Market positioning**: positioning is concerned with how you want CRM to be perceived by each internal market segment. For senior management it may make sense to position it as a sound strategic move that will make their shareholdings more valuable, for others the positioning may be about job enrichment, work satisfaction, process simplification or anything else that the segment values. One positioning will not suit all segments.
- **Marketing mix**: the marketing mix is the set of tools that marketers use to bring about the results they want in their target markets. Figure 12.5 shows how the 7Ps of the marketing mix, first introduced in Chapter 7, can be used for internal marketing purposes. Key elements in the internal marketing mix are communication and networking.[9]

Empowerment

Many strategic CRM implementations make a virtue of creating a culture and climate in which the customer's voice is heard, valued and acted upon. Consequently, they give their customer contact staff a higher level of authority to meet, and even exceed, customer requirements. Some companies make heroes out of employees who have 'gone the extra mile'. However, empowerment is not just a matter of telling employees they are now responsible for managing the customer relationship. Empowerment means equipping employees with the knowledge and skills to match that authority. For example, they need to know how to

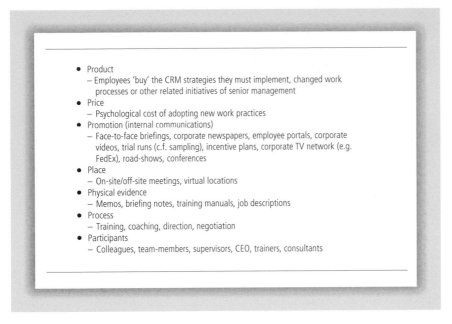

- Product
  - Employees 'buy' the CRM strategies they must implement, changed work processes or other related initiatives of senior management
- Price
  - Psychological cost of adopting new work practices
- Promotion (internal communications)
  - Face-to-face briefings, corporate newspapers, employee portals, corporate videos, trial runs (c.f. sampling), incentive plans, corporate TV network (e.g. FedEx), road-shows, conferences
- Place
  - On-site/off-site meetings, virtual locations
- Physical evidence
  - Memos, briefing notes, training manuals, job descriptions
- Process
  - Training, coaching, direction, negotiation
- Participants
  - Colleagues, team-members, supervisors, CEO, trainers, consultants

Figure 12.5
Using 7Ps as the internal marketing mix

deal constructively with a customer complaint, particularly one that is objectively unjustified. This may involve scripting the dialogue in advance, providing information from a knowledge database on known problems and how they can be resolved, or providing diagnostics tools.

Empowerment ranges from total authority to do what it takes to satisfy and retain a customer, to bounded empowerment where the employee has more limited discretion to act. The boundaries may be financial (e.g. no more than $200 per customer) or product related (e.g. domestic appliances but not financial services).

Empowerment helps create an environment in which employees feel trusted and valued, leading to greater job satisfaction and motivation, which in turn can improve customer satisfaction and retention.[10] However, empowerment is not always an appropriate strategy. Michael Treacey and Fred Wiersema found that successful companies excelled at one of three basic value-delivery disciplines: operational excellence, product leadership and customer intimacy.[11] These are discussed in more detail in Chapter 7. The role of empowerment must be limited in businesses founded on operational excellence. Too much empowerment might slow down and impede the operational processes that create excellence. Empowerment is much better suited to organizations dedicated to customer intimacy.

The service–profit chain

In the section above, you read about the link between satisfied employees and satisfied customers. Many companies believe that happy employees make happy customers make happy shareholders. Among them are

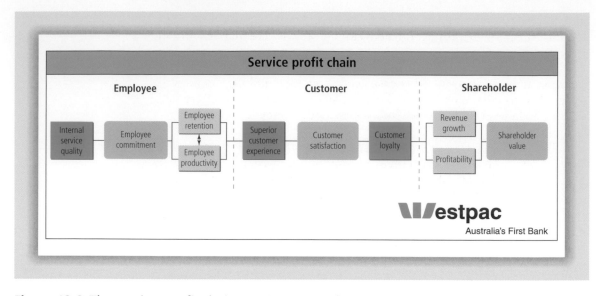

Figure 12.6 The service–profit chain at Westpac Bank

Marriott Hotels, Virgin Airline, Westpac Bank (see Figure 12.6), Taylor Nelson SOFRES (a market research company), Sears Roebuck and Volvo. They believe that if employees are satisfied at work they will deliver excellent experience to their internal and external customers. This in turn will drive up customer retention rates and improve business performance.

The connections between business performance, customer satisfaction and employee satisfaction were first spelt out in the service–profit chain, a model developed by a group of Harvard professors.[12]

As originally specified, the model suggests linkages between internal service quality (the quality of service we receive from our colleagues in the workplace), employee satisfaction, value delivered to customers, external customer satisfaction, customer loyalty and business performance. The model does not claim cause and effect relationships between these variables. It simply finds evidence of correlation. Businesses like AC Nielsen, the international market research company, for example, find the model very attractive. It provides them with an organizing framework for running their business. They claim:

> 'We live and breathe the service–profit chain, understanding our customers are fundamental to our success – satisfied employees make satisfied clients, make happy shareholders'.[13]

There is some evidence to support this claim. Some is generated by practitioners and consultants, some by academics.[14] Ben Schneider and David Bowen have found that a climate for service and a climate for employee wellbeing are highly correlated with customer perceptions of service quality. Put another way, the experiences that employees have at work are associated with the experiences of customers. Sears Roebuck, the retailer, has found a high inverse correlation between customer satisfaction and employee turnover. The stores with highest employee turnover had the lowest customer satisfaction, and vice versa. The research also found that increases in employee attitude correlated strongly with increases in both customer satisfaction and revenue growth.[15]

Sears has developed a measurement model linking employee experience to customer experience to business performance. They call this the TPI (Total Performance Indicators) model. They report:

> 'We use the TPI at every level of the company, in every store and facility; and nearly every manager has some portion of his or her compensation at risk on the basis of non-financial measures ... (I)n the course of the last 12 months, employee satisfaction on the Sears TPI has risen by almost 4 per cent and customer satisfaction by 4 per cent ... if our model is correct – and its predictive record is very good – that 4 per cent improvement in customer satisfaction translates into more than $200 million in additional revenues in the past 12 months'.

Elsewhere, research on the linkages between components in the service–profit chain has met with mixed results. For example, one grocery retailing study found no correlation between employee satisfaction and customer satisfaction, and worryingly reported a negative correlation between employee satisfaction and profit margin![16] Other banking industry research concluded: 'Branches with favourable employee attitude and climate scores have elevated levels of customer satisfaction and sales achievement, and branches with higher levels of customer satisfaction also have stronger sales'. However, the effect was small and barely significant.[17] Another study by the Institute of Employment Studies found that employee commitment was connected to company profitability in three ways:

1. directly through employee behaviours
2. indirectly through customer satisfaction
3. indirectly through a reduction in staff absenteeism and turnover.[18]

Although research continues, the service–profit chain is proving to be a useful framework for many businesses.

Employee relationship management (ERM) software applications

A number of leading CRM application vendors also offer employee relationship management (ERM) modules. Other terms for ERM are human capital management and talent management. ERM involves the application of CRM-like concepts, processes, tools and technologies to the internal market, i.e. the workforce. An Oracle white paper describes ERM as follows.

> Employee relationship management (ERM) provides applications, content and services that enhance the value of the employee to the organization and directly affect the activities by which employees create value for the customer. Companies today are realizing that, just as they need a single, comprehensive view of their customers (such as that provided by customer relationship management (CRM) solutions) they would also benefit from having a single view of their employees and from providing that view to the employees themselves.[19]

Just as CRM strives to build long-term relationships with valued customers, ERM strives to build long-term relationships with valued employees. ERMs two main internal user groups are employees and managers. Managers can use ERM to help them with a number of people management tasks: recruitment, training, performance management and remuneration, for example. ERM enables managers to communicate with their teams, align employees with the overall goals of the business, share information and build a common understanding. ERM also offers support to employees through workflow modelling that depicts how tasks should be performed, provision of job-related information and collaboration with colleagues.

A key technology for many ERM applications is the employee portal. Employee portals are one stop shops that provide access to all the role-relevant resources employees need to do their jobs effectively and efficiently, whether they are managers or reports. As with many commercial websites, portals often allow employees to customize their own homepage so that role relevant information is readily accessible. See Case 12.1.[20]

Case 12.1

ERM in the US Navy

Traditionally, the US Navy's sailors have been motivated by the desire to serve their country and have a rewarding career. Nevertheless, the military is always concerned with sailor morale, due in part to the unique circumstances of its 'employees' being separated from their families for extended periods of time. The happier the Navy can keep its sailors, the more effective it believes they will be and the less likely they are to quit for civilian life. As the complexity and technical nature of military equipment has increased, the return on the investment of recruiting and training qualified sailors has become more critical. This translates directly into the issue of sailor retention. For the Navy to spend large amounts of time and money to recruit and train sailors for increasingly technical jobs, only to watch them leave the military for the civilian sector after a few years, is clearly counterproductive, very expensive, and a serious issue in terms of military readiness. The US Navy has therefore embarked on building a relationship with its sailors that fosters improved morale, maximizes job satisfaction, and promotes sailor retention.

Family communications	1.76
General interest information	3.17
Career and training information	3.25
Job-related information	3.95
Health and fitness information	4.58
Military news	5.12
Shipmate news	6.16

(1 = high preference; 7 = low preference)

Sailor preferences for personalized communications

One part of the solution has been to use technology to create sailor-specific, personalized, web pages on a Navy Internet portal. This was expected to create an environment in which each sailor felt that the Navy knew and cared about him or her personally. Researchers investigated what kinds of personalized communications would be of interest to sailors. Top of the list of preferences, as shown in the inset table were family communications, such as e-mails and birthday reminders, and general interest information, such as hometown news, favorite sports teams' scores and quotes of particular stocks.

Summary

In this chapter you have learned about the importance of managing relationships with owners/investors and employees. Owners and investors are an important source of capital, in return for which they expect growth in shareholder value. Any expectations that they will enjoy a fast return on their investment in CRM may need to be moderated because strategic CRM implementations may not earn a return for between three and five years, and operational CRM might have a payback horizon of one to two years. Companies that have high levels of investor churn because of dissatisfaction with returns on CRM investment can pursue one or more of four ways to create a stable group of long-term oriented investors: educate current investors, shift the investor mix to institutions that avoid investor churn, attract the right kind of core owner and operate as a privately owned company.

Employees are critical to the successful deployment of CRM. People design and implement the CRM strategy. They use technology tactically. Many companies recognize the importance of their people in creating value for customers and company alike. It is often necessary to market the CRM project's vision, strategy and objectives to employees to achieve initial buy-in and ongoing commitment. This deployment of marketing strategies and tactics to the workforce is known as internal marketing.

A growing number of companies give their customer contact the authority to meet, and even exceed, customer requirements. This is known as empowerment, and it involves equipping employees with the knowledge and skills to match the authority.

Many companies, particularly in the service sector, believe that employee satisfaction is a necessary precondition for customer satisfaction and excellent business performance. They believe that if employees are satisfied at work, they will deliver excellent experience to their internal and external customers. This in turn will drive up customer retention rates and improve business performance. These connections between business performance, customer satisfaction and employee satisfaction are spelt out in the service–profit chain.

References

1. Doyle, P. (2000) *Value-based marketing: marketing strategies for corporate growth and shareholder value.* Chichester: John Wiley.
2. Reichheld, F.F. and Teal, T. (1996) *The loyalty effect: the hidden force behind growth, profits, and lasting value.* Boston, MA: Harvard Business School Press.
3. Ang, L., Buttle, F., (2002) ROI on CRM: a customer journey approach, ANZMAC Annual Conference, Melbourne
4. Ferron, J. (2000) The customer-centric organization in the automobile industry: focus for the 21st century. In: S. Brown (ed.). *Customer Relationship Management. A strategic imperative in the world of e-business.* Toronto: John Wiley, pp. 189–211.
5. http://www.pepsico.com/PEP_Investors/AnnualReports/06/PepsiCo2006Annual.pdf. Accessed 18 November 2007.
6. Berry, L.L. (1981) The employee as customer. *Journal of Retail Banking,* Vol. 3 March, pp. 25–28.
7. Ahmed, P.K. and Rafiq, M. (2002) *Internal Marketing: tools and concepts for customer-focussed management.* Oxford: Butterworth Heinemann.
8. Judd, V.C. (1987) Differentiate with the 5th P: People. *Industrial Marketing Management,* Vol. 16, pp. 241–247.
9. Gilmore, A. and Carson, D. (1995) Internal marketing: the missing half of the marketing programme. In: W.J. Glynn and J.G. Barnes (eds.). *Understanding services management.* Chichester: John Wiley.
10. Bowen, D.E. and Lawler, E.E. (1992) The empowerment of service workers: what, why, how and when. *Sloan Management Review,* Spring, pp. 31–39.

11. Treacey, M. and Wiersema, F. (1995) *The discipline of market leaders: choose your customers, narrow your focus, dominate your market.* Reading, MA: Addison-Wesley.

12. Heskett, J.L., Jones, T.O., Loveman, G.W. Sasser, W.E. Jr and Schlesinger, L.A. (1994) Putting the service–profit chain to work. *Harvard Business Review*, March–April, pp. 164–174; Rucci, A., Kirn, S.P. and Quinn R.T. (1998) The employee–customer profit chain at Sears. *Harvard Business Review*, January–February, pp. 82–97; Loveman, G.W. (1998) Employee satisfaction, customer loyalty and financial performance. *Journal of Service Research*, Vol. 1, August, pp. 18–31.

13. For more details refer to http://www.acnielsen.com.au/

14. Dennis McCarthy's 1997 book *The loyalty link: how loyal employees create loyal customers* (New York: John Wiley) is an example of the consultant's approach. He writes 'the abstract nature of these terms (customer loyalty and employee loyalty) makes it difficult to prove empirically that such a link exists, but there is a preponderance of indirect evidence'. He then cites many examples of associations between employee satisfaction, employee retention and customer loyalty.

15. Rucci, A., Kirn, S.P. and Quinn, R.T. (1998) The employee–customer profit chain at Sears. *Harvard Business Review*, January–February, pp. 82–97.

16. Silvestro, R. and Cross, S. (2000) Applying the service–profit chain in a retail environment. *International Journal of Service Industry Management*, Vol. 11(3), pp. 244–268.

17. Geladel, G.A. and Young, S. (2005) Test of a service profit chain model in the retail banking sector. *Journal of Occupational and Organizational Psychology*, Vol. 78, pp. 1–22.

18. Barber, L., Hayday, S. and Bevan, S. (1999) From people to profits. Institute of Employment Studies Report 355.

19. Linking Employee Relationship Management to Customer Relationship Management. Oracle White Paper, 2006. http://www.oracle.com/applications/crm/siebel/resources/erm-white-paper.pdf. Accessed 18 November 2007.

20. Gillensen, M.L. and Sanders, T.C. (2005) Employee relationship management: applying the concept of personalization to US Navy sailors. *Information Systems Management*, Winter, pp. 45–50.

Chapter 13

Information technology for customer relationship management

By the end of this chapter you will understand:

1. the range of CRM technologies
2. the role that technology plays in the achievement of CRM outcomes
3. the structure of the CRM ecosystem
4. the main application areas of CRM
5. the role that analytics play in CRM technology
6. the importance of integration, knowledge management and workflow to CRM outcomes.

Introduction

Our definition of CRM stresses that CRM is a technology-enabled approach to management of the customer interface. In this chapter we present an introduction to CRM technologies.[1] Subsequent chapters take a more detailed look at sales-force automation, marketing automation and service automation.

Origins of CRM technology

The building blocks of today's CRM technology have been in place for several decades. CRM has evolved from a range of standalone technologies including call centres, sales-force automation systems and customer information files (CIF), some of which date back to the 1970s and earlier.

In the late 1980s, several organizations attempted to consolidate some of these disparate technologies. For example, the CIF that was central to many insurance companies and banks started to be seen as a source of marketing information, rather than a basic record of a customer's accounts. Call centres began being used for outbound calls such as up-selling customers rather than just responding to inbound service calls. The customer started to be recognized as a single entity across all customer-facing departments, leading to the idea of a 'single view of the customer' (Figure 13.1), whereby appropriate customer-related data is made available at all customer touchpoints and channels.

Customer expectations have also played a direct role in the emergence of CRM technology. As customers moved from one industry to the next they took their increased expectations with them. 'I am recognized by my airline', they'd say. 'So I expect to be recognized by my energy

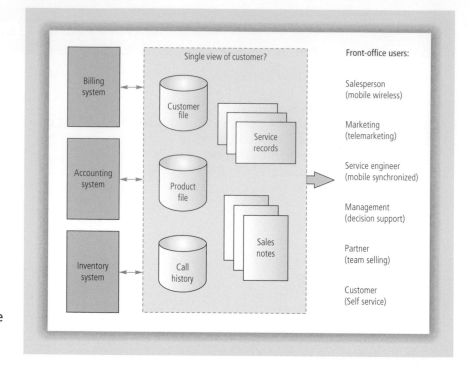

Figure 13.1
A single view of the customer for front-office applications

utility'. CRM spread rapidly from the early adopter industries, such as banks and telecommunications companies, to consumer goods and healthcare. Organizations started to realize that they needed a central view of the customer, and an understanding of the value of the customer, if they were to compete effectively.

These early attempts at the creation of a consolidated customer view were often internally-focused, rather than aimed at improving customer experience. The ultimate goal became multichannel CRM, whereby customer contact channels such as sales, channel partners, marketing and the service centre were consolidated into a single view of the customer, across all touchpoints and communication media including face-to-face, voice telephony, e-mail, web and wireless (Figure 13.2). Customers, after all, expect a continuous, consistent dialogue with a company, irrespective of the systems and departments within. This is the idea of a 'single view for the customer' (Figure 13.3).

Multichannel CRM presents a significant technical challenge. The technology required to support remote field salespeople is very different to the technology required to support a large, high-volume call centre. This technical challenge made it difficult to provide technology support for all of the customer channels in one system.

The emphasis on obtaining a single view of the customer is dependent on the effective deployment of operational CRM. Recently, the emphasis has moved toward understanding the value of the customer, and increasing the value of each interaction with the customer. This requires

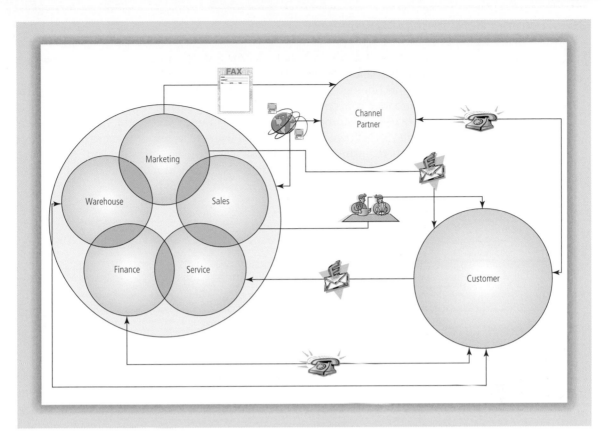

Figure 13.2 The challenge of multiple different channels of communication between an organization, its partners and its customers[2]

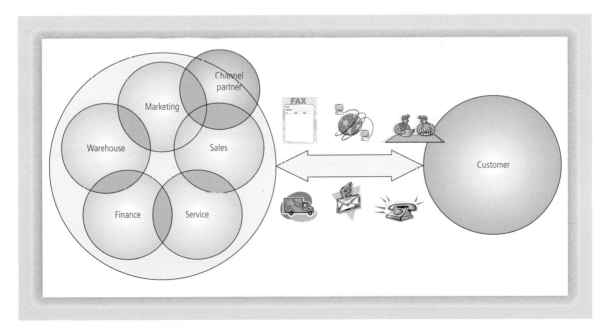

Figure 13.3 The customer expectation – consolidation of channels into a single, consistent dialogue[3]

sophisticated analytical tools, leading to the recent focus on analytical, rather than operational CRM.

Web technologies also had a significant role to play in the emergence of a broader conception of CRM, encompassing users other than direct employees (customers, channel partners, investors). Web browsers (Figure 13.4) allowed these external users to access and share information, without requiring specialist software to be installed on their own computers, leading to extra-enterprise CRM functions such as customer self-service, partner portals and investor portals.

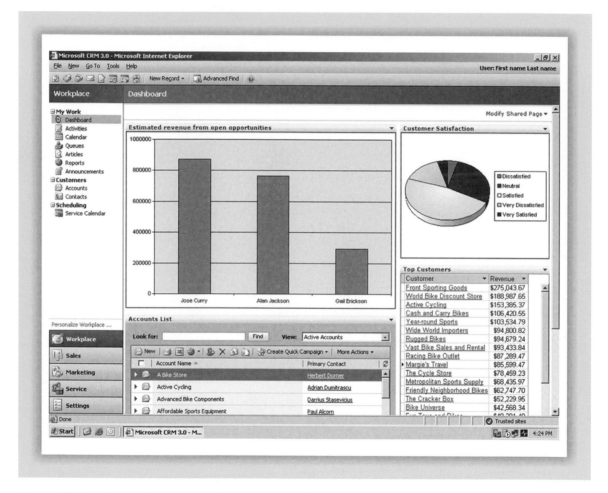

Figure 13.4 Microsoft CRM web browser interface

CRM technologies, therefore, are much more than a simple suite of applications. CRM must be flexible enough to stay in touch with a changing audience (the customer). It must reflect different requirements in different industries, as first discussed in Chapter 1. It must be accessible to external stakeholders and mobile professionals, such as salespeople and field technicians. It must operate over any communication channel, and it must integrate with other systems to provide a single view of, and for, the customer. Finally, it must be implemented in such a way that appropriate work processes and skills are deployed, as many of the objectives of CRM cannot be solved by technology alone.

The CRM ecosystem

The CRM ecosystem is made up of three major groups: CRM solutions providers, hardware and infrastructure vendors, and service providers (Figure 13.5).

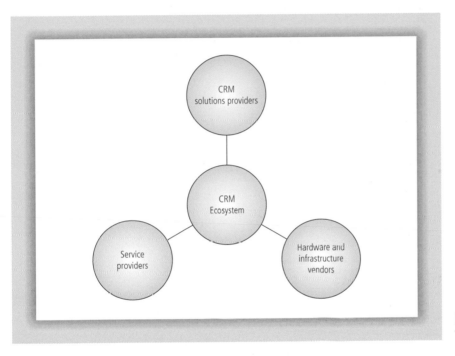

Figure 13.5
The CRM ecosystem

CRM solutions providers

The best known members of the CRM ecosystem are the CRM solution providers. Oracle, SAP, salesforce.com, Microsoft, and E.piphany are some well known examples. The independent research organization, Forrester, reports that worldwide revenue for CRM solution providers reached US$8.4 billion in 2006 and is forecast to grow to US$10.9 billion by 2010.[4]

CRM solutions can be clustered into three groups, as discussed below and shown in Tables 13.1 and 13.2:

- **Enterprise CRM suites:** this category comprises vendor solutions primarily targeted toward organizations with revenues of more than US$1 billion per year and/or more than 1000 employees. CRM vendors focused on enterprise class organizations typically offer a full

Enterprise CRM suites	Mid-market CRM suites
Amdocs CRM	Entellium
Chordiant Cx	GoldMine Corporate Edition
Onyx CRM	Maximizer Enterprise
Oracle's E-Business Suite CRM	Microsoft Dynamics CRM
Oracle's Siebel CRM	NetSuite
Oracle's PeopleSoft CRM	Oracle's Siebel CRM Professional Edition
Infor CRM E.piphany	Oracle's Siebel CRM On Demand
Pegasystems Customer Process Manager	Pivotal CRM
mySAP CRM	RightNow
	Sugar Enterprise
	SageCRM
	salesforce.com
	Soffront CRM Suite

Table 13.1
Enterprise CRM
suites and mid-
market CRM suites

Analytics tools	Customer service tools
SAS	ATG
SPSS	Applix
Teradata	eGain
	Graham Technologies
Customer data management tools	KANA
Dun & Bradstreet	KNOVA
Initiate	Unipress
Purisma	
Siperian	**Marketing automation tools**
VisionWare	Aprimo
	Unica
Partner channel management and collaboration	
BlueRoads	**Sales force automation tools**
Click Commerce	Sage Saleslogix
Comergent (Sterling Commerce)	Saratoga

Table 13.2 CRM
speciality tools

range of functionalities, can scale to serve large user populations and offer support for many industries, languages and currencies. They offer their products primarily through the traditional on-premise license model. However, several of the leading players now offer hosted or SaaS deployment options.

- **Midmarket CRM suites:** this category comprises vendor solutions primarily targeted towards small and medium-sized businesses: organizations with revenues of less than US$1 billion per year and/ or less than 1000 employees. CRM vendors in this group also offer a breadth of CRM functionalities, but these often have more limited capabilities in specific areas and are simpler to use than solutions built for the large enterprise market. These vendors are less suitable for large-scale global deployments. Vendors in this group also offer a variety of deployment options, including on-premise license and SaaS.
- **CRM speciality tools:** this category comprises vendors that offer solutions with narrow functional breadth but deep specialty capabilities, for both enterprise and mid-market organizations. Speciality CRM tools are available for marketing automation, sales-force automation (SFA), customer service, partner channel management and collaboration, customer analytics and customer data management.[5]

The CRM solutions companies, however, are only a small proportion of the overall CRM ecosystem. CRM software must run on hardware platforms such as Unix or Intel-based computers and it must integrate with communications infrastructure such as telephony for call centres, web and e-mail systems. Hence, hardware and infrastructure vendors are also an important part of the CRM ecosystem.

Hardware and infrastructure vendors

For CRM goals to be achieved there often needs to be a high level of emphasis on hardware and infrastructure. Call centres, for example, need tight integration between the software on the customer service agent's desktop and the automated call distributor (ACD) or switch hardware. Calls may need to be prioritized and routed based on CRM metrics, such as customer value or the customer's propensity to churn. Handheld devices carried by salespeople need to be synchronized with the central CRM database. Hardware vendors such as IBM, Blackberry, Dell and Hewlett-Packard provide a range of solutions across the hardware spectrum, while infrastructure vendors such as Avaya, Genesys and Siemens provide telephony and CRM-related infrastructure solutions.

Service providers

The services component of the CRM ecosystem is the largest and the least clearly defined. The use of service providers in a CRM implementation is often a critical factor in overall success of the implementation. Much of the CRM journey involves changes to strategy, business processes, organizational structures, skills and technical infrastructure, so good external advice and implementation can mean the difference between success and failure. Furthermore, some aspects of the front office, such as the call centre, may be outsourced either technically or as an entire business process. Service providers for CRM can be segmented, as shown in Table 13.3.

Service	Details	Examples of service providers
Strategy consulting	Consulting support for the formulation of customer strategy, contact strategy, channel strategy, CRM strategy	McKinsey, Peppers and Rogers
Business consulting	Services around business process re-engineering, process improvement and best practices for CRM	Accenture, Bearing Point, CGEY
Application consulting	Design and development of application modifications, project management of software package implementation and training	CRM solutions companies, Accenture, CGEY, Bearing Point, IBM
Technical consulting	Design and implementation of technical infrastructure and integration of this infrastructure with the existing business processes and applications	Unisys, IBM, Logica
Outsource service providers	Technology outsourcers and business process outsourcers	EDS, IBM, CSC, Acxiom

Table 13.3 CRM service providers

CRM solutions

Most CRM solutions, whether from enterprise, mid-market or speciality providers, are broadly aligned with the primary front-office functions of marketing, sales and service. However, not all CRM applications sit squarely in one or other of these functional areas. For example, some CRM modules focus on customers or products, rather than the operational processes performed by the marketing, sales and service departments. Customer and product management applications offer a suite of dedicated functions and modules that sit across sales, marketing and service. Companies that market, sell or service through channel partners use PRM (partner relationship management), a module of many CRM solutions. Finally, CRM analytics are often regarded as a separate suite of applications, with specialist solutions and vendors, as noted in Table 13.2.

The following sections outline the main elements of each of these application areas. Modern CRM applications are extremely rich in features and functions, far beyond what can be practically presented here.

Customer and product management

Customer and product management applications may be components of a broader CRM application, or they may be built into a focused sales, service or marketing application. It is vital that the database recognize important attributes of, variance within, and relationships between, customers and products, as indicated in Figures 13.6 and 13.7. For example, B2B organizations are not all the same: they vary in size, structure, buying roles and transactional histories. Similarly, not all products are the same. Off the shelf retail products are simple to classify and understand, each having a unique identification number, but customizable products such as cars or computers, made of a wide range of chosen components, are less easy to classify and understand. Company and product management systems are often industry-specific or company-specific.

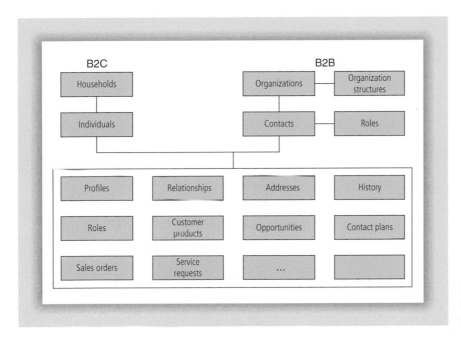

Figure 13.6
CRM components – customers

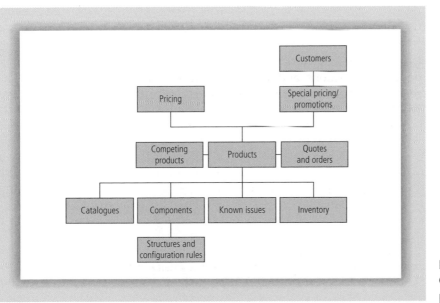

Figure 13.7
CRM components – products

Marketing

CRMs deployment for marketing purposes enables customers or prospects to be segmented, lists to be generated, campaigns to be run and assessed, and leads to be allocated. Marketers also use CRM to help create marketing plans, manage marketing budgets and loyalty programmes, launch new products and administer channel partner relationships. Marketing applications must also enable customer communications to be delivered and integrated across many communication channels, including e-mail, newsletters, telemarketing, conventional direct mail and web marketing. In all cases, the CRM focus on segmenting and personalizing the marketing effort is made possible by the sophistication of the underlying applications and the availability of customer-related data. Figure 13.8 shows a number of elements that typically form part of CRMs deployment for marketing purposes.

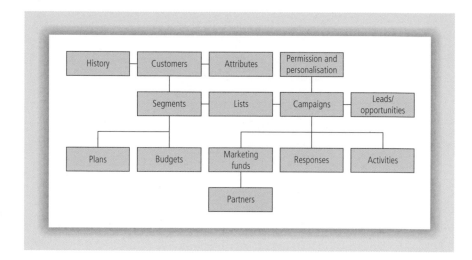

Figure 13.8
CRM components –
marketing
automation

Sales

CRM sales applications typically support many different types of selling, ranging from complex selling in the business-to-business environment, to business-to-consumer telesales and browser-enabled self-service sales. These different types of selling could involve a team of people over time, channel partners, specific sales methodologies and territory management. Whatever the context, however, the focus is on managing the opportunity from initial identification through to close. Opportunity management applications track the sale as it progresses along the sales pipeline, and allow quotes, orders and forecasts to be generated from a single source.

The implementation of sales-force automation technology is often accompanied by the implementation of a sales methodology (Figure 13.9). Without a methodology, salespeople will all use the system differently,

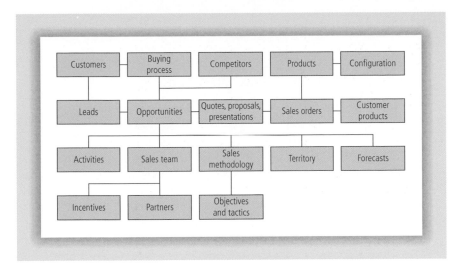

Figure 13.9
CRM components – sales-force automation

making sales management and prioritization of resources very difficult. There are a number of sales methodologies available, and some CRM solutions have them pre-integrated. Selling over the web also presents a unique set of challenges. It requires some specialist applications such as shopping carts, storefronts, graphical catalogues and secure checkout. The emergence of product configurators has made it possible to sell complex products over the web. Selling often involves complex incentive and commission schemes, and these can be modelled in the CRM application to allow salespeople to assess the impact of winning a sale on their own personal compensation.

Finally, a key technology to support selling processes is mobile synchronization or wireless, which allows salespeople access to the CRM system while out of the office and on the road.

Service and support

Service and support applications in CRM are also highly variable. Companies that service complex industrial products employ service engineers located in the field to visit customer sites, whereas companies that service consumers with a complaint require centralized teleservicing and a current knowledge base. The central element in CRM-enabled service is the service request or trouble ticket. This is used to track the service event through to completion, including service orders and issue resolutions.

As with sales-force automation, field service also requires mobile technologies. In service, however, despatch and scheduling applications may be used. Scripts may be deployed (as in marketing and sales) in a teleservicing application to help agents to deliver a consistent customer dialogue.

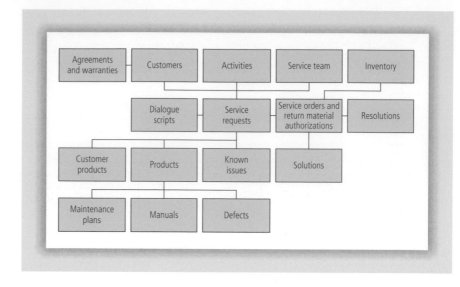

Figure 13.10
CRM components –
service automation

Partner relationship management (PRM)

Many companies market and sell through channel members or service through specialist partners. This is known as collaborative CRM. Channel members and partners all require support if they are to manage the relationship with the end customer effectively (Figure 13.11). In addition to sales, marketing and service functionality, as described above, managing the partner relationship requires specialist functionality such as partner qualification and sign up, developing joint business plans and objectives, measuring performance, partner training, administration of marketing funds and rebates, and specialist partner incentive schemes.

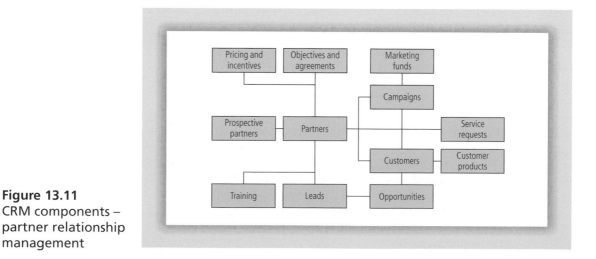

Figure 13.11
CRM components –
partner relationship
management

PRM most often requires a portal to be established in order to give partners access to the CRM system in a controlled, secure, yet collaborative way (Figure 13.12). Data security and administration are also important functions, to ensure that competing partners cannot see each other's data and opportunities, and to enable individual partners to administer their own users through the portal.

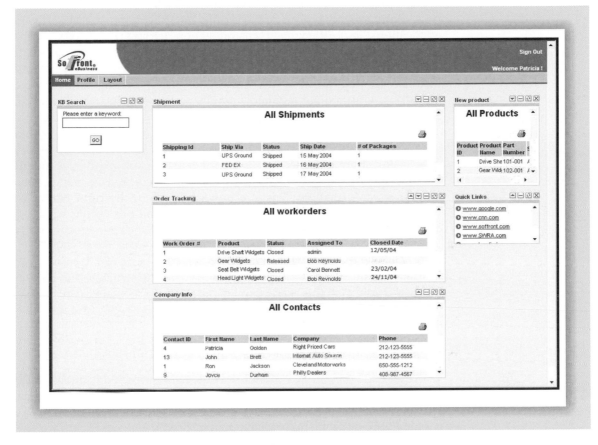

Figure 13.12 Example of a partner portal[6]

CRM analytics

CRM analytics has grown in importance over the last few years. Organizations have realized that merely streamlining the customer-facing operations in sales, marketing and service is not enough. Analytics can provide a deeper insight into the customer, reflected in key CRM metrics such as customer value, satisfaction and propensity to churn. The three levels of analysis in today's CRM systems, in increasing order of complexity, are standard reporting, online analytical processing (OLAP) and data mining.

Standard reporting

Reporting is an essential element of an effective CRM system. The foundation of CRM is an understanding and differentiation of customers – something which depends on good customer-related information. Reporting can take the form of simple lists of information, such as key accounts and annual revenues, to more sophisticated reports on certain performance metrics.

Reporting can be standardized (predefined), or query-based (ad hoc). Standardized reports are typically integrated into CRM software applications, but often need customization to suit the needs of the organization. Some customization of the report can be done when it is run, for example in selecting options or filtering criteria, but the end result is limited to what the report designers envisaged. For some industries, legislation or regulators require certain reports to be produced. Sometimes customized reports can be expensive to design and create.

Query-based reporting, on the other hand, presents the user with a selection of tools which can then be used to construct a specific report. This is far more flexible, but it is not suitable for regular, standard operational level reporting due to the time required to set up the request for information. This is a powerful tool in the right hands, as it allows specific reports to be requested, for example: 'show me all of the customers that have expired on their maintenance agreement, in my territory, with annual revenues above $50 000'.

As the requirement for analysis grows, the standard transactional information in the core CRM database may not be structured to deliver the best results; for this reason, online analytical processing (OLAP) has become an essential part of CRM.

Online analytical processing (OLAP)

OLAP technologies allow warehoused data to be subjected to analysis and ad hoc inquiry. Warehoused data is stored in one or more star schema, allowing users to drill down into graphs and tables to analyse how a certain figure or problem may have arisen. The format used is known as a star schema because it contains a central fact table surrounded by several dimension tables, giving it the appearance of a star, as in Figure 13.13.

A data warehouse will typically contain several star schemas, each organized around a central fact table based on customers, opportunities, service requests, activities and so on. The customer schema, for example, may contain information such as customer sales revenue figures, volumes, cost of sales, profit margins, discounts and promotional expense. OLAP users perform analysis against one or more schemas to answer a query. The schema format lends itself to ad hoc analysis, allowing the user to drill down into summarized information to investigate the underlying detail.

Two leading OLAP products are Hyperion's Essbase (Hyperion is now part of Oracle) and Oracle's Express Server. Some vendors prefer to use the term business intelligence rather than OLAP.

OLAP is valuable to a range of CRM users who have different types of questions to ask of the warehoused data (Figure 13.14). Salespeople

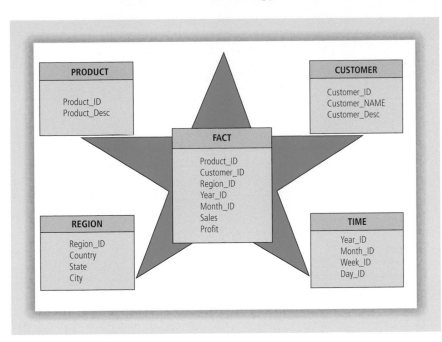

Figure 13.13
Star schema of data stored in a data warehouse[7]

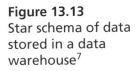

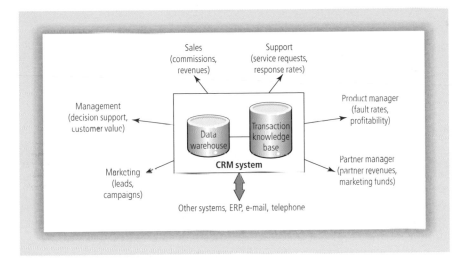

Figure 13.14
Different users demand different reports using OLAP technology[8]

can analyse their territory to determine revenue and profitability by customer. Service people can analyse call response rates and times. Partner managers can analyse the performance of partners by comparing marketing fund approvals to partner-generated revenues.

OLAP tools can also support decisions in real-time. For example, propensity-to-buy measures can be delivered to the call centre agent while the customer is on the telephone. This allows a tailored offer to be made that is more likely to receive a positive response from the customer. Real-time CRM is the result, an approach advocated by specialist vendors such as E.piphany (Figure 13.15).

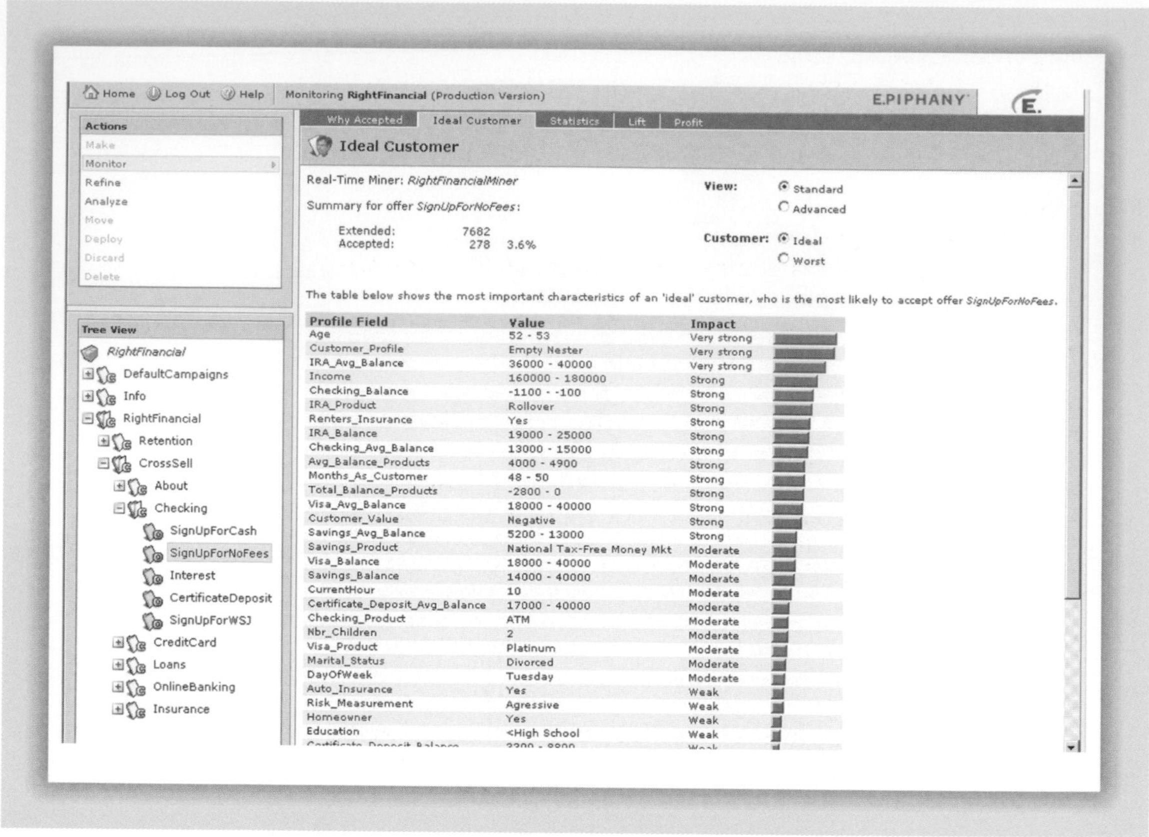

Figure 13.15
Real-time CRM analytics[9]

An important element in CRM analytics is the information delivery mechanism. Information can be made available on the desktop in a web browser interface with graphical layout and drill-down. This approach requires the user to search for a result. Another method of delivery involves setting trigger points (e.g. when a customer logs more than a certain number of service calls in a month). The analytics application then pushes the related information to the user via e-mail or another alert mechanism. This approach, also known as 'publish and subscribe', is a powerful management tool.

Data mining

Data mining provides considerable CRM analytical power that is highly valued in some industries. Banking, telecommunications, insurance, public sector, retail and utilities all require analysis of huge volumes of consumer data, a task that is very difficult without data mining. The data mining process seeks to identify patterns and relationships in the data, using selection, exploration and modelling processes. The results include, for example, churn scoring (likelihood that the customer will leave), fraud propensity or credit risk, customer value scoring and campaign effectiveness scoring.

A number of CRM vendors specialize in advanced analytical and data mining applications (Table 13.2). SAS Institute, for example, markets an 'Intelligence Architecture' which comprises:

- data warehousing (storage)
- business intelligence (delivery)
- analytical intelligence (data mining, predictive modelling, forecasting, simulation and optimization).

Analytical applications such as these are important in CRM. For example, customer profitability can only be used as a performance metric if it can be measured. Data mining in conjunction with an activity-based costing system allows performance against this KPI to be assessed. Operational CRM applications can also draw upon customer value or churn scores during customer dialogue, to assist in targeting and prioritizing customer offers.

CRM architecture

A key consideration in effective CRM is the way in which the system is constructed, or the 'architecture'. Unlike purely internal systems, CRM systems must be able to operate in the office, out of the office and over the web. They must tie together multiple communication channels, each using very different technologies (web, e-mail, telephone), and they must perform well enough, and be flexible enough, to suit a constantly changing, potentially growing user community.

Very few CRM implementations are standalone; they are nearly always integrated with other inhouse systems, including back-office systems. The challenges faced by the CRM architecture, therefore, are significant. CRM architecture can become a major limitation to the delivery of desired CRM outcomes. CRM project managers must consider architectural issues, as it can be very difficult and costly, and perhaps impossible, to change the architecture of a system once it is installed.

Multichannel CRM

There are two perspectives on multichannel CRM that have developed over the last decade: multiple communication technology channels and multiple organizational touchpoints

The challenge here is that customers may choose to browse your website for information, e-mail you for pricing, and call you to discuss discounts – expecting consistency across the whole dialogue. Multichannel CRM technology is necessary in order to deliver an enhanced customer experience, including a feeling of recognition and consistency of service across all channels and touchpoints.

Multiple communication technology channels

Whether the customer chooses to communicate with your organization by telephone, e-mail, web chat or face-to-face, CRM technology lets you create and track a consistent dialogue that reflects the value of the customer. Strategically significant customers may expect to get priority, irrespective of the communication channel they choose. They expect their inbound telephone calls and e-mails to go to the top of the list. To achieve this, in particular where e-mails from high value customers take priority over telephone calls from lower value customers, requires a central CRM database and a technology known as universal queuing. Universal queuing lists all communications in a single queue, irrespective of their origin or technology medium, and prioritizes response based on customer value or some other variable. In order to be effectively implemented, universal queuing requires the integration of the communications infrastructure (telephone, e-mail and web systems) with the CRM application (source of customer value metrics).

Multiple organizational touchpoints

The communications with a customer take place not only in different technology channels, but also with different people within your organization. Marketing sends out customer offers, sales representatives call to negotiate terms, and the customer calls the service desk for assistance. The marketing offer should be visible in order for the customer service agent to treat the customer correctly. This is even more important if the service desk is to perform a blended function, and cross-sell the customer an offer at the end of the service call. Finally, channel partners must be included in the communication loop if channel conflict over pricing, leads and commissions is to be avoided. The technology solution for multiple contact channels includes an integrated suite of applications for all departments, customer and external partner web portals, universal implementation across the organization, synchronization technology (to get the information into the field), and a central knowledge base for products, pricing and customer activity. While the technology challenges here are significant, the most difficult aspect of multiple contact channels is often the implementation of business processes across the departments, and externally, to allow a consistent customer dialogue.

Case 13.1

Channel integration at Dow Chemical

Dow Chemical, a leading science and technology organization, handles tens of thousands of customer inquiries each day across a large number of channels such as face-to-face, telephone, e-mail and the Internet. However, customer information being received through these channels was rarely consolidated. Without a comprehensive view of its customers Dow had difficulty in delivering consistent levels of service and in cross-selling other products and services.

To address this problem Dow implemented a major CRM strategy utilizing Siebel software in conjunction with a new call centre. The implementation of the strategy involved substantial redesign of Dow's operations and IT infrastructure. The management consulting firm Accenture was also involved in implementing the strategy, which took 18 months to complete.

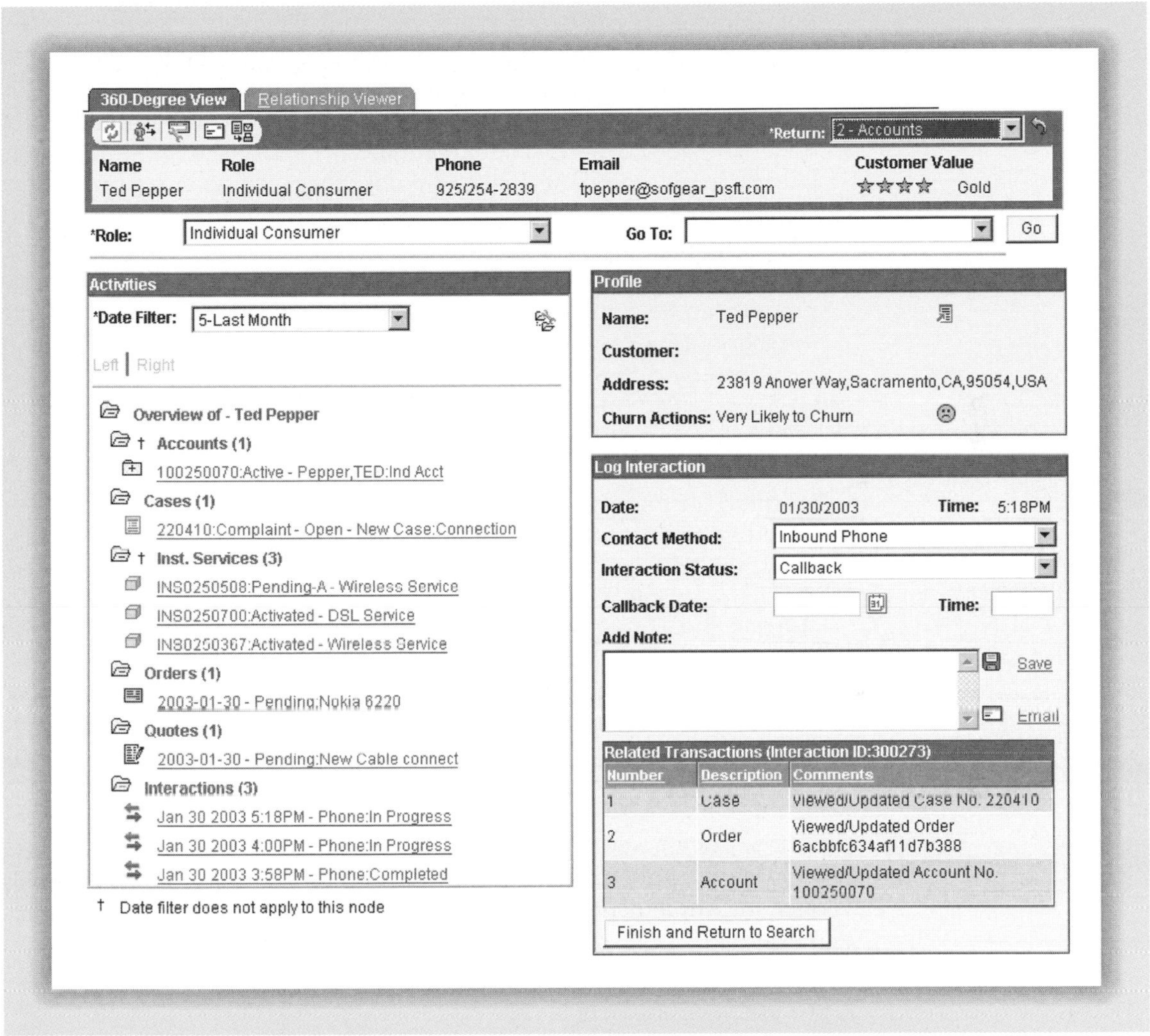

Figure 13.16 Multichannel (360 degree) view of the customer[10]

Mobile and wireless solutions

Many businesses operate in the field, with salespeople, merchandisers, meter readers and service technicians making calls on customers' home or business premises. These people play a significant role in delivering excellent customer experience. They can only do this if they are equipped with the latest customer, product and technical information. The two main technologies that are available to support such mobile professionals are mobile (synchronized) and wireless (online).

- **Mobile synchronized** solutions include a handheld or laptop device with a small resident database that is a replica of the particular individual's information in the main CRM system. These systems are not online or permanently connected, but they rely on sophisticated synchronization technology to filter the information that flows onto the relatively small handheld device. The user synchronizes the device when convenient, for example before leaving home, office or depot in the morning. The advantage of such systems is that they operate in environments that could not otherwise sustain a permanent connection, such as aeroplanes, remote areas and basements. Mobile CRM clients can be as functional as their connected in-the-office counterparts. The disadvantage of mobile is that the synchronization process can be complex and unreliable, or may not scale well to large numbers of users with some vendor technologies. The mobile client may employ different technology to the connected client, and so may be functionally inferior. Another disadvantage is that information is only as current as the last time it was synchronized. Despite this, the mobile synchronized solution is currently the most widespread and accepted for mobile professionals.
- **Wireless online** solutions also typically involve a handheld device. However, this device is connected to the main system using a wireless data connection. Technologies such as 3G, 4G and Bluetooth have enhanced the wireless online experience. Modern wireless broadband networks have largely removed the cost and performance penalties that were previously associated with wireless online solutions, especially in metropolitan areas. The advantage of being continuously online, with all the ensuing benefits of data currency, may offset the relatively minor connection and data cost differences.

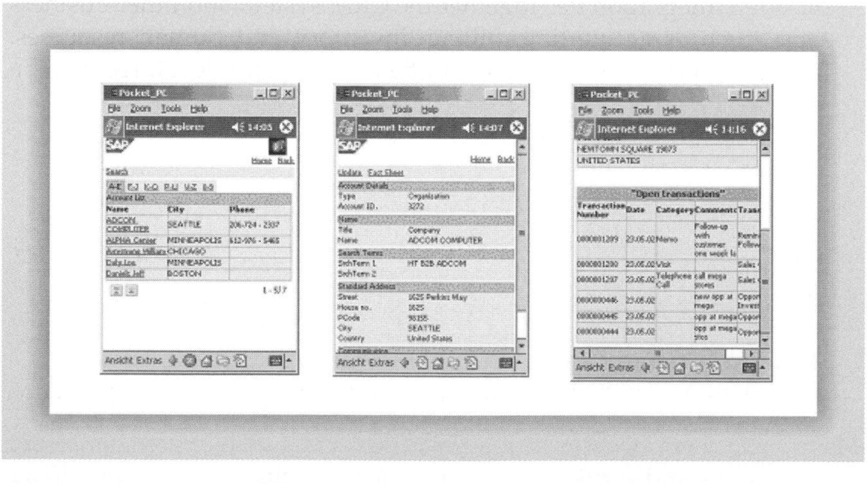

Figure 13.17
Sample handheld
screen views[11]

Integration

Integration is a major IT topic in its own right. Specialist integration middleware providers, such as Webmethods, IBM, SeeBeyond and Tibco, play an essential role in large-scale, complex CRM projects.[12] However, not all CRM integration requirements are complex. The integration challenge is largely a function of the complexity of the applications environment and the need for timeliness of information transfer. This gives rise to the two main types of integration: batch and real-time.

- **Batch processing** is technically simpler than real-time, and can handle larger volumes with less impact on system performance. Batch processing stores information in a file or batch, and then moves the information across the interface into the destination system in one go. However, the delay in moving the information may be costly in terms of revenues lost and inadequate customer experience. Many batch processes only run overnight, meaning the information is always a day old in the destination system. International organizations that trade across time zones face a more complicated task, in that batch processing has to be synchronized with night time in different geographies. In general, it is preferable to use batch integration where it will suffice, for example when transferring information that does not change often, such as part number details.
- **Real-time integration** takes place immediately. For example once a customer record is updated in one system, the change is immediately reflected in the destination system. Some forms of integration, for example telephony integration, must always be real-time, as the customer is on the phone at the time.

Whatever the integration method – batch or real-time – CRM systems generally face four integration challenges.

Application integration

Application integration ties together the CRM system and other business systems, such as accounting, billing, inventory and human resources. This type of integration can be either batch (for example, all records are changed at the end of day) or real-time (when an order comes in, it is put through to the warehouse immediately).

Application integration can be provided as standard by the CRM or other system vendors. However, in many cases this standard integration requires modification. Integration can also be handbuilt, although this becomes costly over time, as the interface between systems must be rebuilt each time a software upgrade is performed. Complex integration situations, where there are many applications requiring integration, normally require specialist integration middleware solutions that handle the flow of information or messages between applications. These solutions typically deploy standard systems connectors for the most common applications.

Telephony integration

Telephony integration ties the CRM application into the telephone system, allowing inbound calls to be routed to the right person based on caller profile, and outbound calls to be automatically made from the call centre desktop. At financial services organization Capital One, this has meant that calls from customers who have not used their credit card for the last two months are routed to a customer retention specialist. At Qantas Airlines, if the call is from a customer who has recently made a booking, it is routed to reservations; otherwise it goes to general customer service. The effectiveness of the integration solution for telephony is essential to the success of large-scale contact centres. In addition, technologies such as universal queuing and predictive dialling can be deployed to further refine the contact handling process.

Predictive dialling technologies are aimed at optimizing the productivity of call centre agents. These technologies monitor the call times, and predict when an agent is likely to complete the current call. The system will then dial the number of the next call, anticipating a pickup by the customer at the precise moment that an agent will complete the current call, hence minimizing unproductive time. While these systems can increase call rates, they must be carefully managed to ensure the quality and effectiveness of the customer interaction are satisfactory, and that agents do not suffer burnout from the increased workload.

E-mail integration

This is a similar form of integration to telephony in that it streamlines communications with the customer. It normally requires quite different technologies to be deployed. E-mail integration can involve both the generation of e-mails as a result of an internal workflow process (e.g. once an order is ready for shipment, automatically e-mail the customer to advise despatch details), and automated e-mail routing and response.

E-mail response applications have developed quite sophisticated capabilities. Simple applications include automatic acknowledgements, such as responding to an inbound e-mail to the service desk, advising that the e-mail has been received, and the associated service request tracking number. More sophisticated applications can be designed to read inbound e-mails, recognize key phrases or patterns and automatically respond with the most probable answer (see Figure 13.19). These systems can learn over time. However, they can create a negative customer experience when the customer receives a response that does not address their issue.

Web integration

A significant challenge for many organizations implementing CRM is the integration of the website. Most modern business have a website, and

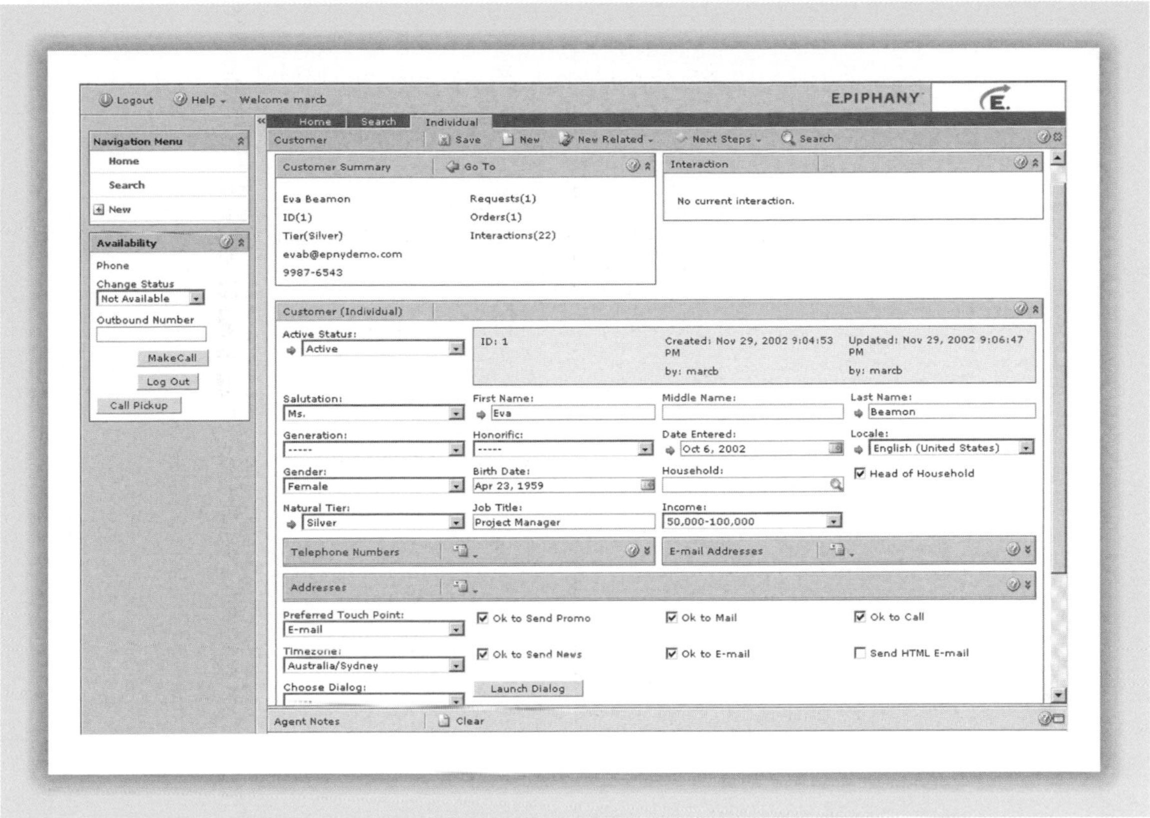

Figure 13.18 Call centre service application showing telephony integration on the left, in the window titled 'Availability'[13]

this website contains large amounts of content that is duplicated in the CRM system (customer registration details, solution knowledge base, product information, price lists, etc). The ideal position is for the website to draw this information from the CRM system, using integration technologies, or for the web application to be part of the core CRM system. Any unnecessary duplication of information will most likely result in errors and increased work, not to mention an unsatisfactory experience for the customer when, for example, the call centre advises a different price to the one on the website.

Web integration may also involve web chat or web collaboration. These technologies allow an organization to assist the customer over the web, without them having to leave the web page they are in. Examples include a simple call back over a telephone line, using a number provided by the customer, web text chat whereby the customer and the agent can have a dialogue over the web using chat windows, and interactive collaboration where the agent can effectively take control of the customer's mouse pointer and help them to fill in a form or find a document.

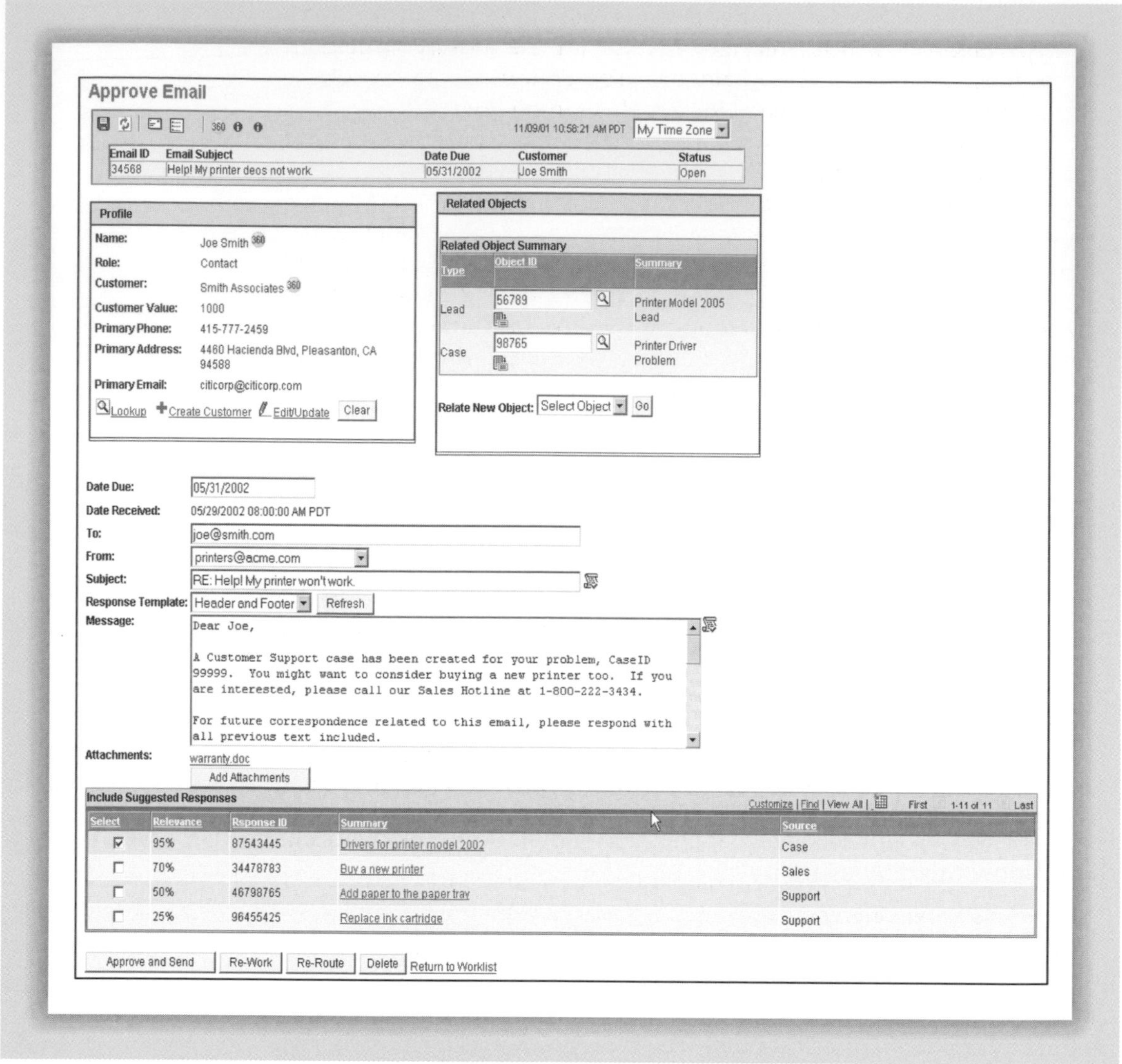

Figure 13.19 E-mail response screenshot[14]

Web browsers

Web browser technology has become an essential ingredient of modern CRM systems, because of their ubiquitous accessibility to customers and channel partners. Conventional client/server technologies are not suitable for customers or partners, as they require the customer or partner client PC to have CRM software installed on it. An organization can neither expect, nor support, large numbers of customers having to install and maintain the company's CRM software. Browser-based systems, on the other hand, require only a standard browser (perhaps of a certain release level) to be installed on the client machine. The CRM application then typically communicates with the web browser using HTML (hypertext markup language) or DHTML (dynamic HTML).

Browser technologies have other benefits that are important to CRM. The hyperlink-driven user interface is ideal for the loosely structured flow of most customer-facing dialogues. The ubiquitous nature of the web also makes it relatively easy for people to learn how to navigate in such an application. This is particularly important with customer- and partner-facing applications.

Web technologies also play an important role in integration and mobile solutions. XML (extensible markup language), a standard, flexible format for the description of documents over the web, is becoming a standard language for integration between applications. The CRM application may communicate with the accounting system, for example, using XML. Wireless mobile solutions are also implemented using web servers and WML (a compact, wireless form of HTML) as a means of transferring information to and from the mobile device.

Knowledge management

A central contributor to effective CRM is storing and leveraging customer-related knowledge. Note the use of the expression 'customer-related'. We are not just talking about customer knowledge. Knowledge about customers includes not only structured data such as contact history and account balances, but unstructured information such as letters and faxes from the customer, and notes on telephone conversations. Customer-related data also includes a wealth of other types of information that is useful in marketing, selling and servicing the customer. This ranges across product features and benefits, price lists, competitors' offerings, market research, service issues, business processes, company policies and much more.

Knowledge management can be defined as follows:

> Knowledge management is the organizational practice of consciously gathering, organizing, storing, interpreting, distributing and judiciously applying that knowledge to fulfil the mission of the organization.

The achievement of the CRM vision depends largely on how well knowledge is deployed at customer touchpoints. In Chapter 4 you read about six attributes of good quality data, captured in the mnemonic STARTS: shareable, transportable, accurate, relevant, timely, and secure. Information available at the touchpoints needs to satisfy those six same criteria.

Information needs to be **shareable** if several users require access to the same data at the same time, as might happen in the case of product specification data. Information also needs to be **transportable** from storage location to user. Data need to be made available wherever and whenever users require, on the website and on a service engineer's laptop. Information also needs to be suitably **accurate**. Price lists and transaction histories need to be absolutely up to date, whereas it might be acceptable for market-related data such as industry sales forecasts to be 12 months out of date. **Relevant** information needs to be available at the touchpoints. Sales representatives do not want to wade through masses of irrelevant information before they find what they need. **Timely** knowledge is available when needed. Knowledge that is important for competitive advantage needs to be **secure**.

The STARTS attributes have driven many companies to develop an IT-based knowledge management system which is capable of capturing, storing, organizing, interpreting (using data-mining tools) and distributing knowledge to users at customer touchpoints, so that marketing, sales and service objectives are accomplished. Knowledge bases need to be quickly accessed and searched for answers to ad hoc queries. Without a shareable, editable and searchable knowledge base, service people may resolve an issue but never share this solution with colleagues. A key element in being able to solve future customer issues is a way of storing symptoms verses resolutions, and categorizing service requests so they can be filtered and analysed. This knowledge base can be used for solution searching and issue resolution in the future, by service agents, partners and customers over the web on an intranet or extranet.

Automated workflow

Many customer-related processes can be predefined and automated in modern CRM applications, meaning that business rules that are critical to the success of sales, marketing and service no longer need to be manually managed. Workflow technologies can also be programmed to monitor for predefined conditions. They then respond to these conditions in a predictable and satisfactory manner (Figure 13.20).

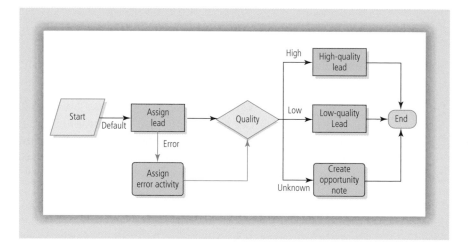

Figure 13.20 Example of a workflow process for lead assignment[15]

Automated workflow engineering applies to many CRM processes, including the following:

- **Service enquiry escalation:** 'if a service call is 20 hours old and is high severity, and is for a high value customer, and the status is not resolved, page the service manager'

- **E-mail response:** 'when an e-mail comes in from a customer in the southern region, automatically respond with the following…'
- **Lead assignment:** 'when a lead comes in from the website, look at the product being offered, the territory, and the current workloads of my salespeople, and assign the lead to the best person'
- **Dialogue scripting:** 'when a customer calls in, prompt the call centre agent with a standard welcome script. Register the customer's response, then determine the best course of action, and offer the agent a script accordingly. Continue this process to increase the chance of up-selling the customer'
- **Log-in navigation:** 'if the customer does not offer their password, automatically navigate the user to the customer identification screen'
- **System integration:** 'if the customer submits a confirmed order, automatically post it to the fulfilment system for verification and despatch'.

Workflow functionality is usually embedded into enterprise and mid-market CRM applications, and speciality CRM applications such as sales, marketing and service automation.

Summary

In this chapter you've learned about the technologies that support the achievement of CRM outcomes. Today's CRM technology has evolved from a range of standalone technologies, some of which date back to the 1970s and earlier. However, since the 1980s, some organizations have consolidated these disparate technologies into unified CRM offerings. The CRM ecosystem is made up of three major groups: CRM solutions providers, hardware and infrastructure vendors, and service providers. Most CRM solutions, whether from enterprise, mid-market or speciality providers, are broadly aligned with the primary front-office functions of marketing, sales and service. CRM analytics has grown in importance over the last few years. Organizations have realized that analytics can provide a deeper insight into customers, for example, their value, satisfaction and propensity to churn. Most CRM technologies allow users to receive a number of forms of management report, based, in order of complexity, on standard reporting formats, online analytical processing (OLAP) and data mining.

A key consideration in effective CRM is the system's architecture. Unlike internal systems, CRM systems must be able to operate in the office, out of the office, over the web, and they must tie together multiple communication channels using technologies such as the web, e-mail and telephone. Very few CRM implementations standalone – they are nearly always integrated with other inhouse systems, including back-office systems. Many marketing, selling and service processes are predefined and automated in modern CRM applications, using workflow technologies. Another important technological contribution to effective CRM is storing and leveraging customer-related knowledge. Many companies have invested in knowledge management systems as a consequence.

In sum, CRM information technology enables consistent customer interaction across multiple channels of communication, encompasses mobile and web technologies, customer knowledge management and analytics, process automation though workflow technologies, integration with other systems and technologies, and a broad suite of applications, over marketing, sales, service and partners, all of which may be customized or pre-configured for industry-specific requirements.

References

1. Much of this chapter is based on materials compiled originally by John Turnbull, founder and Managing Director of Customer Connect Australia, for the first edition of this book. Refer to Chapter 3 in Buttle, F. (2004) *Customer Relationship management: concepts and tools.* Oxford: Elsevier.
2. Courtesy of CustomerConnect Australia, www.customerconnect. com.au
3. Courtesy of CustomerConnect Australia, www.customerconnect. com.au
4. Forrester, Inc. (2006) CRM market size and forecast: 2006 to 2010. www.forrester.com
5. www.oracle.com/corporate/analyst/reports/ent_apps/crm/forrester-crm-0207.pdf Accessed 28 November 2007.
6. Courtesy of Soffront CRM, www.soffront.com
7. http://hubpages.com/hub/Star_schema. Accessed 28 November 2007.
8. www.customerconnect.com.au
9. Courtesy of E.piphany, which is now part of Infor CRM http://go.infor.com/inforcrm/
10. Courtesy of PeopleSoft, www.peoplesoft.com
11. Courtesy of SAP, www.sap.com
12. See Gartner Inc. (2007) Report highlight for market trends: portal, process and middleware software, worldwide, 2006–2011. www. gartner.com. Accessed 10 November 2007.
13. Courtesy of E.piphany, www.epiphany.com
14. Courtesy of PeopleSoft, www.peoplesoft.com
15. Courtesy of Siebel Systems, www.siebel.com

Chapter 14
Sales-force automation

By the end of this chapter you will understand:

1. what is meant by sales-force automation (SFA)
2. the members of the SFA ecosystem
3. the benefits derived from SFA
4. the functionality that is available in SFA software applications
5. what needs to be done to encourage salespeople to adopt SFA.

Introduction

This is the first of three chapters that look at CRM technologies. This chapter is about technologies used by salespeople and their managers. Subsequent chapters review marketing automation and service automation.

Sales-force automation (SFA) has offered technological support to sales people and managers since the beginning of the 1990s. SFA is now so widely adopted in business-to-business environments that it is seen as a 'competitive imperative'[1] that offers 'competitive parity'.[2] In other words, SFA is just a regular feature of the selling landscape.

Salespeople are found in a wide variety of contexts: in the field calling on business and institutional customers, in offices, contact centres and call centres receiving incoming orders and making outbound sales calls, in retail business-to-customer settings, in the street selling door-to-door, and even in the home where party planners sell a variety of merchandise ranging from adult sex aids to cleaning products. All these sales contexts deploy SFA in some form or other.

The SFA ecosystem is made up of three components: SFA solutions providers, hardware and infrastructure vendors, and associated service providers. The technology enables companies to collect, store, analyse, distribute and use customer-related data for sales purposes. Customer-related data like this is the key to customer orientation[3] and the development of long-term mutually beneficial relationships with customers.[4] SFA software from solutions providers enables sales representatives and their managers to manage sales pipelines, track contacts and configure products, among many other things. SFA software also provides reports for sales representatives and managers. This chapter starts by defining the field and identifying members of the SFA ecosystem.

What is SFA?

The term sales-force automation (SFA) can be defined as:

> Sales-force automation is the application of computerized technologies to support salespeople and sales management in the achievement of their work-related objectives.

Hardware and software are the key technological elements of SFA. Hardware includes desktop, laptop and handheld devices and contact or call centre telephony technology. Software comprises both 'point' solutions that are designed to assist in a single area of selling or sales management, and integrated solutions that offer a range of functionality. The integrated packages can be dedicated to sales-force applications only, or can be incorporated into comprehensive CRM suites that operate over the three front-office areas of marketing, service and sales.

All SFA software is designed so that pertinent customer-related data can be captured, stored, analysed and distributed to sales people and sales managers in order for them to become more effective or efficient in the pursuit of their objectives.

The SFA ecosystem

The SFA ecosystem consists of SFA solutions providers, hardware and infrastructure vendors, and service providers.

SFA solutions providers

SFA solutions providers can be classified in a number of ways. Some are SFA specialists. They compete against enterprise and mid-market CRM suites that include SFA modules, and enterprise suite vendors that offer a full range of IT solutions to support business, including supply chain management (SCM), enterprise resource planning (ERP) and customer relationship management (CRM). A number of illustrative examples are listed in Table 14.1.

SFA specialists	SFA as part of CRM suite	SFA as part of Enterprise suite
Selectica	Onyx	Oracle (including PeopleSoft and Siebel suites)
EzRoute	Pivotal	SAP
Salesnet	Salesforce.com	Epicor
CallWizard	SalesLogix	Deltek
Selltech	ACCPAC	Fourth Shift
CyberForms	NetCRM	Intentia

Table 14.1
Classification of SFA vendors

Some SFA specialists focus on particular areas of functionality within SFA. Selectica, for example, builds customized configurators. A configurator is a software-based application engine that allows companies to configure complex products and services based on pre-defined rules. Sometimes, customers interact directly with configurators. For example, the Dell Computer website allows customers to build their own personal computers (PCs). Configurators guide users through the buying and specification process, offering only valid options and features at each step. This can deliver benefits to customers, salespeople and management. Customers can define and build their preferred customized solutions, reducing cost and meeting specifications. Salespeople no longer need to master comprehensive product or service technical data, because these are built into the engine. Training costs for salespeople are therefore reduced. The potential for incorrectly specifying a solution for a customer is decreased. Configurators enable mass customization (see Case 14.1).

Case 14.1

Product configuration at General Motors

Lou Adler is responsible for helping car dealers configure, order and price cars. For more than 15 years he lugged three binders between dealerships. One binder listed current models. Another listed available options. The third listed price information. It took Adler 20 minutes to configure each vehicle. Some dealerships asked him to configure 300 vehicles per sales call. It took a long time, and ultimately about 25 per cent of orders were rejected by the factory as impossible to build. Today, Adler takes two minutes to configure, price and order each car. He uses a product configurator called GM PROSPEC which has virtually eliminated factory rejection.

Many of the vendors offering SFA as part of broader CRM suites started out as SFA specialists, for example Siebel and salesforce.com. These brands now offer a wide range of marketing, service and sales automation.

Hardware and infrastructure vendors

The performance requirements of SFA applications can create significant challenges for both hardware and technology infrastructure. Whereas office-bound salespeople and sales managers might be happy to use desktop or laptop computers, field sales representatives often want lighter, handheld devices, such as Microsoft-based Windows Pocket PC, Palm Pilot or Blackberry. Where companies have geographically dispersed external salespeople, SFA systems must be able to operate out of the office and over the web. Mobile or wireless solutions are necessary, as the data held on portable devices must be regularly synchronized with the central database. SFA applications often need to integrate with a number of communication channels which use different technologies (e.g. web, e-mail or telephone). In growing industries and companies, SFA applications must be supported by hardware and infrastructure that can sustain increased numbers of users.

Services

The services component of the SFA ecosystem is very diverse. When a sales-force automation project is undertaken, service costs may significantly add to overall project expenditure. SFA project leaders might buy services from providers that re-engineer selling processes, manage projects, train salespeople, consult on organizational structure or conduct customer portfolio analysis. Service providers can contribute significantly both to SFA project costs and to the probability of success.

The hardware and software for a sales-force automation project may account for between 10 and 50 per cent of the overall costs. The balance is made up of service costs. Although some software vendor case studies suggest that payback is achievable within days, many projects take between 12 and 24 months to implement, let alone to yield a return. It has been suggested that the average implementation period is 21 months[5] and that users need over 100 hours experience with the systems before they could claim to have mastered it.[6]

SFA software functionality

SFA applications offer a range of functionality, as listed in Table 14.2. Not all solutions provide the full complement of sales-related functionality. In the next few paragraphs, we'll describe this functionality in more detail.

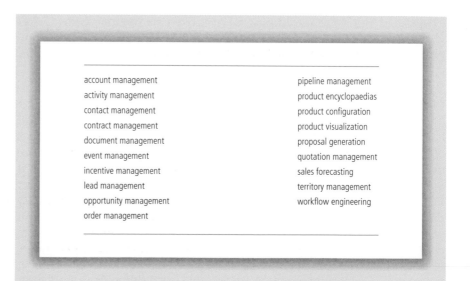

account management	pipeline management
activity management	product encyclopaedias
contact management	product configuration
contract management	product visualization
document management	proposal generation
event management	quotation management
incentive management	sales forecasting
lead management	territory management
opportunity management	workflow engineering
order management	

Table 14.2
Functionality
offered by SFA
software

Account management

Account management offers sales representatives and managers a complete view of the customer relationship including contacts, contact history, completed transactions, current orders, shipments, enquiries, service history, opportunities and quotations. This allows sales representatives and account managers to keep track of all their obligations in respect of every account for which they are responsible, whether this is an opportunity to be closed, an order or a service enquiry. Figure 14.1 is an account management screenshot from CRM vendor salesforce.com. You will see that it shows account details, contacts, opportunities, activities and service cases that are unresolved.

Activity management

Activity management keeps sales representatives and managers aware of all activities, whether complete or pending, related to an account, contact or opportunity, by establishing to-do lists, setting priorities, monitoring progress and programming alerts. Activities include, for example, preparation of quotations, scheduling of sales calls and following up enquiries.

Contact management

Contact management functionality includes tools for building, sharing and updating contact lists, making appointments, time setting, and task, event and contact tracking. Contact list data includes names, phone numbers, addresses, preference data and e-mail addresses for people and companies, as well as a history of inbound and outbound communications. Figure 14.2 is an illustration of a contact management page from a CRM vendor.

Contract management

Contract management functionality enables representatives and managers to create, track, progress, accelerate, monitor and control contracts with customers. Contract management helps manage a contract's lifespan by shortening approval cycles for contracts, renewing contracts sooner and reducing administrative costs. The software may use security controls to ensure only approved people have access to contracts.

Document management

Companies generate and use many documents as they sell to customers, for example brochures, product specifications, price lists, competitive comparisons and templates for preparing quotations. Document management software allows companies to manage these documents, keep them current and ensure that they are available to representatives and managers when needed. Some systems allow all documents to be 'attached' to the account or contact, thus facilitating faster and fuller recall of past interactions.

Event management software

This software enables representatives and managers to plan, implement, control and evaluate events such as conferences, seminars, trade shows,

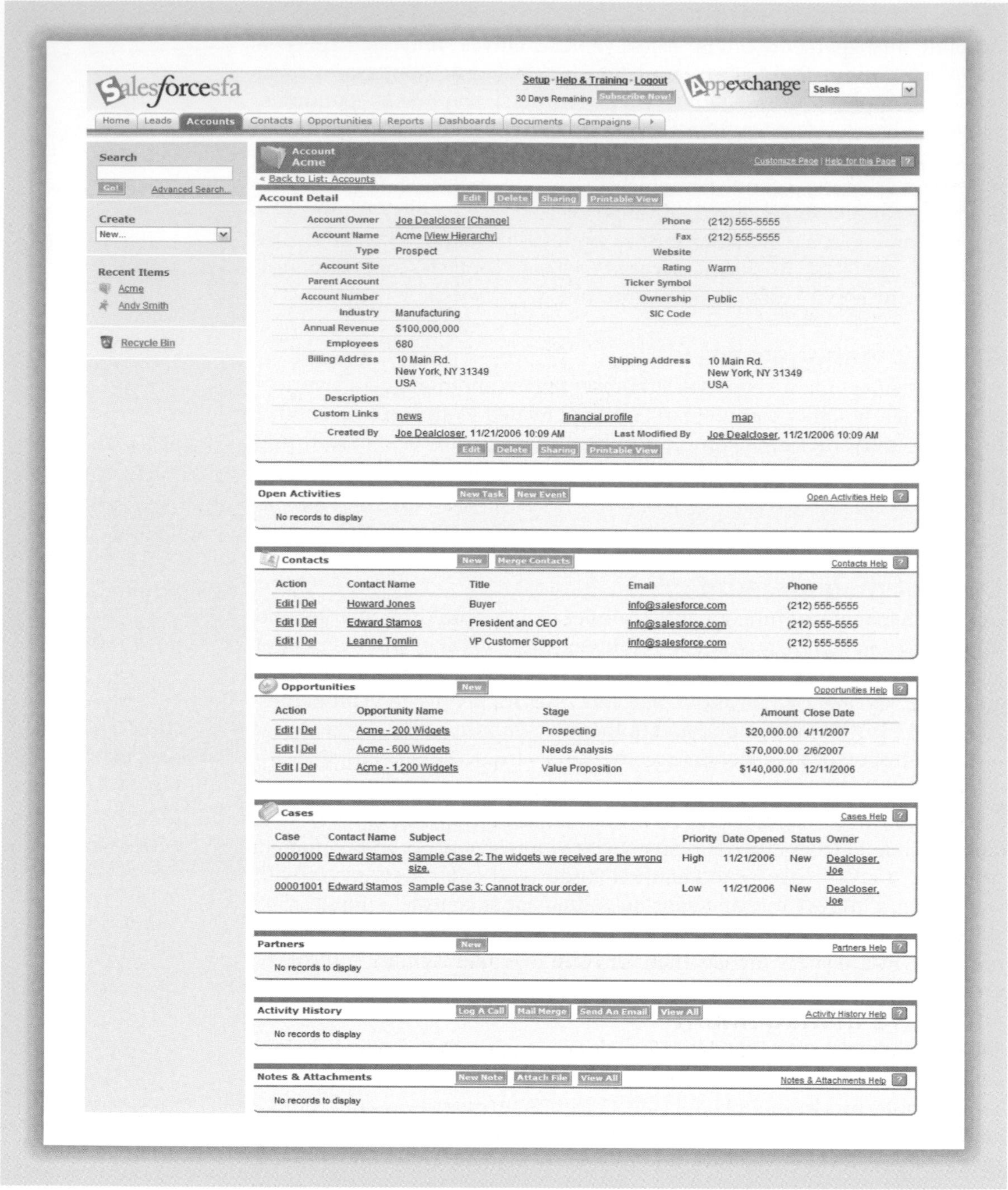

Figure 14.1 Account management screenshot[7]

exhibitions and webinars, whether run solo or jointly with customers or other partners. Some events, such as conferences, can be very complex and involve many stakeholders, such as sponsors, exhibitors, security partners, police, accommodation partners, travel partners, catering

Figure 14.2
Contact
management
screenshot

partners, lighting and sound contractors, speakers, invitees and the general public. Indeed, some major events are planned many years in advance; you only need to consider the Olympics or FIFA World Cup to appreciate the grand scale of some major events. Few, if any, sales-related events reach a comparable level of complexity, but events to which customers and key partners are invited must run smoothly or the company risks being regarded as unprofessional.

Event management software contains a range of tools that can be useful to sales managers and others organizing events. These include an event calendar, online registration, partner management tools, event reports and analytics, attendee communication and management tools, badge creation, activity lists for exhibitors and venue management tools. Figure 14.3 is an illustrative event management screenshot from PCGuild.

Incentive management

Incentive management is an issue for sales managers who use commissions to lift, direct and reward sales representatives' efforts. In many companies, commissions are calculated using standalone spreadsheets. When part of a sales-force automation solution, incentive management eliminates the need to re-enter or transfer data from spreadsheets, leading to better visibility, accuracy and higher efficiency. Incentive management applications can be linked into back-office payroll applications that automate payment.

Lead management

Lead management allows companies to create, assign and track sales leads. Leads either expire or convert into qualified opportunities. User-defined rules allow leads to be allocated to representatives and account managers on the basis of role, territory, product expertise or

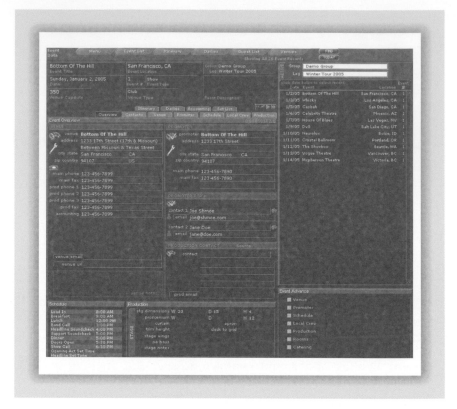

Figure 14.3
Event management
screenshot[8]

other variables. Lead management allows for more equitable workload distribution across a sales team, and uses security controls to ensure that representatives can only access their own leads.

Opportunity management

An opportunity is a record of a potential sale or any other type of revenue generation. Opportunity management software enables representatives and managers to create an opportunity record in the database and monitor progress against a predefined selling methodology. Salespeople follow the steps as if following a checklist, ensuring that all opportunities are handled consistently. Sales representatives can view their own opportunities linked to additional information such as contacts, activities, products, proposals, projects, presentations, quotations, competitors, estimated revenue, cost of sales, probability of closure, sales stage and so on. Opportunity management functionality allows representatives to estimate their future bonuses or commissions. Managers can then receive reports on the progress of opportunities as they move towards closure, broken down by salesperson, territory, type, date or other criteria. Figure 14.5 shows an opportunity management report. Note the selling model in the window on the left, at the bottom of the screen, and the probability of closing the opportunity at the top of the screen.

Figure 14.4
Lead management screenshot[9]

Order management

Order management functionality allows representatives to convert quotations and estimates into correctly priced orders once a customer has agreed to buy. If this is done in front of a customer, the order can be loaded into production or picked from a warehouse more quickly. Order management software may include a quotation engine, a pricing module and a product configurator. With visibility through a portal, the customer, representative and manager have access to the same, up to date, order information.

Pipeline management

Pipeline management is the process of managing the entire sales cycle, from identifying prospects, estimating sales potential, managing leads, forecasting sales, initiating and maintaining customer relationships, right through to closure. It relies on accurate, up-to-date opportunity information, such as the potential size and close date for each opportunity.

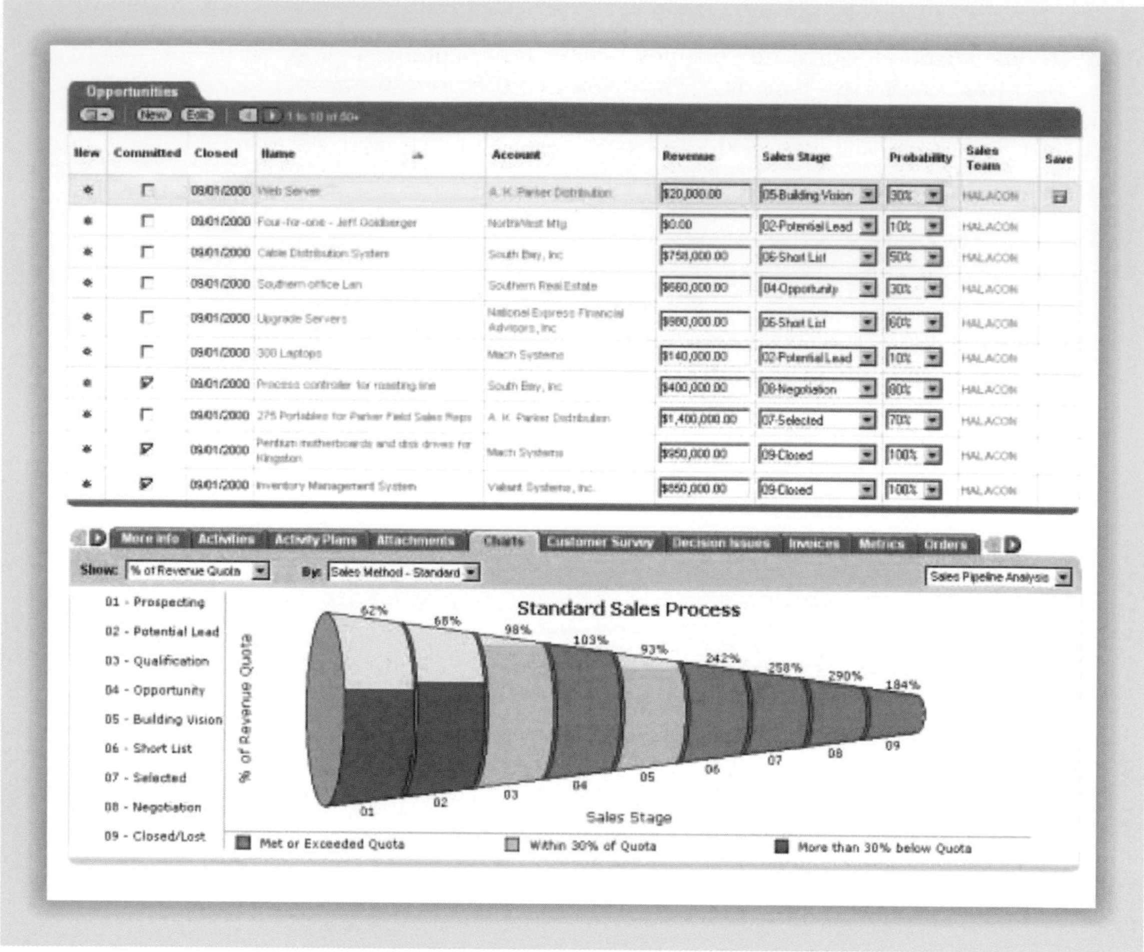

Figure 14.5
Opportunity management report[10]

A well-defined sales pipeline helps minimize lost opportunities and breakdowns in the sales process.

Product encyclopaedias

A product encyclopaedia is a searchable electronic product catalogue that generally contains product names, stock numbers, images and specifications. These can be stored on representatives' computers and/or made available to customers online.

Product configuration

Product configuration applications enable salespeople, or customers themselves, automatically to design and price customized products, services or solutions. Configurators are useful when the product is particularly complex or when customization is an important part of the value proposition.

Product visualization

Product visualization software enables sales representatives and customers to produce realistic images of products before they are manufactured. This is a useful application when linked to a product configurator. The image can take the form of a simulated photograph, three-dimensional model or technical drawing, and can include other related documentation such as specifications or prices.

Proposal generation

This allows users to create customized proposals for customers. Users draw from a database of information to create proposals which, typically, are composed of several parts, some of which are customized, including cover page and letter, introduction, objectives, products, product features, services, prices, specifications, pictures, drawings, people, experience, resumes, references, approach, schedule, organization, scope of work and appendices.

Quotation management

Quotation management software allows representatives and managers to quote for opportunities. This may be part of a broader order management capability. The software allows users to create, edit, approve and produce costed, customized, proposals quickly and reliably. Some vendors enable users to create multimedia proposals with audio, animation and video. One survey suggests that proposals produced with software have a much higher win rate (46 per cent) than proposals produced manually (26 per cent).[11]

Sales forecasting

Sales forecasting applications offer sales representatives and managers a number of qualitative and quantitative processes to help forecast sales revenues and close rates. Among the qualitative methods are sales team estimates, and among the quantitative methods are time-series analysis and regression models (covered in Chapter 5). Accurate sales forecasts help resource allocation throughout the business.

Territory management

Territory management software allows sales managers to create, adjust and balance sales territories, so that sales representatives have equivalent workloads and/or opportunities. Some territory management applications come with a territory management methodology which users can follow when establishing sales territories.[12] Some applications link to geographic mapping or geodemographic software. The software enables companies to match sales coverage to market opportunity, create sales territory hierarchies (e.g. cities, states, regions) and reduce the cost of selling by reducing travel time. Call cycle scheduling, calendaring and lead management is often enabled by the software.

Workflow engineering

Workflow engineering software is useful for designing sales-related processes, such as the lead management process and the event

406 Customer Relationship Management

management process. It can even be used to design the selling process itself – the series of steps that a sales representative must follow in shifting a prospect from initial awareness to closing the deal.

Although we have thus far discussed a generic set of sales-related functionality, SFA software is also designed for context-specific applications. For example, sales representatives selling liquor to a retail store might employ software that recommends planograms, optimizes the allocation of retail display space, audits inventory levels, recommends prices and controls cooperative promotional support. In some contexts graphics, video and sound support is important. Some SFA vendors offer functionality designed for salespeople in particular industries. Siebel, for example, offers customized solutions for over a dozen different industries ranging from aerospace and defence to transportation. SAP have pre-configured applications for over two dozen industry contexts.

Most SFA applications can generate a wide range of standard and customized reports which are useful to salespeople, sales managers and executive management, as shown in Table 14.3. Salesforce.com, for example, offers over 50 standard reports and also enables users to construct their own customized reports using wizards. These deliver charts, tables, text and other graphics to receivers' devices. Dashboards deliver real-time sales data to executives that can be refreshed at a single click. Customized dashboards ensure that people receive reports matched to their roles and responsibilities. Drill down capabilities mean that users can thoroughly investigate the reasons behind results in dashboard reports. Furthermore, dashboards can be integrated with third-party analytics to deliver deeper analysis of sales performance and problems.

Table 14.3
Examples of reports available from SFA software

cost-to-serve	sales cycles
customer profitability	share of market
lead conversion	share of wallet
pipeline progress	sales person productivity
quotation performance	win–loss rates

SFA adoption

Generally, a company's determination to adopt SFA follows a two-step process. First senior management decides to invest in SFA and, secondly, sales representatives and their managers decide to use SFA. Both groups, senior managers and users, will anticipate benefits from SFA and unless those benefits are delivered SFA may be abandoned.[13]

Benefits from SFA

Vendors and consultants claim a number of benefits from SFA implementation, including accelerated cashflow, shorter sales cycles leading to faster inventory turnover, improved customer relations, improved salesperson productivity, increased sales revenue, market share growth, higher win rates, reduced cost of sales, more closing opportunities and improved profitability. These benefits appeal to differing SFA stakeholders:

- **sales people**: shorter sales cycles, more closing opportunities, higher win rates
- **sales managers**: improved salesperson productivity, improved customer relations, accurate reporting, reduced cost of sales
- **senior management**: accelerated cashflow, increased sales revenue, market share growth, improved profitability.

In addition to these measurable outcomes, there may be additional benefits such as less rework, more timely information and better quality management reports. Software vendor case histories of SFA implementations offer testimonials to SFAs impacts (see Case 14.2 Freight Traders).

Independent research, summarized in Table 14.4, suggests that the primary motivation for implementing SFA is improved efficiency, although not every SFA implementation has specified formal goals.[14]

Motivation	% of sample reporting
Improve efficiencies	72
Improve customer contact	44
Increase sales	33
Reduce costs	26
Improve accuracy	21

Table 14.4
Motivations for implementing SFA[15]

Case 14.2

Freight Traders enjoys benefits from SFA

Freight Traders, a subsidiary of global food manufacturer Mars Incorporated, is a web-based logistics consultancy that connects shippers to carriers. The company facilitates the transit of cargo between the two parties. Customers include Kellogg's, Lever Faberge and Sainsbury's Supermarket Group. Garry Mansell is Managing Director.

'We had the system up and running in three days', says Mansell. 'Within eight days the whole company was using it across multiple countries. Ease of use and speed of implementation were everything I expected of a web-based solution'. Major benefits include far greater customer, lead and prospect visibility. 'We operate dispersed account teams and they now have a single view of customers and prospects'. Another major benefit is accessibility. 'Regardless of where I am in the world, I only have to log on to see how our business is doing', he says. 'The reporting tools are really useful to our business', continues Mansell, 'we don't need to waste time chasing sales teams for reports. Once we input the information, reports are automated and can be tailored to our requirements'. Mansell finds these reports a valuable tool to the running of the business. It helps the company focus on maximizing resources by identifying where and when the best sales opportunities arise and responding to them. Freight Traders uses salesforce.com to communicate best practices across the organization. 'Because the system is so transparent we can show clearly what works best with a particular company, country or industry and share that vital intelligence across the organization. All the information is contained in our salesforce.com account'.

Source: Salesforce.com[16]

How SFA changes sales performance

There have been a number of independent assessments of the effects of SFA on sales performance.[17] One empirical investigation of a pharmaceutical company's operations in three countries finds a clear relationship between SFA adoption and salesperson performance. The researchers conclude: 'Does the use of sales-force automation really contribute to higher sales performance? With overall sales growing and with 16.4 per cent of the variance in sales explained by the use of sales-force automation systems, this study suggests the answer is 'yes'.'[18] Another investigation found that use of SFA was associated with improvements in sales representatives' selling skills, knowledge and performance. This research found positive correlations between SFA implementation and sales representatives' market knowledge, technical knowledge, targeting skills, adaptive selling and call productivity. Essentially sales representatives with SFA support became more adaptable and productive. Sales representatives' use of SFA accounted for a small, yet significant, portion (7 per cent) of their sales performance.[19] However, not all research indicates positive outcomes from the implementation of SFA.[20] It seems likely that SFA will have more impact on sales performance when a number of conditions are met.[21] These include:

1. salespeople find that SFA is easy to use
2. salespeople find the technology useful because it fits their roles well
3. availability of appropriate-to-task SFA training
4. users have accurate expectations about what SFA will deliver
5. users have a positive attitude towards innovation
6. users have a positive attitude towards technology

7. availability of user support after roll-out, for example, a helpdesk
8. involvement of user groups, including sales representatives and managers, during project planning and technology selection
9. deployment of a multidisciplinary team in the project planning phases
10. senior management support for SFA.

It is SFA users, not technology firms, who decide what is easy to use. Some ease-of-use considerations include screen design, the use of a graphical user interface (GUI), system navigation, online help, user documentation, data synchronization and system support. Screen layouts that are clean, bright, appear uncluttered and are easy to navigate are appreciated. User interfaces are best if purpose-built for a particular screen layout. For example, it is not acceptable to take a PC screen design and merely cut it to size to fit a PDA screen. A graphical user interface essentially involves the use of a pointing device and graphical icons to control a computer. The most common GUI is the Microsoft Windows system, which is deployed throughout the Microsoft Office suite and related products. The basic components of a GUI are a pointer on the screen, a pointing device such as a mouse, graphical icons that represent commands, files or windows, a desktop where these icons are assembled, windows which divide a computer screen allowing several files or programmes to be run simultaneously, and menus which allow users to execute commands. System navigation is good if users can move from field to field, screen to screen, and function to function with no difficulty. Online help that is available at field-level, as well as screen-level, is valued by users because it means they can resolve questions quickly. User documentation that includes screenshots and textual explanation is appreciated, as is simple, fast, data synchronization and general system support through training and a helpdesk.

Summary

Sales-force automation is a competitive necessity which involves the application of technology to support salespeople and their managers. Broadly, SFA enables members of sales teams to become more efficient and effective in their job roles. The SFA ecosystem includes a wide range of software, hardware, infrastructure and service organizations. SFA software offers an enormous range of functionality, including account management, activity management, contact management, contract management, document management, event management, incentive management, lead management, opportunity management, order management, pipeline management, product encyclopaedias, product configuration, product visualization, proposal generation, quotation management, sales forecasting, territory management and workflow engineering.

Three stakeholder groups – salespeople, sales mangers, and senior management – have a particular interest in generating benefits from SFA adoption and each may have a different take on success. For a salesperson, success might mean 'increased commission' or 'more time released from administrative tasks for selling'. For a sales manager, success might be 'better management of underperforming reps'. For senior management, success might be 'improved market share and reduced cost-to-serve'.

None of these benefits are likely to be delivered if salespeople fail to adopt the technology. Adoption is more likely if salespeople find the technology is useful, easy to use and they receive appropriate training.

References

1. Morgan, A. and Inks, S.A. (2001) Technology and the sales force. *Industrial Marketing Management*, Vol. 30(5), pp. 463–472.
2. Engle, R.L. and Barnes, M.L. (2000) Sales force automation usage, effectiveness, and cost-benefit in Germany, England and the United States. *Journal of Business and Industrial Marketing*, Vol. 15(4), pp. 216–242.
3. Lambe, C.J. and Spekman, R. (1997) National account management: large account selling or buyer-seller alliance? *Journal of Personal Selling and Sales Management*, Vol. 17(4), Fall , pp. 61–74.
4. Grönroos, C. (2000) *Service marketing and management: a customer relationship management approach*, 2nd edn. Chichester: John Wiley.
5. Taylor, T.C. (1994) Valuable insights on sales automation progress. *Sales Process Engineering and Automation Review*, December, pp. 19–21.
6. Conner, K.R. and Rumelt, R.P. (1991) Software piracy: an analysis of protection strategies. *Management Science*, Vol. 37(2), February, pp. 125–139.
7. Copyright © 2008. SAS Institute Inc. All rights reserved. Reproduced with permission of SAS Institute Inc., Cary, NC, USA.
8. Courtesy of PCGuild, http://www.pcguild.com/database.html
9. Courtesy of salesboom.com, www.salesboom.com
10. Courtesy of Siebel Systems, http://www.oracle.com/applications/crm/siebel/resources/siebel-salesforce-sales-data-sheet.pdf. Accessed 25 January 2008.
11. http://www.realmarket.com/news/pragmatech121102.html. Accessed 21 November 2007.
12. http://download-uk.oracle.com/docs/cd/B11454_01/11.5.9/acrobat/jty115ig.pdf
13. Speier, C. and Venkatash, V. (2002) The hidden minefields in the adoption of sales force automation technologies. *Journal of Marketing*, Vol. 66(3), July, pp. 98–111.
14. Erffmeyer, R.C. and Johnson, D.A. (2001) An exploratory study of sales force automation practices: expectations and realities. *Journal of Personal Selling and Sales Management*, Vol. 21(2), Spring, pp. 167–175; Ingram, T.N., LaForge, R.W. and Leigh, T.W. (2002) Selling in the new millennium: a joint agenda. *Industrial Marketing Management*, Vol. 31(7), pp. 559–567.

15. Erffmeyer, R.C. and Johnson, D.A. (2001) An exploratory study of sales force automation practices: expectations and realities. *Journal of Personal Selling and Sales Management*, Vol. 21(2), Spring, pp. 167–175.

16. http://www.salesforce.com/customers/casestudy.jsp?customer= ft. Accessed 26 August 2005

17. Erffmeyer, R.C. and Johnson, D.A. (2001) An exploratory study of sales force automation practices: expectations and realities. *Journal of Personal Selling and Sales Management*, Vol. 21(2), Spring, pp. 167–175; Engle, R.L. and Barnes, M.L. (2000) Sales force automation usage, effectiveness, and cost-benefit in Germany, England and the United States. *Journal of Business and Industrial Marketing*, Vol. 15(4), pp. 216–242; Ahearne, M. and Schillewaert, N. (2001) *The acceptance of information technology in the sales force*. eBusiness Research Center, Working paper 10–2000. Penn State University.

18. Engle, R.L. and Barnes, M.L. (2000) Sales force automation usage, effectiveness, and cost-benefit in Germany, England and the United States. *Journal of Business and Industrial Marketing*, Vol. 15(4), pp. 216–242.

19. Ahearne, M. and Schillewaert, N. (2001). *The acceptance of information technology in the sales force*. eBusiness Research Center, Working paper 10–2000. Penn State University.

20. See review of SFA research in Buttle, F., Ang, L. and Iriana, R. (2006) Sales force automation: review, critique research agenda. *International Journal of Management Reviews*, Vol. 8(4), pp. 213–231.

21. This section draws on Buttle, F., Ang, L. and Iriana, R. (2006) Sales force automation: review, critique research agenda. *International Journal of Management Reviews*, Vol. 8(4), pp. 213–231.

Chapter 15
Marketing automation

By the end of this chapter you will understand:

1. what is meant by marketing automation (MA)
2. the benefits that MA can deliver to organizations
3. the functionality available within MA software.

Introduction

This is the second of three chapters that look at CRM technologies. This chapter is about technologies used by marketers. The preceding chapter reviewed sales-force automation and the next examines service automation. The chapter starts with a definition of marketing automation (MA) and then describes some of the functionality that is available in MA software.

What is marketing automation?

Marketing practices have historically been very *ad hoc*. Some of the major companies, particularly fast-moving consumer goods companies such as Unilever and Procter and Gamble, have bucked the trend and developed marketing processes which brand managers and market managers are obliged to follow. However, they are the exception. In general, marketers have not been structured in the way that they plan, implement, evaluate and control their marketing strategies and tactics. Marketing automation has brought increased rigour to marketing processes. The term marketing automation (MA) can be defined as follows:

> Marketing automation is the application of computerized technologies to support marketers and marketing management in the achievement of their work-related objectives.

A very wide range of marketing positions can make use of MA including marketing managers, campaign managers, market analysts, market managers, promotions managers, database marketers and direct marketing managers.

Hardware and software are the key technological elements of MA. Hardware includes desktop, laptop and handheld devices. Software comprises both 'point' solutions that are designed to assist in a single area of marketing or marketing management, and integrated solutions that offer a range of functionality. Some integrated packages are dedicated to marketing applications only; others are incorporated into broader CRM solutions that operate over the three front-office areas of marketing, service and sales.

Benefits of marketing automation

Marketing automation can deliver several benefits. These include:

- **Enhanced marketing efficiency**: the replication of marketing processes delivers greater control over costs. When marketers use manual systems and ad hoc processes there can be considerable inefficiencies. MA enables companies to develop more streamlined, cost-efficient processes that can be operated by any marketing incumbent, whether experienced or new to the role.
- **Greater marketing productivity**: in the days before MA marketers might have been expected to run a modest number of advertising campaigns and sales promotions in a single year. MA enables companies to run dozens, even thousands, of campaigns and events through multiple channels simultaneously.
- **More effective marketing**: MA allows marketers to employ what is known as closed-loop marketing (CLM). CLM is based on a plan–do–measure–learn cycle, as illustrated in Figure 15.1. Marketers plan a campaign or event, implement the plan, measure the outcomes, learn from the outcomes and subsequently modify the next campaign or event. CLM ensures that companies learn continuously from their marketing activities, achieving higher levels of marketing effectiveness. Companies can also identify and abandon failing marketing initiatives before they drain financial resources.

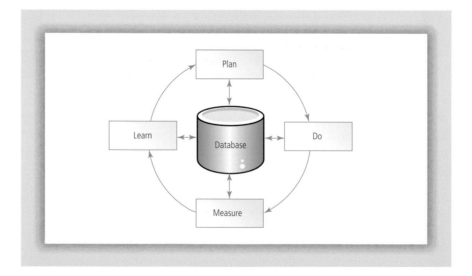

Figure 15.1
Closed-loop
marketing

- **Enhanced responsiveness**: marketers have traditionally created and implemented annual marketing plans with campaigns and promotions planned and scheduled many months ahead. MA allows marketers to respond instantly to opportunities, even if they are not part of a plan. MA functionality enables companies to engage in real-time marketing, responding immediately to an identified opportunity. For example, when a female customer buys baby clothes from a catalogue for the first time, marketers can send an automated invitation to the customer to join a mother and baby club which offers additional customer benefits to new mothers.
- **Improved marketing intelligence**: embedded reporting and analytics functionality provides valuable management insights into markets, customers, campaigns, events and so on, leading to enhanced efficiency and effectiveness.
- **Improved customer experience**: customers receive personalized, relevant communications and offers at appropriate times. MA means less spam, from the customer's perspective.

Software applications for marketing

Marketing automation applications offer a range of functionality, as listed in Table 15.1. The table lists both macromarketing automation solutions that offer a wide range of functionality, and micromarketing automation solutions that offer a narrow range of functionality. The macro solutions, such as enterprise marketing management, deliver

Asset management	Market segmentation
Campaign management	Marketing analytics
Customer segmentation	Marketing optimization
Direct mail campaign management	Marketing performance management
Document management	Marketing resource management
Email campaign management	Partner marketing
Enterprise marketing management	Product lifecycle management
Event-based marketing	Search engine optimization
Internet marketing	Telemarketing
Keyword marketing	Trigger marketing
Lead generation	Web analytics
Loyalty management	Workflow engineering

Table 15.1
Functionality offered by MA software

much of the functionality present in the micro solutions. In the next few paragraphs, we'll describe this functionality in more detail.

Asset management

Asset management enables companies to identify and track the assets that customers purchase, license, use, install or download. Assets can be tangible, intangible or blended. The pallet hire company, CHEP, uses asset management to track where its tangible assets, pallets, are in their network, whether at customer sites, depots or in transit, and to ensure that customers are only billed for the periods when the pallets are in use by that customer. Jim Beam uses asset management to track the use of its intangible asset, the Jim Beam brand, by other manufacturers. NXT uses asset management to track the licensed use of its blended tangible and intangible assets, manufacturing processes and technology, by other companies that want to manufacture flat panel speakers. Asset management can also be used to track and monitor the use of marketing assets such as point-of-sale materials and exhibition kiosks by customers, partners or sales representatives.

Campaign management

Campaign management automates the processes involved in planning, implementing, measuring and learning from communication programmes targeted at prospects or customers. Campaigns may be used to raise awareness, influence emotions or motivate behaviours, such as buying a product or visiting a website. The key elements of campaign management software are workflow, segmentation and targeting, personalization, execution, measurement, modelling and reporting.

- **Workflow**: before any campaign is run, the overall campaign development process must be designed. Workflow establishes the order in which tasks have to be performed. The tasks may include setting measurable objectives, setting a budget, getting approvals, creating a database of contacts, selecting contacts, creating a core message, testing the core message, customizing the message for individual recipients, selecting communication channels, executing the campaign, measuring response, reporting outcomes and reviewing and learning from the campaign.
- **Segmentation and targeting**: the customer base or source list can be divided into subsets so that one or more subsets can be subjected to a customized campaign. Segmentation is the process of identifying subsets; targeting is the selection of the subset(s) that will receive the material. A common approach to segmentation is to partition customers based on recency of purchase, frequency of purchase and monetary value of purchase, targeting different offers at different subsets.
- **Personalization**: core messages and offers are tailored for individual recipients.
- **Execution**: the campaign is run when the message is delivered through the selected communication channels. Campaigns can be run

in many channels, independently, consecutively or simultaneously by direct mail, e-mail, telephone, fax or text message.
- **Measurement**: the results from the campaign are assessed at segment and individual recipient level. Measures focus on whether the objectives originally set have been achieved.
- **Modelling**: is the process of interpreting campaign results statistically, so that future campaigns can be based on statistical insight into what works and what does not.
- **Reporting**: campaign results are computed and delivered in standard or customized management reports to relevant parties.

The ability to run integrated marketing campaigns over multiple channels, optimize campaigns and integrate with sales and service applications are important considerations for large-enterprise users of campaign management.

Case 15.1

Campaign management at Harrah's Entertainment

Harrah's Entertainment is the world's largest gaming organization. Through Harrah's Total Rewards programme customers earn credits each time they visit and play. Accumulated credits are traded for rewards, cash, coupons or complementary services, and tallied to determine customer loyalty levels of gold, platinum or diamond. Associated services and privileges become increasingly valuable at each higher level.

The Total Rewards programme is a key component of Harrah's CRM strategy and underpins the company's marketing campaigns. Customer-related data, gained primarily from card use, is enriched from other data sources so that Harrah's obtains detailed understanding of their customer profiles and behaviours.

Harrah's first established a data-based marketing approach in 1998. Using historical data, which showed how often customers visited and how much they spent, these early modelling efforts provided basic segmentation based on various demographic trends. Currently Harrah's applies predictive analytics to the customer-related data which can generate an accurate estimate of each customer's potential value.

Historical data shows how often a customer visits Harrah's casinos, but predictive models will reveal which customers are also likely to visit other casinos in the market. Based on share of wallet estimates, Harrah's can target them with campaigns that attempt to increase their loyalty to Harrah's casinos. As a consequence, Harrah's was able to increase its share of customers' gaming budgets from 36 per cent in 1998 to 45 per cent in 2005.

Source: SAS[1]

According to independent analysts, Gartner Inc., leading solutions for multichannel campaign management include SAS, Teradata and Affinium campaign management from Unica.[2] Affinium, for example, is a comprehensive campaign management solution that allows companies to create, test, deploy and analyse multiwave, multichannel personalized communications. It offers optional modules for e-mail authoring and execution, real-time personalization, distributed campaign execution and cross-campaign optimization. This and similar products allow organizations to deliver personalized, one-to-one marketing messages across all touchpoints. Key features include:

- a web-based interface
- workflow for designing, executing and analysing, transactional, real-time, event-triggered and scheduled communications
- integrated customer analytics and predictive models for enhanced targeting
- automated response tracking
- the ability to merge and transform campaign data across databases and operational systems
- built-in and repeatable processes that speed training and time to market.

Customer segmentation

Customer segmentation is the practice of partitioning customers into homogenous subsets so that each subset can be addressed as a unique marketing audience. Historically, segmentation by marketers has been very intuitive. However, as you read in Chapter 5, when customer segmentation is performed from a CRM perspective, it is much more data-based. Both consumers and organizational customers can be grouped into clusters, based on a wide range of user attributes and usage attributes. In the data-driven world of CRM, marketers often need to use statistical processes to help them identify clusters of customers. Among the widely employed statistical processes are cluster analysis, discriminant analysis, classification and regression trees (CART) and chi-square automatic interaction detection (CHAID).[3]

Cluster analysis aims to sort cases (customers, in this instance) into groups, or clusters, so that the degree of association is strong between members of the same cluster and weak between members of different clusters. Cluster analysis can reveal associations between customers which, although not previously evident, are nevertheless sensible and useful once discovered.

Discriminant analysis is used to determine which variables discriminate between two or more naturally occurring groups. For example, a marketer may want to investigate which variables discriminate between buyers of standard size packs and buyers of economy size packs. A large number of variables are entered into the statistical routine and discriminant analysis is able to identify the variables which discriminate between purchasers of the two pack sizes. Those variables can then be regarded as predictors of pack size purchase.

CART is a non-parametric statistical methodology for resolving classification problems involving either categorical (nominal or ordinal) or continuous (interval or ratio) dependent variables. If the dependent variable is categorical (e.g. buy/not buy), CART produces a classification tree. If the dependent variable is continuous (buys x, y … n occasions), it produces a regression tree (see Figure 15.2).

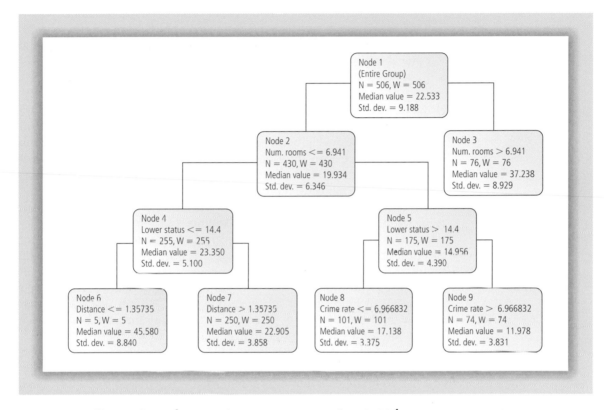

Figure 15.2 Illustration of regression tree output using CART[4]

CHAID is used to explore the relationships between a dependent variable (e.g. buyers or non-buyers of a product) and a number of possible predictor variables (such as age, gender, post-code, marital status, income, educational attainment, occupational status) that themselves may interact. The output of a CHAID analysis is a tree diagram that discriminates between buyers and non-buyers on the basis of the other variables.

Once customers have been clustered they can be treated to a range of customized and personalized communications and offers over time, designed to build value, multi-product ownership and loyalty. It is important to continue to find new ways of segmenting the customer base, as new clusters will often signal additional opportunities for value creation.

Direct mail campaign management

Direct mail campaign management is a specific form of campaign management in which the communication medium is direct mail. According to the World Postal Union:

> 'Worldwide postal statistics show very low growth in letter mail volumes. One exception, however, has been direct mail, which is experiencing significant growth in many parts of the world. Evidence shows that this growth has reached double digits in some developing countries. Even in more mature markets, there are still expectations of growth'.[5]

However, according to Euromonitor, UK spending on direct mail reached £2.6 billion in 2004 and forecasters were predicting that spending would stabilize at these levels because of direct mail's association with junk mail.[6] The Direct Mail Information Service (DMIS) reports 2005 direct mail expenditures of £2.3 billion, split between consumer (77 per cent) and business (23 per cent) mailings.[7]

Direct mail has many applications including lead generation, lead conversion, building awareness, up-selling and cross-selling, customer retention, database building or image enhancement. Important contributors to direct mail success are the list, the creative execution, the offer and the timing. Making the right offer to the right person at the right time in the right way will produce greater success. Automated processes can help deliver all these outcomes. A high quality list that is clean and contemporary, a creative execution that catches the eye and promotes action, an offer that is determined by the list member's propensity to buy and that is personalized, will achieve greater success that the conventional mass mailouts that have been marketing's tradition. The old cry that 'it's a numbers game' has been replaced by a clear focus on customized, personalized offers. The average response rate for both business and consumer mailings is around 8.5 per cent; about one in 12 recipients does what the mailer wants them to do, whether that is register for an event, redeem a coupon or call a toll-free number. Response rates range from below 1 per cent to over 30 per cent (for government mailings).[8] Many companies elect to outsource direct mail campaigns to third-party service providers, who are themselves big users of marketing automation.

Document management

Companies generate and use many documents in their marketing activities. These include brochures, product specifications, price lists and competitive comparisons. Document management software allows companies to manage these documents, keep them current and ensure that they are available to marketing people when needed. Typically, these documents are held in a central repository and made available to users in their browsers.

E-mail campaign management

E-mail campaign management is a specific form of campaign management in which the communication medium is e-mail. E-mail is cheap, easy to use and ubiquitous. Over 90 per cent of Internet users have one or more e-mail addresses.[9] E-mail marketing is a massive industry. In the US alone, eMarketer estimates that spending on e-mail marketing will grow from $338 million in 2006 to $616 million in 2011.[10] Legitimate e-mail marketing is tainted by the widespread use of e-mail spam, that is, unsolicited bulk e-mail. Fifty per cent or more of e-mail messages are spam. The typical legitimate opt-in (or permission-based) e-mail marketing message contains text and a link through to a website. Open and click-through rates, the most commonly used e-mail marketing metrics, provide marketers with some insight into how an e-mail message has performed. These metrics can be combined into a click-to-open rate (CTOR) that measures click-through rates as a percentage of messages opened, instead of messages delivered. As with all customer communications, it is very important to specify clear objectives. If the objective is to sell 100 units, reporting success in terms of CTOR makes little sense.

There is a significant and growing volume of research into the effectiveness of e-mail marketing. The corporate website, www.e-maillabs.com, the E-mail Experience Council (www.e-mailexperience.org) and the E-mail Statistics Center (www.e-mailstatcenter.com) act as gateways to many of these resources. Among the statistics they cite are the following, which collectively indicate the potential of, and problems with, e-mail:

- for every dollar spent on e-mail marketing in 2007, marketers obtained $48 return on investment (ROI), compared to $7 for print catalogues
- the US e-mail marketing industry is estimated at $3 billion in 2007, inclusive of $1.15 billion for all the technology, agency, consultant and service providers
- e-mail generated sales in the US will show a compound annual growth of 14.9% from 2006 to 2011
- the average order conversion rate of e-mail is 6%
- permission e-mail marketing now accounts for 27% of the e-mail that consumers receive in their primary personal inboxes, up from 16% in 2003
- one in five e-mail is invisible and ineffective due to blocked images
- 45% of click-through landing pages do not repeat the promotional copy found in the e-mail, thus failing to reinforce the call-to-action that prompted the e-mail recipient to click on the link in the first place
- only 10% of e-mail campaigns are fully individualized in terms of salutation, images, timing and promotion.

There are many e-mail campaign management software packages, either standalone or integrated into more comprehensive campaign management or MA offerings. eGain is a leading vendor that divides the campaign management process into six steps (see Figure 15.3).

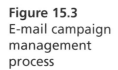

Figure 15.3
E-mail campaign
management
process

Enterprise marketing management

The analysts, Gartner Inc., describe enterprise marketing management (EMM) thus:

> 'EMM encompasses the business strategy, process automation and technologies required to operate a marketing department effectively, align resources, execute customer-centric strategies and improve marketing performance. It is best suited for large organizations with 50 or more people in marketing. This includes functionality for campaign management, lead management, MRM (marketing resource management) and analytics. However, EMM is more than simply the sum of "parts" (such as campaign management plus MRM). EMM also emphasizes the architecture and platform for role-based distribution of information, content, functionality, data and analysis for performance management. Critical elements of this platform include SOA (service oriented architecture), composite application functionality, data repository for structured and non-structured data, marketing data models and analytical toolsets'.[11]

The EMM market is immature in terms of both vendor offerings and user adoption. Companies like Aprimo, Siebel and Unica are offering these comprehensive suites of marketing applications. The ultimate purpose of EMM technology is to help marketers align their analysis, planning, implementation and control activities so that they can become more effective, efficient and accountable.

Event-based marketing

Event-based marketing occurs when an event triggers a communication or offer. Event-based campaigns are usually initiated by customer behaviours or contextual conditions. For example, a customer who uses a credit card less than six times in a three month period might receive an invitation to participate in a frequency reward programme designed to encourage repeated use. A bank customer who deposits $50 000 or more into a savings account might receive an offer of investment advice from a licensed financial planner. Contextual conditions such as a birthday, registration of a child's birth, change of address and religious festivals also provide opportunities for marketers to run context-specific campaigns.

Internet marketing

Internet marketing can be defined as follows:

> Internet marketing is the process of creating value by building and maintaining online customer relationships.

According to Rafi Mohammed and his colleagues, Internet marketing can be thought of as a seven-stage process (Figure 15.4). Internet marketing applications range across these seven stages, some more comprehensively than others.

Internet marketing software enables users to perform a wide range of online activities designed to generate website traffic and make it profitable. Users can do the following: develop and manage online content, create a pleasing online customer experience, obtain search engine listings, perform search engine optimization, implement keyword marketing, obtain customer information, customize web pages (known as dynamic web pages) and visitor communications, run online advertising campaigns using the likes of Google Adwords, manage pay-per-click programmes, operate affiliate marketing programmes, run e-mail campaigns and perform web analytics.

Keyword marketing

Keyword marketing is the practice of generating website traffic from Internet users who have entered keywords into search engines such as Google, Yahoo!, AOL, Ask.com and Live search (formerly MSN). A company that is interested in improving its complaint management processes might use the keywords 'complaint-handling' and 'ISO 10002' to search the web for useful information. The keywords will lead to thousands of listings. Keyword marketing software applications enable companies to feature early in these listings. Some keyword marketing involves purchasing advertising space, typically banners and text links, on the search results page. The other major form of keyword marketing is search engine optimization (SEO), which aims to get unpaid listings on

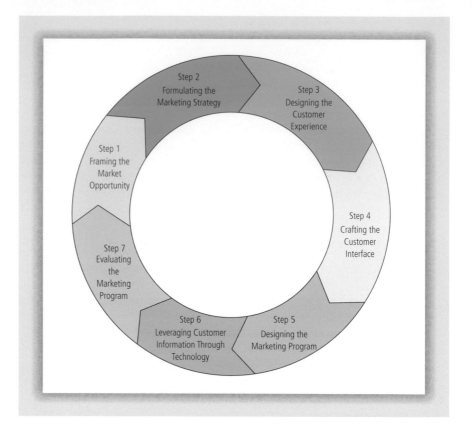

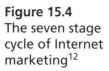

Figure 15.4
The seven stage
cycle of Internet
marketing[12]

the early search results pages. Google pages feature both. Advertisements that have been bought appear on the right hand of the search results page and SEO listings appear on the left. We cover SEO later in this chapter.

Lead generation

Lead generation is an important marketing objective, particularly in business-to-business contexts. Salespeople challenged to grow the numbers of customers served need to be presented with high-quality leads for follow-up. Marketers can deploy campaigns, events, seminars, webinars and other tactics to generate leads.

Loyalty management

The development of customer loyalty is a goal of many CRM programmes (see Figure 15.5). The availability of loyalty management applications is a direct response to this need. Loyalty, or frequency, programmes are important to several constituencies; the brand owner who operates the programme, the member who collects and redeems credits, and the channel partner who transacts with the member.

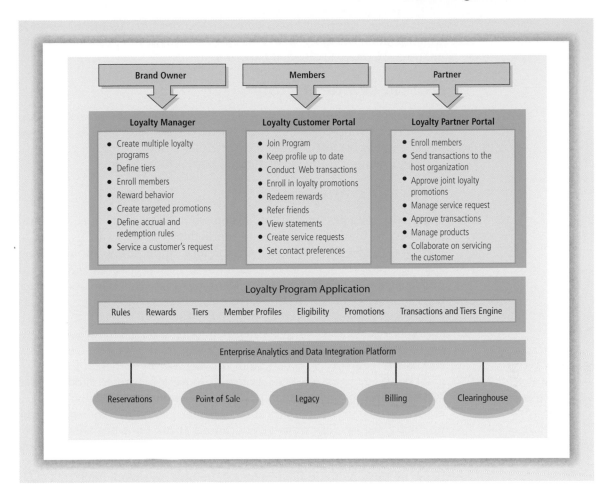

Figure 15.5 Siebel's loyalty management software application

Many loyalty programmes are very simple, particularly when the brand owner has a single retail site, hands a rewards card to the customer and stamps the card when a purchase is made, for example 'Buy 5 cups of coffee, get the next one free'. However, there are other programmes which are operationally and technologically complex. Consider the Nectar loyalty programme operating in the UK. Nectar is the UKs largest coalition loyalty programme, with half of all UK households having a Nectar card. The Loyalty Management Group (LMG) owns and operates the Nectar brand. Over 15 consumer brands including BP, Debenhams, Hertz, Ford and the Automobile Association are members of the coalition. Consumers acquire points with purchases and can redeem them on a number of treats, including spa days, movie and theatre tickets and luxurious holiday breaks. There are around 6000 retail outlets where the card can be used to earn points. Nineteen Nectar cards are swiped every second of the day. The technology challenge is massive and ranges across many of the issues in Figure 15.5; partner web application, member web application, contact centre, loyalty programme administration, transaction processing, data warehousing, campaign management, account management, rewards administration, member analytics, partner analytics, report engines and multiple interfaces to different partner systems.

Market segmentation

Market segmentation is the practice of partitioning markets into homogenous subsets, so that each subset can be addressed as a unique marketing opportunity. The same principles discussed in the context of customer segmentation and earlier in Chapter 5 apply here.

Marketing analytics

Marketing analytics is the application of mathematical and statistical processes to marketing problems. Marketing analytics can be used to explore, describe and explain. Exploratory applications of marketing analytics provide insights into, and understanding about, issues and problems. For example, you might want to explore the issue of customer defection rates: do some sales territories, customer groups or products experience higher levels than normal? You would want to analyse customer-related data to get a better understanding of the issue. This might lead you towards defining a problem more precisely, identifying alternative courses of action and developing hypotheses to test or identifying key variables or relationships to explore further. A descriptive application of marketing analytics would involve the depiction of some marketing phenomenon, such as a customer group, market segment or product category. Descriptive applications focus on who, what, where and when. Some descriptive analyses are cross-sectional, others are longitudinal. A cross-sectional analysis involves description at a single point in time. Longitudinal analyses involve repeated data collection about the same variables over time, so that you can get a better sense of what changes. An explanatory application of marketing analytics would seek to obtain evidence of a cause–effect relationship. Analytics are used to explain why something has happened or to predict what might happen.

As noted in Chapter 13, there are three types of analytics: standard reports, online analytical processing (OLAP) and data mining. Standardized reports integrated into marketing automation may meet basic descriptive needs, but as the requirement for analysis grows they may be insufficient. OLAP offers more analytical power, in that it enables users to drill down into graphs and tables. Data mining offers the most powerful statistical routines including:

- descriptive statistics (frequency, mean, median, mode, variance, standard deviation)
- data reduction
- bivariate statistical analysis (cross-tabulation, regression, correlation)
- multivariate statistical analysis (multiple regression, factor analysis, discriminant analysis, factor analysis, cluster analysis, multi-dimensional scaling, conjoint analysis)
- decision trees and neural networks
- data visualization that presents results in tables, charts and graphs.

Data mining can be used to answer questions such as:

- What segments do my customers fall into and what are their characteristics?
- Which customers are most likely to respond to my promotion?
- What is the lifetime value of my customer?
- Which customer is at risk of defection?
- What is the best channel to reach each customer segment?

Data mining can be used to produce:

- **scores**: the likelihood a customer will purchase a product
- **predictions**: how much a customer will spend in the coming year
- **descriptions**: what characteristics define profitable customers
- **profiles**: the common characteristics of each customer segment.[13]

Marketing analytics are built into the comprehensive CRM and MA suites available from vendors like SAP and Oracle. Specialist organizations like SAS and Teradata also operate in this segment.

Marketing optimization

Campaign management solutions are very popular, but most cannot handle a complex environment in which a fixed amount of campaign spend has to be distributed over many offers in many channels to many customer segments, with a view to achieving some overarching commercial goal such as maximum sales or contribution to profit. Marketing optimization is a mathematically-based solution to this problem. Users of marketing optimization software do not need to understand the complex optimization algorithm that underpins this application.

Marketing optimization software allows you to select an overall goal, such as sales or profit margin maximization, and specify all of the constraints of your marketing campaign strategy, such as budget, customer contact policy (e.g. no more than three offers per customer per year), channels available (e.g. direct mail, e-mail, text message, telemarketing), minimal cell size per offer (e.g. target customer segment size of at least 250 persons) product-specific volume requirements (e.g. must sell 10 000 gizmos this quarter), customer segments' propensities to buy different products, and channel constraints (e.g. call centre can only make 200 outbound calls per week), to name but a few. The software then determines which customers should get which offer through which channel to ensure your campaign objectives are met.

Marketing optimization software also lets you explore any number of 'what-if' scenarios by changing constraints and objectives before committing any marketing resources. The more advanced marketing optimization technology operates in real-time, allowing your website to present the right offer and your call centre agent to offer the right promotion during each customer interaction.

In short, marketing optimization enables marketers to extract the best return, however defined, from their campaign spend while taking account of a range of constraints such as budgets, customer segments, propensity to buy, contact policies, channel availability and channel capacity (see Figure 15.6).

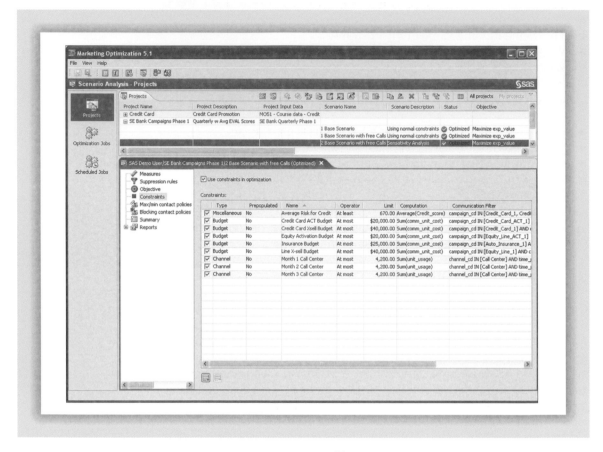

Figure 15.6 Constraints for marketing optimization[14]

Marketing performance management (MPM)

Marketing performance management (MPM) software enables companies to measure their marketing performance through analysis and reports and improve outcomes over time through closed-loop marketing. Senior management is progressively becoming more demanding that marketers be accountable for their expenditure, and MPM helps marketers meet that expectation. MPM, which is typically focused on analysis of marketing tactics such as events and campaigns, is routinely built into most MA applications. It enables marketers to:

- assess the effectiveness of marketing campaigns and events by:
  - measuring expenditure and response rates
  - reporting variance between planned and achieved campaign/event responses and expenditure
  - tracking cost per lead, cost per sale and revenue per lead

- evaluate the effectiveness of different offers, channels and creative executions, thereby enabling marketers to identify the most successful strategies and continually fine-tune their programmes
- forecast ROI from current and future campaigns/events based on the performance of past campaigns/events.

Some of the more advanced MPM applications focus on more strategic aspects of marketing performance measurement. For example, SASs MPM product is able to deliver a range of reports against a number of KPIs, including:

- marketing programme metrics that report on the efficiency and effectiveness of marketing tactics
- customer metrics that report customer satisfaction, value, churn, migration, etc.
- business/financial metrics (sales, profitability, cost, etc.) that give executives a better insight into marketing's financial impact
- marketing process metrics that focus on process efficiency to identify best practices and areas for improvement.

The core components of MPM software are analytics (discussed above) and a reporting process. Reports are typically delivered online in charts, tables, dashboards and text.

Marketing resource management

Marketing resource management applications consist of a range of automated tools that enable marketers to manage their marketing processes and assets more effectively, and to work at greater speed and with improved control. MRM toolkits may include modules for:

- marketing planning and budgeting
- new product launch
- marketing event calendaring
- event planning and registration
- project management
- campaign planning
- collateral production, proofing and approval
- digital asset management, including brands, trademarks, logos and collateral material
- expense and budget management
- time management
- media buying
- procurement.

These tools, like other CRM applications, can be accessed on demand or licensed for installation on your company's own hardware. Investment in MRM is more justified if marketing budgets are high; if you need to align implementation across several branches or offices; if collateral material is subject to frequent change; if brands, trademarks and logos are highly valued assets that need to be protected; if you run more than one event simultaneously; if you run more than six campaigns in a year; if you launch more than one new product a year; if you need to facilitate collaboration across departments on projects, events and campaigns.

Partner marketing

Partner marketing solutions enable companies to coordinate and work collaboratively with channel partners and others. Sometimes partner marketing is referred to as partner or trade management. Many companies market and sell to and through channel members, such as travel agents or value added resellers, or service end-users through specialist partners, such as third-party contact centres. Partner marketing solutions allow companies to synchronize the planning and execution of local, regional or global marketing activities by providing partners with controlled access to brand and marketing resources through a portal.

Partner marketing solutions are used to manage processes such as partner qualification and sign up, development of joint business plans and objectives, cooperative advertising and promotions, lead management, co-branding of collateral and point-of-sale materials, measuring partner performance, partner training, administration of marketing funds and specialist partner incentive schemes.

Microsoft Canada's partner website describes the value of partnering with this message to their partners: 'Your goals: Increase profitability. Decrease business costs. Our goal: To provide the resources needed to reach yours' (see Figure 15.7).

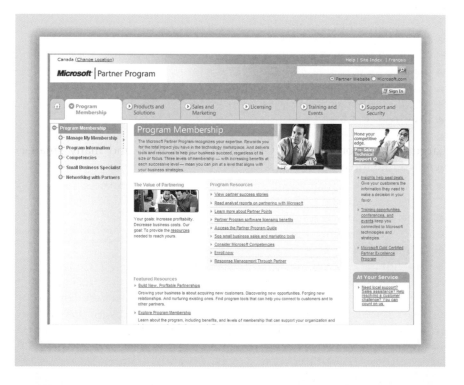

Figure 15.7
Microsoft Canada's partner website

Product lifecycle management

Many products progress through a series of stages from their initial market introduction to their eventual withdrawal. Product lifecycle management (PLM) applications aim to help marketers manage lifecycle stages effectively and profitably.

PLM software solutions facilitate collaborative intra- and extra-enterprise engineering, product development and improved management of projects, product portfolios, documents and quality. PLM applications can provide a single source of all product-related information to use in the innovation, design, engineering, feasibility, launch and market development processes.

PLM applications offer a wide range of functionality, including:

- concept evaluation process
- new product development and approval process
- new product launch process
- product costing process
- product sourcing process
- product compliance process (compliance with legal, regulatory and voluntary standards)
- quality function deployment (QFD) process
- channel member qualification and recruitment process
- collaborative extra-enterprise product development process
- computer-aided design (CAD)
- computer-aided engineering (CAE)
- computer-aided manufacturing (CAM)
- product portfolio analysis (e.g. BCG matrix)
- engineering data management
- product delisting process
- workflow engineering
- project management and scheduling
- action item management
- document management
- product record.

Large corporations such as Oracle, SAP and IBM, and many smaller vendors operate in this field.

Search engine optimization

Search engine optimization can be defined as follows:

> Search engine optimization (SEO) is the practice of improving the quantity and quality of website traffic generated by search engines.

Usually, the higher ranking results that appear earlier in the listings generate more visitors. SEO aims, therefore, to achieve high rankings, preferably on the first or second pages. The major search engines use web crawlers, also known as web spiders or web robots, to browse the

World Wide Web methodically. Crawlers visit websites, read the site's visible content and meta tags, and visit linked links, reading content and meta tags there also. The crawler dumps all the data into a central depository, where it is indexed. The crawler returns to the sites to check for any changed information at periods that are determined by the search engine's management. Unlike visible content, meta tags provide information about who created the page, how often it is updated, what the page is about and which keywords represent the page's content.

A website's position on a results page is determined by that search engine's ranking algorithm. Algorithms are formulae composed of a set of weighted criteria; Google's algorithm considers over 200 variables. Each search engine has its own algorithm which is a trade secret and/or patented.

SEO software can help users tailor their website so that it meets the criteria that the search engine algorithms employ, therefore giving the site a high ranking. The most successful websites employ methods such as strategic keywords that are well matched to the content of the site, strategic meta tags, website structure (each page having its own keyword/s), search engine placement and link relevance.

Web masters need to understand the site's marketing goals, the products that are being sold on site, the geographies being served and the keywords employed by users of search engines. They can then ensure that the right keywords and meta tags are used, the right links are embedded in the site and the site is submitted to the right search engines.

Case 15.2

Filtrex implements search engine optimization

Filtrex (not their real name) is a commercial reseller of industrial air filters that had invested in e-commerce to generate incremental sales of their products. Sales were poor and there was little return on the initial investment. The reseller hired an SEO consulting firm to develop their online sales channel. The goals were to increase order volume and change the product mix to increase sales of higher-margin items. The online air filter market is very competitive, and Filtrex's major competitors were already using a combination of search engine optimization (SEO) and pay-per-click (PPC) marketing to generate traffic and sales. The consultant researched, developed and implemented a plan to increase Filtrex's sales using a combination of creative website design and the application of advanced SEO techniques. Within three months the results were as follows:

- order numbers increased by 525%
- average order spend increased by over 50%
- number of unique visitors to the website increased by over 100%
- the conversion rate from website visitor to customer increased from 1.3% to over 10%.

Source: Braveheart Design Inc[15]

Telemarketing

Telemarketing can be defined as follows:

> Telemarketing is the use of the telephone to identify and qualify prospects, and to sell and service the needs of customers.

Telemarketing takes two forms: inbound (calls from customers) and outbound (calls to customers). Some call centres perform a blended function with agents both making and receiving calls. Telemarketing is widely employed in both B2C and B2B environments, but is subject to legislative control due to its intrusive nature. For example, both the USA and Australia operate a 'Do Not Call' register on which telephone account holders can list their numbers. With a few exceptions, such as charities, political organizations and research firms, marketers are not allowed to call listed numbers and penalties apply if this rule is breached.

Telemarketing software applications offer a wide range of functionality over landlines, mobile networks and VoIP (Voice over Internet Protocol):

- autodialling
- predictive dialling
- automated voice-messaging
- contact list management
- agent management
- Do Not Call compliance
- screen pop with caller ID
- scripting, including objection response
- computer-aided telephone interviewing (CATI)
- interactive voice response (IVR).

Autodiallers queue a list of calls and automatically dial the next number, either when the current call is finished or the agent presses a hot key. Predictive diallers predict when an agent is about to conclude a call, and autodial the next call in anticipation. Automated voice messagers (or messengers) will make telephone calls automatically to a contact list and convey a message to them. This can be used for lead generation, debt collection, political canvassing and reminding customers about appointments. Telemarketing software that integrates with campaign management and event-based marketing applications enables agents to make real-time offers to customers. In-call online access to a searchable knowledge base enables agents to resolve issues and enquiries quickly.

Trigger marketing

Trigger marketing is the practice of responding to some event in a way that is designed to achieve some marketing goal, such as make a sale, identify a cross-sell opportunity, prevent negative word-of-mouth or promote positive word-of-mouth. The event triggers the response.

As noted in the section on event-based marketing, the triggers are usually customer behaviours or contextual conditions. Opportunities for trigger marketing occur throughout the customer lifecycle. When a customer first makes a purchase you might respond with a thank you e-mail or letter. When a customer complains and you believe you've resolved it well, you might follow-up with a survey to find out the complainant's level of satisfaction with your complaints-handling process. When a customer is won back, having been lost to a competitor for a while, you might respond with a 'welcome back' note.

Trigger marketing software can be trained to identify events and either to send an automated response, such as an e-mail, digitally-personalized direct mail piece or text message, or to feed the information through to a salesperson or customer service agent for follow-up. Trigger marketing ensures that the communication is relevant to the recipient, because it is a contextualized response to an event in the customer's life. For example, when a customer is approaching their credit limit you might send an e-mail notifying them so they can avoid fees and charges. This would surely be welcomed.

Case 15.3

Trigger-based marketing at HPES

HPES provides education and training products and services to Hewlett-Packard's clients. Its offering includes partner training, virtual classrooms and a number of distance learning solutions, as well as accreditation programmes. In 2005 HP noticed that attaching HPES products and services to hardware sales enabled their customers to gain more from their purchase while the customer, in turn, became far more loyal and profitable to HP.

HP created a pilot study to assess whether or not trigger-based marketing could be used to identify opportunities to attach HPES products and services to existing sales opportunities.

HP sales teams had been reluctant to sell HPES products and services, so the pilot study set out to identify the correct points in the sales cycle to send sales representatives an appropriate trigger-based communication to encourage them, and provide them with the information, to make incremental HPES sales.

The HP CRM team collaborated with an external consultancy to explore the customer and sales data that resided in the CRM system. The result was a bespoke set of event-based rules that would trigger a personalized communication from HPES to the representative.

The e-mail contained information to assist in the conversion of the sale, while attaching a relevant HPES solution. The resultant communication was tracked and the results fed back into the Siebel CRM system to determine sales value and ROI measure. The 12-week pilot generated $450 000 of incremental revenue. An extended (EMEA) pilot generated additional revenue of $2 million and a projected sales uplift across EMEA of $8.2 million. The pilot achieved a 60 per cent response rate by HP sales representatives to the personalized automated communication and lifted the perception of HPES within the HP sales team.

Source: TW Connect[16]

Web analytics

Web analytics report the behavior of website visitors. Routine reports (see Figure 15.8) generally detail web traffic data, but may also include performance data from campaigns and events that involve the website, for example the number of click-throughs from a web link inserted in a campaign e-mail. Two main technologies collect data: logfile analysis and page tagging. Web servers record all website activity in a logfile which can be read by web log analysis software. Logfile analysis can deliver inaccurate readings of human website visitors because of caching and visits by web spiders from search engines. This prompted the introduction of page tagging as an alternative form of generating website data. Page tagging requires webmasters to insert some extra Javascript or HTML code onto web pages, so that analytics software can identify how many visitors originate from search engines, the search terms used and whether they arrived from paid-for or free listings.

Three different types of statistics provide insight into a website's performance: frequency counts (e.g. the number of visitors), ratios (e.g. page views per visit) and KPIs (key performance indicators, which can either be a frequency count or ratio). The Web Analytics Association has

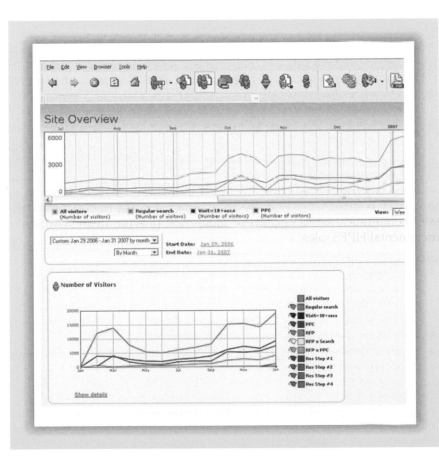

Figure 15.8
Web analytics
report[18]

defined a number of important terms that are used by web analytics vendors.[17] These include:

- **building block terms**: page, page view, visit/session, unique visitor, new visitor, repeat visitor, return visitor
- **visit characterization terms**: entry page, landing page, exit page, visit duration referrer, internal referrer, external referrer, search referrer, visit referrer, original referrer, click-through, click-through rate/ratio, page views per visit
- **content characterization terms**: page exit ratio, single page visit, single page view visits, bounces, bounce rate
- **conversion metrics terms**: event, conversion.

Vendors of web analytics services and software make widespread use of the following measures:

- **Hit**: a request for a file from the web server. This information is only available in log analysis. You should be aware that the number of hits is a misleading measure of a site's popularity, because most web pages are made up of many files, each of which is counted as a hit as the page is downloaded. Most web analytics tools allow users to specify the file types that count as a page (known as analyst-definable content) and to request reports accordingly.
- **Page view**: the number of times a page (as defined by the analyst) is viewed.
- **Visit or session**: an interaction by an individual with a website consisting of one of more requests for analyst-definable content. A visit usually contains multiple hits (in log analysis) and page views.
- **First visit or first session**: a visit from a user who has not made any previous visits.
- **Unique visitor**: the number of individuals who make one or more visits to a site within a defined reporting period (e.g. day or month), making requests on the web server (log analysis) or viewing pages (page tagging). Because most sites do not require log-in, cookies are generally used instead (see below for more information on cookies).
- **Repeat visitor**: a visitor that has made at least two visits to the website in a reporting period.
- **New visitor**: a visitor that has not made any previous visits to the website.
- **Impression**: when a page loads onto a visitor's screen. Advertisers measure the reach of their online advertisements by tracking advertisement impressions, or the number of times their advertisements are loaded onto a visitor's screen.
- **Singleton**: a visit when only a single page is viewed.
- **Bounce rate**: the percentage of visits that enter and exit on the same page, without browsing other pages.

A cookie is a small file of information (normally less than 1k) that a website places on a visitor's computer hard drive so that it can recognize the visitor on subsequent visits. There are two kinds of cookies: session cookies and persistent cookies. Session cookies are erased when the user

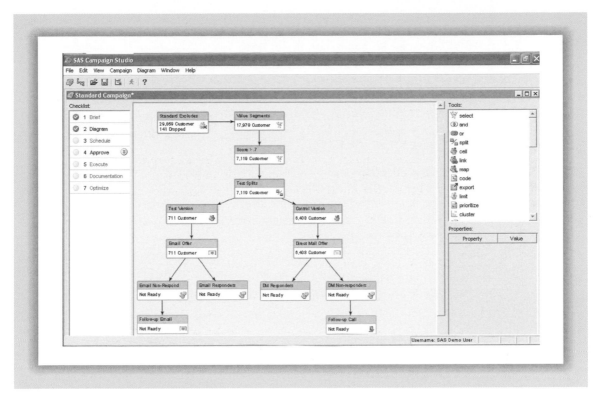

Figure 15.9 Campaign workflow[19]

goes offline. Web analysis, however, relies on persistent cookies that are stored on the visitor's hard drive until they expire (persistent cookies have expiry dates) or until the user deletes the cookie. Companies such as Omniture, Google Analytics and WebTrends are well-known players in this market.

Workflow engineering

Workflow engineering software is useful for designing marketing-related processes, such as the campaigning process (see Figure 15.9), event-based marketing process or the marketing planning process.

Summary

Marketing automation is the application of computerized technologies to support marketers and marketing management in the achievement of their work-related objectives. Many marketing positions can make use of marketing automation including marketing managers, campaign managers, market analysts, market managers, promotions managers, database marketers and direct marketing managers. Hardware and software are the key technological elements of MA. Hardware includes desktop, laptop and handheld devices. Software comprises both 'point' solutions that are designed to assist in a single area of marketing or marketing management and integrated solutions that offer a range of functionality.

Marketing automation can deliver several benefits, including enhanced marketing efficiency, greater marketing productivity, more effective marketing, enhanced responsiveness, improved marketing intelligence and a better customer experience.

Marketing automation software applications help users in asset management, campaign management, customer segmentation, direct mail campaign management, document management, e-mail campaign management, enterprise marketing management, event-based marketing, Internet marketing, keyword marketing, lead generation, loyalty management, market segmentation, marketing analytics, marketing optimization, marketing performance management, marketing resource management, partner marketing, product lifecycle management, search engine optimization, telemarketing, trigger marketing, web analytics and workflow engineering.

References

1. http://www.sas.com/success/harrahs.html. Accessed 25 January 2008.
2. Gartner Inc. (2007) Magic quadrant for multi-channel campaign management, 1Q07.
3. Saunders, J. (1994) Cluster analysis. In: G.J. Hooley and M.K. Hussey (eds.). *Quantitative methods in marketing*. London: Dryden Press, pp. 13–28.
4. Courtesy of Phillip H.Sherrod (http://www.dtreg.com).
5. http://www.upu.int/direct_mail/en/index.shtml. Accessed 13 January 2007.
6. Euromonitor. (2005) *Direct marketing in the UK.*
7. http://www.dmis.co.uk/. Accessed 13 January 2007.
8. http://www.dmis.co.uk/pdfs/Response_Rates_Survey_2006.pdf. Accessed 13 December 2007.
9. http://www.e-maillabs.com/tools/e-mail-marketing-statistics. html#e-mailusage. Accessed 13 December 2007.
10. http://www.emarketer.com/Reports/All/Emarketer_2000382. aspx?src = report_more_info_sitesearch. Accessed 13 December 2007.
11. http://mediaproducts.gartner.com/reprints/unica/article11/ article11.html. Accessed 17 December 2007.
12. Mohammed, R.A., Fisher, R.J., Jaworski, B.J. and Paddison, G.J. (2002) *Internet marketing: building advantage in a networked economy.* New York: McGraw-Hill.
13. http://www.teradata.com/t/pdf.aspx?a = 83673&b = 84891. Accessed 17 January 2007.
14. Copyright © 2008 SAS Institute Inc. All rights reserved. Reproduced with permission of SAS Institute Inc., Cary, NC, USA.

15. Braveheart Design Inc. http://www.braveheartdesign.com/casestudies/filters.htm. Accessed 17 December 2007.
16. TW Connect Ltd. http://www.twconnect.co.uk/upload/file/158/79244/FILENAME/HP_Education.pdf. Accessed 26 January 2008.
17. http://www.webanalyticsassociation.org/attachments/committees/5/WAA-Standards-Analytics-Definitions-Volume-I-20070816.pdf. Accessed 18 December 2007.
18. http://www.customfitonline.com/solutions/web-analytics.htm. Accessed 18 December 2007. Used with permission.
19. Copyright © 2008 SAS Institute Inc. All rights reserved. Reproduced with permission of SAS Institute Inc., Cary, NC, USA.

Chapter 16
Service automation

By the end of this chapter you will understand:

1. what is meant by customer service
2. what is meant by service automation (SA)
3. the benefits that SA can deliver to organizations
4. the functionality available within SA software.

Introduction

This is the last of three chapters that look at CRM technologies. This chapter is about the technologies used in customer service departments or by service staff. The preceding two chapters reviewed sales-force automation and marketing automation. This chapter starts by defining customer service and service automation (SA) before describing some of the functionality that is available in SA software.

What is customer service?

As customers we all understand and appreciate when we have experienced excellent customer service. The people who serve us are friendly, responsive, empathetic and do the right things well, whether it is answering a question, offering advice or accepting the return of faulty merchandise. Equally we can all recognize poor customer service, delivered by surly, unapproachable, dogmatic, inflexible staff working with poor information and hampered by outdated technology.

Customer service has been a necessary preoccupation of service organizations because they have understood that customers are responsive to the quality of the service they experience. However, the quality of customer service is just as important for agriculturalists, miners and goods manufacturers. This is particularly so when there is product parity and customers are unable to discern meaningful differences between alternative suppliers or brands. For most customers one brand of carpet is much like another. Carpet manufacturers and retailers find it hard to differentiate in terms of meaningful product-related variables; they therefore use service-related variables such as prepurchase advice, measurement, delivery, removal of old floor coverings and fitting of new carpet, to win business from customers.

Customer service standards can be assessed by customers when a service is being performed, as well as after the service has been delivered. The service experience, as perceived from the dentist's chair during service delivery, might be very different from the assessment a few days later.

Customer service can be experienced at any stage of the customer activity cycle: before, during or after purchase.[1] In a B2C context the purchaser of a laptop computer might call a number of retailers for advice prior to selecting a store to visit; while in the store he or she might ask the store clerk to demonstrate a number of shortlisted machines; after the purchase has been made he or she might need to call the manufacturer's helpdesk for advice on how to obtain service under warranty. In a B2B context a company purchasing new manufacturing equipment might need prepurchase engineering advice, assistance during purchase with removal of existing equipment and postpurchase assistance with operator training.

In Chapter 7 you read about two important models of service quality that are used by companies to understand and satisfy customers' service expectations. The Nordic model, originated by Christian Grönroos and developed by others, identifies three components of service quality: technical, functional and reputational.[2] Technical quality can be thought of as the 'what' of service quality. Was the dishwasher water leak fixed by the technician? Functional quality can be thought of as the 'how' of service quality. Did the technician turn up on time and act courteously? Reputational quality is not only a product of technical and functional quality, in that reputation derives from performance. Reputation can also predispose customers towards forming particular perceptions of quality, for better or worse. The SERVQUAL model, developed by A. 'Parsu' Parasuraman and colleagues in North America, claims there are five core components of service quality: reliability, assurance, tangibles, empathy and responsiveness.[3]

Customers who receive service from technology-enabled manufacturers or service providers, such as those with CRM systems in place, experience a further form of quality that can be thought of as integrative quality. Integrative quality is determined by the way the various elements of the product and service delivery system work together. High integrative quality means that the processes, people and technology complement each other, working efficiently and effectively to deliver excellent customer service. Good people either working with ill-defined processes or supported by dated technologies find it very difficult to deliver excellent customer service.

Fred Wiersema has researched the attributes that companies renowned for excellent customer service have in common. He identifies six common attributes, all of which are important from a CRM perspective.[4]

1. Customer service is pervasive. It is everyone's responsibility; it is neither delegated nor relegated to a single department or function.
2. Their operations run smoothly with minimal product and service defect rates, allowing them to focus on pleasing customers.
3. They are always looking for ways to improve.
4. Customer service lies at the heart of the value proposition. Customer service is the main selling point.
5. They build personal relationships with customers.

6. They employ the latest IT to allow their customers to interact with them more conveniently; to develop a profound understanding of what customers need and want; to track activities and processes that influence customer experience.

From a CRM perspective these are all important, but the last three in particular. Customer service is the key element of these companies' value propositions and is an important component of strategic CRM. They understand that customers are responsive to excellent customer service, whatever the basic product or service they create. They also build personal relationships with customers. They understand the needs and requirements of customers at an individual level, and they recognize and respond to events in the customer's life using analytical CRM. Finally, they employ the latest information technology, which allows customers to interact with them whenever they want through multiple channels, an important component of operational CRM. IT also enables them to learn about and respond to customer requirements and to track interactions and processes that connect them to their customers.

What is service automation?

The term service automation (SA) can be defined as follows:

Service automation is the application of computerized technologies to support service staff and management in the achievement of their work-related objectives.

According to the International Customer Service Association, customer service departments are responsible for managing inbound call centre operations, complaint handling and resolution, order entry and processing, providing field sales support, managing outbound call centre operations, and acting as liaison to other departments.[5] It is in these and related activities that SA is deployed.

Service automation is used in five major contexts:

- contact centres
- call centres
- helpdesks
- field service
- web self-service.

Contact centres are configured to communicate with customers across multiple channels, including voice telephony, mail, e-mail, SMS, instant messaging, web collaboration and fax. Service agents need to be able to access an entire communication history, regardless of channel, when communicating with customers about service issues. Channel integration is, therefore, an important feature of contact centre technologies. Technologies for inbound and outbound customer communication, including e-mail response management systems, are widely deployed in contact centre contexts. Contact centre staff may be called on to handle inbound service-related calls, participate in outbound marketing campaigns, respond to e-mail and engage in web chat.

Call centres are generally dedicated to voice telephony communications, whether through a public switched telephone network, cell phone network or VoIP. Agents operating in call centres require a different skill-set from those operating in multichannel contact centres. There is a less compelling need for excellent literacy skills such as reading and writing; they do, however, need excellent listening and responding skills.

Helpdesks are usually associated with IT environments where assistance is offered to IT users. SA applications, such as case management, job management and service level management, are used in this setting. Helpdesk solutions often comply with, and support, third-party standards such as information technology infrastructure library (ITIL) and the information technology service management (ITSM) reference model.

Field service is widespread in both B2C and B2B environments. Service engineers for white goods, such as dishwashers and washing machines, or brown goods, such as televisions and hi-fi installations, visit consumers' homes to install, maintain or repair products. In the B2B context, technicians and engineers visit factories, depots, warehouses, workshops, offices and other workplaces before, during and after purchase to help customers specify, select, procure, install, service and decommission a wide range of machines and systems, ranging from photocopiers, to forklifts, to IT infrastructure. Service automation applied to field service operations involves technologies such as job management, scheduling, mapping and spare parts management. Unlike their office-bound colleagues, field service staff needs access to SA applications and data on their laptops, handheld devices, smart phones and cell phones. Technology firms such as Oracle, SAP, Corrigo, ServicePower, Ventyx, Astea, TOA and @Road all provide specific software applications for field service technicians.

Many companies now offer web-based self-service to customers. Customers can place orders, pay, track service issues, or perform service diagnostics online at any time of day or night.

In addition to engineers and technicians, others may also be involved in providing customer service aided by service automation: customer service agents, sales representatives, sales administration and marketers, for example. Customer-centric organizations may take the view that all employees should be able to deliver excellent customer service, including the ability to handle an enquiry, create a trouble-ticket, or resolve a complaint.

Infrastructure, data, devices and software are the key technological elements of service automation. Infrastructure plays an important role in enabling service to be delivered. When service is delivered through a central call centre or contact centre, in a multichannel environment, there needs to be close integration between various communication systems including telephony, e-mail and web. A customer may browse the web to find out how to obtain service and then communicate the service request by voice telephony into a call centre. However, the customer may expect to receive the initial notification of service appointment time by e-mail and any change to that time by text message. Call centres need integration between the software on the customer service agent's desktop and the automated call distributor (ACD) or switch hardware, so that calls are prioritized and routed appropriately.

Access to the right customer-related data, to enable the service agent to identify and fix the issue promptly, is critical to the delivery of responsive customer service. Customer-related data includes both structured data, such as contact history, account balances and agreed service levels, and unstructured data, such as e-mails and agent notes on telephone conversations. Being able to draw on a searchable database of service issues and fixes allows the agent to resolve problems quickly and completely.

Where service is delivered by a distributed workforce, smaller, lighter, devices such as laptops, Windows-enabled handheld devices and smart phones or cell phones such as Blackberries, tend to be employed; these are typically not found in call and contact centres. Synchronization is also an issue for a distributed service team. Periodic synchronization with the central CRM database enables service engineers and others to ensure that they are fully apprised of their daily scheduled appointments. In addition it is important for service engineers to have the most current service manuals in their laptops.

Benefits from service automation

Service automation has an important role to play in allowing companies to deliver excellent customer service. SA can deliver several benefits, including the following:

- **Enhanced service effectiveness**: service requests can be completed more quickly to the customer's satisfaction by ensuring that requests are handled at the first point of contact, or routed to the right service engineer or customer service agent, who is able to draw on an up to date knowledge base to resolve the issue.
- **Greater service productivity**: call and contact centre management systems ensure that the optimal numbers of agents are scheduled and that their time is used productively. Field service applications ensure that workload is equitably and optimally distributed.
- **Improved customer experience**: agents have full visibility into the customer history and service request and can ensure that service delivery is appropriate to customer status or agreed service levels.

Case 16.1

Service automation at ICEE

The ICEE Company is a division of J&J Snack Foods and is located in Ontario, California. Its flagship product is the ICEE, a flavoured frozen ice beverage that is carbonated and comes in various flavours. ICEE also produces other slushies, beverages and ice pops under both the ICEE and Slush Puppie brands. The company serves over 300 million Icees per year.

ICEE employs 800 people with 400 field technicians who service 30 000 ICEE machines across the US. In the year 2000 ICEE began to scrutinize the inefficiencies they found in the ICEE machine repair process. The company's existing process was very inefficient and error-prone. The challenges were to transform the inefficient paper-based machine repair processes, shorten billing cycles, capture accurate inventory and customer data electronically and transmit in real-time, respond to customer requests more quickly, eliminate an ineffective paper-based parts inventory system and reallocate despatchers time.

After researching several alternatives, ICEE concluded that a real-time wireless data solution would provide them with many more benefits than a batch system, which would require technicians to connect to a landline and synchronize data at the beginning and end of each day. The final solution comprised a wireless handheld device from Symbol Technologies, coupled with Countermind's Mobile Intelligence Field Service Automation Solution, which was tailored to reflect ICEE's business process. This application runs on AT&T's GSM/GPRS network.

Now, all repair data is captured electronically on handheld devices. Billing cycles are reduced because manual data entry is eliminated. Complete job information is available to field technicians in real-time. Field technicians can complete more work orders in a day, improving productivity and customer satisfaction. Parts inventory is managed more effectively and accurately.

Source: AT&T[6]

Software applications for service

Service automation applications offer a range of functionality, as listed in Table 16.1. Note that different SA vendors use the terms issue, case,

Table 16.1
Functionality offered by service automation software

Activity management	Mapping and driving directions
Agent management	Outbound communications management
Case assignment	Queuing and routing
Case management	Scheduling
Contract management	Scripting
Customer self-service	Service analytics
E-mail response management	Service level management
Escalation	Spare parts management
Inbound communications management	Web collaboration
Invoicing	Workflow engineering
Job management	

incident, trouble ticket and service request synonymously to describe the different customer problems that service agents are called on to fix. The table lists both macro-software application solutions that offer a wide range of functionality and micro-software application solutions that offer a narrow range of functionality. The macro solutions, such as case management, deliver much of the functionality present in the micro solutions. In the next few paragraphs, we'll describe this functionality in more detail.

Activity management

This enables service staff to review their workload, to-do list and priorities as directed by their manager or scheduler, and to report back on progress and issue resolution. Some applications allow activities to be updated in real-time by despatchers and routed to the technician, so that work can be reprioritized. Alerts can be set so that appointments are not missed or to notify agents and their managers that issues are unresolved or service levels are about to be, or have been, violated. The despatch process typically uses wireless messaging, requiring the technician to carry an 'always-on' PDA or cell-phone, and a laptop with service manuals and diagnostic tools.

Agent management

Agent management is a high priority for call and contact centre managers. Managers want to employ the lowest number of staff compatible with the desired level of customer service. Too few agents and customers will be dissatisfied with wait-times; too many agents and payroll costs will be unnecessarily high. Customers and managers both want issues to be resolved quickly by agents. Technologies that contribute to this outcome include queuing, scripting and knowledge management, which are discussed elsewhere. Agent managers are faced with the challenge of managing globally dispersed service agents, employed both inhouse and outsourced, operating in different times zones, languages and currencies. Dashboards provide managers with visibility into the performance of both contact centres and individual agents. Performance data include volumes received (e.g. calls, e-mails), average queuing time, percentage handled, average speed of answer (measured in seconds and/or rings), average handle time and abandon rates.

Case assignment

Case assignment applications ensure that each enquiry or issue gets routed to the right agent or technician for resolution. Customer service agents might, for example, be organized according to language skills. When an e-mail enquiry is received in Urdu it is assigned to the agent competent in that language. Field technicians might be organized according to product category. When a service request is received to fix a printer, it is assigned to a technician who is knowledgeable about that product class, not to a more expensive photocopier expert.

Case management

Case management covers the full cycle of activities involved, from receiving initial notification of a matter of concern to a customer to its final resolution and the case file being closed. Case management is also known as incident management and issue management. Case management processes are typically designed using workflow applications within SA software. Workflow depicts the activities that must be performed, the sequence in which they occur and sometimes includes the standards to which the activities must comply. Cases, incidents or issues are initiated by the creation of a trouble ticket. Customers may be allowed to do this by web form or by e-mailing or calling a service or contact centre. The ticket is assigned to a service engineer. The software automatically communicates with the customer at different trigger events, such as scheduling of appointments, or follow-up after the case is closed. Case management software is often associated with a service knowledge base that enables technicians to diagnose and fix problems quickly.

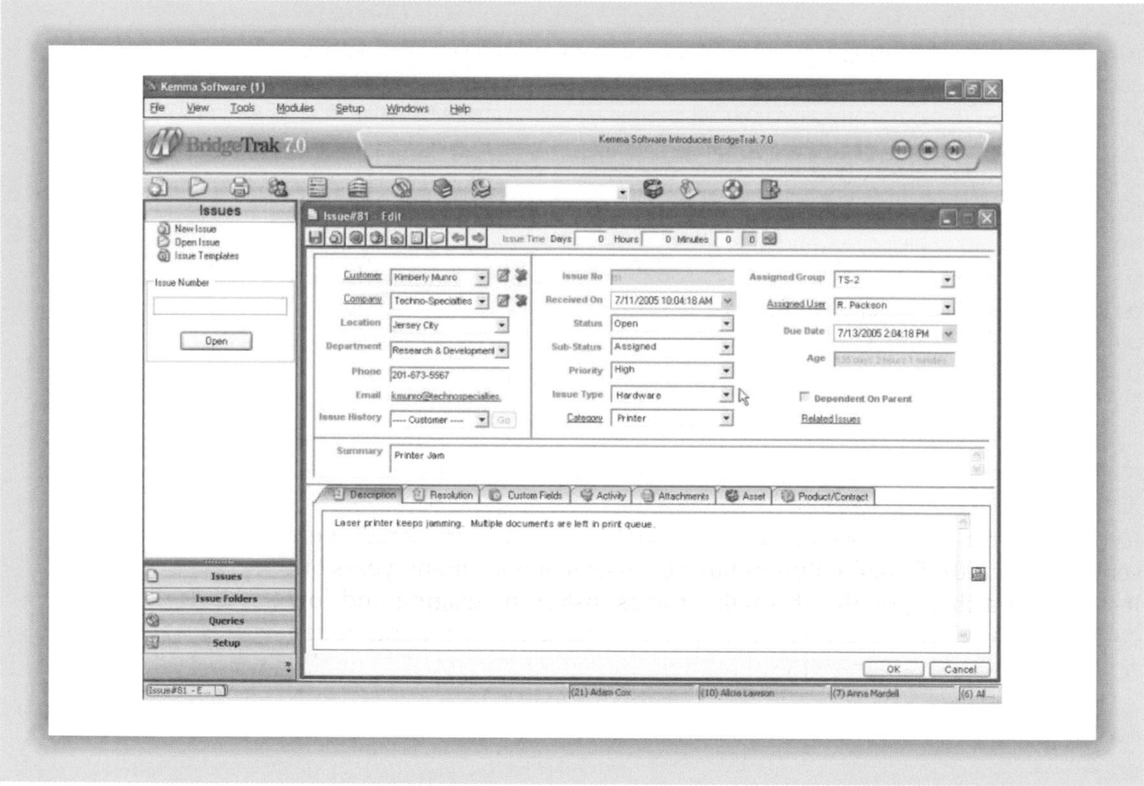

Figure 16.1 Trouble-ticket screenshot[7]

Contract management

Contract management functionality enables service engineers and managers to create, track, progress, accelerate, monitor and control service contracts with customers. Many companies now sell extended service contracts to customers when warranty periods have expired. Some industries, such as office photocopier suppliers, rely on extended service contracts as the primary profit stream, selling machines at a loss and recouping the cost over several years of service.

Customer self-service

Customer self-service is an attractive option for companies because it transfers the responsibility and cost of service to the customer. Customers who self-serve are much less likely to place demands on contact centre, call centre, helpdesk or field service staff. Customers are typically more competent at self-serving when transactions are involved (e.g. online banking or music downloads). However, they are less competent when problem resolution is concerned. In some sectors, it is commonplace to be able to place orders online and track the progress of the order. For example, customers can track and trace the location of packages they have sent or are expecting to receive. The website, www.track-trace.com, serves as a central track and trace clearing house for couriers DHL, UPS, TNT, FedEx and dozens of other market participants. Extranet-enabled portals are the technology of choice for companies wanting to enable customers to self-serve. Customers can transact online, place orders, pay accounts and check order and shipment progress on any day and at any time. Companies that place their knowledge base, or parts thereof, online also facilitate problem resolution by customers. Customers can browse for answers to their queries or solutions to their problems. In the event that this is unsuccessful, companies can allow customers to use an online web form to create a case or an issue for the company to follow-up and resolve or offer web collaboration (see below).

E-mail response management

E-mail response management systems (ERMS) are an increasingly important part of the service automation landscape. E-mail is widely used for both interpersonal and intercompany communications. IDC, the technology analyst, reported that nearly 100 billion e-mail messages were sent daily in 2007. E-mail volumes have been growing for many years but it is expected that growth rates will slow as instant messaging and low cost or free VoIP calls become more common, particularly among young adults.[8] ERMS are not only useful for handling inbound e-mails, but also for delivering outbound e-mails and SMS messages. Company collateral, packaging and websites often list e-mail addresses for individuals and departments. As many as 90 per cent of companies' websites list e-mail contacts for customer support.[9] In addition, many companies have generic e-mail addresses such as info@, sales@ and support@. Customers increasingly expect companies to offer an e-mail communication channel, not just for general communications but specifically for service-related issues. They also expect companies to respond promptly to incoming e-mails. One survey indicates room for improvement in this regard, with 37 per cent of Fortune 100 companies failing completely to respond to e-mails.[10] As individuals, many of us use Outlook or Notes for e-mail. While these may be suitable for small volumes of e-mail, they lack functionality that is useful for higher volume, business-related purposes, such as queuing, routing, intelligent autoresponders, personalization, knowledge-based integration, productivity tools such as templates and multi-language spell checkers, and e-mail analytics. These are typically part of commercial ERMS.

Effective deployment of an ERMS is often accompanied by the publication of service levels. Published service levels such as 'We respond to all e-mails within 24 hours' help to manage customers' service expectations and motivate employees to act accordingly. Service levels can vary between customer segments and product categories. For example, service issues raised by more valued customers, or related to newly launched products, might receive a faster response.

ERMS are designed up to manage the reception, interpretation, routing, response and storage of incoming e-mail securely and effectively. Rather than using generic e-mail boxes, many companies have opted to receive customer service requests using preconfigured web forms. These require customers to select responses to a number of predetermined questions using dropdown menus, check boxes and radio buttons. Space may also be provided for customers to key in free text. Log-in data or cookies allow companies to respond to web form service requests according to customer-related metrics, such as customer value and purchase history. Where companies choose to receive customer e-mails into generic e-mail boxes, there needs to be a manual or automated system for reading and responding to them, routing them to responsible individuals where necessary. First generation automated readers typically are trained to recognize keywords and respond accordingly. Second generation readers recognize patterns across the entire e-mail text rather than simply recognizing keywords. Pattern recognition has the added advantage of being able to detect the emotional tone of an e-mail, so that a particularly angry customer might be identified and receive an immediate response. ERMS also have specialized spam recognition and filtering features and antivirus tools. It is estimated that about 40 per cent of e-mails are spam.[11]

Routing rules in ERMS allow incoming e-mails to be routed into queues for particular agents or departments. Most ERMS allow clients to configure routing rules using an administrative user interface that can only be accessed by authorized administrators. Routing rules can push e-mails to particular queues based on agent workload, agent language skills, agent product knowledge, subject matter expertise, customer value or other variables. This speeds up resolution times and helps meet service levels. Routing also allows more important service requests, perhaps from more valued customers, to be escalated for resolution by higher authorities.

The response time and response content are two important issues that customers consider in assessing service quality. ERMS can be set up to issue an immediate, personalized acknowledgment and case (tracking) number on receipt of a service-related e-mail. These autoresponses can also be used to set out the service promise, for example, that you will resolve the issue within seven days. ERMS can also be used to keep the customer informed of progress in the resolution of the service request.

From the company's point of view, a number of service metrics shed light on the effectiveness of their e-mail management processes: numbers of e-mails in queues, average response time, service level compliance and agent productivity. From a service delivery perspective the most important measure is customer satisfaction with response time and content.

Escalation

Escalation ensures that issues get escalated according to internally determined rules. Higher levels of authority typically have greater discretion to resolve issues. For example, a frontline customer service agent might be required to escalate issues that have a potentially high cost or reputational consequence to higher levels of management. Workflow rules can be applied to determine escalation levels and actions appropriate to any given circumstances. A health insurance specialist escalates issues based on their cost implications as follows:

Level	Limit
Customer service agent	<$50
Team leader	<$100
Business unit manager	>$500
Executive manager	>$2000

Agents in the frontline are trained to recognize issues that fall outside of the normal rules for health insurance provision and to escalate those issues accordingly.

Inbound communications management (ICM)

Inbound communications management (ICM) applications are widely deployed in contact centre contexts. The technology allows companies to receive, route, queue and distribute incoming communications from any channel (voice telephony, e-mail, fax, instant message, SMS, fax or web form) to agents in any location including a contact centre, in the field or at home. A unified queue, issue/content recognition, intelligent routing and knowledge-base integration allow agents to deliver a consistent customer experience and to respond effectively to service requests, whatever the communication channel. Additional technologies that support service delivery in this multichannel environment include computer telephony integration (CTI), interactive voice response (IVR), scripting, call recording, problem diagnostics and service analytics. As with other CRM applications, ICM is available on demand (hosted) or on premise (installed on the user's hardware). According to Gartner Inc.'s analysis of 16 vendors' solutions, Oracle is the leader in providing contact centre management solutions, with Microsoft and salesforce.com challenging. Other technology firms such as Amdocs, SAP, Chordiant, RightNow and Pegasystems also operate in this space.[12]

Case 16.2

Service centre automation at Coca Cola

Coca Cola Bottling Unit (CCBU), a soft drinks manufacturer and distributor, is based in Lambeg, Northern Ireland. The company employs over 400 people and has 14 000 customers. The service support team deals with a range of incoming calls that include complaints, orders, enquiries, delivery and pricing.

The decision to install a single customer service touchpoint dates back to 1996 when a customer satisfaction survey indicated that although customers generally felt they were receiving good service, they wanted a single contact point for customer service.

CCBUs lack of a single contact point meant that inbound calls were not logged in a uniform way. This in turn hindered analysis of call content and frequency and lead to variance in the quality and consistency of responses to service queries. In addition, the company had no way of tracking if the advice given had resolved the problem.

The company resolved these problems by introducing a single touchpoint for all service issues and implementing the service automation product, HEAT. The support centre is split between customer services and customer complaints. HEAT is used to monitor product codes found on packaging and products; when the support team finds three or more complaints that refer to any of these items then an alert message is sent direct to the incident team who investigate the situation.

CCBU installed service level agreements (SLAs), scripted responses and screen customization to ensure high levels of customer service. CCBUs implementation of SLAs means that if a call has not been resolved within a specified period of time it is automatically escalated. The system ensures all calls are logged and are therefore measurable. The customer service team underwent intensive training. Every new employee is trained in first level response across the board, which enables everyone within the company to close standard queries and improve the service customers receive.

Source: FrontRange Solutions UK[13]

Invoicing

Invoicing is a useful application for service technicians who are called to site to provide out of warranty service. Having completed the job to the customer's satisfaction and captured the customer's signature electronically, the invoice can be raised on the spot covering fixed charges, labour and parts, improving cashflow and reducing customer service issues relating to invoicing errors.

Job management

Job management applications offer a range of functionality that is useful to service managers and technicians when planning and performing field service repairs, preventive maintenance, meter readings, inspections,

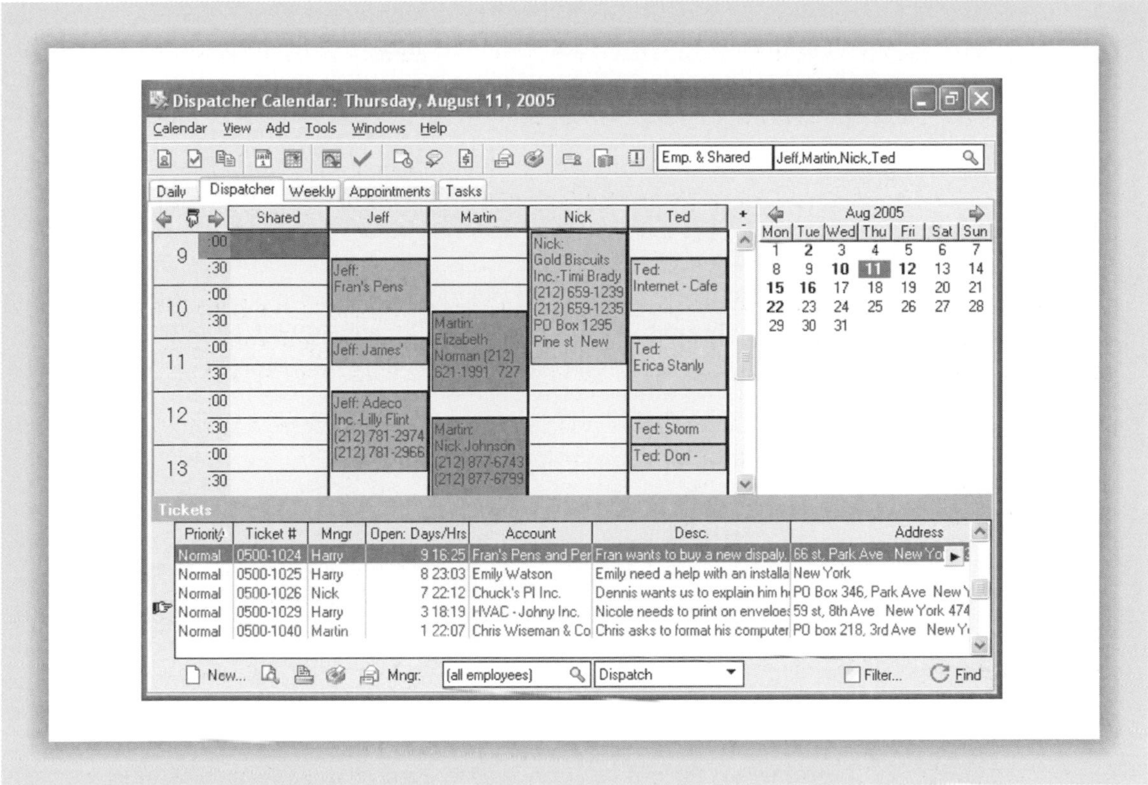

Figure 16.2 Job management screenshot

installations, upgrades and other service tasks. Functionality ranges over cost estimation, quotation generation, creation of trouble tickets, job planning, travel time and distance calculation, job clustering (to reduce travel time), calendaring, scheduling, spare parts management, job progress tracking, invoicing, service level management, technician despatch, time management and product configuration (see Figure 16.2).

Solutions that provide mapping and driving directions are very useful for service engineers who need to visit customers' homes or business premises. Taking into account the engineer's point of origin, service locations, job priorities, service level agreements and other variables, mapping solutions can minimize travel times and distances to ensure that service tasks are performed optimally.

Outbound communications management

Outbound communications management software applications are used in a service environment to acknowledge service requests, make and confirm service appointments, advise on the progress of a service task, invoice for out of warranty service and follow-up after service to ensure that the customer is satisfied. Customer preferences can be considered when selecting the communication medium, whether telephone, e-mail or SMS. The technology firm, KANA, provides outbound communications management applications, and comments that it is possible to convert successful service interactions into up-sell and cross-sell opportunities with follow-up outbound e-mails and SMS messages.[14]

Queuing and routing

Queuing and routing applications allow issues to be routed to agents with particular expertise and positioned in that agent's queue according to some criterion. Routing is usually determined by case assignment rules (see above) and position in the queue is determined by customer value or some other metric. The objective of queuing and routing is to ensure that every service issue is presented to the most appropriate agent for handling and resolution.

Scheduling

This involves planning and organizing a service technician's activity plan for a day, a week or any other period. A technician's schedule contains details on the customer, location, time, product and issue. Some scheduling applications take into account a range of considerations to ensure that the right technician is sent to service the customer. These include travel time and distance, technician availability, technician skills, customer access hours, service level agreement, availability of spare parts and the technician's hourly rates of pay. Optimization engines allow schedules to be changed as new service tickets are created, priorities change and technicians or parts become (un)available. Optimization reduces service costs while maintaining service performance levels. Scheduled tasks can be released in batches for days or weeks or drip-fed to technicians for the coming few hours (see Figure 16.3).

Scripting

Scripting enables customer service agents to converse intelligently with customers to diagnose and resolve problems, even though they may be untrained as technicians. Scripts can be designed so that they flex dynamically according to customer response. Scripts also reduce agent training time.

Service analytics

Service analytics provide managers with information on how effectively and efficiently customer service generally, and individual agents or technicians specifically, are operating. Important metrics for managers of field service operations include, for example, technician utilization, parts inventory, travel time, first time fix rate (FTFR), mean time to resolve (MMTR) and job backlog. FTFR tells managers how many cases were resolved at the technician's first call. MMTR measures time elapsed between notification of the service request to the company and

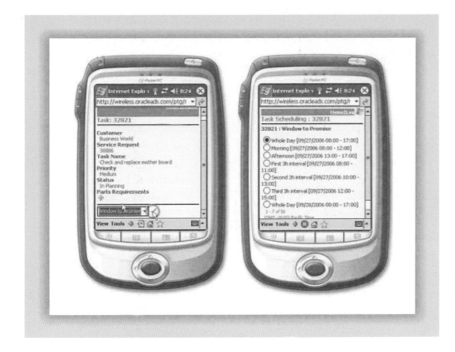

Figure 16.3
Task schedule
delivered to a
Pocket PC[15]

its final resolution. With this information managers can obtain new
resources, reassign staff, offer training, or recalibrate key performance
indicators to enhance service delivery. Many SA applications incorporate
embedded analytics that produce standard reports and enable OLAP to
be performed.

Service level management

Service level management applications allow managers to control the
level of service that is offered to customers, and technicians to deliver
the agreed level of service. As introduced in Chapter 7, a service level
agreement is a contractual commitment between a service provider and
a customer that specifies the mutual responsibilities of both parties with
respect to the services that will be provided and the standards at which
they will be performed. Service levels can be agreed for a number of
variables including availability (the percentage of time that the service
is available over an agreed time period), usage (the number of service
users that can be served simultaneously) and responsiveness (the speed
with which a demand for service is fulfilled). Service levels, however,
are not always subject to negotiation with customers. Many companies
simply offered tiered levels of service to customers based on some metric
of their own choice, typically customer value as measured by customer
profitability or sales. Technicians that understand the entitlements
of customers can service to the specified limit and even up-sell the
customer to a higher level of service. Establishing service levels can also

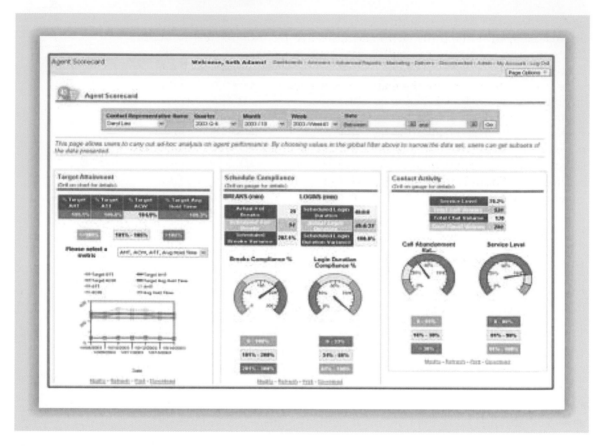

Figure 16.4
Contact centre telephony dashboard with meters showing key information[16]

help human resource management measure people's performance and compute incentives for meeting service level goals.

Spare parts management

Spare parts management is an important application for field technicians. They can see what parts they have with them on the road, check the inventory levels held by other technicians and at regional and central warehouses, order new parts, transfer parts from colleagues, manage excess and defective parts, and check on the progress of orders, thereby ensuring that when they turn up at a job they are properly equipped. Managers can use this application to ensure that appropriate levels of parts inventory are maintained. Too few parts and jobs cannot be completed; too many and inventory costs are unnecessarily high.

Web collaboration

Web collaboration between customer and service agent is enabled by technologies that use instant messaging (web chat 'request call back' or 'click to talk') or allow both parties to co-browse web pages. This allows the agent to help the customer to resolve the issue in real-time. Customer service agents can collaborate with a number of customers simultaneously or can prioritize based on customer value or some other metric. Transcripts of the chat can be retained and attached to the customer file. Web collaboration is often used as an escalation option for customers who cannot find a solution to their issue through a self-service portal. Web collaboration may reduce online abandonment rates, increase problem resolution and customer satisfaction, and provide up-sell and cross-sell opportunities. In countries with excellent broadband services (e.g. South Korea) web chat with text, voice and even web-cam is being used for problem-resolution, up-sell and cross-sell.

Workflow engineering

Workflow engineering software is useful for designing service-related processes, such as problem diagnosis and issue escalation. Workflow for field service operations will define how service requests are validated, how service tickets are issued, how tickets are allocated, how problems will be diagnosed, how parts will be ordered, how problems will be fixed, how customers will be invoiced and so on.

Summary

Service automation is the application of computerized technologies to support service managers and customer service agents in contact and call centres, and helpdesk staff and mobile service staff operating in the field, to achieve their work-related objectives. Companies and their customers can experience three main benefits from service automation: enhanced service effectiveness, greater service productivity and improved customer experience. Service automation applications offer a range of functionality to service managers and technicians: activity management, agent management, case assignment, case management, contract management, customer self-service, e-mail response management, escalation, inbound communications management, invoicing, job management, mapping and driving directions, outbound communications management, queuing and routing, scripting, scheduling, service analytics, service level management, spare parts management, web collaboration and workflow engineering.

References

1. Vandermerwe, S. (1993) Jumping into the customer activity cycle: a new role for customer services in the 1990s. *Columbia Journal of World Business*, Vol. 28 (Summer, 2), pp. 46–66.
2. Grönroos, C. (1984) A service quality model and its marketing implications. *European Journal of Marketing*, Vol. 18, pp. 36–44.

3. Parasuraman, A. Zeithaml, V.A. Berry, L.L. A conceptual model of service quality and its implications for future research. *Journal of Marketing*, Vol. 49, Fall, pp. 41–50; Parasuraman, A., Zeithaml, V.A. and Berry, L.L. (1988) SERVQUAL: a multiple-item scale for measuring consumers' perceptions of service quality. *Journal of Retailing*, Vol. 64(1), pp. 22–37; Parasuraman, A., Zeithaml, V.A. and Berry, L.L. (1991) Refinement and reassessment of the SERVQUAL scale. *Journal of Retailing*, Vol. 64, pp. 12–40; Parasuraman, A., Zeithaml, V.A. and Berry, L.L. (1994) Reassessment of expectations as a comparison standard in measuring service quality: implications for future research. *Journal of Marketing*, Vol. 58(1), pp. 111–132.

4. Wiersema, F. (1998) *Customer service: extraordinary results at Southwest Airlines, Charles Schwab, Land's End, American Express, Staples and USAA*. New York: Harper Collins.

5. International Customer Service Association. (2002) *Measuring customer service performance: final results.*

6. www.wireless.att.com/businesscenter/en_US/pdf/ICEECaseStudy.pdf. Accessed 27 January 2008.

7. Courtesy of ScriptLogic Corporation. http://www.filebuzz.com/software_screenshot/full/20119-bridgetrak_help_desk_software.jpg. Accessed 27 January 2008.

8. http://www.idc.com/getdoc.jsp?containerId=prUS20639307&pageType=PRINTFRIENDLY. Accessed 15 January 2008.

9. Talisma Corporation. (2007) Winning strategies for e-mail management. White paper.

10. CustomerRespect.com report cited in eGain (2004). Mission-critical customer service: 10 best practices for success. eGain Corporation, August.

11. Talisma Corporation. (2007) Winning strategies for e-mail management. White paper.

12. Gartner Inc. (2007) Magic quadrant for CRM customer service contact centers. March.

13. http://heat.frontrange.co.uk/common/Files/Xtra_Sites/HEAT/casestudy_HEAT_Coca_Cola.pdf. Accessed 28 January 2008.

14. www.kana.com/solutions.php?tid=105. Accessed 27 December 2007.

15. Oracle Mobile Field Service data sheet, 2006.

16. Oracle Contact Centre Telephony Analytics data sheet, 2006.

Chapter 17
Organizational issues and customer relationship management

By the end of this chapter you will understand:

1. how various organizational roles use CRM tools
2. several ways of organizing the customer interface to achieve CRM objectives, including functional, geographic, brand or product, market or customer and matrix organizations
3. how IT acts as a proxy for structure in the networked or virtual organization
4. the role of key account management structures in CRM.

Introduction

In this chapter you will learn about several front-office roles in which CRM plays an important role, and how companies organize their customer interface to achieve their CRM objectives. We will examine several roles that make significant use of CRM tools: sales representative, account manager, marketing manager, market analyst, campaign manager, market manager, customer relationship manager and customer service agent.

The chapter also examines organizational structures as they relate to CRM implementations. Organizational structures serve both to enable and to constrain business outcomes. For example, it is very difficult to promote creativity in a rule-bound bureaucracy. Conversely, a bureaucracy is highly conducive to obtaining compliance to standardized business processes. Similarly, it is a struggle to become customer-centric in a functional organization where specialists report upwards within silos, but do not share customer insight horizontally across silos. Consequently, there is no single correct structure that is suitable for all organizations. What is right depends upon the strategic goals of the business and we turn to this issue later in the chapter. First we review some of the roles that use CRM tools.

Organizational roles and CRM

Earlier in the book, we identified four different forms of CRM: strategic, operational, analytical and collaborative. Strategic CRM is focused on the development of a customer-centric business culture that is dedicated to winning and keeping customers by creating and delivering value better than competitors. Operational CRM focuses on the automation of customer-facing processes such as selling, marketing and customer service. Analytical CRM focuses on the intelligent mining of customer-related data for strategic or tactical purposes. Collaborative CRM applies technology across organizational boundaries with a view to optimizing company, partner and customer value. These different forms of CRM vary in their significance for the roles we examine here: sales representative, account manager, marketing manager, market analyst, campaign manager, market manager, customer relationship manager, and customer service agent.

Sales representative

Not all sales representatives perform the same role. For example, there are sales representatives who act as:

- **deliverer**: the representative who delivers bottled water for the office water cooler
- **order taker**: the shop assistant in an electrical goods retail store
- **missionary**: the pharmaceutical company representative whose job is principally to nurture relationships with doctors and specialists
- **technician**: the engineer who consults to clients considering the purchase of cranes and hoists
- **demand creator**: the representative who sells 'unsought goods and services', that is, products that have to be sold, rather than products that are sought after and bought, for example advertising space, insurance or encyclopaedias
- **solution vendor**: the representative who sells computer networks, or enterprise CRM suites.[1]

The selling challenge also ranges from taking stock fill orders that maintain inventory levels of basic commodities, to team selling of high-technology military systems to national governments. Some representatives focus on winning new accounts (hunters) and others focus on nurturing existing accounts (farmers). Whatever the sales role, representatives are typically exposed to operational CRM and use sales-force automation solutions that help them maintain contacts, keep track of opportunities and manage their territories and accounts.

Account manager

Whereas sales representatives may be organized to serve geographic territories, or to sell specific product categories, account managers are committed to serving nominated customers or groups of customers. Account managers occupy boundary-spanning roles. That is, they have a foot in two camps: that of their employer and that of their customer. The account manager must ensure that the employer understands the requirements of the customer, and that the customer understands what the account manager's company can do for them. Account managers are usually responsible for developing, maintaining and improving the profitability of relationships with clients. They may operate alone or enjoy the support of an account team, offering specialist help to the customer and account manager. Leads are generally fed to account managers. Like sales representatives, account managers make good use of sales-force automation, particularly account management, contact management, pipeline management and sales forecasting.

Marketing manager

The detailed job descriptions of marketing managers vary enormously, but one thing that they have in common is that their core goal is to manage demand. Some marketers try to decrease demand (e.g. health agency marketers for tobacco products), some try to redistribute demand (e.g. hoteliers shifting over-demand from high season to the shoulders and off season), but most try to increase demand. By increasing demand, marketers have an impact on shareholder value.[2] A number of marketing decisions are important elements of strategic CRM, as was pointed out in Chapter 12, including target market selection and value proposition development. Marketing practitioners strive to develop value propositions that targeted customers prefer over competitors. Many marketers conduct market and customer analysis, develop product, brand or category plans, generate leads and align their marketing efforts with channel partners. This exposes them to operational CRM in the form of marketing automation modules for customer and market segmentation, lead management, marketing resource management and product lifecycle management; to analytical CRM as they perform analysis on market, customer and environmental data in order to identify opportunities and threats; and to partner relationship management (PRM) applications as they engage in collaborative CRM with their channel partners.

Market analyst

Market analysts generally occupy entry level or junior positions, yet this belies the importance of their role. Although analysts have no line management responsibility for sales or profit, the ability to make sense of, or interpret, market and customer data provides a foundation for line management decisions such as target market selection, product design and communication and channel choice. Fluency with marketing analytics or web analytics is essential for market analysts, who need to be able to choose the right analytical approach for different types of data: nominal, ordinal, interval and ratio.

Campaign manager

Campaign managers are responsible for planning, implementing, evaluating and reporting on marketing campaigns targeted at prospects and customers, whether consumers or organizations, across a range of channels including direct mail, e-mail, web and text messaging. Campaign managers are generally charged with achieving KPIs such as lead generation, customer acquisition, cross-sales and customer retention. They are expected to work with a number of internal stakeholders including line managers in marketing, sales and customer development roles, IT management, data analysts and privacy officers. Managing relationships with external stakeholders, such as direct mail vendors, e-mail marketers, creative agencies and print suppliers, also falls to campaign managers. Unsurprisingly, campaign managers use operational CRM modules for campaign management, e-mail and direct mail campaign management and marketing optimization. In the absence of inhouse or external specialist analytics expertise, they might also be expected to use marketing analytics and web analytics to target and evaluate their campaigns.

Market manager

The word market is used in a number of ways. The traditional use is to describe a meeting place for buyers and sellers. The word is still used in the same way, for example, you might have a local 'Farmers' Market' where farmers sell direct to the public. The word is also used to describe customers and vendors buying and selling a particular product class, such as the car market or the wheat market. Market also refers to customer groupings, irrespective of product class, such as the DINK (double-income, no kids) market or the German market.

Market managers are generally responsible for business operations for particular geographic areas, market segments or product classes. Respective examples are market manager (Asia-Pacific), market manager (SOHO (small office, home office)) or market manager (Aircraft Tyres). Given the focus on geography, customer or product, almost any operational CRM application might be used by a market manager. The geographic market manager might use territory management, a customer market manager might use account management and a product market manager might use a product encyclopaedia application.

Customer relationship manager

Customer relationship managers are becoming more widespread; they can be found in many business-to-business (B2B) companies and in a smaller number of business-to-consumer industries, such as personal banking and wealth management. Customer relationship managers are responsible for maintaining and growing the value of specified customer relationships. They have to be skilled at identifying new opportunities to grow share-of-customer by cross-selling and up-selling. In a B2B context, they need to understand customers' businesses, processes and products and to be able to identify when their employer's products and services might be of value. At heart, customer relationship managers need to listen effectively, understand customer needs, recognize opportunities and respond appropriately. They make use of operational CRM applications, such as account management, contact management, opportunity management, order management, proposal generation, quotation management and sales forecasting.

Customer service agent

Customer service agents generally operate out of call and contact centres, working with a range of communications technologies. CSAs can perform inbound, outbound or blended communications roles. Inbound CSAs handle service matters such as account queries, complaints and service requests. Outbound CSAs work collaboratively with campaign managers and marketing teams. Depending on their role, CSAs use operational CRM systems that range across sales, marketing and service applications.

We now turn to the issue of organizational structures for CRM implementations.

Strategic goals of CRM

The expression 'strategy before structure' comes from the work of Alfred Chandler.[3] He was stressing the point that organizations should decide their strategic goals before designing the structure of the organization to achieve those goals. Companies adopting CRM as their core business strategy need to create an organizational structure that achieves three major outcomes through its marketing, selling and service functions:

- the acquisition of carefully targeted customers or market segments
- the retention and development of strategically significant customers or market segments
- the continuous development and delivery of competitively superior value propositions and experiences to the selected customers.

No organization can expect to achieve these outcomes alone. All have to work in close cooperation with suppliers, partners and other members of their business network. This means that the organizational structure has to facilitate the cooperation of several normally autonomous organizations.

These goals have to be achieved in an environment of increasing turbulence. Between the end of World War Two and the 1970s the business environment was relatively stable. Businesses could develop strategies and structures that only infrequently needed revision. Today's environment is one in which there is immense volatility: deregulation, global competition, new technologies providing additional routes to market, the emergence of new national market economies and highly demanding and well-educated customers. Structures need to be invented that allow organizations to sense and respond to change with great speed.

Conventional customer management structures

We will start by considering a standalone company as it organizes to achieve these three CRM goals. This company is presented with a number of alternative structures:

1. functional organization structure
2. geographical organization structure

3. product, brand or category organization structure
4. market or customer-based organization structure
5. matrix organization structure.

Functional structure

A functional structure has sales, marketing and service specialists reporting to a functional head such as a director or vice president of sales and marketing. The specialists might include market analyst, market researcher, campaign manager, account manager, service engineer, and sales support specialist. Small- to medium-sized businesses with narrow product ranges tend to prefer the functional organization. The three core disciplines that interface with customers, sales, marketing and service, may or may not coordinate their efforts and share their customer knowledge by depositing it in a common customer database. From a CRM perspective it would be better if they did. Elsewhere in a functionally organized business there will be other specialists whose decisions can impact on customer acquisition, retention and experience, for example, specialists in operations, human resources and accounts receivable. These experts would also benefit from having access to customer information. Very often, functional specialists feel a sense of loyalty to their discipline rather than their customers.

Geographical structure

A geographical structure organizes some or all of the three core CRM disciplines, marketing, selling and service, on territorial lines. Selling and service are more commonly geographically dispersed than marketing. International companies often organize geographically around the Americas, EMEA (Europe, Middle East and Africa) and Asia-Pacific regions. Smaller companies may organize around national, regional or local areas.

Where customers are geographically dispersed and value face-to-face contact with salespeople, there is a clear benefit in salespeople also being geographically dispersed. Where service needs to be delivered at remote locations, service may also be distributed geographically. Because selling and service costs can be very high, companies try to find ways to perform these activities more cost-effectively. Some companies sell face-to-face to their most important customers and offer a telesales service to others. Others provide service through centralized contact centres that might either be outsourced or company operated. Websites that enable customers to service their own requirements can also reduce cost. Technology companies such as EMC have found ways to reduce service costs by developing a technology-enabled remote problem-sensing and problem-solution capability (see Case 17.1).

One disadvantage of this approach, from a CRM perspective, is that there may be many different customer types in a single geographic area. A salesperson selling industrial chemicals might have to call on companies from several industries such as textiles, paint or consumer goods manufacture. The applications of the sold product may be diverse;

the buying criteria of the customers may be quite different. Some may regard the product as mission critical; others may regard it insignificant. The problem is multiplied if a salesperson sells many products to many customer groups. The salesperson develops neither customer nor product expertise.

Case 17.1

EMC delivers remote customer service

EMC sells information storage, systems, networks and services worldwide. EMC provides proactive and pre-emptive customer service. EMC systems are configured to identify problems. If an EMC system detects an error or unexpected event, no matter how small, it will automatically call home to the support centre that is available 24/7. Staff immediately research the issue by dialling back into the system. Over 90 per cent of service calls are resolved remotely, most often without the customer even being aware there has been a problem or there being any impact on the information system.

Product, brand or category structure

A product or brand organization structure is common in companies that produce a wide variety of products, especially when they have different marketing, sales or service requirements. This sort of structure is common in large consumer goods companies, such as Procter and Gamble and Unilever, and in diversified business-to-business companies. Product or brand managers are generally responsible for developing marketing strategy for their products, and then coordinating the efforts of specialists in marketing research, advertising, selling, merchandising, sales promotion and service, to ensure that the strategic objectives are achieved. Normally, brand and product managers have to compete for company resources to support their brands, through an annual planning cycle inviting the brand managers to submit and defend their marketing plans. Resources are spread thinly across many brands and the company risks becoming focused on products rather than customers. Procter and Gamble found that brand managers became isolated, competing vigorously against each other, focusing on their own goals rather than those of the corporation. Brands competed against each other, creating cannibalization.[4]

Many multibrand companies have found that brand management is an expensive way to market their offerings. In a worst-case scenario, different brand managers might be calling on the same customer on the same day. This certainly gives the impression of a lack of coordination and a disregard for the value of the customer's time. The customer may also experience varying levels of service from the different brand or product managers. Some companies have tried to coordinate their product marketing efforts by appointing product group managers to an oversight role.

More recently, some leading companies have moved to a category management structure. Procter and Gamble did this in the 1980s in response to the problems outlined earlier. Kraft markets a number of different brands, including Louis Rich cold meat cuts and Oscar Mayer hot dogs. The company has now appointed category business directors who coordinate a team of functional experts focused on each major category (Figure 17.1). Brand managers sit on the category team. The category team works with a customer team that is dedicated to each major customer to ensure that the category offer generates profit for both Kraft and the customer. The customer team works closely with customers to help them learn how to benefit more from intelligent product assortment, shelf position and promotion decisions. They also help retailers to understand better and exploit their own customer data. Also dedicated to each category is a process team that is responsible for ensuring that business processes are aligned with customer requirements. Typically, the process team addresses issues of quality management and logistics. This sort of structure attempts to integrate product, functional and customer considerations.

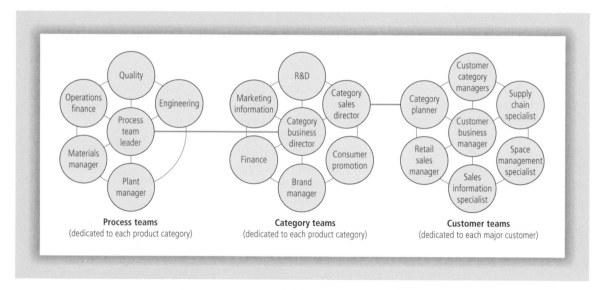

Figure 17.1 Category management at Kraft[5]

Market or customer structure

Market or customer-based organization structures are common when companies serve different customers or customer groups that are felt to have different requirements or buying practices. Dell, for example, sells to SOHO (small office, home office), medium-sized businesses, large businesses and government/institutional markets. IBM has refocused its selling efforts on 14 different customer groups. Royal Bank of Canada has rebuilt its organization to focus on customers, not product lines. Market- or customer-based managers come in many forms: market managers, segment managers, account managers and customer business managers, for example. The roles are responsible for becoming expert on market and customer requirements and for ensuring that the organization creates and delivers the right value proposition for the customer. Recently, there has been a trend towards national, key or global account management that we look at in more detail later in the chapter.

Matrix structure

A matrix organization is often the preferred structural solution when a company has several different product lines serving several different customer groups. A matrix typically has market- or customer-based managers on one side and product managers on the other side of the matrix, as in Figure 17.2. In the high-tech industries, another common matrix structure is geography against industry. The sales team includes a salesperson and a pre-sales consultant. Salespeople are organized into geographic territories, but pre-sales consultants are organized by industry. This allows customers to have not only a geographically convenient point of face-to-face contact, but also an industry specialist on whose expertise they can draw.

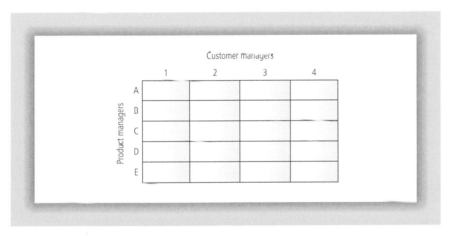

Figure 17.2
A matrix
organization

A variation that is commonly found in multichannel organizations is the replacement of customer managers with channel managers. Multichannel retailers can have several routes to market: stores, catalogues, online retailing, perhaps even a television shopping channel. Financial services institutions also have many channels: branch networks, call centres, agency outlets and corporate websites. Matrix organizations have been popular since the 1970s, when they were felt to facilitate both horizontal and vertical communication, therefore improving coordination and reducing inefficiencies.

Market or customer managers in matrices are responsible for developing and maintaining profitable relationships with external customers. Generally, they view product managers in the matrix as suppliers. Sometimes the internal product manager will compete against external suppliers to become the market manager's preferred supplier. Then, market managers will form internal customer–supplier relationships, negotiate prices and agree service levels just as they would with outside suppliers. Pricing internal transfers can be a tricky decision. One of two approaches is taken: either the internal supplier sells at external market prices (as if they were marketing to an external customer, and aiming to make a profit), or they sell at an internally agreed transfer price that enables market managers to return a profit on their external transactions and relationships. This price then allows the market manager more flexibility in negotiating price with the external customer.

As an alternative to, or in some cases a prelude to, the development of a matrix organization, many companies have opted for the use of cross-functional teams. A cross-functional team is usually established when a project has implications that span normal functional, product or market lines. A cross-functional team, as we saw in Chapter 3, is often used to consider the implications of the adoption of CRM. It will consist of experts from marketing, sales, service, technology, finance and general management.

Network and virtual organizations

Business networks compete, not just standalone companies. Virgin Atlantic's network competes with the networks of American Airlines and British Airways. Indeed, some members of Virgin Atlantic's network may also be part of British Airways' and American Airlines' networks.

In this networked world, it is no longer a simple matter to know where an organization's boundary lies. This brings us to the role of IT in organizational design. The role of IT in a stable corporate environment is to allow senior management to control information and decision making.[6] As environments become more turbulent and as companies attempt to forge network relationships, the role of IT has changed. Its role is now to provide information that enables the company and its network members to:

- sense and respond rapidly to changes in the business environment
- collaborate to develop and deliver better customer value propositions
- enhance and share their learning about customers
- improve their individual and joint cost profiles.

The B-2 stealth bomber, for example, was the product of network collaboration. IT was a substitute for a more formalized and centralized organization structure linking the four contributing organizations. It has been suggested that IT functioned as a proxy for organizational structure in two ways:

> 'First, the information systems aided coordination directly by making information-processing less costly. Secondly, this enhanced information-processing made the governance of the project more efficient'.[7]

IT therefore has a number of influences on organizational design. It allows information to be shared not only right across an organization – vertically, horizontally and laterally – but also outside an organization with network members. Structure therefore no longer has to be tied to traditional vertical reporting relationships. IT also enables organizations to adapt the decentralized and networked structures that are necessary if they are to respond successfully to both environmental turbulence and customer expectations.

Customers do not want to learn how the organizations they patronize are structured. They do not want to have queries rerouted from one silo or specialist to another in search of a solution. Customers who hear the words: 'That's not my department. I'll put you through to the right person', or find themselves looping through IVR menus in search of a solution are likely to be dissatisfied customers. Customers want their needs, demands and expectations to be met. Companies therefore need to create an organization structure that enables their products, services and information to be ubiquitously and immediately available in the channels that customers patronize. Traditional structures, particularly those that are functional, geographical or product-based, struggle to meet these standards.

Structures that are IT-enabled are more likely to meet customer requirements. For example, a web-based banking service is open every day and hour of the year. A typical branch-based service is open less than one third of the time. If the branch network were to replicate the scale of the web-based service, it would require three times the staffing levels with a concomitant increase in management structure. Even then, this could not match the convenience of a home-accessed banking service, or its price. Datamonitor, for example, suggests that a branch-based transaction costs a bank 120 times the cost of an Internet transaction.[8] Some or all of these transaction cost savings can be passed on to customers as improved prices.

At its most advanced, the IT-enabled organization is able to take any sales or service query from any customer through any channel and resolve it immediately. Among the preferred characteristics of such a design are:

- a customer interface that is consistent across channels and easy to use whatever the technology or device
- a first point of contact that takes responsibility for resolving the query
- a back-end architecture that enables the contact point to obtain relevant customer and product information immediately.

These IT-enabled structures eliminate the need for conventional silo-based geography-, function- and product-based arrangements.

Person-to-person contacts

Interpersonal contacts between people from the seller and buyer dyad are important, whether they are conducted face-to-face or mediated by technology such as phone, fax and e-mail. On the seller's side these contacts are important for identifying customer needs, requirements and preferences, for understanding and managing customer expectations, for solving problems and showing commitment. Over the life of a relationship, such personal contacts contribute to the reduction of uncertainty and the creation of close social bonds. Interpersonal communication also underpins the development of product and process adaptations that serve as investments in the relationship. These act as structural bonds.

Relationships between individuals on buyer and seller sides tend to be hierarchically matched.[9] Sales representatives meet with buyers, general managers meet with general managers. Researchers have also identified three main patterns of interorganizational contact.[10]

1. **Controlled contact pattern**: where all contacts are physically channelled through a single point of contact, typically a salesperson on the seller's side or a buyer on the customer side. This individual manages all the contacts on the other side of the dyad. There are two forms of this pattern:
   - seller-controlled
   - buyer-controlled.
2. **Coordinated contact pattern**: many different departments or individuals have direct personal contacts with departments or individuals on the other side, but there is one department or person, usually a buyer or sales representative, who is involved in and coordinates all these contacts. There are three forms of this pattern:
   - seller coordinated pattern
   - buyer coordinated pattern
   - seller and buyer coordinated pattern.
3. **Stratified contact pattern**: where individuals and departments on both sides of the dyad manage their own contacts with their equivalents on the other side of the dyad.

These established patterns are breaking down under the influence of new technologies. Now it is possible to have many-to-many communications between contacts on the buyer's and seller's sides, enabled by web technologies. The coordination of these contacts is one of the features of CRM application software. Modern communication technologies, such as e-mail and the web, require the use of multichannel consolidation infrastructures if all types of communication are to be consolidated into a single record of interorganizational contact.

Key account management

Many B2B companies have adopted a market-based customer management structure, variously called key account management, national account management, regional account management or global account management. We use the term key account management (KAM) to cover all four forms. KAM is a structure that facilitates the implementation of CRM at the level of the business unit.

A key account is an account that is strategically significant. This normally means that it presently or potentially contributes significantly to the achievement of company objectives, such as profitability. It may also be a high volume account, a benchmark customer, an inspiration, or a door opener, as described in Chapter 5.

Companies choose one of two ways to implement KAM. Either a single dedicated person is responsible for managing the relationship, or a team is assigned as in the Kraft example mentioned earlier. The team membership might be fully dedicated to a single key account or may work on several accounts. Generally, this is under the leadership of a dedicated account director. The motivation to adopt a KAM structure comes from recognition of a number of business conditions:

1. **Concentration of buying power** lies in fewer hands. Big companies are becoming bigger. They control a higher share of corporate purchasing. Smaller companies are cooperating to create purchasing power and leverage purchasing economies. Even major competitors are collaborating to secure better inputs. For example, Procter and Gamble and Unilever, rivals on the supermarket shelf, are cooperating to buy raw materials and input goods such as chemicals and packaging.
2. **Globalization**: as companies become global they want to deal with global suppliers, if only for mission critical purchases. Global companies expect to procure centrally, but require goods and services to be provided locally.
3. **Vendor reduction programmes**: customers are reducing the number of companies they buy from, as they learn to enjoy the benefits of improved relationships with fewer vendors.
4. **More demanding customers**: customers are demanding that suppliers become leaner. This means they eliminate non-value adding activities. The corollary is that they want suppliers to supply exactly what they want. This may mean more reliable, more responsive customer services and just-in-time delivery.

A supplier may decide that it wants to introduce a KAM system, but it is generally the customer who decides whether to permit this sort of relationship to develop. If customers feel that their needs are better met outside of a KAM-based relationship, they are unlikely to participate in a KAM programme.

According to one study, suppliers are finding considerable benefits in the adoption of KAM.[11]

- doing large amounts of business with a few customers offers considerable opportunities to improve efficiency and effectiveness
- selling at a relationship level can spawn disproportionately high and beneficial volume, turnover and profit
- repeat business can be considerably cheaper to win than new business
- long-term relationships enable the use of facilitating technologies, such as EDI and shared databases
- familiarity and trust reduce the need for checking and make it easier to do business.

Although the research suggests major benefits for sellers, the companies that succeed at KAM are those that perform better at a whole range of management activities, including selecting strategic customers, growing key accounts and locking out the competition.

'Companies that are most effective at developing strategic customer relationships spend more time and effort thinking about their customers' profiles, direction and future needs than the least effective … (T)hey spend relatively less time and effort considering how their strategic customers will benefit themselves as suppliers'.[12]

Concentration of buying power has lead to buyers taking charge of relationships. Many companies have supplier accreditation and certification processes in place. To be shortlisted as a potential supplier, vendors often have to invest in satisfying these criteria. Buyers increasingly have documented processes that compel vendors to deal with specific members of a decision-making unit at specific times in the buying process. Under these circumstances, sellers may not have the chance to exhibit their exceptional selling capabilities. What they must do, however, is demonstrate their relationship management capabilities.

KAM differs from regular business-to-business account management in a number of important ways. First, the focus is not on margins earned on each individual transaction; rather the emphasis is on building a mutually valuable long-term relationship. The effect of this is that a more trusting, cooperative, non-adversarial relationship develops. Secondly, key account plans are more strategic. They look forward five or more years. Non-key accounts are subjected to more tactical campaigning designed to lift sales in the short term. Thirdly, the KAM (team) is in continuous contact, very often across several functions and at multiple levels of hierarchy. Special access is often provided to customer senior management. Contact with non-key accounts tends to be less frequent and less layered. Fourthly, suppliers make investments in key accounts that serve as structural bonds. Indeed, even the allocation of a dedicated key account manager or team represents an investment in the customer. Additionally, suppliers are much more likely to adapt elements of their value proposition such as products, inventory levels, price, service levels and processes for key accounts. Some additional elements might be added to the value proposition for key accounts. This might include vendor-managed inventory, joint production planning, staff training and assistance with the customer's product development and marketing strategies.

KAM can be thought of as a form of investment management, where the manager makes decisions about which accounts merit most investment, and what forms that investment should take.

Researchers have made efforts to understand how KAM develops over time.[13] Figure 17.3 shows KAM developing through several stages as suppliers and customers become more closely aligned. As the relationship becomes more collaborative, and as the level of involvement between the two parties grows, the commitment to more advanced forms of KAM grows.

In the pre-KAM stage, a prospective key account – one that shows signs of being strategically significant – has been identified. Because the prospect is supplied by other vendors, the major task is to motivate a

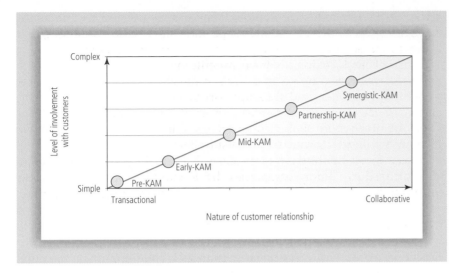

Figure 17.3
A model of KAM
development

modified re-buy, most likely by identifying ways in which the new solution meets customer requirements better. In the early KAM stage, the new supplier has won a small share of customer spend, and is on trial. The early KAM structure often takes the form of a bow-tie (Figure 17.4), in which the only contact is between single representatives of each company, typically account manager and buyer. These contacts act as gatekeepers, liaising with their own colleagues as needed.

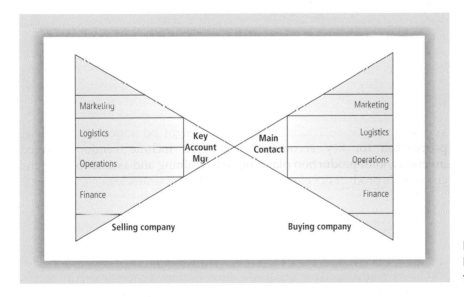

Figure 17.4
Bow-tie structure
for early KAM

The bow-tie is a very fragile arrangement. If either party doesn't get on well with the other, the relationship might not evolve. If either moves on or retires, the relationship may be severed. The ability of the supplier company to understand the customer depends on the skills of one person alone. If that person doesn't record what is known in a customer database, it might be lost forever. Customers will sometimes refuse vendors access to other contacts. This is often designed to demonstrate power.

As it becomes clearer that the relationship is paying off for both parties, it may migrate to mid-KAM status. The customer has come to trust the supplier, and the supplier has shown commitment to the customer. The supplier is now a preferred, though not sole supplier. There are other, more senior, contacts between the organizations. As the relationship heads towards partnership KAM status, the relationship becomes more established. The customer views the supplier as a strategic resource. Information is shared to enable the parties to resolve problems jointly. Customers might invite suppliers to go 'open book' so that cost structures are transparent. Pricing is stable and determined by the tenure and value of the relationship. Innovations are offered to key accounts first before being introduced to other customers. There is functional alignment, as specialists talk to their counterparts on the other side. There is much more contact between the companies at every level. The job of the key account manager is to coordinate all these contacts to ensure that the account objectives are achieved. This sort of relationship is often represented as a diamond (Figure 17.5).

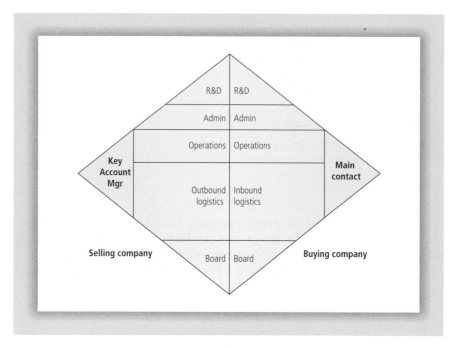

Figure 17.5
Diamond structure for partnership KAM

The most advanced form of KAM, identified as synergistic KAM, occurs when a symbiotic relationship has developed. As Figure 17.6 suggests, the boundaries between the two organizations are blurred as both sides share resources and people to work on mutually valued projects. These might be cost reduction projects, new product development projects, quality assurance projects or other ventures beyond the scope of their present relationship.

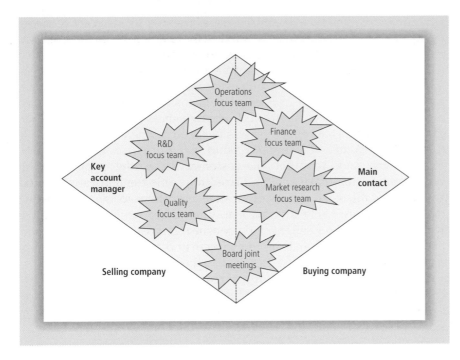

Figure 17.6
Virtual organization
for synergistic KAM

This developmental model does not suggest that all KAM arrangements migrate along the pathway towards synergistic KAM. KAM will only advance as far as the parties want. If either party finds they are not benefiting from the arrangement, it can be reversed and become more transactional. Key account status might be withdrawn if the customer ceases being strategically significant, purchases from a major competitor of the supplier, becomes financially unstable, displays unethical behaviours or demands too many concessions, making the relationship unprofitable.

There are also situations that can lead to relationship dissolution. This might happen if the customer finds that the supplier has acted opportunistically, thereby breaking trust. Opportunistic behaviours might include ramping up price, betraying confidences to third parties, supplying the customer's major competitors or artificially restricting supply. Suppliers can also 'sack' customers, for example, when it is clear that there is no prospect of making a profit from the relationship even if it were to be re-engineered to reduce cost.

Progress along the KAM pathway may also be limited by either party's relationships with other companies. It may be impossible for a vending machine company to develop a strong relationship with PepsiCo, if it already has a strong relationship with Coca Cola.

Team selling

Team selling is a form of selling that is often associated with the more advanced forms of KAM. A key account team is assembled that consists of a number of specialists that can sense and respond to customer concerns over a variety of issues. The team might, for example, include people from engineering, logistics, research and development and sales. Collaborative team selling may even cross organizational boundaries. Representatives from two or more partnering organizations can come together to pitch for new business or service an established customer. Partner relationship management systems facilitate such arrangements by making customer, project and product information available to all partners.

These teams may be thought of as a multiperson selling centre, in much the same way that the customer has a multiperson buying centre or decision-making unit. The selling centre might have a fixed composition throughout the relationship with the customer, though the make-up is more likely to vary. For example, at the beginning of the relationship a 'hunter' might initially win the account. Later a 'farmer' takes over and builds the team to maintain and manage the relationship for mutual benefit.

Major decisions for team selling concern the composition of the team, coordination of team efforts and measurement of team performance. Coordination can be achieved through conformance to a cultural norm (for example, a focus on customer satisfaction, or mutual benefit), formal rules and plans, deference to hierarchical direction, improved communication facilitated by committee meetings or IT. Intranets can be especially useful in this respect.

Summary

This chapter has examined a number of organizational issues, as they relate to the implementation of CRM.

We found that different forms of CRM – strategic, operational, analytical and collaborative – touch on a number of roles with varying degrees of significance: sales representative, account manager, marketing manager, market analyst, campaign manager, market manager, customer relationship manager, customer service agent and key account manager.

Agreeing the CRM strategy is a necessary prelude to deciding on structure. There are a number of conventional organizational models for the customer-facing parts of a business: sales, marketing and service. They can be organized around functions, geography, products, markets or they can take a matrix form. As organizational boundaries become blurred, CRM strategies can be seen as being delivered by networks and virtual organizations, where IT serves as a proxy for structure. Sharing information across the network acts in the same way as organizational structure to facilitate the achievement of objectives.

One important market-based approach to organizational structure is key account management. Key accounts are strategically significant customers which the selling company is prepared to invest in. Key account management can be thought of as comprising a number of forms of structures. Early key account management often is thought of as a bow-tie structure; later stages of development can be characterized as a diamond shape. The ultimate form of key account management happens when corporate boundaries dissolve and the buyer and seller work together on projects of mutual interest. Team selling may be an important part of key account management.

References

1. McMurray, R.N. (1961) The mystique of super-salesmanship. *Harvard Business Review*, Vol. March–April, p. 114.
2. Doyle, P. (2000) *Value-based marketing: marketing strategies for corporate growth and shareholder value*. Chichester: John Wiley.
3. Chandler, A.D. Jr (1962) *Strategy and Structure: Concepts in the History of the Industrial Enterprise*. Casender, MA: MIT Press.
4. Martinsons, A.G.B. and Martinsons, M.G. (1994) In search of structural excellence. *Leadership and Organization Development Journal*, Vol. 15(2), pp. 24–28.
5. George, Michael, Anthony Freeling & David Court 'Reinventing the Marketing Organization' McKinsey Quarterly, No. 4, 1994.
6. Whisler, T.L. (1970) *The impact of computers on organizations*. New York: Praeger.
7. Argyres, N.S. (1999) N.S. The impact of information technology on co-ordination: evidence from the B-2 Stealth bomber. *Organization Science*, Vol. 10(2), pp. 162–180.
8. Datamonitor. (1999) *Banking and e-commerce: more than just another distribution channel*. Special report. New York: Datamonitor.
9. Cunningham, M.T. and Homse, E. (1986) Controlling the marketing–purchasing interface: resource development and organisational implications. *Industrial Marketing and Purchasing*, Vol. 1(2), pp. 3–27.
10. Cunningham, M.T. and Homse, E. (1986) Controlling the marketing–purchasing interface: resource development and organisational implications. *Industrial Marketing and Purchasing*, Vol. 1(2), pp. 3–27.
11. Policy Publications (1998) *Developing strategic customers and key accounts*. Bedford: Policy Publications, (author John Hurcombe).
12. Quotation attributed to John Hurcombe, author of *Developing strategic customers and key accounts*. Bedford: Policy Publications, in a press release.
13. Millman A.F. and Wilson K.J. (1995) From key account selling to key account management. *Journal of Marketing Science*, Vol. 1(1), pp. 8–21; Macdonald, M. and Rogers, B. (1996) *Key Account Management*. Oxford: Butterworth-Heinemann.

Index